PHILODEMUS, ON ANGER

WRITINGS FROM THE GRECO-ROMAN WORLD

General Editors
John T. Fitzgerald and Clare K. Rothschild

Editorial Board
Andrew Cain
Margaret M. Mitchell
Teresa Morgan
Ilaria L. E. Ramelli
David T. Runia
Karin Schlapbach

Number 45
Volume Editor
Elizabeth Asmis

PHILODEMUS, *ON ANGER*

*Introduction, Greek Text,
and Translation by*

David Armstrong and Michael McOsker

Copyright © 2020 by SBL Press

All rights reserved. No part of this work may be reproduced or transmitted in any form or by any means, electronic or mechanical, including photocopying and recording, or by means of any information storage or retrieval system, except as may be expressly permitted by the 1976 Copyright Act or in writing from the publisher. Requests for permission should be addressed in writing to the Rights and Permissions Office, SBL Press, 825 Houston Mill Road, Atlanta, GA 30329 USA.

Library of Congress Cataloging-in-Publication Data

Names: Philodemus, approximately 110 B.C.–approximately 40 B.C., author. | Armstrong, David, 1940– translator, editor. | McOsker, Michael, translator, editor. | Philodemus, approximately 110 B.C.–approximately 40 B.C. De ira. 2020. | Philodemus, approximately 110 B.C.–approximately 40 B.C. De ira. English. 2020.
Title: Philodemus, On anger / by David Armstrong and Michael McOsker.
Other titles: On anger | Writings from the Greco-Roman world ; 45.
Description: Atlanta : Atlanta : SBL Press, 2020. | Series: Writings from the Greco-Roman world ; 45 | Includes bibliographical references and index.
Identifiers: 2019059288 (print) | LCCN 2019059289 (ebook) | ISBN 9781628372694 (paperback) | ISBN 9780884144274 (hardback) | ISBN 9780884144281 (ebook)
Subjects: LCSH: Anger—Early works to 1800.
Classification: LCC B598.P43 D3813 2020 (print) | LCC B598.P43 (ebook) | DDC 152.4/7—dc23
LC record available at https://lccn.loc.gov/2019059288
LC ebook record available at https://lccn.loc.gov/2019059289

David Armstrong:
to his husband, Marcos David Jimenez

Michael McOsker:
to Molly, δῖα γυναικῶν

Contents

Preface ix
Abbreviations xi

Introduction 1
   1. Philodemus: Life and Works   1
   2. Previous Philosophical Scholarship   10
   3. Plato and Aristotle on Anger   20
   4. The Stoic and Epicurean Reactions   32
   5. Philodemus's Natural and Empty Anger   40
   6. The Structure and Analysis of *On Anger*   45
       6.1. The Initial Fragments (Frags. 1–16)   46
       6.2. Anger, Reasoning, and the Critique of Timasagoras
            (Frags. 17–33 and Cols. 1–7)   47
            Excursus 1: Timasagoras and Philodemus's Reply   53
       6.3. The Diatribe (Cols. 8–31.24)   58
       6.4. The Peripatetics (Cols. 31.24–34.6)   64
       6.5. The "Anger" of Sages and Their Students
            (Cols. 34.16–37.9)   66
            Excursus 2: Nicasicrates   72
       6.6. On the Painfulness of Natural Anger (Cols. 37.16–44.35)   73
       6.7. The Maximalists (Cols. 44.35–50.8)   77
   7. The Epicurean Context of *On Anger* and the History of
      Philodemus's Theory   80
      Excursus 3: *Diatheseis*: Physical and Moral Dispositions in
      Epicureanism   91
      Excursus 4: Epicurus, *On Nature* 25   94
   8. The Papyrus and the *Disegni*   98
   9. The Order and Contents of the *Cornici*   99
  10. Column Tops in Columns 1–50   107
  11. Stichometry and the Length of the Roll   110

	12. The Subscription	112
	13. Paleography, the Scribe, Errors, and Corrections	114
	14. Philodemus's Style	119
	14.1. Grammar and Vocabulary	119
	14.2. Hiatus	121
	14.3. Prose Rhythm	122
	14.4. Style	127
	15. Previous Textual Scholarship	130
	16. Principles of Our Edition and Translation	133
	17. Concordance of Fragments and Numerations across Editions	136

Sigla 139

Text, Translation, and Notes 141
    The Initial Fragments (Frags. 1–16)   142
    Anger, Reasoning, and the Critique of Timasagoras
        (Frags. 17–33, Cols. 1–7)   154
    The Diatribe (Cols. 8–31.24)   196
    The Peripatetics (Cols. 31.24–34.8)   260
    The "Anger" of Sages and Their Students (Cols. 34.16–37.9)   266
    On the Painfulness of Natural Anger (Cols. 37.16–44.35)   274
    The Maximalists (Cols. 44.35–50.8)   296

Bibliography 315
Index Verborum 337

Preface

In creating a new text and translation of *On Anger* we have incurred a great debt of gratitude to many colleagues and predecessors. We thank Giovanni Indelli especially for generously allowing us to make his text the base for our own. His excellent and meticulous Italian translation, the first into any modern language, and his wide-ranging and learned philological commentary have been our guide and first resort at every step. Indelli restored this text to the literary and philosophical world, after it had been for decades a mere name. In the wake of Indelli's edition, *On Anger* enjoyed not only new accessibility but even reached an unexpected prominence, as studies of the philosophy and psychology of the emotions in antiquity began to multiply. A new wave in the interpretation of *On Anger* began immediately, with a number of significant contributions.

Our friends and colleagues, particularly Elizabeth Asmis, Francesco Verde, and John Fitzgerald, have been a tremendous help in keeping us up to the minute. We mention with very special gratitude Gaia Barbieri, Jeffrey Fish, and W. Ben Henry, who graciously provided us with newly reedited columns of Philodemus's *On Epicurus*, *On the Good King according to Homer*, and *On Frank Speech* (respectively) from their publications. Gianluca Del Mastro and Marzia D'Angelo checked readings for us. Kilian Fleischer made a draft of his edition of the *Index Academicorum* available to us and kindly sent us a number of his articles. Ben Henry and Richard Janko read the whole text and apparatus and gave us the benefit of their advice, as well as a number of corrections and their own proposals. Richard also helped read the proofs. Liz Asmis, Enrico Piergiacomi, David Kaufman, and Francesco Verde read the whole work and gave us valuable advice about philosophical topics and points of interpretation. Sarah Hendriks gave us information about the Oxford *disegni* and advice about dealing with fragments and stratified papyri. The staff of the *officina dei papiri* in Naples were constantly helpful. We also owe a debt of gratitude to Brigham Young University's Ancient Textual Imaging Group and the Biblioteca Nazionale di Napoli for sharing the "multispectral images" of the Herculaneum Papyri. The Classics Department of the University of Texas, Austin, has also supported us with grants that paid us to begin work and Edwin Robert to set up our draft for the Index Verborum. Special recognition is due to Bob Buller, our tireless typesetter. We heartily thank all of them.

Michael first began working on the *On Anger* in the fall of 2013, while supported by a *borsa di studio* from the *Centro internazionale per lo studio dei papiri ercolanesi*, and CISPE continued its support for another fellowship in the summer of 2017. He would like to thank Professors Longo Auricchio, Indelli, Leone, and Del Mastro, as well as Mariacristina Fimiani, Matilde Fiorillo, and Antonio Parisi, as well as David Kaufman. But he is most grateful to David Armstrong for inviting him to participate in the first place.

David first made a working English translation, with brief notes, of Indelli's text in the mid-1990s, and read through it with care and in detail with Voula Tsouna not long after. Some of the conclusions arrived at then influenced her chapter on the *On Anger* in *The Ethics of Philodemus* (2007, 195–238), as she acknowledges (195 n.1). A similar read-through with David Kaufman, in spring 2012 while David A. was on a fellowship at the Princeton Center for Hellenic Studies, made it look possible to publish this material, and when Michael offered his papyrological expertise as coauthor in late 2013, we were ready to begin. Now that it's done, we find, with some surprise, that we have argued out nearly every word and sentence of what follows and agreed on it, so it's truly a joint production. There are no minority reports. The errors left in it are also due to none of the people we thank above but are entirely ours.

Those wishing the swiftest possible overview of Philodemus's position should read §§4 and 5 of the introduction. We have done all we can to double-check references, but due to the pandemic and closure of university libraries, some works were unavailable.

Abbreviations

Primary Sources

Adol. poet. aud.	Plutarch, *Quomodo adolescens poetas audire debeat*
Aff.	Chrysippus, *De affectibus*
Aff. Dig.	Galen, *De affectuum dignotione et curatione*
Alc. 2	[Plato], *Alcibiades 2*
Amic.	Cicero, *De amicitia*
Ann.	Tacitus, *Annales*
Anon.Lond.	Anonymus Londinensis
AP	*Anthologia Palatina*
Att.	Cicero, *Epistulae ad Atticum*
Ax.	[Plato], *Axiochus*
Bib. hist.	Diodorus Siculus, *Bibliotheca historica*
Cap.	Plutarch, *De capienda ex inimicis utilitate*
Carm.	Catullus, *Carmina*
Caus. puls.	Galen, *De causis pulsuum*
Cels.	Origen, *Contra Celsum*
Chr.	Proclus, *Chrestomathia*
Cohib. ira.	Plutarch, *De cohibenda ira*
Cont.	Polystratus, *De contemptu*
Cyr.	Xenophon, *Cyropaedia*
Deipn.	Athenaeus, *Deipnosophistae*
Dial.	Seneca, *Dialogi*
Diatr.	Epictetus, *Diatribai*
Ep.	*Epistula(e)*
Epic.	Philodemus, *De Epicuro liber primus (?) et secundus*
Epigr.	Martial, *Epigrammata*
Epigr. Bob.	*Epigrammata Bobiensia*
Epin.	[Plato], *Epinomis*
Eth. nic.	Aristotle, *Ethica nicomachea*

Fam.	Cicero, *Epistulae ad familiares*
Fin.	Cicero, *De finibus*
Garr.	Plutarch, *De garrulitate*
Geogr.	Strabo, *Geographica*
Gnom. vat.	Epicurus, *Gnomologium vaticanum*
Hdt.	Epicurus, *Epistola ad Herodotum*
Hipp.	Euripides, *Hippolytus*
Hist.	*Historiae*
Hist. Rom.	Velleius, *Historiae Romanae*
Id.	Theocritus, *Idylls*
Il.	Homer, *Ilias*
Imag.	Philostratus, *Imagines*
Ir.	Philodemus, *De ira* (*On Anger*); Seneca, *De ira*
Kyr. dox.	Epicurus, *Kyria doxai*
Leg.	Plato, *Leges*
Lib.	Philodemus, *De libertate dicendi* (*On Frank Speech*)
Luc.	Cicero, *Lucullus*
Math.	Sextus, *Adversus mathematicos*
Men.	Epicurus, *Epistula ad Menoeceum*
Mort.	Philodemus, *De morte* (*On Death*)
Mus.	Philodemus, *De musica* (*On Music*)
Nat.	Epicurus, *De natura*
Nat. an.	Aelian, *De natura animalium*
Nat. d.	Cicero, *De natura deorum*
Nat. hom.	Nemesius, *De natura hominis*
Od.	Homer, *Odyssea*
Off.	Cicero, *De officiis*
Or.	*Oratio*
Phileb.	Plato, *Philebus*
Piet.	Philodemus, *De pietate* (*On Piety*)
Pis.	Cicero, *In Pisonem*
Plac.	Galen, *De placitis Hippocratis et Platonis libri IX*
Plen.	Galen, *De plenitudine*
Poem.	Philodemus, *De poematis* (*On Poems*)
Pol.	Aristotle, *Politica*
Prot.	Plato, *Protagoras*
Praep. ev.	Eusebius, *Praeparatio evangelica*
Prov. cons.	Cicero, *De provinciis consularibus*
Pyr.	Sextus, *Pyrrhoniae hypotyposes*

Quaest. conv.	Plutarch, *Quaestionum convivialum libri IX*
Rer. nat.	Lucretius, *De rerum natura*
Resp.	Plato, *Respublica*
Rhet.	Aristotle, *Rhetorica*; Philodemus, *Volumina rhetorica*
Rom.	Plutarch, *Romulus*
Sat.	Horace, *Satirae*; Juvenal, *Satirae*
Sign.	Philodemus, *De signis* (*On Signs*)
Sup.	Philodemus, *De superbia* (*On Arrogance*)
Tusc.	Cicero, *Tusculanae disputationes*
Var. hist.	Aelian, *Varia historia*
Vit. Apoll.	Philostratus, *Vita Apollonii*
Vit. phil.	Diogenes Laertius, *Vitae philosophorum*

Secondary Sources

ACl	*Acta Classica*
AfP	*Archiv für Papyrusforschung*
AJP	*American Journal of Philology*
A.O.P.	Archivio dell'Officina dei papiri, in the Biblioteca Nazionale di Napoli
ASNP	*Annali della Scuola Normale Superiore di Pisa, Cl. di Lettere e Filosofia*
BASP	*Bulletin of the American Society of Papyrologists*
BETL	Bibliotheca Ephemeridum Theologicarum Lovaniensium
BFC	*Bollettino di Filologia Classica*
BICS	*Bulletin of the Institute of Classical Studies*
BPW	*Berliner philologische Wochenschrift*
BSGRT	Bibliotheca Scriptorum Graecorum et Romanorum Teubneriana
C&M	*Classica et mediaevalia*
CA	*Classical Antiquity*
CErc	*Cronache Ercolanesi*
ClAnt	*Classical Antiquity*
CP	*Classical Philology*
CQ	*Classical Quarterly*
CR	*Classical Review*

D.-K.	Diels, Hermann, and Walther Kranz, eds. *Die Fragmente der Vorsokratiker* ed. 6th ed. Berlin: Weidmann, 1951.
DPA	Goulet, Richard, et al., eds. *Dictionnaire des philosophes antiques*. 6 vols. Paris: CNRS Éditions, 1989–2018. Cited by initial letter and number of philosopher followed by the editor's name in parentheses.
GB	*Gräzer Beiträge: Zeitschrift für klassische Altertumswissenschaft*
GRBS	*Greek, Roman and Byzantine Studies*
HE	Gow, A. S. F., and Denys L. Page. *The Greek Anthology: Hellenistic Epigrams*. Cambridge: Cambridge University Press, 1965.
HV	*Herculanensium Voluminum Pars Prima*
HV^2	*Herculanensium Voluminum Quae Supersunt Collectio Altera*
lib. inc.	*liber incertus* (a book whose title or number is not known)
MGH	*Memoria Graeca Herculanensis*
Mnemosyne	*Mnemosyne: A Journal of Classical Studies*
NF	New Fragment
NovTSup	Supplements to Novum Testamentum
OCD	Hornblower, Simon, and Antony Spawforth, eds. *Oxford Classical Dictionary*. 4th ed. Oxford: Oxford University Press, 2012.
OSAP	*Oxford Studies in Ancient Philosophy*
PapLup	*Papyrologica Lupiensia*
P.Herc.	Herculaneum papyrus
PhR	*Philosophical Review*
REA	*Revue des études anciennes*
RhM	*Rheinisches Museum für Philologie*
RFIC	*Revista di Filologia e d'Istruzione Classica*
SB	Preisigke, Friedrich, et al., eds. *Sammelbuch griechischer Urkunden aus Ägypten*. 21 vols. Wiesbaden: Harrassowitz, 1915–2002.
SBLTT	Society of Biblical Literature Texts and Translations
SVF	J. von Arnim, *Stoicorum Veterum Fragmenta* (Stuttgart I-III, 1903-5, IV 1924). Cited by Stoic, volume

	number, and fragment number, e.g. as follows: Antipater *SVF* III.65.
TAPA	*Transactions of the American Philological Association*
VC	*Vigiliae christianae*
WGRW	Writings from the Greco-Roman World
WJA	*Würzburger Jahrbücher für die Altertumswissenschaft*
YCS	*Yale Classical Studies*
ZPE	*Zeitschrift für Papyrologie und Epigraphik*

Introduction

1. Philodemus: Life and Works

Philodemus was born circa 110 in Gadara (now Umm Qais, Jordan), in the Seleucid kingdom of Syria, just south of the Sea of Galilee.[1] Gadara was a center of Greek culture that had already produced distinguished writers as natives and would produce more. Menippus the satirist (fl. ca. 250) was already legendary, and Meleager the epigrammatist and "Menippean" prose satirist was an older contemporary. We have no details about Philodemus's early life or education, but Meleager's successful career abroad may tell us something about Philodemus's education.[2] During his

---

1. All dates are BCE unless other noted. For much of the chronology and discussion, see Dorandi 1987; Sider 1997, 3–24; and now above all Fleischer 2017c. For the history of the Epicurean school in general, see Clay 2009; Sedley 2009; and Erler 2009. For the history and archaeology of Gadara and its significance as Philodemus's and Meleager's birthplace, see Fitzgerald's survey (2004). For more detailed archeological reports, see Weber 2002 and the papers in Hoffman and Kerner 2002.

2. Note Meleager's use of words from two local languages in *AP* 7.418 = 4 HE and references to Jewish customs in *AP* 5.160. The city is described in 7.417 = 2 HE as Ἀτθὶς ἐν Ἀccυρίοιc ναιομένα Γάδαρα ("Gadara, an Athens built among Assyrians"). A later grave epigram (1070 in Peek 1988) calls Gadara πατρὶc δέ μου καὶ πᾶcι κοινὴ Γάδαρα χρηcτομουcία ("my fatherland and one common to all, Gadara, devoted to the Muses"); see also Sider 1997, 4–5. A lemmatist to the Palatine manuscript of the Greek anthology puts Meleager's floruit under "the last Seleucus," Seleucus VI Epiphanes (96/95–94/93 BCE), who died, like many other Seleucid princes of this era, in a civil war with a rival Seleucid. This may be the publication date of his collection of his own and earlier epigrams, the *Garland*. Presumably Meleager is given a Seleucid date for his floruit because he was so proud of Gadara and even of being Syrian and Phoenician; see Isaac 2017, 127–33 and 153–58. He was educated in Tyre as well as Gadara and spent his old age in Kos (*AP* 7.418.1–2 and 419.5–6). For the latest survey of his life and work, see Prioux 2019, 389 and n. 3. There are already imitations of his epigrams in Latin by about 80 BCE.

childhood and youth, the authority of the Seleucids was collapsing, after Antiochus VII Sidetes (r. 138–129), the last Seleucid king of any stature, was defeated and died during a war with Parthia. The area around Gadara was wracked by the wars of Alexander Yannai (Jannaeus), the Hasmonean king of Judea (r. 103–76). Gadara itself was at some point besieged and captured, perhaps even sacked, and remained under Hasmonaean control for decades. The date of the conquest is controversial: as early as 101 or as late as 82.[3] In 64/63, Pompey conquered Syria and made it a Roman province. Although Gadara quickly regained prosperity under Roman rule, the city was almost certainly at a low point in its history until then.[4] It was now given a high rank among the cities of the new province, partly through the influence of Pompey's trusted freedman Demetrius of Gadara.[5]

Philodemus had long since left Gadara by then and had started his philosophical studies abroad, probably in his teens or twenties. We have gained many details about Philodemus's life from recent work on the so-called *Index Academicorum* (or *History of the Academy*, primarily preserved in P.Herc. 1021).[6] Fleischer points out that the *Index* can be dated to 67–57.[7] Philodemus probably first spent time in Alexandria (90?–ca. 85) and then certainly in Athens (ca. 85–ca. 75), while he was studying with Zeno of Sidon (ca. 160–75, scholarch of the Garden ca. 100–75).[8]

---

3. For discussion, see Fitzgerald 2004, 359–63; he prefers a date earlier in this period.

4. See Fitzgerald 2004, 359–69.

5. Fitzgerald 2004, 365 and n. 101.

6. The *Index* is Philodemus's history of the Platonic Academy in Athens, arranged as brief biographies of the scholarchs, ending with the dates of their death and followed by lists of their most important students, from Plato's lifetime to Philodemus's own. It is preserved by two papyri, P.Herc. 164 and 1021. P.Herc. 164 is the finished copy but in a terrible state of preservation. The latter is a draft, with extensive additions in the margins and on the back, but it is in much better condition. The last full edition of the text (Dorandi 1991) has been partially superseded by the work of Puglia (2000), Blank (2007b), and the ongoing work of Fleischer (2015, 2016, 2017a, 2017c, 2017d, 2018). Fleischer is currently producing a new edition of the whole text. We have given an English translation of the relevant passages.

7. It refers to Antiochus as (recently?) dead and Dio of Alexandria as still alive, whence the range of dates given.

8. The dates for Philodemus's stay in Alexandria are a guess; we have no firm evidence for its beginning, but its end can be dated with confidence to 85 or 83. Similarly, we have no evidence for any of Philodemus's movements, if there were any, after he left Gadara and before he reached Alexandria. On Zeno's birthdate, see Fleischer 2019.

At the end of the *Index* (33.1–34.2), Philodemus discusses Philo of Larissa (159/158–84/83 BCE), scholarch of the Academy from 110/109 to at least 88, when he fled to Italy at the beginning of the Athenian revolt against Rome in 88–86.[9] He died in the influenza epidemic of 84/83. Here Philodemus notes his own arrival in Athens almost in passing, as he comes to the question of Philo's successor: "and [*name illegible*], I think from Ceos, was already presiding over the school when I arrived by sea from Alexandria" (34.2–7). As Fleischer notes, the person who "was already presiding" at the Academy whose place of birth Philodemus does not remember for certain sounds like a caretaker, and Philodemus's arrival should be dated to 85 or 83, just before or just after Philo's death.[10] He probably could not have gone to Athens before Sulla took the city in March 86 after a siege; we might suspect he would not have moved there soon afterward either.

Before we move on to Athens, we should dwell briefly on several friends that Philodemus could have made during his Alexandrian period. Philodemus got to know Antiochus of Ascalon (ca. 125–67) personally, if not in Alexandria, then certainly in Athens.[11] He was also friendly with several of his students, "especially my close friends (cυνήθειc) Aristo and Dio, both of Alexandria, and Cratippus of Pergamum; of these, Aristo and Cratippus, having studied with [*name lost*] ... enthusiasm ... became Peripatetics, but Dio is still one of the Old Academy" (that is, he is still a follower of Antiochus and Aristus), "and I hear just recently from Dio that quite a number of Stoics ... to Alexandria..." (35.7–19).[12] He may have been in Alexandria in 87 for Antiochus's famous reading of Philo's new

---

9. On Philo, see in general *DPA* P148 (Goulet) and Brittain 2006, updated by Fleischer 2017b and 2017c; for detailed discussion, see Brittain 2001.

10. The date depends on the exact interpretation given to ἤδη and what "taking over the school" (διακατεῖχεν) means: they could refer to a caretaker who took over in Philo's absence or to the next scholarch to take office after Philo's death. Fleischer inclines to the former understanding, as do we. The former understanding puts Philodemus's arrival in Athens in 85, the latter in 83.

11. "He (Antiochus) spent most of his life on embassies to Rome and to the generals in the provinces and in the end died in Mesopotamia [probably in the winter of 68/67], still working devotedly for and with Lucius Lucullus and beloved by many people, as also by me," Philodemus says, "and having himself given us a favorable reception" (*Index* 34.35–35.2). On Antiochus as a philosopher, see *DPA* A200 (Dorandi) and Sedley 2012.

12. On Aristus, see *DPA* A406 (Dorandi). On philosophical "networking"

Italian works, which provoked a response from Antiochus in the form of the treatise *Sosus* and led to the foundation of Antiochus's rival school, which he called the "Old Academy." Cicero (*Luc.* 11–12) does not record Philodemus as a participant, but Philodemus later knew three of the Academics involved: Dio, who remained loyal to Antiochus; and Aristo and Cratippus, who became Peripatetics.

All three were of some importance. Dio of Alexandria returned home after studying in Athens but had influential friends in Italy that he visited often. At the end of his life he headed an embassy to Rome in 57 to protest the planned restoration of Ptolemy XII Auletes, who was in exile there.[13] He was soon poisoned by assassins, along with most of the delegation. Aristo of Alexandria wrote a treatise *On the Nile,* which Strabo used as one of his sources (*Geogr.* 17.1.5).[14] Cratippus had a remarkably distinguished later career and enjoyed a level of patronage that dwarfed Philodemus's.[15] Cicero called him the foremost Peripatetic philosopher of the age (*Off.* 3.5) and also obtained Roman citizenship for him, as M. Tullius Cratippus; later, in 44, he sent his son Marcus to study with him in Athens. After Pharsalia, Pompey chose Cratippus to offer him philosophical consolation and *therapeia*. After the death of Caesar, Brutus, already a close friend, attended Cratippus's lectures in Athens.

These philosophers were part of a renaissance of the Peripatos, which had passed some time out of the limelight. Philodemus's friendship with them may help explain his interest in Peripatetic views of anger (cols. 31–34), including "some of the Peripatetics, whom we have also mentioned earlier by name" (31.24–27). The earlier passage may have been extensive.[16] The Peripatetic school of Zeno's and Philodemus's days in Athens was in a flourishing state and worth debating; the school was making converts around the time of Philodemus's arrival there. Additionally, we see that Philodemus kept up friendships and correspondences with philosophers of other schools. We also see that debate was fierce, despite the extramural friendships.

---

between Athens and Alexandria in the last two centuries BCE, see Lévy 2012, 290–92; and Fleischer 2016.

13. On Dio, see *DPA* D304 (Dorandi).
14. On Aristo, see *DPA* A393 (Caujolle-Zaslawksy and Goulet).
15. On Cratippus, see *DPA* C208 (Dorandi).
16. Our frags. 7–13 may contain its remains; see introduction, §6.1.

Philodemus's own principal teacher in Athens, to whom he remained loyal for the rest of his life, was Zeno of Sidon.[17] He would have studied Epicureanism at the Garden from 83 (or 85) until he finished his studies or until the death of Zeno (ca. 75).[18] He may have met Cicero during his time there, when Cicero and Atticus attended Zeno's lectures around 78/79.[19] Unfortunately, little is known for sure about Zeno and his views.[20] Philodemus then moved west, becoming part of what Sedley (2003) calls the "decentralization of philosophy" from Athens in the late second and early first century BCE. He spent time in Sicily, and there may have been a malicious story in circulation that his property was seized and he was exiled from Himera because his "impiety" was blamed for a plague.[21]

At some point, probably around 71 or a bit earlier, Philodemus came from Sicily to Rome, where he was soon accepted into the entourage of L. Calpurnius Piso Caesoninus (consul 58), the father of Julius Caesar's wife Calpurnia.[22] Cicero claims (*Pis.* 68 and 70) that Philodemus, when he first met him, was in awe of the youthful (*adulescens*) Piso for being "a senator of the Roman people." This suggests that Piso was at the first rank one achieved as a senator, quaestor, when they met; according to Broughton,

---

17. On Zeno, see the collection of fragments by Angeli and Colaizzo 1979, as well as the discussions in *DPA* Z24 (Angeli) and Blank 2019, §2.2.5.1.2. The fragments are translated into French with notes at Delattre and Pigeaud 2010, 233–37 and 1163–69. For his birthdate, see n. 8 above.

18. Dorandi (1996) conjectured that Philodemus left Athens because he was passed over for the scholarchate, but see now Fleischer 2018 (Philodemus was almost certainly too young). It may still be that there is a connection between Zeno's death and Philodemus's departure from Athens.

19. See Cicero, *Tusc.* 3.38 and *Fin.* 1.15–16.

20. Three texts by Philodemus—*On Frank Criticism* (P.Herc. 1473) and two books from a treatise on sensation in at least three books (P.Herc. 1003 and P.Herc. 1389)—bear a note in their end titles that they are "from Zeno's lectures" (ἐκ τῶν Ζήνωνος ϲχολῶν). It is not clear how significantly Philodemus edited or otherwise intervened in the material nor what this implies about other works by Philodemus that do not bear this note.

21. *Index* 34.8–11, reading ἕωϲ προ[c]ῆν with Blank (followed by Fleischer) instead of Dorandi's earlier πρ[ώι]ην. For the story about Himera, see Sider 1997, 9–10; Rawson 1985, 36 n. 90; and now Fleischer 2017c, 77–79. Sider reconstructed the story of Philodemus's stay at Himera and his flight from there to Italy from three separate passages in the Suda, but if anything traumatic happened to him in Sicily it is not obvious from his own words in the *Index*.

22. For Piso's philosophical interests, see *DPA* P189 (Boudon-Millet).

he was quaestor in 70.²³ Presumably Philodemus joined his entourage at that time. So far as we can tell, they remained connected for the rest of their lives.²⁴ Philodemus dedicated to Piso a brilliant little poem inviting his wealthy patron to a simple dinner with philosophers, on the occasion of a celebration of Epicurus's birthday, the εἰκάς, on the twentieth day of the month.²⁵ Because of this connection, Philodemus was mentioned without being named by Cicero in two speeches, the *In Pisonem* and the *De provinciis consularibus*.²⁶ These texts show that Philodemus not only lived with Piso for many years as a companion and near family member "who rarely left the fellow's side," (*Pis.* 68: *nec fere ab isto umquam decederet*) but accompanied him to Macedonia when Piso was proconsul there from 57 to 55. It is probable that Philodemus's *On the Good King according to Homer* was written in Piso's honor, perhaps, as Braund infers, to celebrate his consulship or proconsulship in Macedonia.²⁷

---

23. Piso was of high enough birth that he never lost an election (*Pis.* 2), so he arrived at all the stages of the *cursus honorum* as soon as he was of legal age. This was called being elected "in one's proper year" (*anno suo*). So he will have been quaestor at age 30, in 70, and consul at age 43 in 58, thus born no later than 101; see Broughton 1951–1986, 1:129, 2:47.

24. For a possible explanation for Philodemus's arrival in Italy, see Dorandi 1997. Sider (1997, 7–8) suggests that Philodemus was in Italy by 70, because of a present-tense reference to Zeno of Sidon in *On Rhetoric* 2, at P.Herc. 1674, 53.10-1 (Longo Auricchio 1977, 152–53; cf. 57.13–17, Longo Auricchio 1977, 160–61), but this could be a citational present tense.

25. Epigram 27 (Sider 1997). As Sider shows in his commentary (1997, 153), this poem alone created a mini-genre, the "invitation to a simple supper," imitated in Catullus 13; Horace, *Odes* 1.20, 4.12; *Ep.* 1.5; as well as Martial, *Epigr.* 5.78, 10.48, and 11.52; and Juvenal, *Sat.* 11.56–76.

26. Asconius identifies him in his commentary to the *In Pisonem* as *Epicureus illa aetate nobilissimus* (§68, Clark 1907, 16,12; *nobilissimus* does not look like an inference from Cicero's text), and the inference that he is in question in the other speech at *Prov. cons.* 14 is safe. In that passage, Cicero argues that Piso was held back from claiming a triumph after his victories as governor of Macedon by the clever Greek philosophers that appeared with him continually in public, whereas they were kept behind the stage in Rome. Gardner (1958) rightly annotates this plural with "Philodemus," but Grillo (2015) overlooks this.

27. See, e.g., Braund 1996, 31–34. Braund favors dating *On the Good King* to the proconsulship of 57–55; the whole chapter ("Kings, Proconsuls, Emperors," 22–40) deals with the quasi-monarchic style characteristic of proconsular government and the relevance to it of philosophical treatises on kingship.

If our Piso was the one who served as propraetor in Spain in 61 (there is a good deal of uncertainty on that point), Philodemus may have gone with him there also as personal philosopher.[28] If so, we gain a bit more insight into Philodemus's situation. Catullus (*Carm.* 28, 47) reports the complaints of his friends, Veranius and Fabullus, who are treated badly in comparison with Porcius and Socration. Philodemus has long been suggested for the real identity of "Socration,"[29] and "Porcius" is an appropriate pseudonym for another Epicurean companion.[30] Indeed, Catullus and Philodemus are wittily playing on the names of Socrates and his wife Xanthippe: many of Philodemus's erotic epigrams are dedicated to Xanthippe (presumably a pseudonym) because she is the most famous "wife of a philosopher," so Catullus calls Philodemus Socration, "Socrates Jr.," in his own poems. Incidentally, despite Catullus's complaints, Philodemus and "Porcius" could probably expect better treatment as personal friends of Piso than could Fabullus and Veranius as members of his staff. They may have served as envoys or personal agents and so warranted description as "right hands" of Piso, which Catullus, outraged on his friends' behalf, travesties as "left hands" in his poem (*Carm.* 48.2).[31]

In Italy, Philodemus was a busy teacher and polemicist. He counted among his students several leading literary and political lights beyond Piso and his family. He taught Virgil and his lifelong friends Plotius Tucca, Varius Rufus, and Quintilius Varus and dedicated works to the four of them together.[32] He was also in the patronage circle of C. Vibius Pansa

---

28. For longer treatment and bibliography, see Sider 1997, 23–24. See especially Syme 1956.

29. From Friedrich (1908, 228) onward. See also Tait (1941, 36–47), Landolfi (1982), and Sider (1997, 23–24), and, contra the identification, Shapiro (2014). Sociation transliterates Σωκράτιον, the diminutive, not Σωκρατίων.

30. Like Horace's *Epicuri de grege porcus* ("a pig from the herd of Epicurus," *Ep.* 1.4.14–15) and Cicero's *Epicure noster, ex hara producte, non ex schola* ("our Epicurus, brought out from the sty, not the school," *Pis.* 37, with Nisbet 1961, 98). Kroll (1923, 86–87, on Catullus, *Carm.* 47.1) took Porcius to be the Porcius Cato who was tribune of the plebs in 56; while Fordyce (1961, 210–11) does not accept the identification, he, too, takes the name to be a gentilic rather than a pseudonym.

31. But the joking insults of *Carm.* 28 suggest that Catullus is not too upset at his friends' situation.

32. Philodemus dedicates P.Herc.Paris 2, a book *On Slander*, to them; see Gigante and Capasso 1989. On these figures in general, see the articles in *The Virgil Encyclopedia*. Piso's daughter, Calpurnia Caesaris (born ca. 75), was an Epicurean,

Caetronianus (consul 43), an Epicurean to whom he dedicated the fourth book of *On Rhetoric*.[33] Horace would later pay Philodemus the compliment of a citation (*Sat.* 1.2.121, published 35) and many imitations.[34] Cicero probably used him as a source for the first two Epicurean books of *De finibus* and for the doctrines of the Epicurean Velleius in *De natura deorum* 1.[35] An Oxyrhynchus papyrus (P.Oxy. 54.3724) contains a list of epigram beginnings, mostly Philodemus's, and testifies to the wide circulation of his poetry, which would later be anthologized by Philip of Thessalonica in his *Garland*. Cicero cites his epigrams as well known even to the members of his senatorial audience (*Pis.* 70) and says that his poetry is "so pleasing, polished, and elegant that nothing could be imagined more artful" (*ita festivum, ita concinnum, ita elegans, ut nihil fieri possit argutius*). However, despite his lasting fame as a poet, Philodemus is mentioned only once in later philosophical literature, by Diogenes Laertius (*Vit. phil.* 10.3), who cites his *Syntaxis* of philosophers for a detail.

---

and so probably was her much younger half-brother L. Calpurnius Piso Pontifex (48 BCE–32 CE, consul 15, the probable dedicatee of Horace's *Ars poetica*). The latter was praised by Velleius (*Hist. Rom.* 2.198) and Tacitus (*Ann.* 6.10) for his mild temper and love of leisure and his equally impressive devotion to business when necessary. This may be a standard way to praise an Epicurean of the governing class (see Swan 1976). Pontifex is satirized by Seneca (*Ep.* 83.14) for his supposed addiction to wine, but (again) this did not affect his diligence at work. This may be a hostile parody of the standard way to praise an Epicurean. For details of the identification, see Armstrong 1993, 200–201 and n. 29; 2014, 93–94 with n. 5. On Philodemus and Virgil, see the introduction to Armstrong et al., 2004.

33. See Dorandi 1996.

34. On Philodemus's literary influence, see Tait 1941; Cameron (1993, 385–87) noted that *Epigr. Bob.* 32 is a translation of Sider's epigram 3, and Sider (1997, 67) plausibly suggests that *Epigr. Bob.* 35 is a translation of a lost epigram. These translations, made in the fourth or fifth century CE, testify to Philodemus's continuing popularity.

35. If Cicero and Philodemus became acquainted in Cicero's student days in Athens, Cicero's use of Philodemus as a source is easy to explain; see Cicero, *Fin.* 2.119, where the Epicurean advocate Torquatus mentions Philodemus and Siro, also one of Virgil's teachers, as the authorities he will consult to find further arguments against Cicero's attack on his Epicureanism. For the *De natura deorum*, see Diels 1879, 529–50; and Obbink 2001; 2002, esp. 196–97. Philodemus's authorship of the *On Piety* is open to question: only the initial *phi* of the author's name is legible on the papyrus, and Cicero requests Phaedrus's *On the Gods* at *Att.* 13.39 (see also *Fam.* 13.1), which makes Phaedrus another possible author.

The last datable event in Philodemus's writings may have happened in 40: Mark Antony's import of pygmies from Hyria, mentioned as a recent event.[36] He would have been already about seventy at that point and probably did not live much longer. Horace's present-tense reference in the first book of the *Satires* (1.2.121) may, but need not, mean that he was still living at the time it was published in 35.

Philodemus's surviving treatises were found between 1752 and 1754 CE in the Villa dei Papiri just outside of Herculaneum beneath Vesuvius. They had been carbonized and buried in the eruption.[37] The villa may have been owned by Piso himself, but only the presence of Philodemus's books there connects the man and the place. The library is made up primarily of Philodemus's own treatises, followed by Epicurus, then Demetrius Laco, an Epicurean probably of the generation before Philodemus. At least some of it descends from Philodemus's own papers, as the working copy of the *Index Academicorum* shows, but the vicissitudes that his collection underwent before the eruption are unknown. An important datum is the inclusion of up to three copies of Epicurus's *On Nature* (three copies of one book are attested and two copies of several others); one of the copies is probably from the third century and so must have been brought to Italy from Athens. The existence of these copies probably indicates the existence of a reading group or teaching circle, for which multiple copies of the same text would be useful.

Most of Philodemus's surviving works deal with ethics and aesthetics. This is not to say that he had no concern with physics—his *On Sensations* and *On Signs* both show proficiency in the topic—but we do not know of any treatise dedicated completely to physics. *On Anger* (*De ira*) had a sibling treatise in *On Gratitude* (unfortunately, extremely damaged), for anger and gratitude, *orgē* and *kharis,* were paired in the first *Kyria Doxa*: they are as necessary for humanity as they are irrelevant to the gods.[38] *On Anger* is also closely related to *On Frank Speech*, which is concerned with Epicurean didactic strategies and practices and which it cites at 35.24–25. We do not know if these three works belonged together in an *ensemble*.

---

36. Mentioned at *Sign.* 2.15–18; see Carruesco 2010 and Longo Auricchio 2013.

37. For the library and its relationship to the villa, see Dorandi 2017 and Capasso forthcoming. For a recent survey of archeological work on the villa, see the essays in Zarmakoupi 2010, especially De Simone 2010 and Guidobaldi and Esposito 2010; see also the essays in Lapatin 2019.

38. For an edition, see Tepedino Guerra 1977; see also §6.7 below.

What survives of *On Anger* does not refer explicitly to datable events or even to specifically Roman or Italian customs.[39]

2. Previous Philosophical Scholarship[40]

Giovanni Indelli's 1988 edition of *On Anger* finally broke down the barriers to study by providing a fully realized edition with commentary and translation—the foundation for a growing secondary literature.[41] We thank Indelli especially for generously allowing us to make his text the base for our own when we were beginning our edition in 2013. His excellent and meticulous Italian translation, the first into any modern language, and his wide-ranging and learned philological commentary have been our guide and first resort at every step. Indelli's edition restored this text to the literary and philosophical world of modern classical studies after it had been for decades an empty name.

Before Indelli's edition, the secondary literature of *On Anger* was devoted primarily to establishing the text, but there were two exceptions, both still of interest. The first of these was the Latin *Praefatio* to Karl Wilke's edition of 1914, especially his paraphrase of the contents, his discussion of Philodemus's adversaries Timasagoras and Nicasicrates, and his argument for Chrysippus as a major source for *On Anger*. The other was Hermann Ringeltaube's rival analysis of *On Anger* (1913, 38–50),

---

39. Unless the vivid passage of *On Anger* about cruelty to slaves provoking them to become runaways or revolt (24.17–36) represents Roman rather than Greek customs; see n. 143. If so, this would be the only such instance in *On Anger*. *On Property Management* implicitly refers to Roman customs and explicitly mentions one at 25.38–40; see Tsouna 2012, 70–71. Citations of Philodemus's works are by column.line number unless identified as a fragment.

40. The history of scholarship on the text of the *On Anger* is summarized in §15.

41. The most useful general treatments of Philodemus's philosophical position in *On Anger* are Annas 1989; 1992, 189–99; 1993, 188–200, esp. 195–200; Asmis 1990, 2393–99; 2011; Delattre 2009b; Fowler 1997; Procopé 1993; Sorabji 2000, 202–5; Spinelli and Verde forthcoming; Tsouna 2001, 2003, 2007a (especially the chapter devoted to *On Anger*, 195–238), 2007b, and 2012. On the question of the relationship between *On Anger* and the portrayal of Aeneas and Turnus's anger in Virgil's *Aeneid*, see Erler 1992b; Fish 2004; Galinsky 1988, 1994; Gill 2003; Indelli 2001, 2004; Polleichtner 2009; for a different view, see Fowler 1997. On Philodemus's influence on Horace's *Satires*, see Armstrong 2014 and 2016, as well as Yona 2015, 2017, 2018a, 2018b, and 2018c.

which gives a radically different view.[42] Wilke, like many scholars of his day, regarded Philodemus's own thought, and indeed Epicureanism itself, as of very minor interest compared to the fragments of other philosophers and writers that might be extracted from On Anger and from Herculaneum texts in general. His elaborate and careful reading of the papyrus is illuminated by a wide study of ancient writings on anger and makes his text still indispensable for critics. Philodemus's casual mention of Chrysippus's *Therapeutikos Logos* and Bion of Borysthenes's *On Anger* as classics of the diatribe against anger (1.16–19) gave Wilke the ambition of resurrecting, from Philodemus's own diatribe (8–31.24), not just quotations and paraphrases from Chrysippus's treatise but even its general order and arrangement, which he claims was identical with Philodemus's (1914, l–li).[43] Wilke also believed, following Crönert, that it was possible to identify not merely humorous imitations of Bion but actual quotations from Bion in the text (1914, liv). The implication is that Philodemus was merely a lazy paraphraser of Chrysippus's *Therapeutikos Logos*.[44]

Wilke's progress in editing *On Anger*, from his visit to Naples to read the papyrus in 1911 to the appearance of his Teubner text in 1914, seems to have been followed closely by Ringeltaube and his teachers. Ringeltaube believed, as we do, that there are multiple sources for *On Anger*, of which

---

42. Karl Julius August Wilke (1880–1916) was also the editor of Polystratus's *On Irrational Contempt of Popular Opinions* (Teubner, 1905), which was his dissertation at Kiel under the great early Herculaneum papyrologist Siegfried Sudhaus (1863–1914). Wilke and Sudhaus were both killed in World War I. Hermann Ringeltaube, born in 1890, also served in World War I and survived until at least the 1950s but published nothing further. His 1913 treatise was his dissertation, written at Göttingen under Max Pohlenz (1872–1962). Paul Wendland (1864–1915), one of his examiners, had taught at Kiel with Sudhaus before moving to Göttingen and had stayed au courant with Herculaneum work in general.

43. This ambition was helped along by the fact that frag. 19 appears to paraphrase Chrisyppus (*SVF* 3.478). See our note ad loc.

44. Wilke (1914, liii): *Philodemus, vel potius Zeno, quem ille sectatur, cum iram describeret, omnia fere ex Chrysippi curatorio libro hausisse mihi videtur; his perpauca ex Epicureorum scholis addidit; nonnulla denique lumina orationis ex Bione adspersit* ("Philodemus, or rather Zeno, whom he is following, when he describes anger, seems to me to have drawn nearly all his material from Chrysippus's *Therapeutikos*, adding a very small amount of material from Epicurean sources and scattering in a few striking sayings from Bion"). Wilke (1914, ilv) and Jensen (1911) even considered Philodemus's rhetorical use of *praeteritiones* such as "Why should I say more?" as a sign that he was abridging his source at that point.

Chrysippus may be one, but that Philodemus's arrangement and content are original throughout and entirely Epicurean. Philodemus's diatribe against anger, Ringeltaube argued, cannot be used to isolate new fragments of Chrysippus or Bion. The rhetorical genre of diatribe, and specifically of the diatribe against anger, was older than both, going back to the Sophists (and thence perhaps to archaic iambos), and its commonplaces had been passed on from writer to writer so long and used for so many purposes that source criticism is impossible. As Ringeltaube puts it:

> In fact, every other writer "on anger" that we have is full of similar material, as no reader can fail to notice. But no one would dare take all this and ascribe it to Bion, and there is no ascribing this material to any one source, for "Bionean" diatribe was so popular in all the philosophical sects and so overworked, that the same topics, expressed in nearly the same words and illustrated by the same *exempla*, are found in all examples that survive of such writing. Certainly Paul Wendland is right to say ... "it is enough to identify the philosophical tendency and genre to which any given diatribe's ideas belong, but to look for a named source would be fruitless and indeed misguided." Philosophers of all kinds were constantly arguing about these much-studied matters and took up the forms of argument they found worked out in ethical tracts for popular audiences, but their doctrine was nonetheless that of their teachers.[45]

Modern scholarship on Chrysippus and his *Therapeutikos Logos* leaves *On Anger* and Philodemus entirely out of account. So also, the passages in *On Anger* once taken by Buecheler, Crönert, and Hense to be quotations from Bion of Borysthenes have disappeared from the editions and scholarship on that author.[46]

Ringeltaube was also the first to argue that Philodemus's opponents Nicasicrates, Timasagoras, and the "maximalists" were all fellow Epi-

---

45. 1913, 39, our translation here and elsewhere; the quotation of Wendland is from his 1895, 62. On the futility of source hunting in the diatribe genre, see also Ringeltaube 1913, 32 and 76–77.

46. Hense's supposed fragments of Bion are gone from the standard modern edition (Kindstrand 1976) and from the secondary literature. So also, Tieleman's book on Chrysippus's *On Emotions* hardly mentions Philodemus and cites *On Anger* only once, in passing (2003, 179), and that in spite of the imagery borrowed from Chrysippus in frag. 19 (see our notes) and the storm of medical imagery in the first eleven columns of *On Anger*, which no doubt parallels similar uses of medical imagery of the *Therapeutikos Logos*; see Tieleman's general account of its fragments (2003, 140–97).

cureans, so that the treatise is almost entirely a conversation between Epicureans (1913, 40–46). This has become the accepted account.[47] We have contributed further arguments to it by following Ringeltaube's technique, which was to mark off the opponents' own words as Philodemus cites them and analyze them for Epicurean technical language. We found still more such technical language in all three.

Ringeltaube also analyzes the history of the definition of anger from Aristotle onward and notes that *On Anger* teaches a purely Epicurean definition that differs significantly from those of Aristotle and the Stoics. He formulates the definition, using key terms from Philodemus's text, as follows: "Anger is an irritation following on suppositions that people are harming or intending to harm one" (διερεθιςμὸς ἐπακολουθῶν ὑπολήψεciν βλαπτόντων ἢ βλάψειν μελλόντων, 1913, 46–47); he also notes that *harm* (βλάβη) is an important word in the Epicurean vocabulary (1913, 47 n. 1).[48] The omnipresence of a definition such as this as crucial to understanding the various parts of *On Anger* is a major theme of our interpretation as well. But at this early stage, with the crucial distinction between "empty anger" and "natural anger" still unarticulated, the definition is not yet precise enough.

After Ringeltaube and Wilke, we must skip over the next seventy years to Indelli's 1988 edition and begin anew, for there seems to be no further extended literary or philosophical analysis of *On Anger* as a whole in the secondary literature. Philippson's 1916 article on the treatise is almost entirely textual, though he promised a longer, interpretive treatment (never to appear).[49] However, the interpretive tradition after 1988 does a great deal to make up for lost time.

We begin with Annas (1989), who is the first writer on *On Anger* to articulate the distinction of empty and natural anger in the work. She shows that Philodemus assigns to empty anger almost all the bad behaviors

---

47. Asmis (1990, 2011) is a significant holdout; see excursus 1 below for more details.

48. Wilke did not see any important difference between the Peripatetic, Stoic, and Epicurean definitions of anger: "this appears to have been Philodemus's very unoriginal definition: 'anger is a desire to get vengeance on a person harming one intentionally'" (1914, li: *Philodemo … haec fere definitio tritissima fuisse videtur*: ὀργὴ ἐπιθυμία τοῦ μετελθεῖν τον βλάπτοντα ἑκουcίως).

49. There are attempts to trace the influence of Philodemus (or his sources) in other writers on anger, e.g., Fillion-Lahille (1970) and (1984, 221–36) on possible echoes of *On Anger* in Seneca's *On Anger*.

and negative outcomes that had been the subject of the diatribe tradition and that he limits natural anger to a pleasureless impulse toward punishment, accepted only with pain, and as an unenjoyable duty, like agreeing to drink some bitter drug or undergo a surgical operation. Philodemus's view, Annas notes, is not some middle view between Stoic refusal of all emotion and Peripatetic acceptance that anger includes the pleasure of vengeance. It is worked out principally as a quarrel between his own and other, differing opinions within the Epicurean school itself. This is, in essence, Ringeltaube's view and our own.

Annas (1989, 153–59) is also the first to articulate fully the relevance to *On Anger* of Epicurus's classification of desires as empty and natural (*Men.* 127; *Kyr. dox.* 29–30).[50] Interpreters must realize that most or all of what Philodemus calls empty anger entails empty desire, in this case, the empty desire for the pleasures of revenge or even of punishment as good things in themselves. That anger can give you any real pleasure is an empty belief, and therefore a desire for the pleasure of vengeance is always an unnatural (and thus unnecessary) desire. Natural anger is never accompanied by pleasure or enjoyment or the hope of it; revenge is forbidden, and punishment is not a pleasure. That means, for Annas, that the "desire" involved in natural anger is too special to be easily analyzed by the three categories natural and necessary, natural but unnecessary, and unnatural. Natural anger is just "something necessary, something we cannot avoid....

---

50. *Men.* 127: "We must reckon that, of the desires (*epithumiai*), some are natural, some are empty; and of natural desires, some are necessary, some merely natural; and of those that are necessary, some are necessary for happiness, some for the comfort of the body, some for life itself" (ἀναλογιστέον δὲ ὡς τῶν ἐπιθυμιῶν αἱ μέν εἰσι φυσικαί, αἱ δὲ κεναί, καὶ τῶν φυσικῶν αἱ μὲν ἀναγκαῖαι, αἱ δὲ φυσικαὶ μόνον. τῶν δὲ ἀναγκαίων αἱ μὲν πρὸς εὐδαιμονίαν εἰσὶν ἀναγκαῖαι, αἱ δὲ πρὸς τὴν τοῦ σώματος ἀοχλησίαν, αἱ δὲ πρὸς αὐτὸ τὸ ζῆν).

Kyr. dox. 29: "of desires, some are natural and necessary, some are natural but not necessary; and some neither natural nor necessary, but come about because of empty opinion" (τῶν ἐπιθυμιῶν αἱ μέν εἰσι φυσικαὶ καὶ ⟨ἀναγκαῖαι, αἱ δὲ φυσικαὶ καὶ⟩ οὐκ ἀναγκαῖαι, αἱ δὲ οὔτε φυσικαὶ οὔτε ἀναγκαῖαι, ἀλλὰ παρὰ κενὴν δόξαν γινόμεναι).

Kyr. dox. 30: "In the case of those physical desires that do not lead to physical pain if left unfulfilled and yet there is intense (*syntonos*) eagerness, they are due to empty opinion, and it is not because of their nature that they refuse to be dissipated but because of the person's own empty opinion" (ἐν αἷς τῶν φυσικῶν ἐπιθυμιῶν, μὴ ἐπ' ἀλγοῦν δὲ ἐπαναγουσῶν, ἐὰν μὴ συντελεσθῶσιν, ὑπάρχει ἡ σπουδὴ σύντονος, παρὰ κενὴν δόξαν αὗται γίνονται, καὶ οὐ παρὰ τὴν ἑαυτῶν φύσιν οὐ διαχέονται ἀλλὰ παρὰ τὴν τοῦ ἀνθρώπου κενοδοξίαν).

There is … no point in trying to get rid of this desire, any more than in trying to get rid of the desire for food or drink; you won't succeed, because it is part of what you are, one of your human needs" (Annas 1989, 159–60).

Annas believes that Philodemus's natural anger is a limited and tranquil emotion, more suited to arguments between philosophers or their students. We do not agree, but certainly there are passages in the text that show why she and others have thought so. It is true that Philodemus makes clear that anger, as something painful, is self-limiting in the sage or the good person. It is also the case, as we will show, that two important passages of the surviving text presuppose a school or educational context. We agree with Annas that anger among Epicurean students like Philodemus's own and among good people, including sages, is a main theme in *On Anger* and is related, as an explicit cross-reference at 36.22–28 shows, to the parallel treatise on Epicurean education *On Frank Speech* (*De libertate dicendi*).[51] Annas concludes from these passages that anger is not a heroic emotion for Philodemus but a merely scholastic one:

> Epicurean anger seems to show itself principally in the philosophical life of the Garden, in teaching and disputes; its scope overlaps with that of frankness, to which Philodemus devotes another work. Achilles' kind of anger is ruled out; one should not feel like that, principally because one should not care about the kind of thing Achilles cared about. To get into combat because of a sense of injured honor is already to have left the Garden. (1989, 162).

---

51. See especially 18.35–21.36 (with our discussion below at pp. 61–62), a passage that Ringeltaube singled out for evocation of an ancient classroom: "in these words, we seem to be transported back to an ancient philosopher's lecture hall, to such a style, grave and severe, as befits a teacher's classroom as he warns his students against indulgence in anger. Does not there seem to breathe on us in these words the very air of Philodemus's own preceptor Zeno's teaching, of the man who is called by Cicero (*Tusc.* 3.38) *acriculus senex*, the sharp-tempered old man?" (1913, 39); see also n. 160 below. We feel that Ringeltaube appreciated the style and tone better than Procopé, who said (1998, 174): "it reeks of the Epicurean lecture-room.… So much is clear from the unattractive and slovenly prose. Its failings of style may be blamed on gaps in the papyrus and on insensitive attempts to restore them. But that is not the whole story" (of Philodemus's faults as a writer). We think the diatribe is witty, ironic, self-aware, and amusing, with affinities to Horace and Lucilius. For comparisons with Horatian diatribe satire, see Armstrong 2014.

That, we will show, is a misunderstanding. Although no Epicurean will get angry for the reason that Achilles got angry (i.e., injured honor), the essence of natural anger is punishment of those who intentionally caused real harm and the removal of the possibility of further harm caused by the offenders or any others who might imitate them (41.2–8). This suggests that, when Epicurean sages act in anger, they act vigorously and decisively. As for heroic action, *On Anger* assumes the relevance of both Homeric epics, tragedy, and comedy to the discussion of anger. Philodemus, like every other ancient philosopher of anger, privileges Odysseus's temperance and self-control over Achilles's violent emotions; he is skeptical about the violence of Achilles's empty anger but confident in the validity of Odysseus's natural anger, even against the suitors and the maids.[52]

Eventually Annas came to think that Epicurean anger and gratitude are both merely cold and formal pretenses of emotion; as she puts it, "we think that things like retaliation and gratitude matter, and to a good Epicurean they do not."[53] This does not seem right; of course punishment and gratitude matter to the sage. Punishment, as we saw, is intended to stop the offenders and anyone tempted by their example, which implies a serious response (41.2–8). Gratitude is the foundation of true friendship, and the strict performance of its obligations is necessary not just to the secure life but to the pleasant life.[54] But anger and gratitude are always feelings one assents to in the service of security, friendship, and pleasure and not ends in themselves. That is why they matter so much and also why they are not the whole story.

John Procopé's pioneering account of the treatise (1993) has influenced us in many details, perhaps most of all his use of a passage from Demetrius Laco, a contemporary of Philodemus's own teacher, Zeno of Sidon. In the treatise conventionally called *On Textual and Exegetical Problems in Epicurus*, Demetrius Laco specifies four possible meanings

---

52. Thus Erler's essay (1992b) on the relevance of *On Anger* to Virgil, who we know studied with Philodemus, is deliberately titled "Der Zorn des Heldens" ("the anger of the hero"). For further arguments, see that essay and Fish 2004, as well as our notes on frag. 31, with a newly edited passage from Philodemus's *On the Good King according to Homer* that Fish has kindly provided to us.

53. Annas 1992, 192–99, at 198; 1993, 194–99. For counterarguments to this view, see Armstrong 2008, 84–88.

54. On the crucial interrelationship of practical *kharis* and more ideal forms of *philia* in Epicureanism, see Armstrong 2016.

that an Epicurean could give to the term "by nature"; Procopé explains how they relate to Philodemus's term "natural anger."[55] In context (cols. 66–68), Demetrius is defending Epicurus's refusal to call parental affection natural. What is natural is (1) what comes about by unperverted natural instinct (*adiastrophōs*), such as needing nourishment; (2) what comes about by unavoidable necessity (*katēnangkasmenōs*), such as being liable to pain; (3) what comes about to our advantage (*sumpherontōs*), such as pursuing the virtues; and (4) the natural or "first" uses of words (*prōtai anaphōnēseis*), which give the best and simplest match with what is signified by the word. Procopé argues, and we accept, that three of these qualifiers (2-4) are relevant to *On Anger*.[56] If natural anger, in Philodemus's theory, has these three characteristics, we can see better why it is as necessary as it is natural: an emotion prompting self-defense against harm, felt by correct natural instinct, and one that must be available to every human being, even sages.[57]

Sorabji (2000, 201–3) argues that Philodemus's natural anger, which is described as "biting" in the treatise, can be compared with the "bites" of the Stoic pre-emotions or *propatheiai* and otherwise corresponds to the unemotional feelings of the Stoic sage.[58] But Stoic pre-emotions are precisely those that do not as yet lead to action, in contrast with Philodemus's view that natural anger must lead to action (cf. 41.2–8). It is important to establish, against critics such as Sorabji and Annas, that natural anger in its full sense is an unwelcome impulse toward deterrent punishment that can and must be inflicted decisively, that it comes about through serious provocation, and that it involves a serious response. Moreover, the only reason the sage is not greatly angered when he is intentionally and greatly harmed is that to him "nor is any external thing all that important, seeing that he is not liable to great [*tarakhais*] disturbances even through the presence of great pains, and much less through his fits of angers" (42.4–12). But this

---

55. For our account, see below, pp. 40–45. This passage has become standard in interpreting *On Anger*; see Procopé 1998, 179–80; Tsouna 2007a, 224–25; and Armstrong 2008, 83–84, 101–5, and 109, where Demetrius's categories of the natural are applied to the fear of death as described in Philodemus's *On Death*, as well as to natural anger as described in *On Anger*.

56. Sense 1 is also relevant: simply retaliating against harm intentionally done to us may be an instinctive and undistorted natural reaction, self-defense. See p. 42.

57. For discussion of the philosophical argument in *Textual Problems* 66–68, see McConnell 2017 and McOsker forthcoming a.

58. On *propatheiai*, see also Graver 2007, 85–108.

raises quite high the requirement for the sage's calm endurance of suffering; it is really the same argument from the sages' invulnerability as the argument that they are happy even on the torturer's rack.[59] The question is whether we should feel overwhelming transports of natural anger, not whether we should feel it as a genuine, fully experienced emotion (see Armstrong 2008, 87).

Voula Tsouna, in her very helpful chapter on Philodemus's *On Anger* (2007a, 195–238), argued strongly that Philodemus's natural anger is a real and active emotion. As she makes clear, "desire for revenge" is the most certain sign of empty anger. Chrysippus had given examples of a confused pleasure in anger itself, a pleasure so malevolently attractive that the angry person even gets angry with inanimate things, such as that of the man who bites the key for failing to open the door for him (frag. 19, cf. Chrysippus in *SVF* 3.478). Choleric and unreflective persons find the pleasure of what they imagine to be vengeance against an enemy so great that they go on the attack on any provocation, still blind to the consequences of their emotionally confused actions. Tsouna gives a good account of the section on diatribe and the diatribe itself (2007a, 204–17) and shows how Epicurean training in *epilogismos* (rational appraisal) and other rational techniques helps people to avoid empty emotion, while not abandoning natural emotion (2007a, 52–73).[60] She proves that by "bites" and "gnawings" Philodemus does not mean transient irritations or Stoic pre-emotions but real emotions that are based on reliable cognitions and can issue in significant acts (2007a, 32–51), and she has a helpful analysis of natural anger, as seen in the later columns of *On Anger* (2007a, 221–30).

Elizabeth Asmis's 2011 discussion of the necessity of natural anger in *On Anger* has been equally helpful to us. The last lines of the treatise say that a supposition of intentional harm is a necessary condition of anger but not a sufficient condition, just as being literate and numerate is necessary to be a sage but not sufficient. Procopé thought this was a weak and ineffective way to end the argument; the whole finale is "hurried and slapdash, as though the author had lost interest and decided that he had

---

59. Reported at Diogenes Laertius, *Vit. phil.* 10.118. Tsouna (2007a, 228) rightly cites Epicurus's famous deathbed letter as a parallel (frag. 138 [Usener 1887, 143] = frag. [52] at Arrighetti 1972, 427, *apud* Diogenes Laertius, *Vit. phil.* 10.22).

60. For the meaning of *epilogismos*, see Schofield 1996; Erler 2003. On consequences of anger, see below, n. 120.

gone on long enough" (1998, 188), but Asmis shows it to be a pointed and striking conclusion. Indeed, it constitutes a tacit appeal to the audience to think back through the whole treatise and see that Philodemus has indeed required much more as prerequisites for natural anger than merely a supposition of harm. The sage or the good person has to become good at reasoning and reflection, to develop a temperament and character that prevents careless and injudicious responses to provocation; however, even after all that precaution and self-searching, there remains a natural anger that will be accepted and acted on at some point by every person, the sage included. "What must be added to the assumption of harm to make anger follow in every case? To judge by Philodemus's illustration, the answer is: a lot" (Asmis 2011, 153). We do not agree with Asmis that there is a further distinction between necessary and unnecessary natural anger, based on the greatness of the provocation.[61] In our view, empty anger, in the strict sense, is always unnatural and unnecessary, and natural anger, in the strict sense, is always natural and necessary.

We are most indebted to Asmis, however, for her detailed exposition of the many ways in which the anger of fools ("useless persons," as she renders *mataioi*) differs from that of the wise and good. "An emotion is a feeling joined to a cognitive disposition. When the disposition is good, the emotion is good, even though the feeling itself may be bad. Conversely, when the disposition is bad, the emotion is bad, even if there is a feeling of pleasure" (2011, 162). Natural anger requires "a rich set of insights.... The assumption of harm is a very minor requirement: what is needed in addition is a complex set of judgments, *arising from a good disposition*, concerning the nature of the harm and the appropriate response to it" (2011, 171, emphasis added). This sums up the emphasis in *On Anger* on disposition and character in Philodemus's analyses of natural and empty anger. We are also indebted to Asmis's discussion of how Philodemus's definitions of natural and empty anger are influenced by and respond to the earlier definitions of the Peripatetics and Stoics (2011, 159–76, especially 171–76).

---

61. Asmis 2011, 176–82. Empty anger in *On Anger*, we would argue, is always unnatural (and thus unnecessary), whether it is provoked by trifles, middling offenses, or threats to life and limb. Natural anger, by contrast, is always both natural and necessary, whether it is about serious offences (*blabai*) or, in a milder form, a necessary part of the process of teaching and offering therapy to students, see below §6.3. Consequently, there are only two kinds of anger: natural and empty.

In the following analysis, we take for granted several points that seem to us already well established in the literature of *On Anger*. Now that we have reedited the fragments and arranged them in better order, we find it thematic that, at least in the later fragments (frags. 21–32), fools think their anger to be compulsory just because they suppose that harm has been done to them. But if that is all that they take into account, Philodemus argues, their anger is neither compulsory nor necessary. Without the richer mental context that Asmis describes, the fools' anger will indeed be empty and unnecessary. "A rich set of insights" and an alert and reflective disposition is indeed required as the context for natural anger. So the ironic challenge that Asmis sees in the treatise's final sentences, that we already know the supposition of intentional harm is insufficient, goes even further when we reread fragments 19–32. Badly damaged as they are, they clearly argue that only fools believe that the mere supposition that they have been harmed is a sufficient cause for anger. Anger on that basis alone is never compulsory. Asmis's intuition that the last sentence or two of *On Anger* is an ironic challenge to the reader or hearer to remember all the different requirements for natural anger beside "a supposition of harm" is still further vindicated.

These are some of the assumptions with which one must begin in explaining *On Anger*. Perhaps the most important aspect, and the one where we feel our attempts have been the most productive, is seeing what Philodemus's definition or sketch definition of anger really is, both for itself and in its historical context.

3. Plato and Aristotle on Anger[62]

The philosophical and literary interest of *On Anger* depends on its detailed working out of a polemical definition of anger—in more strictly Epicurean terms, a "sketch" (ὑπογραφή, *hypographē*) of the "preconception" (πρόληψις, *prolēpsis*) of anger that the Epicureans set up against Aristotle's definition of anger in the *Rhetoric*.[63] Aristotle's definition, in turn, was a response to a problem posed in Plato's *Philebus* about the mixture of pleasure and pain

---

62. For a summary of the topic, see Price 2009.
63. On *prolēpsis*, see Verde 2013a, 64–72, with further bibliography at 248–50; on *prolēpsis* and *hypographē*, see Fine 2014, 226–56. Beyond Verde's introduction to Epicureanism, see also O'Keefe 2010; Long 1986; and the primary sources gathered in Long and Sedley 1987, 1:87–90 and 2:91–93. For the Epicurean hostility to Academic,

in our emotions. Additionally, the *Protagoras* appears to have influenced Epicurus in at least two ways: his definition of the "hedonic calculus" (or, as Epicurus calls it, *symmetrēsis*, *Men.* 129–130) is couched in language much like that of Socrates's pioneering statement of this concept to Protagoras at *Prot.* 354a–357e. Similarly, Protagoras's Great Speech in the dialogue pioneers the theory of punishment as deterrence. Aristotle argued that both the pain of anger, that of experiencing intentional and undeserved slight (ὀλιγωρία), and the pleasure mixed with it, that of first imagining and then executing revenge (τιμωρία), are morally acceptable if not allowed to become excessive.

In *On Anger*, Philodemus does not directly engage with Plato's *Protagoras* or *Philebus* or with Aristotle's *Rhetoric* or *Nicomachean Ethics*, but they are essential background for his ideas. Not because Philodemus had read these texts or, in Aristotle's case, even seen copies of them, but because their language about the emotions profoundly influenced Epicurus and his circle. Plato's and Aristotle's vocabulary for describing and defining anger, revenge, and punishment influences Philodemus's language and arguments at every point in this treatise.

Protagoras's Great Speech, where he pioneers the theory of punishment as deterrence, already contains much of the terminology and even phraseology found in *On Anger*'s central theory: that natural anger does not aim at the pleasure of vengeance but only at the calm, practical infliction of deterrent punishment "for the sake of the future":

> In the case of evils that people believe each other to have by nature or by fortune, such as being ugly or short or weak, no one gets angry at [θυμοῦται], reproves [νουθετεῖ], teaches, or punishes [κολάζει] them for having these evils, so that they will not be like that any longer; people just pity them. Who is so absurd as to do anything like that to the ugly or the short or the weak? For I think they know these things come to people by nature and fortune, for good or bad. But as for things that they think are goods that come to people from practice and exercise and teaching, that is where you see fits of anger [θυμοί] and punishments [κολάсεις] and reproofs [νουθετήсεις], things like wrongdoing and impiety and in general everything opposite to civic virtue.
>
> There everyone gets angry with everyone else and tries to reprove them, obviously because civic virtue can be acquired by teaching and

Peripatetic, and Stoic lists of definitions and the use of *hypographē* instead, see Asmis 1984, 35–47; Besnier 1994; Giovacchini 2003; and Tsouna 2016.

practice. If you are willing, Socrates, to consider what "to punish wrongdoers" means, that itself will teach you that humans think virtue can be acquired. No one punishes a human just to punish and just because one did wrong, except for a person who, like a beast, unreasoningly [ἀλογίστως] goes after revenge [τιμωρεῖται]. A person who punishes with reason [μετὰ λόγου] does not take vengeance because of a past offense because one cannot make what has been done to be undone. One punishes for the sake of the future, so that the person will neither offend again, nor will any other who has seen that person receiving his punishment [τοῦ μέλλοντος χάριν, ἵνα μὴ αὖθις ἀδικήσηι μήτε οὗτος μήτε ἄλλος ὁ τοῦτον ἰδὼν κολασθέντα]. (Plato, *Prot.* 323d–324b)

Here we find almost exactly the same distinction as Philodemus makes in *On Anger* between punishment (κόλασις), the objective of natural anger, and revenge, the objective of some kinds of empty anger. Revenge is never compulsory to those who can reason. The good Epicurean, who has learned the techniques of *logismos* and *epilogismos*, reflection and appraisal, punishes for a reason, with the goal of deterrence, as is characteristic of natural anger, rather than seeking revenge for any or no reason—except one's own pleasure, as happens in empty anger. That is the same idea as in the *Protagoras* passage.

Further, Protagoras says that the offender, once punished, "will neither offend again, nor will any other who has seen that person receiving his punishment." This passage helps explain Philodemus's own statement, couched in rather difficult Greek, of what is achieved by punishment: εἰ δ' ἀλλότριον καὶ γινώσκει, διότι κολασθεὶς ἀνασταλήσεται καὶ τοὺς ἄλλους ἐπιστήσει, μανικῶς οὐκ ἂν ἔλθοι πά[λι]ν καθ' ἕνα γέ τινα τρόπο[ν] δακών. τὸ δὲ τοιοῦτο[ν ὀ]ργὴν [κ]αλοῦμεν (41.2–9), which must mean that, "if it is an alienated feeling (i.e., if he feels alienated)—and he knows that, when punished, the person will be stopped cold and will deter the others—it would be insane not to come back in one way or another, gritting his teeth (as he does so)."[64] That sort of thing, Philodemus adds, "is what we (Epicureans) call anger." The fuller passage in *Protagoras* resolves the ambiguities in Philodemus's more telegraphic one. Natural anger aims at punishment that stops further offense by the offender and "the others," that is, anyone else who has seen the offender punished. Further, Philodemus makes the same distinction as "Protagoras": *only* punishment should be the goal of

---

64. On gritting one's teeth, see Procopé 1998, 191 n. 41; see also our note ad loc.

natural anger, and the pleasure of revenge, or even pleasure in punishing, is a sure indication that something has gone wrong. Natural anger always looks to the future and is focused entirely on the prevention of further harm, either by the offenders or anyone else who might be inspired to follow their lead.

At *Phileb.* 47e, where Plato makes the first surviving list of emotions in Greek philosophy and attempts to define them, Socrates characterizes "anger and fear and desire and mourning and sexual love and jealousy and envy and similar emotions" (ὀργὴν καὶ φόβον καὶ πόθον καὶ θρῆνον καὶ ἔρωτα καὶ ζῆλον καὶ φθόνον καὶ ὅσα τοιαῦτα) as being "kinds of distresses of the soul itself" (αὐτῆς τῆς ψυχῆς ... λύπας τινάς)—which, however, are also "full of irresistible pleasures" (ἡδονῶν μεστάς ... ἀμηχάνων). Socrates gives anger as his first example of this mixed pain and pleasure and uses a quotation from Homer to characterize it: "the line '(sc. anger), which goads on even the most self-controlled man to get angry and is much sweeter than honey pouring down'" (τὸ "[sc. χόλος,] ὅς τ' ἐφέηκε πολύφρονά περ χαλεπῆναι / ὅς τε πολὺ γλυκίων μέλιτος καταλειβομένοιο"; *Il.* 18.108–109).[65]

Socrates and Protarchus are discussing whether pleasures and pains are false if they are based on false opinions and expectations or true if based on true opinions and expectations (*Phileb.* 36c–42a), since in either case we really feel them. Plato makes clear from the start that every definition of emotion should account for both true and false opinions or cogni-

---

65. Plato does not quote Homer's whole passage, "may strife perish from among gods and mortals, and anger, which goads on even the most self-controlled man to get angry and is much sweeter than honey pouring down and can grow up like smoke in men's chests." Achilles is lamenting to his mother Thetis that his anger has brought about the death of Patroclus and will soon bring about his own. By the comparison of anger to smoke, he admits that pleasure in feeling anger broke down his self-control and confused him. The lines have a long afterlife in the theory of anger: Aristotle quotes them at *Rhet.* 2.2, 1378b1–9 (discussed below) and at *Rhet.* 1.11 1370b11–14 in discussing the pleasures of painful emotions: "Even being angry is pleasant; Homer said of anger that it is 'far sweeter than dripping honey,' for no one feels anger against those on whom vengeance cannot be inflicted or those who are far more powerful than oneself" (and thus one can fantasize with pleasure about getting vengeance). Chrysippus also analyzed them in full (*SVF* 2.890, 905–6, 911); see also Tieleman 2003, 157–62. Armstrong has recently shown that these lines were used by Diogenes of Oenoanda in NF 203, which on his and Gronewald's suggestion now reads "for this very reason Homer, poetically calling anger χόλος ['bile'], says it flows more sweetly than honey"; see Hammerstaedt and Smith 2014, 274–75; Smith 1993 and 2003.

tions about whatever has happened, is happening, or is going to happen to provoke an emotional reaction. This distinction between true and false pleasure and pain in emotions is at the root of Philodemus's distinction between empty and natural anger: for Philodemus, empty anger has no sufficient basis in reason and is not based on realities. Plato had said:

> As it turns out, he who has any opinion at all always really has an opinion, even if it is sometimes not based on realities whether present, past, or future … [and] he who feels pleasure at all in any way always really feels pleasure, although it is sometimes not based on realities, whether present or past, and often, perhaps most frequently, on things that will never be realities even in the future…. the same may be said of fears and angers and everything like them, that all those sorts of things are sometimes false. (*Phileb.* 40c8–e5)

As Fortenbaugh says, this passage

> makes clear that Plato saw an intimate relation between emotion and cognition. But it fails to make this relationship clear…. Further clarification was necessary … and we can imagine lively debate in the Academy concerning the way cognition is involved in emotional response. Aristotle was most certainly part of this debate…. he recognized cognition as the efficient cause and formulated a demonstrative account of emotional response. (2002, 11)

This emphasis on cognition can be seen in Aristotle's definition of anger at *Rhet.* 2.2, 1378a30–32:

> ἔστω δὴ ὀργὴ ὄρεξις μετὰ λύπης τιμωρίας φαινομένης διὰ φαινομένην ὀλιγωρίαν εἰς αὐτὸν ἢ τῶν αὐτοῦ, τοῦ ὀλιγωρεῖν μὴ προσήκοντος.
>
> Let anger, therefore, be an appetition, accompanied by pain, for what appears to be vengeance, because of an apparent slight against oneself or one's friends, the slight being unmerited.[66]

As Cooper and others have pointed out, it is necessary to understand φαινομένη as "apparent" rather than "obvious, notorious."[67] That provides

---

66. On Aristotle and the emotions in general, see Dow 2015 and Gastaldi's 2014 commentary on the *Rhetoric*.
67. We take φαινομένη to mean "apparent," i.e. "appears to you," against the mis-

the cognitive element: it appears to the subject that she has been slighted, and she seeks what appears to her to be, what she thinks is, vengeance.[68] On Moss's "phantasist" view (2012, 97), *phantasiai* reliably cause the formation of beliefs, though this process can be interrupted by rational people: seeing my reflection in a funhouse mirror does not make me believe that I am suddenly rail thin and eight feet fall, though it might confuse my cat. Evaluative beliefs of the sort that regularly accompany emotions are formed in this way, though the emotions are provoked by the *phantasiai* and accordingly are nonrational. If Megacleides does not invite Hipparchus to dinner, Hipparchus has the appearance of being slighted, and this leads, if nothing intervenes, to a belief that he has been slighted. At the same time, the appearance of being slighted provokes the mental reaction that we call emotion and a boiling of the blood around his heart. So emotions have a relationship to beliefs in that both come from appearances, but it is the appearance itself, not the belief, that leads to the emotion. (Making emotions depend on beliefs will be a major innovation of both the Stoics and Epicureans.) Reflection and access to a wider range of facts can strengthen or weaken both the emotion and the belief by producing new *phantasiai* or by causing us to change or modify our judgments. One of the most famous of Aristotle's illustrations of how emotion modifies judgment is his comparison of anger to an eager servant who rushes to execute your orders before you finish telling him in detail what they are (*Eth. nic.* 7.6, 1149a25–28). Means to stop the servant from rushing off too soon are listed in *Rhet.* 2.3, which treats how a speaker can calm anger when it is already present.

Clearly taking his cue from Plato, Aristotle puts anger at the head of his list of emotions in the *Rhetoric* and uses the same passage of the *Iliad* as a reference point for the "mixed pleasure and pain" of anger. In fact, the

---

taken translations "manifest" or "conspicuous"; see Harris 1997; Konstan 2003, 101–3. Moss (2012, 95–98) notes that *phantasiai* are preconditions for thoughts and that Aristotle is not always precise on this point. Philodemus's use of *phantasia* in frag. 28 cannot be pinned down with certainty but probably means "belief," as if following Moss's "doxasist" camp.

68. Vengeance has already been defined as a matter of personal fulfillment: διὰ θυμὸν δὲ καὶ ὀργὴν τὰ τιμωρητικά, διαφέρει δὲ τιμωρία καὶ κόλασις· ἡ μὲν γὰρ κόλασις τοῦ πάσχοντος ἕνεκά ἐστιν, ἡ δὲ τιμωρία τοῦ ποιοῦντος, ἵνα πληρωθῆι ("Vengeance works by wrath and anger, but vengeance and punishment differ: punishment is for the sake of the person who suffers it, but vengeance is for the sake of the person who wreaks it, so that he may be satisfied," *Rhet.* 1.10, 1369b11–14).

influence of *Phileb.* 47e is crucial. In the *Rhetoric*, Aristotle puts forth a general definition of emotion:

ἔcτι δὲ τὰ πάθη, δι' ὅcα μεταβάλλοντες διαφέρουcι πρὸc τὰc κρίcειc, οἷc ἕπεται λύπη καὶ ἡδονή, οἷον ὀργὴ ἔλεοc φόβοc καὶ ὅcα ἄλλα τοιαῦτα, καὶ τὰ τούτοιc ἐναντία.

The emotions are all those feelings by which people so change as to make a difference in their judgments and which are attended by pain and pleasure. Such are anger, pity, fear, and the like, with their opposites. (*Rhet.* 2.1, 1378a20–23)

Pain and pleasure cause people to change their judgments by affecting both how the facts of the situation are seen and their response to it, so a speaker who knows how to appeal to an audience's emotions can change their judgment. But Aristotle does not find *both* pleasure and pain in any of the emotions except anger, where he tries to find them when he makes both the pain of being slighted and "a kind of pleasure that comes from the hope of revenge" essential to it.[69] If there is no such hope, anger cannot be felt: "no one can be angry with those they fear or for whom they feel reverence" (*Rhet.* 2.3, 1380a31–32), that is, those on whom revenge is impossible. But beyond pleasure in achieving revenge, and consistent with the Platonic—and Homeric—roots of the definition, Aristotle finds pleasure in imagining revenge:

καὶ πάcηι ὀργῆι ἕπεcθαί τινα ἡδονήν, τὴν ἀπὸ τῆc ἐλπίδοc τοῦ τιμωρήcαcθαι· ἡδὺ μὲν γὰρ τὸ οἴεcθαι τεύξεcθαι ὧν ἐφίεται, οὐδεὶc δὲ τῶν φαινομένων ἀδυνάτων ἐφίεται αὑτῶι, ὁ δ' ὀργιζόμενοc ἐφίεται δυνατῶν αὑτῶι. διὸ καλῶc εἴρηται περὶ θυμοῦ· ὅc τε πολὺ γλυκίων μέλιτοc καταλειβομένοιο ἀνδρῶν ἐν cτήθεccιν ἀέξεται· ἀκολουθεῖ γὰρ καὶ ἡδονή τιc διά τε τοῦτο

---

69. Fortenbaugh 2008, 33–37. On this sort of anomaly in *Rhet.* 2, see Cooper 1999, 410–19. Hatred is said to be painless: "anger is accompanied by pain, hatred is not; the angry man feels pain, but the hater does not" (*Rhet.* 2.4, 1382a2–3). In *Pol.* 1312b26–34 anger is said to be more active (πρακτικώτερον) than hatred, because the pain of anger makes reasoning (λογίζεcθαι) difficult, but hatred does not; see Moss 2012, 81 n. 27. But hatred is not said to be a pleasure, either. All this is probably relevant to Philodemus's view that the sage will never be greatly angered because he cannot be greatly harmed, but he can feel the most intense aversion (ἀλλοτρίωcιc) and hatred (μῖcοc) in return for being harmed (41.39–42.3; cf. 41.15–16).

καὶ διότι διατρίβουςιν ἐν τῶι τιμωρεῖςθαι τῆι διανοίαι· ἡ οὖν τότε γινομένη
φανταςία ἡδονὴν ἐμποιεῖ, ὥςπερ ἡ τῶν ἐνυπνίων.

> and on all anger there follows a kind of pleasure that comes from the hope of getting revenge. For pleasure follows on the thought that one is going to achieve one's desire, but no one desires anything that seems impossible to him, so the angry man desires what is possible for himself. And thus it was well said about anger that "it is something much sweeter than honey dripping down as it swells up in a man's chest...." for in fact a certain pleasure follows, both through that hope and because one is indulging in the pastime of getting revenge in one's imagination; and certainly, the image that then occurs creates pleasure, like the pleasure of one's dreams. (*Rhet.* 2.2, 1378b1–9)

Aristotle's definition of anger, an appetition for revenge on some particular person that is caused by the pain of a slight and generates pleasant visions of vengeance, makes it seem a dangerous thing to nourish. The definition is rendered more disturbingly attractive by revenge's counting as self-realization, a major good in Aristotelian psychology.[70] It is essential to the definition of anger in the *Rhetoric* that one should not only take revenge but, first in fantasy and then in reality, confront the guilty party and shame him for the mistake made in slighting you. In the same vein, Aristotle says that anger is softened in its intensity if the victims think the guilty party will never know that the punishment "was because of them and in requital for their personal wrongs ... and thus Homer was right to say 'tell him it was Odysseus, sacker of cities' (*Od.* 9.504), since Polyphemus would not have suffered vengeance, if he had remained ignorant of who had blinded him and for what" (*Rhet.* 2.3, 1380b20–24). Aristotle goes on to say that angry people also lose interest in vengeance against the

---

70. Aristotle's phrase τεύξεςθαι ὧν ἐφίεται ("to achieve what one desires") echoes archaic elegy, e.g., Theognis 256: "it is the most pleasant of all things to attain what you long for" (τοῦ τις ἐρᾶι τὸ τυχεῖν). Cf. in the discussion in *Rhet.* 1.11, 1370b29–32, of how to appeal to an audience's natural *epithymia* for pleasure: "getting revenge is also a pleasurable thing; for that which it is painful to fail of getting, it is pleasant to get; and angry men are pained beyond measure if they cannot get vengeance but take pleasure in hoping for it," a passage that underlies our frag. 7 (see note ad loc.). On the *Rhet.* 1 passage's morally dangerous definition of anger as an *epithymia*, see Striker 1996, 286–302. The Homeric context—anger and its vocabulary as expressive of a society where honor is fundamental to selfhood and identity—is well set out by Cairns 2003, esp. 39–41.

dead or against those who will never know at whose hands they suffered. Just as Aristotle ignored, for the sake of his argument, the tragic dimension of Achilles's words, he does not mention what was equally obvious to him and his audience: revenge requires that the offender should be made to realize his mistake in offending you personally, and ideally in your own presence, or else something is missing. It was because he felt he needed this pleasure that Odysseus committed an act of hybris against the Cyclops and defied the urgent warning of his shipmates by telling him that it was not "Outis" but "Odysseus of Ithaca, the sacker of cities, the son of Laertes" who had blinded him. By ignoring their warning, Odysseus brought about the vengeance of Poseidon, whom the Cyclops immediately invoked when he was told "who had blinded him and for what." It appears that, in *On the Good King according to Homer*, Philodemus explicitly interpreted Odysseus's reckless boast to the Cyclops as an expression of empty anger.[71] Philodemus argued that Odysseus was made to learn restraint by this episode, as his later behavior showed. His punishment of the suitors was an act of natural anger, it seems, for he refused to boast over the fallen.

Aristotle carefully specifies another limitation on the pleasure of revenge: one must believe, rightly or not, that it can really be achieved. As we saw, "no one feels anger against those on whom vengeance cannot be inflicted or those who are far more powerful than oneself" (*Rhet.* 1.11, 1370b12–14). Philodemus shares this assumption: if the sage "*knows* that, when punished, he (sc. the adversary) will be checked and will rein in others…" (41.3–5). Without the knowledge that he can at least probably inflict punishment, the practicing Epicurean cannot be angry.

It is also important to specify (and this holds for all the philosophers and definitions we are discussing) that anger in the full sense is a feeling that commits one to action, a desire or impulse that "is never an idle wish."[72] Anger of a milder kind—angry outbursts and surly behavior by

---

71. See below, pp. 51–52. Aristotle himself is said to have asked (in the lost *Homeric Problems*) why Odysseus "foolishly insulted" (ἀνοήτωc … ὠλιγώρηcεν) Poseidon in reply to the Cyclops's invocation of him by saying "not even Poseidon shall heal that eye." Though Odysseus had been terribly wronged by the Cyclops, he should not have provoked Poseidon, "for it is not the same thing from a slave to a freeman as from a freeman to a slave, nor to the kindred of gods (τοῖc θεῶν ἐγγὺc οὖcι) from those outside their circle" (*Problemata Homerica* frag. 174 Rose 1886 = Σ$^{HTQ(M)}$ *Od.* 9.525).

72. Fortenbaugh 1985, 222.

sages and their students—is discussed separately by Philodemus in columns 34–37, with explicit reference to the manual for Epicurean teachers, *On Frank Speech* (*De libertate dicendi*). There the language is more like that of Aristotle's later discussion of anger in the *Nicomachean Ethics*.

In *Eth. nic.* 4.5, Aristotle tempered the definition found in *Rhet.* 2 by giving an account in terms of excess and deficiency in anger, not pleasure and pain.[73] The right state is "mildness" (ἡμερότης, the disposition of tame, not wild, animals; cf. *Ir.* 44.26), "though really there is no word for it" (*Eth. nic.* 4.5, 1125b27–29), which, he specifies, is actually the capacity to get angry "on the right grounds and at the right persons and for the right length of time" (4.5, 1125b31–33). The mild person would rather err "by defect," for such a one is "not vengeful but rather inclined to forgive" (4.5, 1125b32–26a2). The defect is "a kind of lack of anger, or whatever one could call it" (εἴτ' ἀοργησία τις εἴθ' ὅτι δή ποτε, 4.5, 1126a3–4; cf. 2.7, 1108a8).[74] Those incapable of anger do not get angry "in the right manner, at the right time, and with the right people" and are blamed because they do not perceive or feel distressed by insults, and "if one is not angered, one cannot defend oneself, and it is slavish to put up with insults to oneself or one's friends" (*Eth. nic.* 4.5, 1126a3–8). The excess is "a kind of irascibility" (ὀργιλότης τις, *Eth. nic.* 4.5, 1125b29–30), and the "irascible" (ὀργίλοι) are those who "get angry too quickly, with the wrong people, over the wrong things, and more deeply than they should, but whose anger is soon over—

---

73. Frede (1996) evaluates Aristotle's change of tone in *Eth. nic.* 4.5 and argues that the relics of Platonism and the *Philebus* in Aristotle's treatment of the emotions as vehicles of pain and pleasure in *Rhet.* 1–2 are useless baggage and ethically dubious. She finds that the treatment of emotions, in line with that of the virtues, by the rule of excess, mean, and deficiency in the *Nicomachean Ethics* is much more coherent with Aristotelian ethics overall. But she admits that Aristotle handed the *Rhet.* 1–2 treatment down unrevised, apparently intentionally. There is a memorable protest against Aristotle's careless overvaluation of revenge and its modern admirers in Burnyeat's 2002 review of Harris 2001, explicitly referencing the events and ongoing effects of September 11, 2001. But the influence of the portrayal of the emotions in *Rhet.* 2 lived on not just in philosophy but in both Greek and Roman rhetoric (see Webb 1997), and that of the treatment of anger in *Eth. nic.* 4.5 was limited to less passionate contexts, as here in cols. 34–37 (also 18–21, the satirical treatment of anger in students of philosophy).

74. The context makes clear that he is improvising or fixing a new meaning on at least some of these terms, which of course live on throughout the literature of anger until late antiquity and beyond, not just in *On Anger* and *On Frank Speech*.

the best thing about them." It is difficult to sustain that kind of anger for long. These people also "do not keep in their anger, but they pay back the insult in front of everyone, because of their sharp temper, and are done" (*Eth. nic.* 4.5, 1126a13–18). Philodemus, however, uses *orgilos* of people with a vicious general disposition to anger (*Ir.* 34.17, 29, 31, 35; 36.20, 33); for him *aorgētos* means "with a good person's, or a sage's, dispositional resistance to empty anger."[75]

Aristotle identifies several types of irascible people. One is the sharp-tempered (ἀκράχολοι; see *Ir.* 36.3; *Lib.* 3b.4) "who get angry over everything and on all occasions: that is why the word is used." Another is the "bitter" (πικροί), who are hard to deal with and stay angry over time.[76] How much better to get vengeance right away: "when one retaliates there is an end to it, for vengeance gets rid of the anger, creating pleasure in place of pain" (*Eth. nic.* 4.5, 1126a21–22; cf. *Ir.* 11.11–12: κἂν μὴ τὴν δίκην αὐτόθεν ἐπιθῶσι). A third type includes those whom "we call those difficult people (χαλεποί; cf. *Ir.* 37.2) ... who cannot be reconciled until they get vengeance or punishment" (*Eth. nic.* 4.5, 1126a26–28). Here Aristotle treats *timōria* (vengeance) and *kolasis* (punishment) as interchangeable, despite taking *kolasis* as the proper "healing" or "cure" for an offense in *Rhet.* 1.[77]

In anger, the deficiency, Aristotle goes on, is to be preferred to the excess, because the excess is apt to happen more often (*Eth. nic.* 4.5, 1126a30: "for going after vengeance is more human").[78] The *Rhetoric*'s definition of anger is mirrored in Philodemus's list of elements for describing the *prolēpsis* of anger, and the language of *Eth. nic.* 4.5 is mirrored in Philodemus's discussions of the sages' and superior students' harmless and merely apparent irascibility (*Ir.* 34–37) and of the empty anger exhibited

---

75. This is explained in detail at 34.31–39; cf. *Lib.* frag. 12.7.

76. Cf. πικρός at *Ir.* 36.34 and *Lib.* frag. 60.4, 2a.7, and 16a.11; and πικρία at *Ir.* 26.14.

77. *Rhet.* 1.14, 1374b33: ἡ γὰρ δίκη καὶ κόλασις ἴασις ("for justice and punishment are the cure"). By contrast, *Ir.* 44.28–35 shows that pleasure in inflicting punishment is always a sign of empty anger.

78. Aristotle seems somewhat equivocal on this point: we praise the *aorgētos* person as being "mild" but the *orgilos* as "manly and fit for command" (*Eth. nic.* 4.5, 1126b1–2: ἀνδρώδεις καὶ δυναμένους ἄρχειν; cf. *Ir.* 31.17). But to be so incapable of anger as to resist being insulted, and to put up with insults to one's friends, is "slavish" (ἀνδραποδῶδες, *Eth. nic.* 4.5, 1126a7–8). The effect is as if Aristotle preferred the excess to the deficiency after all.

by some students, bad enough already and symptomatic of worse to come as they grow up (18–21).[79]

Historically, Aristotle was taken to approve of pleasure in imagining and inflicting vengeance.[80] He was also criticized, and still is, for making mere slights an adequate provocation to anger and for holding that affronts to one's honor and social standing are important even to the good and the wise.[81] But he provides later philosophers with what they thought were more appropriate words to define the grounds for anger: "injustice" (ἀδικία), used by the Stoics; and "harm" (βλάβη), used by the Epicureans. Aristotle was not so committed to slights as the necessary and sufficient cause of anger; to him, as to everyone, if slights are enough to provoke anger, so injustice and assault will be enough, a fortiori. For instance, in the definitions of "misadventure," "culpable error," and "injustice" in *Eth. nic.* 5.8, 1135b17–22, 25–28, and 1136a1, where anger figures importantly, he says:

> ὅταν μὲν οὖν παραλόγως ἡ βλάβη γένηται, ἀτύχημα· ὅταν δὲ μὴ παραλόγως ἄνευ δὲ κακίας, ἁμάρτημα (ἁμαρτάνει μὲν γὰρ ὅταν ἡ ἀρχὴ ἐν αὑτῶι ἦι τῆς αἰτίας, ἀτυχεῖ δ' ὅταν ἔξωθεν)· ὅταν δὲ εἰδὼς μὲν μὴ προβουλεύσας δέ, ἀδίκημα, οἷον ὅσα τε διὰ θυμὸν καὶ ἄλλα πάθη, ὅσα ἀναγκαῖα ἢ φυσικὰ συμβαίνει τοῖς ἀνθρώποις...διὸ καλῶς τὰ ἐκ θυμοῦ οὐκ ἐκ προνοίας κρίνεται· οὐ γὰρ ἄρχει ὁ θυμῶι ποιῶν, ἀλλ' ὁ ὀργίσας. ἔτι δὲ οὐδὲ περὶ τοῦ γενέσθαι ἢ μὴ ἀμφισβητεῖται, ἀλλὰ περὶ τοῦ δικαίου· ἐπὶ φαινομένηι γὰρ ἀδικίαι ἡ ὀργή ἐστιν...ἂν δ' ἐκ προαιρέσεως βλάψηι, ἀδικεῖ.

> When the harm happens contrary to reasonable expectation, it is (1) a misadventure; when it happens according to reasonable expectation but without evil intent, it is (2) a culpable error, for an error is culpable when the cause starts with oneself but only a misadventure when the cause is outside oneself; but when harm is done knowingly but without malice aforethought, it is (3) an injustice, for example, what is done in anger or

---

79. Aristotle's language of anger in *Eth. nic.* 4.5 is also echoed in *On Frank Speech*, which discusses at length the sages' prerogative of confronting and blaming students with the angry and harsh kind of "frank speech." This provides another serious, though not life-threatening, area where the teachers can reluctantly accept the promptings of sincere anger, in order to confront a student and in hopes of his correction. Philodemus cross-references *Lib.* 2a–5b at *Ir.* 36.22–26.

80. For a good survey of Aristotelian passages on anger, see Harris 2001, 193–97.

81. Kaufman forthcoming.

any other emotion *that is natural or necessary* to humankind.[82] ... acts due to anger are rightly considered to be without malice aforethought, for the person who acts in wrath does not start the affair, but rather the person who got him angry does. Also, one is not arguing over whether the fact occurred or not but over its justice, for anger is excited by what appears to be injustice.... but if (the other has intentionally harmed you), he wrongs you.

In specifying what provokes anger here, Aristotle falls naturally into the language the Stoics and Epicureans prefer. What causes anger in a good person, they felt, should be more important than slight or insult: being wronged or harmed. Yet when the Stoics defined anger or the Epicureans sketched out its "preconception" or *prolēpsis*, the language of the *Rhetoric* about the pain of insult and the joy of revenge still shaped the response.

4. The Stoic and Epicurean Reactions

Theophrastus, Aristotle's successor as head of the Peripatetic school, already attempted to save the Peripatetic view of anger from advocating the dangerous pleasure of revenge. He sees nothing wrong with being angry at first, or even enraged, allowing oneself to be inflamed by the guilty party's misdeeds (importantly, not slights). But one should be much more calm and purposeful in seeking redress:

> men of practical wisdom [φρόνηcιc] should do nothing at all in anger, for rage [θυμόc] is most unreasonable and will never do anything with forethought, but drunken with contentiousness, as may happen, it is subject to impulses. Consequently, you ought not to take immediate revenge [τιμωρίαι] for misdeeds [ἁμαρτήματα], either from slaves or from anyone else, in order that you may always do what (seems) best to reason [λογιcμόc], not what is dear to rage, and that you may extract a penalty from your enemies, as a result of which you will harm [βλάψειν] them, without causing yourself distress [cαυτὸν μὴ λυπῶν]. For taking revenge on someone while injuring yourself is no less to pay a penalty than to extract one.[83]

---

82. For Philodemus, natural anger is inescapable (ἀνέκφευκτον, *Ir.* 39.29; 40.4–5, 20) and most necessary (ἀναγκαιότατον, 44.19). Some translators take θυμόc as "sudden anger," but see pp. 77–78 below.

83. Theophrastus, L88, Fortenbaugh 1984, 52 = Stobaeus *Anth.* 3.19.12, trans. Fortenbaugh 1985, 210, slightly altered. For the thought that the vengeful are at risk of

This is already more like the Stoic and Epicurean view that slights are not a serious enough cause to justify anger. Also, Theophrastus wants the response to be guided by *logismos*, reflection and reason, not emotion. He thus tried to preempt the very objection Philodemus brings against "the Peripatetics" in *Ir.* 31.24–33.

Despite attempts such as Theophrastus's to modify it,[84] Aristotle's definition of anger in *Rhet.* 2 lived on, at least in Peripatetic doxography, and influenced the Epicureans' and Stoics' definitions of anger in turn.[85] It is possible that some main details of Philodemus's theory of anger go back to Epicurus and his circle, who knew the *Philebus*, *Rhetoric*, and *Nicomachean Ethics* as important recent texts. But Philodemus's theory also shows signs that Epicureans had developed it over the course of their arguments against the Stoics in the generations after Epicurus's death.

For the Stoics, every emotion begins with a false judgment about a proposition that something is good or bad, which in turn entails an impulse that exceeds the bounds of reason and is disobedient to it.[86] Errors of judgment and wrong opinions are the only sort of cognitions that constitute emotions. Thus all emotions are indeed cognitive, since they are evaluative beliefs, but the values are always false or distorted and entail assenting to the proposition that a merely apparent good or bad is actually good or bad—or, in the case of anger, two such propositions: that someone did something bad to you and that your getting revenge for it is good. Emotions can be divided into four categories: desires and fears for the future and pains and pleasures in the present (ἐπιθυμίαι, φόβοι, λυπαί, and ἡδοναί; see Chrysippus *SVF* 3.377, 385–87, etc.). Under each of these are gathered

---

causing more pain to themselves than to their enemies, see *Ir.* 27.26–39, 42.34–39, and 44.28–32. It was already a commonplace of the diatribe against anger when Philodemus wrote, see Wilke's apparatus of quotations ad locc.

84. For Theophrastus's view of anger, Fortenbaugh (2008, 39–41) is helpful. Theophrastus probably anticipated the Stoics in holding that anger should be motivated by injustice (*adikia*) rather than merely a slight (*oligōria*). Seneca ascribes to him the proposition that the good will be angered by injustices to their own family and friends (*irascuntur boni viri pro suorum iniuriis*, *Ir.* 1.12.3).

85. On the Stoic and Epicurean views of emotions in general, see Gill 2009. For Aristotle's influence on the Epicureans, see in general Verde 2016; for his influence on the Stoics, see now Bénatouïl 2016.

86. See, in general, Chrysippus at *SVF* 3.377–94.

the individual emotions.[87] Anger is now defined as "a desire for vengeance on the person who appears to have wronged us undeservedly" (ἐπιθυμία τιμωρίας τοῦ ἠδικηκέναι δοκοῦντος οὐ προσηκόντως; cf. Chrysippus SVF 3.395–98). This implies that anger continues to include an irrational desire for vengeance, but punishment is not in the definition, for the Stoics give the word *kolasis* a positive value in the few places it appears. Anger is irrational; it cannot set anything right.[88]

Accordingly, the student of Stoicism who thinks she has actually been wronged has to think again. In fact, the sage cannot be wronged and cannot be truly hurt, except momentarily, and without assenting to the proposition that she really was harmed.[89] (For that matter, the sage never really "thinks" something is so; she knows it to be so.) So the student should realize that her emotion rests on an incorrect appraisal of the facts. She is hoping for what appears to her to be something good in what appears to her to be vengeance because of what appears to her to be something bad, specifically an injustice. But none of these appearances corresponds to reality. The student's only recourse is to set things right without emotion, as an athlete recovers position without anger in a match.[90]

It would be wrong, however, to think that the Stoic sage is cold or emotionless. She can feel as intensely as she pleases three εὐπάθειαι, or "rational emotional experiences": χαρά, joy, which corresponds to pleasure; βούλησις, will, which corresponds to desire; and εὐλάβεια, caution, which corresponds to fear. (Nothing corresponds to λυπή, distress.) Like the *genera* of normal emotions, these also cover groups of individual feelings. Moreover, the sage experiences impulses to emotion that a nonphilosophical person experiences, but only as *propatheiai* or pre-emotions. These can be extremely intense, but the sage will not assent to them, so they cannot issue in action. So she certainly understands how emotions lead people wrong: she has felt their attraction even if in the end she refused to act on it.[91]

---

87. On the division and organization of the emotions and *eupatheiai*, see Rabel 1977; Graver 2007, 35–60, with handy charts.

88. *Kolasis* appears at SVF 2.296–97, where it is defined as "setting things right" or "correction" (ἐπανόρθωσις), 2.338–39, and 3.81. What the sage can do is punish without emotion to set things right.

89. Feeling pain is a different matter. See Chrysippus SVF 3.288, 578, and 579; and Seneca, *On the Constancy of the Sage*, passim.

90. The Stoic Antipater of Tarsus (d. 130/129 BCE) is quoted with approval by Philodemus for this comparison in *Ir.* 33.34–40.

91. On *propatheiai*, see Sorabji 2000, 47–51 and 69–71; and Graver 1999 and

The Stoic definition plays against Aristotle's definition to a certain degree.⁹² Defining anger as "assent to the propositions that one has been harmed and that revenge would be good" is a deliberate rewriting of Aristotle's "appetition for what appears to be vengeance upon a person who has apparently slighted us." The Stoics, following Theophrastus, have rejected "slight" as a cause for anger and replaced it with "injustice," and Aristotle's *orexis* has now been deliberately replaced by *epithymia*, which for the Stoics is more strictly a "craving," an emotional desire for something that appears good. But the student has no right to crave, except insofar as her body naturally craves food, drink, and shelter; she has only a right to "wish" (βούλησις).

So by the five words of the Stoic definition, taken in their Stoic meanings, Aristotle's view is systematically negated. There is no such thing as rational or natural anger for the Stoics. That, in fact, is the only aspect of their position that is explicitly mentioned in the surviving parts of *On Anger*. Philodemus asks his Epicurean opponent Nicasicrates, who wanted to avoid even natural anger to the extent possible, if he is not merely abandoning their school's position to "those who take away anger entirely from the sage" (39.23–25). These can only be the Stoics.⁹³

2007, esp. 62–84 and 85–108. As Graver puts it, "we have every reason to think that the Stoics' wise person can experience very powerful feelings when the occasion calls for them. An awareness of having done the right things should evoke not just a mild satisfaction but real, deep joy. The thought of abusing a child should be met with more than unwillingness: aversion should go off like an air-raid siren that arrests one's very being" (2007, 82). Seneca makes clear in *On the Constancy of the Sage* (5.1-2 and 10.1-2) that sages do not feel slights (*contumelia*, i.e., ὀλιγωρία) such as not being admitted by one's patron to his house with the other clients, being ignored or derided when one speaks, or being given a less honorable seat at a dinner party. It takes at least an injury (*iniuria*, i.e., ἀδικία) to give one even a twinge of resentment, and *contumelia* is *tantum delicatis gravis* (only important to the oversensitive).

92. The Stoics also offered definitions of θυμός as "anger at its outset," μῆνις as "anger become inveterate," πικρία as "anger expressed immediately," χόλος as "swelling anger," and κότος as "anger waiting its time for vengeance." Cicero translates this list at *Tusc.* 4.21. But as Graver (2002, 147) notes ad loc., θυμός is being (falsely) etymologized from θυμιάω, and it appears from Nemesius, *Nat. hom.* 20, a later citation of this list, that similarly μῆνις is supposedly from μένω and κότος from κεῖσθαι. As one would expect, these etymologies are all ignored by Philodemus.

93. But Philodemus, like the Stoics, is clear that to feel *epithymia* for vengeance or even for inflicting punishment is always a sign of empty anger (41.36–39; 42.21–32).

The Epicureans avoided definitions (ὅροι), the staples of Stoic teaching and memorization, and preferred to rely on common language backed up by empirically derived "preconceptions" (προλήψεις, *prolēpseis*), by which instances of a previously known general type could be identified.[94] Instead of definitions, they used sketch outlines (ὑπογραφαί, *hypographai*) to indicate the most relevant features of the object or idea in question, but without any pretense to completeness. Using these, they could argue against other schools' definitions and suggest better terms of their own, without making them too fixed and calcified in their language or falling victim to their own criticisms of definitions. Philodemus mentions a *prolēpsis* of anger; he says that it covered both *orgē* and, insofar as the word could be used as a synonym, *thymos* (45.2).[95] On the basis of terms frequently repeated in the section devoted entirely to the Epicurean doctrine of anger (37.16–50.8), we can reconstruct some of its elements. The key words appear to be chosen as a deliberate response to Aristotle's definition, perhaps also to that of the Stoics. Ringeltaube (1913, 46) already isolated ὑπόληψις ἑκουσίας βλάβης ("a supposition of intentional harm") as central to Philodemus's *prolēpsis* of anger. These three words are not found in exactly that form anywhere in *On Anger*, but all three, or synonyms and paraphrases, are used throughout the treatise wherever Philodemus refers to his own views.[96]

Each word of the phrase "supposition of intentional harm" requires some scrutiny. The Epicurean must have a supposition of harm, that is, the opinion that she (or her friend; cf. 41.17–27) has been the victim of a violation of natural justice. Mere slights do not qualify, nor do violations of mere custom or merely conventional law, but even minor harms, insofar as they are really harms, do count. The word *supposition* emphasizes

---

Natural anger offers nothing that we can desire, nothing enjoyable (*apolauston*; cf. 42.22–23, 44.7, [17]).

94. See n. 63 above.

95. "The Founders accept the idea that the wise man will experience *thymos*, not according to that preconception of it, but according to the more general one" (44.41–45.5). They are accused of favoring empty anger, rather than natural anger, if they allow the sage's anger to be intense and prolonged rather than moderate and brief (45.5–10), as Philodemus claims the Founders described it: for them, *thymos* was synonymous with *orgē*.

96. It is clear in frags. 22–33 that Philodemus discussed whether a "supposition of harm" could compel one, by brute necessity, to retaliate (it cannot), but the word *intentionally* does not occur in its technical sense until 40.32–33 and 41.32–34: βλαβεὶς ὑπό τινος ἑκουσίως and διὰ τὸ βλάπτεσθαι καθ' ἑκούσιον τρόπον ὀργίζεται, respectively.

the element of cognitive appraisal, which was already present in Aristotle's definition of anger. A supposition may be true or false, and further reflection can revise it. The Epicureans used *supposition* interchangeably with *opinion* (*doxa*).[97] These suppositions can be refined by further reflection and reasoning, though not all people can or will do so. The Epicurean must believe the harm to be intentionally inflicted; accidents, because they do not reflect the will of an actor, do not qualify.[98] That the harm is intentional is a second cognitive judgment, in addition to the judgment that harm has been done.

The Epicureans had more to say about harm. Epicurus said that "harms from other people come about because of hatred, envy, or scorn, and the sage gets round these by reasoning and reflection."[99] The sage, however virtuous and friendly, may be the object of hatred, envy, or scorn from those who do not respond rationally to her good behavior, and thus she may be in danger of harm. By *logismos*, she can learn to avoid the harm that may result from those people. Nonetheless, if others intentionally harm her, she

---

97. Cf. Diogenes Laertius, *Vit. phil.* 10.34: τὴν δὲ δόξαν καὶ ὑπόληψιν λέγουσιν, ἀληθῆ τέ φασι καὶ ψευδῆ ("they call opinion also supposition, and these may be true or false"). At two points in *On Anger* (6.14; 37.35), the suppositions that provoke empty anger in fools are called not suppositions, as usual, but "false opinion" (ψευδοδοξία) or the result of "false opining" (ψευδοδοξεῖν).

98. The word ἑκουσίως ("intentionally") can be paraphrased both with παρ' ἑαυτόν ("on one's own responsibility") and κατὰ προαίρεσιν ("on purpose"); see n. 220 on 46.18–22, below. The sage is not perfect and is even capable of reacting in anger now and then without fully realizing that an offense was unintentional, an accident (35.24–26).

99. βλάβας ἐξ ἀνθρώπων ἢ διὰ μῖσος ἢ διὰ φθόνον ἢ διὰ καταφρόνησιν γίνεσθαι, ὧν τὸν σοφὸν λογισμῶι περιγίνεσθαι (frag. 536 [Usener 1887, 323] = frag. [I] 117 4 at Arrighetti 1960, 25–27, *apud* Diogenes Laertius, *Vit. phil.* 10.117). "Harm that comes from people," because of their negative opinion of you, corresponds to ἀσφάλεια ἐξ ἀνθρώπων ("safety that comes from people" because of their positive opinion of you), which is the goal of good behavior. Roskam (2007, 36–39) corrects many mistranslations in the previous literature by showing that this is the usual meaning of these two Epicurean phrases. They do not, or do not primarily, mean, "safety *from* other human beings," "harms done *to* other human beings." Diogenes Laertius, *Vit. phil.* 10.117 especially does not mean that the sage overcomes *his own* hatred or envy or contempt for others by *logismos*, though it has been taken that way. See Armstrong 2007, esp. 191–92: "these aren't the sage's emotions.... they are other people's feelings against the sage." What the sage provides for in advance by reason and reflection, and thus overcomes, is the hatred, envy, and contempt provoked by philosophers in laypersons, who are hostile, like Strepsiades in Aristophanes's *Clouds*, to the pretensions of philosophers to superiority.

can and will inflict punishment on them to deter them and others from acting similarly in the future, whenever this is a practical option.

The sage is entitled to do this because of the Epicurean view of natural justice (τὸ τῆc φύcεωc δίκαιον), which is a sort of social contract, i.e. a "guarantee of mutual advantage, with a view to neither harming one another nor being harmed" (cύμβολον τοῦ cυμφέροντοc εἰc τὸ μὴ βλάπτειν ἀλλήλουc μηδὲ βλάπτεcθαι, KD 31).[100] As KD 31–37 argue, this agreement, after primitive societies arrive at it by reasoning from experience, becomes the foundation of justice and a normative guide to the development of laws. All just laws reflect this natural justice, developing it in further detail and clarifying its terms, and they can be adjusted as societies change and develop. There can be unjust laws, which hinder human nonaggression, and laws that are neutral from the point of view of justice, since they neither promote nor hinder it. Accordingly, members of human society, which is founded on a code based in this normative idea of justice, can expect that their good behavior will be matched by good behavior on the part of others. Punishment for harm done is itself not harm, but an attempt to restore justice and set an example for others. In the context of the *On Anger*, anger, in its full sense, requires an intentionally inflicted harm, that is, a damaging violation of just laws, which are those based in the foundational agreement not to harm or be harmed.

The sage will seek to punish only if the Epicurean hedonic calculus (cυμμέτρηcιc, *symmetrēsis*[101]) shows that the punishment will probably bring about the desired end without too much further disturbance. An angry sage only acts while clearly "seeing what the nature of states of affairs really is, not allowing any false beliefs into the *symmetrēseis* of the harm done, and (thus) into the chastisements of those who harm us" (*Ir.* 37.32-39; cf. Epicurus, *Men.* 129).[102] Thus, the sage is in a position to know better than anyone whether the punishment is possible and appropriate. If it is, then she will inflict it to deter further offenses: if the sage is harmed and "when punished, he (the adversary) will be checked and will rein in the

---

100. On Epicurean views of law and justice, see Alberti 1995; Schofield 1999; and Roskam 2012.

101. For the term, see Epicurus, *Men.* 129–130 with Heßler's notes (2014, 251–69).

102. Cf. Aristotle's anger felt "with those whom we should, over the things we should, as and when we should, and as long, and all those things" (*Eth. nic.* 4.5, 1125b31–2).

others, he (the sage) would be insane not to grit his teeth and come back at him in one way or another" (*Ir.* 41.2–8).[103] If the sage cannot carry out the punishment for whatever reason, she simply avoids the wrongdoer in the future.

A further characteristic of natural anger is that no pleasure or desire is felt at the thought of inflicting punishment. One will not feel "great anger [or] a violent desire for revenge" (41.36–39), nor will it be "[as to something enjoyable]—because it offers nothing sweet—but he approaches it as something most necessary but most unpleasurable" (44.16–20). Natural anger is never an *epithymia* (cf. n. 93). Sages use the biting pain (*daknēron*, 37.19) or mental distress (*lypēron*, 37.27–29) of the emotion as a spur to action, to prevent their enemies from repeating their actions. The goal is not pleasure but deterrence. Natural anger cannot be intense, at least in Philodemus's semitechnical sense (see 44.5, 9; 48.6, 10), and it cannot be called *thymos* in the sense of "intense anger" or "rage."[104] Nor is natural anger even an *orexis*, as Aristotle said. It is evidently a painful but natural impulse (φυσικὴ ὁρμή[105]) toward punishment of the guilty and the restoration of justice.

Therefore the Epicurean student must be able to answer the question, "How were you actually harmed?," not "How were you slighted?," as with Aristotle, nor even, "How were you wronged?," as with Theophrastus and the Stoics. She cannot give a mere empty opinion in reply; she must have a mature and considered opinion of how she was harmed. Then she

---

103. The sage's response is, Philodemus implies, the same in cases where someone is harming a friend of the sage or the friend is harming himself or herself; see 41.17–28. It is also the same whatever the tense description: if she "has been," "is being," or "will clearly be" harmed, her right to punish the offender is the same.

104. *Epithymia*, intensity, pleasure seeking, and lust for vengeance can characterize empty anger, on which see §5 below.

105. At 44.7–8, Philodemus says that anger cannot be "an impulse (ὁρμή) (to revenge) as if to something enjoyable," which does not exclude its being an impulse to something painful. At 46.38, we are "impelled (ὁρμᾶν) to anger, as to gratitude, through the corresponding cause." This is the proposition from which his opponents argue, and which, we think, he accepts. At 48.5–6, he attributes to his opponents the proposition that "if we are naturally impelled (φυσικῶς ὁρμῶμεν) to intense gratitude to those who have voluntarily done us good, we are also naturally provoked (ἐκκαλούμεθα φυσικῶς) to intense anger against those who have harmed us intentionally." Here the context makes clear that Philodemus only disagrees with the word *intense* and accepts the rest of the formulation.

must answer a question about the intentions of the person who harmed her. These conditions will be sufficient to prevent her, in many cases, from feeling anger at all. But if she has, in fact, been intentionally harmed, as must be the case at some point with every human, she must also answer the questions "Do you desire revenge for this harm and take pleasure in that desire—which is wrong—or do you accept the pleasureless task of punishment?" and "Is it in your power to inflict that punishment successfully?" That sets the bar still higher. Few of Philodemus's students who tried to demonstrate to him that their anger was "the reasonable anger" (τὴν εὔλογον ὀργήν, 20.24–25) can have satisfied these conditions. By contrast, it is implied that one way to recognize the empty anger of fools is by their mistaking annoyances for actual harm, and another is by their pleasure in taking vengeance.[106]

Sages and good people have an alternative, at any rate, if it appears that punishment for the harm intentionally done them is not in their power to inflict, and their natural anger cannot lead to action. They can, and in any case will, simply feel "alienation" from and "hatred" for the offender, and to any degree of intensity they like (41.39–42.4). At any rate, as we will discuss in more detail later, it is made very clear that natural anger is brief and does not cause great mental disturbance (ταραχή) to them any more than great physical pains do (42.4–12). But it is a feeling that is more than enough to motivate a forceful and decisive response (41.2–8).

5. Philodemus's Natural and Empty Anger

Natural anger is the right kind of anger, the one felt appropriately in response to suitable circumstances and under the correct conditions. The sage must put in a good deal of mental work to ensure that her anger is natural rather than empty, and the experience of anger will never be pleasant. This is the anger of those who understand the current state of affairs,

---

106. Cf. *Kyr. dox.* 29, quoted above in n. 50. Writers such as Annas (1989, 147–53) and Asmis (2011, 153) are right to comment on this passage as essential to understanding *On Anger*. But for us, although Philodemus certainly holds that pleasure in anger is an infallible sign of something wrong with it, it is learning to question one's perceptions and opinions about whether and how one is harmed, by using *logismos* and *epilogismos*, that makes the difference. His emphasis is on moving from empty opinion to reliable opinion and on escaping from empty anger as from every other empty opinion; see below, on the later fragments and cols. 1–7.

who correctly estimate their losses, and who can punish the wrongdoers in a way that matches the offense. Additionally, we hope to show in what senses natural anger can be said to be natural.

A good disposition is important for ensuring that anger is natural, as 37.24–39 shows: "the emotion itself, taken in isolation, is an evil, since it is painful or is analogous to something painful, but if taken in conjunction with one's disposition, we think that it is something that may even be called a good. For it (anger) results from seeing what the nature of states of affairs is and from not having any false beliefs in our comparative calculations of our losses and in our punishments of those who harm us." In other words, her "good disposition" is one trained in empirical reasoning and accustomed to reflection and appraisal of states of affairs.[107] A good disposition assists with the *symmetrēsis* and so allows the sage to correctly evaluate the facts and what is at stake in a question of anger. If her anger survives such reflection and appraisal, in the light of her realistic vision of how things are, and if she thinks she can inflict punishment, it is unavoidable that she will inflict it. In that sense, her anger will be natural.

We can learn more about the later Epicureans' natural anger by better understanding what they mean by the terms *natural* and *naturally*. A passage of a treatise by Demetrius Laco, whose title does not survive but which is conventionally called *On Textual and Exegetical Problems in Epicurus* (col. 67, Puglia 1988), outlines several possible meanings for the term "by nature."[108] The context is Demetrius's defense of Epicurus's argument that parents' love for their children is not natural.[109]

-2 [φύσει γὰρ λέγεται ὁ]	[… man is said to be "by nature" a
-1 [ἄνθρωπος ποριστικὸς τρο-]‖	procurer of fo]od, since he does so
1 φῆς, ἐπειδήπερ ἀδιαστρό-	by unperverted instinct; to be "by
φως, φύσει δὲ πόνων εἶ-	nature" susceptible to pain, since he
ναι δεκτικός, ἐπειδὴ κα-	is so by compulsion; "by nature" to

---

107. On dispositions, see excursus 3.
108. Translated by Procopé 1998, 179. Demetrius was probably a contemporary of Philodemus's teacher Zeno, and papyri of his works are found in the Herculaneum collection; they may have been brought to Italy from Athens, so Cavallo 1983, 58–60. For Demetrius Laco, see *DPA* D60 (Dorandi).
109. On Demetrius's argument, see in general McConnell 2017; McOsker forthcoming a.

τ{αν}ηναγκαϲμένωϲ, φύ-
ϲει δὲ τὴν ἀρετὴν διώ-
κειν, ἐπεὶ ϲυμφερόντωϲ,
φύϲει δὲ τὰϲ πρώταϲ τῶν
ὀνομάτων ἀναφωνήϲειϲ
γεγονέναι λέγομεν, καθὸ…

pursue virtue, since he does so to his advantage; and we say that the first utterances of names were "by nature," since…

Demetrius replies to a Stoic that loving one's children is not compulsory, for it is characteristic of what is compulsory to be involuntary (ἀκούϲιον), and a consequence (παρακολούθημα) of compulsion is an attempt to resist and fight back (ἀντίπραξιϲ), "which is obviously absent from our love for our children" (col. 68.3–9). Thus it fails to meet one of the meanings of "naturally," and Epicurus's opinion is vindicated.

Philodemus, as Procopé argues, applies the last three glosses, "by compulsion," "to his advantage," and "according to the first utterances of names," to natural anger. We suggest that it occurs by unperverted instinct as well.[110] It is compulsory for all, including the sage, because it is unavoidable in practice due to the nature of our souls and the necessity of social interactions. Philodemus explicitly says in *On Anger* that anger is an evil that is "inescapable, and therefore called natural" (ἀνέκφευκτον καὶ διὰ τοῦτο φυϲικὸν λεγόμενον, 39.29–31; cf. 40.18–26). It is something "most necessary and most unpleasant" (ἀναγκαιότατον, ἀηδέϲτατον δέ, 44.19–21), and it cannot be entirely rejected by anyone. Natural anger can suit the third and fourth categories also: it is advantageous, since it prods the Epicurean to self-defense,[111] and it is so-called because the name has the characteristic of "first utterances" or "primal appellations": "direct, one-to-one correspondence with their objects."[112] There is no reason not to apply

---

110. For ἀδιαϲτρόφωϲ, see Epicurus frag. 398 (Usener 1887, 274) *apud* Sextus, *Pyr.* 3.194, a version of the "cradle argument": "for animals from the moment of their birth are impelled, following unperverted instinct (ἀδιάϲτροφα ὁρμᾶν) to pleasure and turn away from pain." The same thought is paraphrased at *Math.* 11.96 (the next testimonium in Usener) "an animal avoids pain and pursues pleasure naturally and untaught (φυϲικῶϲ καὶ ἀδιδάκτωϲ) from the moment it is born, but not as yet enslaved to mere belief (μηδέπω τοῖϲ κατὰ δόξαν δουλεῦον)."

111. In *Kyr. dox.* 36, natural justice is "to our advantage in our dealings with each other" (κατὰ τὸ ϲυμφέρον τῆϲ πρὸϲ ἀλλήλουϲ κοινωνίαϲ). Similarly, natural anger, and its consequence, retaliation against harm, is to our advantage.

112. Procopé 1998, 179–81.

the first gloss ("by unperverted natural impulse"), either, for self-defense certainly can count as a "unperverted natural instinct."[113] Thus Epicurean natural anger is natural in three, perhaps even all four, of the senses listed by Demetrius.

The main thrust of *On Anger*'s argument is that anger for its own sake is never compulsory merely because one supposes oneself intentionally harmed. In a person of reflective disposition, suppositions of intentional harm are always contextualized and submitted to *symmetrēsis*, which requires knowledge and experience of the world and the possible consequences of anger. Only these can tell us whether our anger is natural and whether we can punish the offender (see 37.32–39). If the answer is no, we can simply profess ourselves "alienated," hate and avoid the person who wronged us, and drop the relationship (see 42.1–4); hatred and avoidance are available to the sage who has suffered harm but cannot punish the wrongdoer and guarantee her continuing security. If the answer is yes to both questions, then the anger becomes necessary and inescapable in a completely different way: it would be absurd not to punish the wrongdoer.

As we gain wisdom, anger does not disappear from our lives any more than grief or love, but it is more and more framed in protective layers of cognition and reflection; we are more likely to feel natural anger. Of course, there are various ways in which this ideal progression can go astray: most people do not have the calm and awareness of circumstances and causes that the Epicurean sage does, and even sages can make mistakes. That said, a reflective and aware person, and the sage most of all, can reluctantly "accept" (ἀναδέχεσθαι) anger, however strong one's resistance to it, and can certainly retaliate under the right conditions with confidence.

As we have seen, the opposite of natural anger for Philodemus is empty anger, which is for various reasons wrong, inappropriate, or incorrect to feel. The term is poorly attested and only appears in two passages, both supplemented. The adjective is suggested by the Epicurean habit of using "empty" (κενός) to characterize incorrect, misleading, or valueless things,

---

113. So also in *On Death*, Philodemus calls the fear of death in certain circumstances natural and painful. Anger is inescapable by and for human nature, and it is well that is so, for evils cannot be remedied without the spur it provides. The fear of death is in many cases equally natural because it keeps us alive and for entirely good purposes, and we are not wrong to lament and weep over the frustration of these good purposes; see Armstrong 2004; 2007 82–83,105–9.

such as beliefs or utterances.[114] The first passage is: "so in the same way we were calling em[pty] anger an evil because it results from an utterly base disposition and entails countless troubles, one must say that the natural one is not an evil" (37.39–38.6). The second is found (if our text is right) in Philodemus's argument that Nicasicrates made natural anger more of an evil than it really is, "since he did not compare it with empty (anger)" (39.8). The characteristics of empty anger, the dark twin of natural anger, get far more discussion than those of natural anger, which is probably a sign of the therapeutic goal of the treatise, and the diatribe against anger (8–31.24) is entirely directed against empty anger.

In short, people feel empty anger whenever they are angry in a way that does not meet the high standards set by Philodemus for natural anger. Unreasoning and unreflective anger over a mere supposition of harm is empty anger. Anger at a harm inflicted unintentionally or at a mere annoyance (rather than a harm) or anger that is too intense or that involves a desire for punishment or revenge as if they were pleasurable are all equally sure signs of empty anger.[115] Empty anger can even result if the sage is correct about suffering intentional harm and sets out to punish the wrongdoer with the correct intentions but has incorrectly evaluated the chances of success: in that case, if the sage fails, she will cause herself to be harmed again needlessly. However, if she made a decision for the best reasons available, she can justify herself with the maxim at the end of *Men.* 135, that "it is better to fail with good reasoning than succeed with bad reasoning." It is implied by the section in the diatribe that satirizes the kind of anger and resentment seen in younger philosophical students (18.35–21) that there are minor forms of empty anger that a teacher and therapist can correct before they become inveterate and have more serious consequences, that is, before they become established as a part of a person's *diathesis* (disposition).

---

114. For the use of the term in general, see Usener 1977, s.v. "κενός, (τὸ) κενόν, κενῶς." For empty beliefs, see above n. 50.

115. Even this list is not exhaustive: any deviation from the rules for natural anger could result in empty anger. The sage, for example, will never retaliate if he thinks it is not in his power to do so; he contents himself with "alienation and hatred"; see on *Ir.* 41–42 below. It takes a fool such as Timocrates, the brother of Metrodorus who apostatized from the school and became its unforgiving enemy, to attack someone he knows is stronger than himself; see on 12.26–30. A fool's anger will often be empty because he cannot reliably make all the necessary judgments.

Empty anger can have each of the characteristics opposite to what Demetrius Laco calls natural. It looks compulsory but is not, "because their own (false) suppositions are creating the deceptions that people have suffered the same thing that they suffer in the case of things that are compulsory" (frag. 24.3–10). Empty anger is not beneficial to the persons who feel it (unlike the restoration of justice and deterrence of further harm that natural anger provides). It also provokes one into foolish and self-damaging actions along the way, as illustrated throughout the diatribe section, where it is clear that empty anger stems from incorrect beliefs and values. One of the main signs of empty anger is a failure to contextualize the situation and to look for unwanted consequences and entanglements. The victims of empty anger are unable or unwilling to make use of *logismos* and *epilogismos* and thus cannot see the evils that are "consequent" on their anger. Their anger is wholly unnecessary; reflection and reason would dissolve it.

6. The Structure and Analysis of *On Anger*

In the treatise as we have it, many of the basic materials needed to reconstruct Philodemus's own theory are crowded into the last fourteen columns, and other aspects of his theory are frequently mentioned or alluded to in the course of his arguments throughout the treatise. That is why we have outlined his doctrine in the previous sections before beginning our analysis of the treatise as a whole. Philodemus may have provided his own theory in the beginning, or at least indicated what authority he was following. At 31.24–27, he says that he had already summarized the views of the Peripatetics whom he discusses, and we should assume he did the same for his other opponents as well. Some of this seems to survive in the initial fragments (frags. 7–13), where Philodemus does appear to be refuting the Peripatetics' positive view of vengeance. At 36.20–21, there is another back-reference, apparently to a discussion of varying levels of natural anger of the souls of Epicurean sages. But we have no indication of what other topics Philodemus might have covered in the lost opening columns; a summary of his own positions is a reasonable guess, but there may not have been much room for it, and he begins other treatises without restating school doctrine.

We can identify seven sections in the treatise, discussed individually in §§6.1–7 in what follows. The first (discussed at §6.1) is a very fragmentary section that might have dealt with Epicurean topics and that apparently included an attack on the Peripatetic theory of anger, probably the one Philodemus mentions at 31.24-25. The second (§6.2) is fragmentary but underlines the importance of *logismos* and *epilogismos* to evaluating impressions and suppositions of harm. It may, in fact, be the last part of a response to the Peripatetics or the beginning of the attack on Timasagoras, who denied the usefulness of various Epicurean therapeutic techniques.

The third section (§6.3) is a lengthy model diatribe including a sort of "school scene," a satire of the empty anger seen in younger students of Epicureanism of the kind portrayed in *On Frank Speech*. This section is the single largest in the extant part of the treatise. The fourth (§6.4) is a brief return to a previous attack on the Peripatetics (see §6.1). The fifth (§6.5) is a discussion of anger within Epicurean communities, especially as seen in sages and mature students whose occasional lapses into bad temper are more or less harmless; this section picks up the school atmosphere of that part of the diatribe. The sixth (§6.6) is a defense of Philodemus's concept of natural anger, apparently directed primarily at Nicasicrates but including all of his opponents at once. The seventh and final section (§6.7) is a brief response to certain unnamed, apparently Epicurean opponents, the "maximalists" who held that the sage's anger could be intense and prolonged.

6.1. The Initial Fragments (Frags. 1–16)

Fragments 1–6 form a poorly preserved section where only the keywords "harm" (βλάβη, frag. 1.4), and "get angry" (ὀρ]γίcαcθαι, frag. 6.2-3, 4-5) remain to suggest the topic. Conceivably, this is near the end of an exposition of Epicurean views about anger, either Philodemus's or an Epicurean opponent's.

Fragments 7–13 probably contained an attack, originally twenty or more columns long, on the Peripatetic view of anger, which is referred to and supplemented in columns 31–34 of the surviving text. It is clear from 31–34 that the main point of attack against the Peripatetics was that they supposedly encouraged taking pleasure in revenge, whereas the Epicureans allowed natural anger only as a feeling of pain that helps to motivate punishment. Fragment 7, however it is to be restored, clearly deprecated seeking revenge (τιμ[ω]ρί[αc, l. 5) to relieve one's mental pain (λύπην, l. 2; λυπεῖcθ[αι, l. 8) when one is angry. Fragment 13 seems to conclude just such an argument against revenge: "and they have said nothing new about the whole subject of revenge (τίcεωc, l. 29) and in general..." (ll. 28-31).

According to 31.27, this first attack contained citations of various Peripatetics by name, but these are completely lost.

Fragments 14–16 offer little that is decipherable, but the first part of the name of Philodemus's Epicurean opponent Nicasicrates occurs at fragment 15.15.

6.2. Anger, Reasoning, and the Critique of Timasagoras (Frags. 17–33 and Cols. 1–7)

We suggest that at this point in the treatise Philodemus is discussing the Epicurean account of moral responsibility, which is, in the end, our responsibility to ourselves, to gain security and friendship by using the virtues and thereby to reach the good life. The language of this account distinguishes mere compulsion (ἀνάγκη, τὸ κατηναγκαςμένον) from the freedom and independence of will that we gain by learning the habits of *logismos* and *epilogismos* and by striving, in response to the teaching and example of other Epicureans and good people, to avoid blame and deserve praise. Texts from Epicurus himself, such as *Men.* 132-135 and some of the more securely edited passages of *Nat.* 25 (see excursus 4), underlie Philodemus's discussion.

Fragments 17–19 anticipate Philodemus's full-blown model diatribe against anger (cols. 8–31; see excursus 1 and §6.3 below) by describing the violent behavior and ugly facial expressions and other physical signs characteristic of people in the grip of empty anger. From what follows, the topic may have already been whether people choose to fall into these states of mind or are compelled.

The following fragments (21–33) are of crucial importance to Philodemus's own distinction between empty anger and natural anger. Philodemus makes an argument, badly damaged but evidently running from at least fragment 21 (if the supplement in ll. 14-5 is correct), that fools never fly into fits of empty anger by compulsion, however it may appear to an observer and whatever the persons themselves may claim. Terms for "compulsion" are strewn all over the text in fragments 21–33, and the question of whether empty anger is compulsory is crucial for Philodemus's account.[116] In fact, empty anger comes about because fools

---

116. For compulsion, see Demetrius Laco, *Textual Problems* col. 67, discussed above. For ἀνάγκη, see οὐχ ὑπὸ τῆς ἀ[νάγκης (frag. 21.14-15) (οὐ τῆς ἀνάγκης ἀπεργαζομένης, frag. 24.5). For καταναγκάζω, see frags. 24.8-9; 28.14-15 and 20-21;

(frag. 22.6[117]) act on mistaken suppositions (cf. frag 22.4–5).[118] We have only two damaged but clear statements to support this contention: the first is "(this) proves what is [said], that they experience the same thing as in the case of things that are compulsory, because not necessity, but their own suppositions, create the deceptions" (frag. 24.3–10).

Philodemus immediately gives four examples of what he means. (1) A poor man may always be angry with his one slave because there is no one else he can abuse; as a result, he will be only grudgingly served (frag. 24.10–17). Philodemus comments: "Therefore, because he failed in reasoning (*logismos*), he will fail to get what he needs" (ll. 14–17). This is crucial as well to the other three examples he gives in fragment 24: (2) the rich man who has many slaves and is always punishing them (ll. 17–20); (3) the tyrant who is always beheading people (ll. 20–21); and (4) the person who restrained his temper as a poor man but changes when he becomes a rich man (ll. 21–26). All four fail to reason correctly because of their false suppositions; as a result, they experience empty anger. If they had corrected their incorrect suppositions by *logismos*, they would not feel this empty anger;[119] instead, the foolish person blames the mysterious workings of necessity.

The second significant indication that a mere supposition of harm does not produce natural anger by itself is preserved in fragment 28, where, lacunose as the text is, we can make out the words: "Even if he thinks, as he says, that he app[ears] to have suffered what is com[pulso]ry, and (thinks this?) even apart from all [knowledge] and logical [inquiry] … (it) [has not been made compul]sory. For even if, ten thousand times over, because some one, single harm or appearance of harm has befallen hi[m…" The subject of this sentence is evidently "the fool," who "thinks, as he says," that his anger was compulsory merely because an impression that he has been intentionally harmed has "befallen" him. If so, Philodemus means that in none of these ten thousand cases was anger compulsory on the fool because he was acting "apart from all [knowledge] and reasonable

---

32.2–3 and 16; and 33.15–16; for βε]βιαϲμένον, see frag. 28.11–12; for [ἀνέκ]φευκτον, see frag. 33.19–20.

117. Cf. 42.24; 47.19, 20; literally "people who act in vain" (μάτην).

118. Cf. especially frags. 24.3–10 and 22.4–5; note that φανταϲία is used synonymously with ὑπόληψιϲ at frag. 28.23. See also n. 67 above.

119. Angeli (2000) correctly saw that frag. 24 is crucial to the interpretation of *On Anger* as a whole.

inquiry." Fools' empty anger comes from a failure to reason about their beliefs and actions (frag. 24.14–15). Additionally, they are unaware of the consequences their anger brings (frag. 32), which *logismos* could have predicted.[120]

Anger is one of many cases in which *logismos* frees people from the fool's apparent compulsion. Epicurus praises *logismos* as the source of all happiness:

> for it is not continuous drinking bouts and revels nor enjoying ourselves with women and boys or fish and the other luxuries of the wealthy table that produces the pleasant life, but sober reasoning [νήφων λογιϲμόϲ] that searches out the motives for choice and avoidance and banishes mere opinions, the things from which the greatest disturbance comes to the soul. (*Men.* 132)

In the next paragraph (*Men.* 133) Epicurus specifies that we are not accountable for what happens by "necessity, which is unaccountable, or chance, which is unstable, but what is up to us (τὸ παρ' ἡμᾶϲ) is free, and on those grounds alone do blame and its opposite (praise) follow (παρακολουθεῖν)." So, if the four comic characters in fragment 24 had only used *logismos*, they would have been freed of their apparent compulsion to be angry and would not have "failed to get what [they] need" but seen that it was "up to them" to change. Moreover, as in the passage quoted above from Plato's *Protagoras* (323b–324d), blame and rebuke do not even come into play when our actions or states are really involuntary, such as our stature or the color of our hair, but only where we are capable of personal responsibility for our actions. The practice of *epilogismos* (rational appraisal) does not

---

120. The "consequences" and "entanglements" of anger become a major theme in the first two columnar sections immediately succeeding the fragments, the justification of the diatribe (cols. 1–7) and then the diatribe itself (8.20–31.24). Literally, the consequences "follow" on anger (ἀκολουθοῦ[ϲι]ν, frag. 32.14, ἠκ]ολού[θ]ηκεν, 18) or are "attached" to it (ϲυναφθη-, frag. 32.19–20). The theme of consequences and entailments is maintained by the repetition of these and related roots throughout the introduction to the diatribe (cols. 1–7) and the diatribe itself. For example, παρακολουθέω ("follow as a consequence") is used of the unforeseen consequences of empty anger eleven times in cols. 1–28. Philodemus reminds his audience of these consequences and entailments at 42.16–20: "(the fool's anger) has countless misfortunes both conjoined with it and consequent (καὶ ϲυμπεπλη[γ]μέναϲ καὶ ϲυνακολουθούϲαϲ) on it. But the sage, who sees into these (misfortunes) most clearly, could not fall into (them)."

go unpraised in this passage either: "for who is the superior of a person who believes holy things about the gods, and is entirely free from the fear of death, and has perfectly appraised for himself (ἐπιλελογιϲμένου) what is the *telos* of his nature?" (*Men.* 133).

So *logismos* (reason and reflection) is the key to doing away with empty anger and limiting it to natural anger. Indeed, *logismos* in one surviving saying of Epicurus (frag. 485 [Usener 1887, 305-6] = frag. [238] at Arrighetti 1960, 567) is all but deified: "A person is miserable either through fear or empty, limitless desire; however, when a person bridles these things, he can win that blessed entity for himself, *logismos*" (ἢ γὰρ διὰ φόβον τιϲ κακοδαιμονεῖ ἢ δι' ἀόριϲτον καὶ κενὴν ἐπιθυμίαν· ἅ τιϲ χαλινῶν δύναται τὸν μακάριον ἑαυτῶι περιποιῆϲαι λογιϲμόν). This seems parallel to the famous semideification of Nature in the fragment from Stobaeus: "Thanks be to blessed Nature, that she made what is necessary easy to provide, and what is difficult to provide unnecessary."[121] Compare also the striking argument of Verde (2013b), where, starting from the same texts in *Men.* 132–135, Epicurean *logismos* is exalted in the same manner, as an all but divine personified deliverer, in this case from the power of fortune or the personified figure of Fortune.

There is only one indication in the fragments of a positive example of *epilogismos* being used to defeat empty anger and replace it with natural anger. But that, too, is significant. The very scrappy fragment 31 of *On Anger* has]υϲ ἐπιλέγω[ν ("applying rational appraisal") and τέτλαθι δή, κραδίη, the first words of *Od.* 20.19. This evokes a famous *exemplum*, used twice by Plato (*Phaed.* 94 d–e; *Resp.* 390). Odysseus, still disguised as the beggar, tries to go to sleep but is disgusted with Penelope's maids, who have become the suitors' lovers, and wants to kill them.

> But he smote his breast and rebuked his own heart: "Endure, my heart; a worse thing even than this you endured, on that day when the Cyclops irresistible in strength was eating my brave comrades, and you endured it until your wisdom got you out of the cave, where you thought you would die." So he spoke, rebuking his own heart, and his heart stayed firm, in complete obedience [πείϲηι]. (*Od.* 20.17–24)[122]

---

121. Frag. 469 (Usener 1887, 300) = frag. [240] Arrighetti 1960, 567: χάριϲ τῆι μακαρίαι Φύϲει, ὅτι τὰ ἀναγκαῖα ἐποίηϲεν εὐπόριϲτα, τὰ δὲ δυϲπόριϲτα οὐκ ἀναγκαῖα.

122. The line and the scene, like *Il.* 18.108–110, were favorites with any poet or philosopher interested in the psychology of anger. Plutarch (*Cohib. Ira* 453d1) called

The repeated words "rebuke his own heart" suggest ἐπιλέγω[ν to Philodemus. In the absence of any teacher besides Athena, Odysseus was forced to rebuke his own heart.

We have a more explicit and better-preserved discussion from Philodemus about Odysseus's moral development from feeling empty anger to feeling natural anger in a column from Philodemus's *On the Good King according to Homer*.[123]

24 ὁ ⟨δὲ⟩ [τυ]φλώσας τὸν	But he [sc. Odysseus] who
25 "οὐ͜ι γὰρ Κύκλ͜ιωπες Δ͜ιὸ͜ις αἰ-	blinded the one who foolishly
γ͜ι͜ιόχου ἀλέγουσ͜ιν οὐδ͜ιὲ	said (?) "for the Cyclopes are not
θ͜ιεῶ͜ιν ἄλλων ἐπ͜ιε͜ι͜ὶ ἢ πο-	heedful of aegis-bearing Zeus nor
λὺ φ]έρτεροί ἐσμεν" φ[λυ-	the other gods, since we are far
αρήσα]ντα κ[....]τωι μεν	better" [*Od.* 9.275–276] ...
30 τοιαύτη[.......]ενη[.]ιν	[*ca. 15 words lost*]
.].ιτ.νε[.........	... affirming that he [Odysseus?]
........]ηκέναι φας[κ- ...	[*one or two words missing*] ...
οὐκ ἐ]ῶν ἐπολολύζειν	forbidding crying out in triumph
τοῖ]ς ἐνδίκως τετιμω-	even over those justly avenged,
35 ρη]μένοις, καὶ ἐπιφωνῶν	and exclaiming that "it is not
ὡς "οὐχ ὁσίη φθιμένοισιν	piety to glory over slain men."[124]
37 ἐπ' ἀνδράσιν εὐχετάασθαι."	

One could argue that Philodemus here highlights Odysseus's empty anger, which resulted in his foolish gloating over Polyphemus. But Odysseus's conduct when he returns to Ithaca shows that he had learned from

---

the ability to hold in your anger "keeping to the Homeric 'obedience' (πεῖσα)," as if that single word was enough to recall the whole scene. Cantarella (2013) is a recent monograph on these three words, their context, and their place in the history of the psychology of the individual.

123. Col. 91 Fish = col. 36 Dorandi 1982. We thank Jeffrey Fish for allowing us to use his work in progress. An earlier text of this fragment is discussed in Fish 2004. Working with Dorandi's text, Asmis already suggested that "Philodemus perhaps also has Homer correct Odysseus' vindictiveness toward the blinded Cyclops" (1991, 43). The new text and interpretation take this a step further: Homer shows Odysseus correcting his vindictiveness in general.

124. *Od.* 22.412. The lines are spoken by Odysseus after he restrains Eurykleia from gloating over the slain suitors.

his mistake and changed his behavior, as we see when he forbids Eurycleia from raising a song of victory over the dead suitors. The pleasure of vengeance and self-assertion by openly naming himself that Odysseus experienced in insulting Polyphemus is characteristic of Philodemus's empty anger. Odysseus's later behavior showed that he learned from this failure in self-control to restrain his impulses, and his anger against the suitors was "natural anger," which Philodemus permits. Whether *Od.* 20.19 was quoted at fragment 31.19 of *On Anger* to invoke the whole scene or was presented as a mantra for those tempted to anger, as an act of *epilogismos*, Philodemus probably used the tag to make a similar point. With Athena's help, Odysseus held his anger back until the right time by compelling himself to reason about and repress it.

So *epilogismos*, like *logismos*, has a crucial role to play in the transformation of a bad disposition to empty anger into a good disposition to natural anger, and we will see *epilogismos* praised as having medical virtue throughout columns 1–7 as well.

It is fruitless to speculate in detail about what was lost before and in between the fragments, but we can say that, from the moment the key terms in Philodemus's theory of anger as we explained it above pop up in them, they seem to be already operating as functional items in it, for example, "harm" (frags. 1.4; 28.22–25), "revenge" (frags. 7.5; 13.29); "supposition" (frags. 22.4–5; 24.6), "reason" (*logismos*, frag. 24.14–15), and "saying in reflection" (*epilegō*[*n*, frag. 31.18).

In column 1, Philodemus is already arguing, against Timasagoras, that the diatribe against anger, of which Philodemus says there were classic examples in Chrysippus's *On Emotions* 4 (the so-called *Therapeutic Discourse*, or Θεραπευτικὸς λόγος[125]) and the *On Anger* of Bion of Borysthenes (a younger contemporary of Epicurus), is no mere pointless rhetorical exercise. Chrysippus's treatise was full of vivid and detailed medical imagery, as are *Ir.* 1–11. In fact, the running medical metaphor that Philodemus borrows to defend the diatribe as relevant to philosophical education fits nicely into his materialist system. Everything we do or say affects not just our thoughts, which are not disembodied, but aspects of our physical structure, and the right kind of rebuke is a tonic to that structure. Praise works in the same way, and the use of praise and blame is central to

---

125. The *Therapeutikos Logos* is said by Galen to have been different in scope and perhaps more widely read in antiquity than the other three books of *On Emotions*; see Tieleman 2003, 89–94, 140–42; a survey of what we know of it is at 142–97.

Philodemus's defense of the diatribe as quasimedical therapy: they make both a physical and mental difference by inducing the habits of reasoning, reflection, and appraisal.

Excursus 1: Timasagoras and Philodemus's Reply[126]

We know from column 5 that Timasagoras had censured the Epicurean scholarch Basilides (ca. 250–175 BCE, scholarch from ca. 202) and his student (and perhaps successor) Thespis, for approving of and perhaps even for practicing a literary form that modern scholars often call diatribe.[127] Philodemus claims that Basilides and Thespis responded, which means Timasagoras was their contemporary (5.17–25).

---

126. On Timasagoras, see primarily *DPA* T 140 (Verde) with further bibliography. We prefer to emphasze the lack of data linking Timasagoras (and Nicasicrates; see n. 163 below) explicitly with Rhodes and the Epicurean school there and to leave this and related questions open. We agree that he (and Nicasicrates) were Epicureans, though not of the same persuasion as Philodemus. Timasagoras was a contemporary of Basilides and Thespis.

127. If Basilides and Thespis first introduced the diatribe against anger (and also against erotic love, as mentioned at *Ir.* 7.19 and at *Lib.* frags. 42.2-4; 48.5; 57.2) into the school's literary and educational repertoire, around 200–175 BCE, then Lucretius's diatribes against the fear of death (*Rer. nat.* 3) and erotic love (*Rer. nat.* 4) may be an exception to Sedley's rule (see 1998, 135–44) that Lucretius did not use later Epicureans as a source. Use of the diatribe in the Epicurean school is already assumed in Erler's 2003 study of the role of visualization in certain forms of ἐπιλογιϲμόϲ. However, Hellenistic literary and philosophical quarrels could turn on very small points, and perhaps Timasagoras's quarrel with Basilides and Thespis turned on their merely having said they admired Bion's *On Anger* and Chryippus's *Therapeutikos Logos,* and so did Basilides's and Thespis's response (*Ir.* 5.17–25). For general information and bibliography about Basilides, see *DPA* B16 (Dorandi); for Thespis, see *DPA* T114 (Dorandi).

The "Epicurean diatribe" is at the root of some of the greatest Latin poetry and is practiced, on the same ethical grounds that Philodemus advocates, by Lucretius and Horace; see Armstrong 2014. There is general agreement that Philodemus's *On Death,* which ends, like the third book of Lucretius, with a vivid diatribe against the fear of death, was a source for the lost *De morte* of Virgil's friend Varius Rufus. All the fragments of Varius's poem survive because Virgil imitated them verbally in his own poems, as the ancient commentators noted; for the fragments, see Courtney 1993, 271–75; Hollis 2007, 263–64.

It has been the consensus since Longo Auricchio and Tepedino Guerra (1981, 1982) that Timasagoras was also an Epicurean.[128] As the first column opens, a probable quotation from him is coming to an end: "'... [nor do] I [deny?] this. For it is obvious to all that, just as that is an evil, so is this.' By such arguments, indeed, he (Timasagoras) undertook (to prove) that 'blaming (anger) is ridiculous'" (1.5–10). If he spoke as an Epicurean, Timasagoras meant that all anger, even natural anger, is always painful and never pleasurable and that what is painful is "obviously" an evil. Philodemus's sarcasm is directed entirely to the word *obviously*, which elides the distinction between empty and natural anger.

Timasagoras considered anger, as a painful emotion, to be "obviously" and "entirely" an evil. Later, in response to Nicasicrates, Philodemus carefully indicates that anger, like everything painful, is indeed an evil per se but that circumstances can make yielding to it a nonevil or even a kind of good (37.20–38.34). Timasagoras, and perhaps also Nicasicrates (see excursus 2), thought that the pain of anger is intense enough to be seriously damaging in itself; Philodemus denies that natural anger is ever so painful or intense. However, it is important to note that none of the three believes that the good person or sage will feel any pleasure in anger. Otherwise, it would count as a good in Epicurean terms. On this point, the three are united against the Peripatetics.

Philodemus also disagrees with Timasagoras on the educational value of therapeutic diatribe, and his report has historical as well as philosophical implications. At 5.18–25, Philodemus claims that misfortunes followed as consequences on Timasagoras's "anger toward Basilides and Thespis," even though he claimed his attack on them was made with moderation. What provoked Timasagoras's attack on Basilides and Thespis? It seems that they adopted the therapeutic diatribe from Chrysippus (and, before him, Bion). In Chrysippus's hands, the diatribe had some remarkable features. He discouraged the philosophical therapist from trying to confront grief or anger at its onset and claimed, famously, that he would not need to convert to Stoicism anyone who believed in "the three goods" (those of the soul, of the body, and of external goods; he means a Peripatetic) or someone who believed "that pleasure was the *telos*" (i.e., an Epicurean); he could argue effectively based on his opponents' commitments, philosophi-

---

128. See also our n. 82 to the translation.

cal or otherwise, to convince them of their folly.[129] If Basilides and Thespis introduced Chrysippus's techniques into the Epicurean school, they perhaps included even the appeal to all schools of thought, including their own, but certainly they approved of the diatribe against anger, and perhaps they even wrote in this genre themselves.[130]

Timasagoras's philosophical claim was that diatribe therapy is not useful to the Epicurean teacher. He may have thought, as Cicero and Galen later did, that Chrysippus's medical metaphors for interpersonal therapy were strained, unconvincing, and even false.[131] Moreover, he held that the diatribe against anger is useless to the angry person, who cannot control his emotions. He claimed that the general idea of "putting the consequent evils before one's eyes (πρὸ ὀμμάτων) is ridiculous and raving" (1.20–26). Philodemus reports that Timasagoras says that those in the grip of anger "have become unable to use rational appraisal about their emotions" (7.6–9).[132] That is, he denied that the diatribe could provoke *epilogismos* in a person already angry.

Philodemus thinks that diatribes can induce *epilogismos* even in people who are still in the grip of emotion. The patients, the philosopher's students, will have the consequences and entanglements of their empty anger mercilessly laid before their eyes, and they will be told that their problem is a bad *diathesis* (disposition).[133] By doing this, she will create

---

129. Chrysippus, *SVF* 3.474, second text = Origen, *Cels.* 8.51; cf. Tieleman 2003, 166–70.

130. The genre "diatribe," defined as an informal philosophical lecture attacking vice, usually with imaginary objections by opponents, *exempla* from poetry and history, and satiric humor, is problematic but useful (the problems with the term itself are well summarized by Moles, s.v. "Diatribe," *OCD*). We are among those who "accept that there is such a tradition but demur at the term," as Moles puts it. But for our purposes it is enough that the meaning of ψόγος ὀργῆς, Latin *vituperatio irae*, a diatribe against anger, was clear to any ancient rhetorician, that Philodemus and Timasagoras argue over whether "to blame" (*psegein*) anger, as Bion and Chrysippus did, and that "diatribe" in modern English means an invective, a *psogos*.

131. The details of the reception of Chrysippus's elaborate medical parallels can be found in Tieleman's chapter on the *Therapeutikos* (2003, 140–97). On the requirement of adopting a new lifestyle and regimen, see 162–66.

132. The word ἀνεπιλόγιστος seems to be Timasagoras's; if so, it is probably enough in itself to prove he was a fellow-Epicurean; see n. 82 to the translation.

133. As Tsouna 2003 shows, "putting things before one's eyes" is an educational technique dear to Philodemus, recommended to Epicurean teachers also in *Lib.* frag. 26.4–5, 77(= 78N).2–3, and col. 17a.8–10. Wilke quotes Seneca, *Ir.* 3.3.2: *necessarium*

great fear in the patient, who, once in a position to use *epilogismos*, will realize that it is "up to him," within his power, to adopt his physician's regimen and suggested lifestyle, change his *diathesis*, and set himself free (2.6–15). Emptily angry people fail to use *epilogismos*, and so the evils of anger are "left unappraised," Philodemus claims, and need to be put in sight (3.9–10, 13–14). These angry people are like sick people who fail to see the danger of their illness by "rational appraisal" (ἐπιλογιϲτικῶϲ, 4.11–12); a doctor or therapist can help them. A good method of attacking empty anger is to convict the patient of "false reasonings" (παραλογιϲμοί, 7.14–15). As philosophical therapists, teachers aim to "rationally appraise (ἐπιλογίϲαϲθαι) the purity of this evil, just as we are accustomed to do in the case of erotic desire" (7.16–20), even when a patient is in the grip of anger as they speak. According to Philodemus, without *epilogismos* and its associated visualization techniques, nothing can be done, but with them, it is easy to convince the patient to undergo therapy (col. 4) and to make the patient acknowledge that anger is indeed an evil, though an escapable one, not a compulsion (col. 6). Philodemus and Timasagoras agree that dispositions can be improved but disagree about the timing and tactics for doing so.

There may have been another area of dispute: Timasagoras may have held that diatribe was an invalid medium for therapy in any circumstances, not just when the patients were angry, because it has too much in common with epidictic oratory, which Philodemus considers an art, but a nearly useless one. In Greek rhetorical theory, the epideictic branch of oratory (τὸ πανηγυρικόν) had two major genres, what we call in English diatribe and panegyric: speeches in praise (*epainos*) or blame (*psogos*) of any topic imaginable, sometimes even deliberately paradoxical (in praise of baldness, in blame of wealth).[134] In *Rhet.* 3, Philodemus offers a long paraphrase of a passage of Epicurus's own *On Rhetoric* in which Epicu-

---

est ... ante oculos ponere quantum monstri sit homo in hominem furens ("it is necessary ... to put before their eyes how much of a monster is a human being in a rage at another human being"). One of the many forms of *epilogismos* is certainly visualization, a fact that was rightly emphasized in Erler 2003. A less lively form of it would be the simple logical arguments about the words defining the prolepsis of anger in the three *epilogismoi* at the end, Philodemus, *Ir.* 45–50. See also McConnell 2015, 121–25.

134. *Epainoi* are not at issue in *On Anger*, but they also were used to improve Epicurean students. Laudatory biographies served a similar purpose in the Epicurean school; see Capasso 1988, 37–53; and Heßler 2015.

rus mocked epidictic rhetoric as an amusement fit only for lazy minds.[135] Unlike political and forensic rhetoric, Epicurus claimed, epideictic deals with topics of no immediate urgency and in a style more preoccupied with stylistic effects than with practical advice. Those who pay to learn it find out that they have wasted their money. It is of no use in the law courts or in political assemblies, where practical decisions must be made. How could the diatribe be a valid form for Epicurean philosophers such as Basilides and Thespis to practice, if Epicurus had denied it any utility?

Philodemus argues throughout columns 2–7 that the diatribe can be a vital and healing form of interpersonal philosophical therapy, a useful means of provoking *epilogismos* even in angry people.[136] Haranguing diatribes can put anger's evil consequences before the eyes in a startling and impactful way, but philosophers' attempts are necessarily limited by their skill in handling the genre. The twenty-three columns of colorful and rhetorical imitation-diatribe against anger, which start with three columns continuing the medical analogy Philodemus had invoked in response to Chrysippus, are intended as a demonstration of the technique of relentless enumeration, in which a teacher forces students to visualize all the entailments and consequences of the emotion, to appraise them rationally by *epilogismos*, and eventually to change their own *diatheseis*, the atomic structure of their souls as well as their moral shapes, for the better. Here Philodemus seems to show himself more optimistic than Timasagoras: a therapist can influence an angry person in the midst of her anger and demonstrate her responsibility for her actions and emotion.[137]

Concern for *epilogismos* and improvements in disposition are the connection to the fragments that immediately precede, with their argu-

---

135. Cf. Epicurus, frag. [20] [4] in Arrighetti 1972, 177–81, as well as Hammerstaedt's edition (1992, 26–31) of the passage, which reedits Sudhaus 1892–1896, 2:255–59. This fragment was not available to Usener. There is a shorter version of the same passage at *Rhet.* 2 (P.Herc. 1674 cols. 10.16–11.34, Longo Auricchio 1977, 62–65). David Blank has provided us with his latest version of this text, which contains many improvements. We are not sure, as he and Hammerstaedt (1992, 67) think, that the version in *Rhet.* 2 is actually nearer to Epicurus's original and that that in book 3 may contain numerous expansions and clarifications by Philodemus himself.

136. Except for frag. 31.18 (and the three brief arguments called *epilogismoi* at 46.17 and discussed in cols. 47–50), the root ἐπιλεγ-/ἐπιλογ- appears only in cols. 1–7 of the surviving text.

137. See Kaufman 2014.

ments that anger is not compulsory but within our moral responsibility, a fact that affects our ability to live the pleasant life. Ultimately, the use of praise and blame in Epicurean education, and thus the justification of diatribe as part of that education, relies on the account in Epicurus's *Nat.* 25 of how consciousness and moral responsibility evolve from outside influences that alter the atomic dispositions in our souls (see excursus 4). Our capacity for responsible moral choice evolves from experiencing blame and praise and learning from them—hence the close connection between *On Anger* and the didactic treatise *On Frank Speech*. Above all, by presenting the evils done by anger, the diatribe forces the students into *epilogismos* about their situation, in order to change their behavior and thereby improve their *diatheseis*.

6.3. The Diatribe (Cols. 8–31.24)

The "demo," or model, diatribe began in the lacuna at the top of column 8. As the text resumes, Philodemus begins intensely with a grandiose description of anger as a terrible, possibly fatal disease requiring the work not just of philosophical therapists but of medical doctors in its treatment (cols. 8–11). It gradually lapses into a more satirical and comic style over the course of 12–18.35. In 18.35–21, Philodemus becomes more intimate and conversational, directly addressing an audience of younger students, who now become the diatribe's focus, about the difficulties bad temper causes them as members of a community based on study and friendship. In these columns, the vocabulary and style show abundant parallels with *On Frank Speech*. In columns 22–30, Philodemus returns to a more elevated style, drawing a terrifying picture of how students who fail to heed him will ruin the rest of their youth, their marriages and family lives, and their careers in politics and the law courts; they will risk arson and murder at the hands of their infuriated slaves and finally die, leaving nothing but hatred, curses, and feuds that will poison the succeeding generations of their families. This is because the longer they live, the more corrupt and poisoned their *diatheseis* become. He ends with a forceful peroration, of which only the final few sentences survive (31.10–24).

The opening columns (8–10) are particularly lurid and graphic in their description of anger as a serious illness with extreme physical symptoms. This theme was inspired by Chrysippus and shows the Epicurean therapist frightening his patient into cooperating with a regimen by vividly depicting the consequences of failing to accept that it is up to him to work for a cure. Rage, a type of empty anger, is described in medical terms of "raging fever and swelling and irritation" (8.21–23), restless movements, damage to the lungs, gasping for breath as if one had just run a thousand *stadia*, and irregular heartbeat (8.32–9.1). The catalog of symptoms ("such as hap[pen] to epileptics [as well]," 9.20–21) concludes: "breakings of lungs, pains in the sides, and" (anticlimactically) "many such afflictions that bring death in their wake" (9.31–33), the first of many such rhetorical anticlimaxes.[138] This suits well with his common practice with *exempla*, which Philodemus uses only in drastic abridgement, such as his careless wave of the hand at tragic fratricides: "as many resembling Oedipus's sons and those of Pelops or Pleisthenes and the rest of that family" (the reference is to Atreus, Thyestes, Agamemnon, Aegisthus, Clytaemnestra, and Orestes) and "like countless others, both in the past and now" (14.10–16).[139] Several instances of *praeteritio* have the same effect of *sprezzatura* and self-conscious irony.[140] Philodemus's goal is not to compose a real diatribe but to provide a vivid mockup of the genre for his audience's amusement. Accordingly, he does not go through his *exempla* in detail; allusion is enough.[141]

---

138. E.g., "or something like that" (13.16–17); "going completely out of control about many other things of the sort" (14.27–29); "slighted in similar circumstances" (18.21–22); "or any[thing else] of that sort," (26.2–3); "[or something] like that" (26.33); "and everything [like that]" (28.4–5); and "and do many other unpleasant things" (28.17–18). See Armstrong 2014, 109 nn. 31–32, who argues that this "throwaway" style, with its suggestion that the diatribe tradition could be employed at any length to prove the same point over and over, can be compared with Horace's similar claim that "there is so much more of this kind of stuff, it could wear out even the talkative (Stoic) Fabius" (*cetera de genere hoc, adeo sunt multa, loquacem / delassare valent Fabium, Sat.* 1.1.13–14). Other marks of the throwaway style are *praeteritio* and the phrases ἀφίημι ("I dismiss") used of further details (23.35; 31.21) and ⟨τὸ⟩ βλεπόμενον at 28.35, "what everyone can see" (cf. Timasagoras's πᾶϲι φανερόν, "obvious to all").

139. Cf. the terse list of divine vengeances visited on the innocent in Homer, Aeschylus, and Euripides (*Ir.* 16.18–26) and the clipped references to "Sophocles's Achilles" and "Alexander's dog" in 18.19–20 and 28–31.

140. Specifically, the phrase "why should I mention…?" (τί γὰρ δεῖ λέγειν) makes its first appearance at 13.11–12; it occurs no fewer than four times in the diatribe (also 18.34–35; 20.28; 28.35) and once more in the attack on the Peripatetics (33.24–25).

141. One *exemplum* is drawn from the history of the Epicurean school itself. At 12.22–30, Philodemus says that empty anger can make people attack others who are obviously much stronger than themselves: "their rage (*thymos*) does not allow them to

The tone of unreserved horror at the physical manifestation of anger as a life-threatening illness (cols. 8–10) and insane defiance of powerful enemies (cols. 12–14) starts brightening and moving in the direction of satire as soon as Timocrates, the brother of Metrodorus and a violent critic of Epicurus, makes his appearance in column 12. The tone in which the murder of family members, particularly brothers by brothers, in tragedy is discussed in this column is contemptuous and dismissive, as is that of the irreligious behavior of the angry (col. 14) and the picture of them "pulling their hair out and sobbing over the insults they visited on people and sometimes butchering themselves" (col. 15). At 15.21, the diatribe even becomes somewhat lighthearted, as Philodemus mocks the "heroic" rage of a Phoenician trader, taken from the comic stage, over the loss of a single coin. After a short lacuna we are in the world of mythology, which Philodemus regards with contempt, reviewing Zeus's threatened quarrel with the god Hypnos on some unknown occasion (16.12–14; cf. *Il.* 14.257–259 and *Ir.* 8.10–27 with Indelli 1988, 175, on 16.15–16) and listing the gods' perverse acts of revenge, not just on offenders but also on innocent bystanders: Apollo's revenge of the insult to Chryses in the first book of the *Iliad*, "his sister" Artemis's revenge on the children of her enemy Niobe, Dionysus's revenge on Cadmus for his daughters' blasphemy (16.19–26). In column 17, those who vent their anger "[kicking their] children and ripping up their frocks (χιτωνίϲκουϲ), and abusing absent people out loud as if they were there, and doing a great many things very like those" (17.8–15) are compared to those who go into a full-blown rage at flies and mosquitoes who they think have disrespected them (ὡϲ καταφρονούμενοι, 17.22–23). The sarcastic tone is continued against tragic heroes who "mix [earth] with heaven … like Sophocles's Achilles" because he was not invited to a dinner,

---

distinguish, as Metrodorus tells us Timocrates did to his eldest brother, Mentorides." We would love to know more about Timocrates, Metrodorus's younger brother, at first a convert to Epicurus's doctrines and then a bitter opponent and satirist of the school, whom Sedley (1973) identified as the source of a large number of hostile stories about the Founders by means of his *Euphranta* (Amusing Stories). On quarrels like this in the early school, see below, §7. There is now a large scholarly tradition of speculation about Timocrates, catalogued and reviewed in *DPA* T156 (Angeli). Verde (2017) conjectures (and we agree) that Philodemus's later citation of Metrodorus (*Ir.* 45.8–12), where he uses *thymos* of the sage's anger and specifies that it should be mild and brief, counts as a fragment of his *Timocrates* or *Against Timocrates* (see Diogenes Laertius, *Vit. phil.* 10.23–24, 136).

and "the poets' gods" who go into rages even with "sows"; "Why should I mention kings?" (18.31-35).

In the next lines (18.35 onward) Philodemus turns to discuss Epicurean students in a tone and vocabulary that resemble those of *On Frank Speech*. Some of them (in the third-person) fail to understand the dangers of empty anger visited on their teachers and their fellow students. Ringeltaube (1913, 39) identified this section as an especially vivid portrayal of an ancient lecture hall, an opportunity to visualize Philodemus's own teaching methods.[142] These students show how empty anger can poison a classroom: they are suspicious of their fellow students' motives and cruel to them, cannot stand even gentle criticism, and fly into rages without provocation. They try to pretend that their useless anger is the "reasonable anger" (*eulogos orgē*), the kind that is permissible for Epicureans (20.24-26), a claim their teachers will obviously refuse to take on trust. They blurt out others' secrets (20.26-27). By this behavior, they destroy all possibility of friendships, even with students who would naturally like them otherwise (20.28-34). Like the man in fragment 24 who is always alienating his single slave, "they fail to meet their own needs" from everyone else in the school (21.18-19) and make no friends even to converse with, let alone to study with or accompany them to a barbershop, a theater performance, or a boat trip (21.29-36). This part is aimed squarely at an Epicurean audience who should take a hint about their own behavior regardless of their

---

142. In columns 18.35-21, the terms of art for Epicurean teaching used in *On Frank Speech* are echoed throughout: καθηγητής "teacher," 19.14 (*On Frank Speech* eight times); cχολάζω "study," 19.11-12; cυcχολάζω, "study together," 19.15-6 (*On Frank Speech* twice); ὁμιλέω, "converse together," 21.28 (*On Frank Speech* four times, and ὁμιλία twice); cf. also cυζήτηcιc, 19.26, "study together" (*On Frank Speech* ζητέω five times); and cυλλάληcιc 21.22 "conversation together" (*On Frank Speech* λαλέω four times). Teachers rebuking and correcting: ἐπιτιμάω 19.16 (twelve times in *On Frank Speech*, ἐπιτίμηcιc seven times); διορθόω 19.17 (five times in *On Frank Speech*, διόρθωcιc three times); and ἐπιπλήττω 19.22 (once in *On Frank Speech*, ἐπίπληξιc twice) are key words for "rebuke" and "correct" in the theory of "frank speech" expounded in *On Frank Speech*. Bad attitudes of students: ὑποπτεύω, "suspect," 18.24 (*On Frank Speech* twice); λοιδορέω "revile" 20.20 (*On Frank Speech* three times); πλάττω "make up stories" about another pupil, 20.21 (cf. *On Frank Speech* πλάcμα, three times); ἐκκαλύπτω 20.27 "reveal (secrets)" (cf. *On Frank Speech* frag. 28.11-12, where "to reveal" one's secrets to the teacher is a good thing); ἐρεθίζειν "irritate" (*On Frank Speech* frag. 13.4, cf. ἐρεθιcμός T12M.2, ἐρεθιcτός IIa.6). See also nn. 76 and 156.

actual age. But the empty anger portrayed is still relatively harmless; more serious consequences will only appear as life goes on.

Columns 22–30 return to the threatening style of the beginning. These columns continue to follow the students' lives through marriage and maturity to their death. In street parties of revelers, they are quarrelsome and cause riots by "guffawing and yelling insults" until they go crazy (22.18–24). If they remain bachelors, they become social outcasts; if they marry, it seems (a lacuna occurs here) that they inflict their bad tempers on their wives (22.26–32). They endanger their property because they are liable to waste it in lawsuits for revenge. "For I pass over," Philodemus says, the way they maltreat their slaves, "with their eyes knocked out or often murdered or, if they have good luck, becoming runaways" (23.35–40). Indeed, their slaves are treated so horribly that they are ready to kill the master and his wife and children or burn down his house and destroy his property (23.35–40; 24.17–36).[143] Although they have many opportunities to show kindness, justice, or good temper (24.36–40), Philodemus goes on, the angry people make themselves odious to friend and foe alike. In their fits of anger, they reveal political conspiracies and ruin themselves and others (col. 25). Even spectacles, baths, dinner parties, travel, and every other amusement are spoiled by their temper.

After the usual lacuna opens column 26, we find the miserable angry man shouting at his "[wife] or slave or any[thing else] of that sort, and not just human beings, but dumb brutes, and indeed inanimate things, and well-nigh even [shadows]...." The men who should now be responsible householders have come to something "more bitter even than their angry emotions: both their nature and that which is mixed with it (their nature) are filled with miserable bitterness" (26.10–14). Their fancied pleasure in vengeance is really an unending sequence of "terrors and agonies and disturbances" (26.14–16). They have made themselves a host of enemies in

---

143. Cobet (1878, 378–79) and Harris (2001, 321–22) both argue that cols. 23–24 describe the brutality of Roman and Italian slave-owners of the late Republic and Empire (*Romanorum esse hunc rabiem et Seneca et multis locis Galenus declarant*, so Cobet), not of Greeks. If true, this would be the only such instance in *On Anger*. The *On Household Management* explicitly refers to Roman customs here and there: Armstrong (2016, 193–201), following Asmis 2004. Roskam (2007) has made it clear that statements such as "live unnoticed" and "avoid politics" were not universally applicable rules and would not have prevented Romans from participating in government; see further Benferhat 2005, Armstrong 2011, Fish 2011.

kinsmen and former friends alike and are as liable to commit suicide when their revenge succeeds as when it fails. At 27.18-19, it turns out that they themselves are punished, and their disposition is once more the cause of their failure: "to this unyielding and ungentle and harsh disposition, the most destructive diseases of all, the emotion is yoked" (27.19-23).

There are two more steps in this imaginary life of the angry man: he cannot play a role in city politics, "since neither a juryman nor a council member nor a member of an assembly nor an archon can be just while in the grip of angry emotions" (28.21-26). In the last columns of the diatribe, we see that the sufferers have indeed failed to learn to reason about their experiences. Philodemus's paraphrases of Homer and Democritus at 29.23-29 sum up their fate: "Many times many misfortunes happen both to friends and others who are close [sc. to them], sometimes also to fatherlands and to kingdoms, not only of old when that 'wrath' 'gave the Achaeans myriad pains,'[144] but every day, and nearly, as Democritus says, 'as many' evils 'as one could conceive of' all come about through excessive [fits of anger]." Angry men are never freed from their anger; fits of it "stay with them even until death and are often handed down to children's children" (30.20-24; cf. Democritus B85 D.-K.).

In column 31, Philodemus apparently pointed out that nothing could dissolve these angers and compulsions and their entailments and consequences "but can[onic] reasoning." Here he flourishes the specifically Epicurean term for empirical reasoning, using *prolēpseis*, *symmetrēsis*, and the information of the senses as criteria. He ends with a complex and beautiful period: "On the other hand, everyone is an opponent: the outsider who provokes anger in every imaginable way, parents and every relative who often rejoice as if over brave fellows, and the philosophers, the ones who babble in their attempts to assuage it [anger], and the others who strengthen it by advocacy—and I pass over orators and poets and all that kind of trash."[145] Not just the parents, the relatives, the Stoics, and the Peri-

---

144. *Il.* 1.1-2. On *Anger*, in the surviving text, quotes poetry, or prose written for literary effect, only in the diatribe: *Iliad* (several familiar quotations), an ornate phrase from Plato's *Laws* at 11.19-21; an allusion to a tragedy of Sophocles, probably *Syndeipnoi*, at 18.20. The only exceptions are a maxim of Menander cited, with an air of the impromptu, at 38.27 and *Il.* 8.63 cited at 44.23-25 to help give a feeling of closure to the argument about natural anger. In frag. 31, *Od.* 20.19 is quoted, perhaps to invoke the whole opening scene at 20.1-55.

145. The claim that "parents and every relative" as well as the poets and orators

patetics but Philodemus himself, in his character as poet and (occasional) epidictic orator and composer of diatribes, are magically swept out of the way with the last contemptuous word "trash" (γρυμέαν), as the "diatribe" ends, and the tone of the discourse drops back to that of ordinary exposition.

6.4. The Peripatetics (Cols. 31.24–34.6)

Philodemus returns to his attack on the Peripatetic theory of anger (see above, §6.1). What Philodemus says against the Peripatetics is, for the most part, clearly borrowed from the same hostile (Academic?) source as several passages in Cicero and in Seneca.[146] Frustratingly, we have no clue in the text about the identities of Philodemus's opponents here. After Falcon's edited volume (2016), especially the essays by Hatzimichali, Falcon, and Dillon, we know for certain that the "esoteric" texts of Aristotle, whatever is the truth of the story about their recovery in Sulla's day, were simply not available in Philodemus's lifetime.[147] Perhaps Aristo of Alexandria and Cratippus of Pergamon, Philodemus's friends, or Staseas of Neapolis, the most distinguished Peripatetic teaching in Italy when Philodemus arrived there, are hiding behind the curtain here?[148] In any case, the relatively generous space given the theory and arguments of the Peripatetics in *On Anger* probably reflects the increasing importance of this rival school and developments in its doctrines. But what the Peripatetics claim about anger seems to have only a little to do with what Aristotle himself says in the works that we can read today.

---

are the enemy of those students who try to limit their anger is verbally paraphrased from Adeimantus's and Glaucon's complaint to Socrates at the beginning of *Resp.* 2 (362e5–366b2); see n. 157 to the translation.

146. Especially Cicero, *Tusc.* 4.43–48; Seneca, *Ir.* 1.9; 3.3. The comparison between taking *thymos* out of the soul and cutting out its nerves was originally Plato's (*Resp.* 3.411b–c) and is also cited by Plutarch, *Cohib. ira* 8 (457b–c). Editors of the fragments of Aristotle have sometimes included *Ir.* 31.24–31; see Bloch 1986; Indelli 1988, 206.

147. This has been shown conclusively by Dillon (2016) to be the case for Antiochus of Ascalon and Cicero, in particular. Philodemus's contemporaries simply did not yet know what was said in the works of Aristotle that we have. There is no reason to suspect that Philodemus had any better access. See also Falcon (2013) and Hatzimichali (2011).

148. Cf. *History of the Academy* (col. 35.7–19), and see above §1 for Aristo and Cratippus. For Staseas, see *DPA* S148 (Dorandi).

In Philodemus's summary, the Peripatetics believe that to refuse all anger is to "cut out the nerves of the soul" (31.28–29), without which people cannot defend themselves. Their behavior will consequently be slavish and fawning. Anger "makes one courageous and takes away all shrinking and cowardice" and creates "a spirit of vengeance against one's enemies, a thing that is noble and just and profitable individually and communally and, in addition, pleasurable" (32.23–29). The emphasis on the last word is pointed: finding pleasure in anger means to an Epicurean that it is empty. In short, anger is required to be an effective fighter in battle, and Aristotle's analysis of anger is expanded to cover warfare: the soldiers are motivated by anger because they are, as it were, getting vengeance on their opponents, just as normal people are motivated to get vengeance on those who slight them.[149] Thus "they think that both the rational courage of some people and their irrational, so to speak, 'possession' constitute the angry emotion (*thymos*) that we are talking about" (32.30–35).[150]

For Philodemus, this account wrongly combines "rational courage" and "irrational 'possession,' so to speak" (32.30-5) That is, he thinks that soldiers need to remain calm in battle (they need to exercise rational courage) and that the anger discussed by the Peripatetics is like an irrational fit of possession and therefore empty. Soldiers regularly win battles without anger, and it often provokes them into foolish behavior (32.35–33.7).[151] To make the rational element in the soul out to be the "general" and make the emotions its "soldiers," as apparently the Peripatetics did in their treatise, is absurd for Philodemus.[152] They will be disobedient and take their general prisoner, then do all kinds of evil (33.22–28). The soul will be nerveless, quick to collapse, and unhealthy (33.28–34).

At this point (33.34–40), Philodemus recruits Antipater of Tarsus (d. 130/129), a Stoic scholarch who wrote a treatise *On Anger*, to the cause.[153] Antipater had said that we are not angry in real life when we fight against

---

149. According to Seneca, *On Anger* 1.9.2–4, Aristotle already used the "soldiers" metaphor, which may mean that this whole analysis of anger in war was originally his.

150. It is not clear whether this sentence is to be taken as Philodemus's inference about their views or a continuation of his report of them.

151. 32.36–39: for parallels with Cicero, Seneca, and Plutarch, see Ringeltaube 1913, 39; and Wilke's (1914) apparatus, with Indelli's discussion (1988, 207–8).

152. To be clear, Philodemus may object not to the metaphor as applied to the rational and irrational parts of the soul but rather to its use regarding emotions.

153. Cf. Athenaeus, *Deipn.* 14.643f–644a = Antipater *SVF* 3.65.

wild animals or engage in sports, and are the better for it. Additionally, anger is useless to teachers of the arts in correcting their students (33.40–34.5; cf. *Lib.* frag. 12). The end of this section and the beginning of the next are lost in the lacuna in column 34. Perhaps Philodemus, or Antipater, was about to say that the same is true of teachers of philosophy. The implication of quoting a Stoic against the Peripatetics is that here, as in the diatribe, Stoic arguments against all anger can be usefully deployed by Epicureans against empty anger, leaving the possibility of natural anger in the good person and the sage undiminished.

Philodemus's use of Antipater's comparison of angry instructors in other fields, such as athletics, horse training, and apprenticeships, forms a tidy, even elegant, transition to the next topic: the role of anger in Epicurean education.

6.5. The "Anger" of Sages and Their Students (Cols. 34.16–37.9)

The discussion here returns to anger as manifested by Epicurean sages, teachers, and students, as in columns 18–21. This section could be read as an amusing pair of sketches in the manner of Theophrastus's *Characters*. Philodemus wittily describes the kinds of angry behavior to be expected and forgiven, first in a sage (34.16–36.30), then in an ordinary Epicurean layperson (36.31–37.9). Ordinary manifestations of hot temper, even by sages, do not count as empty anger, evidence of a bad *diathesis*, or moral irresponsibility (34.18–24). Just as Lucretius claims that "a life worthy of the gods" (that of a sage) can be lived without obliterating all the vestiges of one's original constitution, Philodemus asserts that there is nothing wrong with a sage's having an overbalance of fire in his disposition, even to the point of giving the "impression" now and then of being irascible or angry as if from a vicious disposition.[154] The Epicurean sage is not the Stoic sage;

---

154. For Philodemus's *On Arrogance* (P.Herc. 222), cols. 10–24, which summarize similar character sketches by one Ariston (probably the Peripatetic, of Keos), see Rusten 2003, 160–75; and Ranocchia 2007a, 138–49. In the *Characters* tradition, to be "inconsiderate" (*authadēs*), "a know-it-all" (*panteidēmōn*), "contemptuous" (*hyperoptēs*), and the like may be annoying and undignified, but they do not make you a vicious so much as an eccentric person. The influence of Theophrastus's *Characters* on Philodemus is well treated in Tsouna 2007a, 143–62; see also Fortenbaugh 1985, 219–22; Kondo 1971; and Gargiulo 1981.

some human flaws remain.¹⁵⁵ In his teaching, the sage can exhibit quite a lot of harshness without compromising his status as a sage (cf. *Lib.* 2a–6a). He can rebuke his disciples intensely and often, even revile them, before realizing fully that the bad conduct was an accident (35.24–26).¹⁵⁶ Again, the sage is not perfect. He can remain aloof in his relations with the public, conduct tempestuous philosophical arguments in his writings and lectures, offend friends through his frankness or refusal of their requests, and lose his temper with his slaves without losing his status as a wise person—and these actions are not necessarily indicative of anger in the full sense in any case.¹⁵⁷ As Philodemus says at 39.38–40.2, these outbursts "bring only some little amount of embarrassment upon those who will make out that [anger] is both natural and, in the case of the sage, brief."

At 36.20–26, Philodemus says that some sages are more prone to natural anger than others or harsher in their use of *parrhēsia* on their students. For this topic, he refers his audience to his own *On Frank Speech* for a more detailed treatment. There are, in fact, significant parallel passages in *Lib.* 3b and 5a, and fragments 45, 49, 60, 62, 70, and 87 (Olivieri 1914) that are crucial to understanding Philodemus's meaning here.¹⁵⁸

---

155. On the Epicurean sage, see Verde forthcoming. On the Stoic sage, see Brouwer 2014.

156. The words ἐπιτίμηϲιϲ (35.18) and λοιδορία (cf. 35.22 and 36.36) are theme words for the negative side of the therapist's task in *On Frank Speech* (ἐπιτιμ- twenty-three times, λοιδορ- five times).

157. In 36.6–17, Philodemus may have said that none of this counts as empty anger or indicates a vicious disposition. Perhaps he said "but (it was) without" (ἄνευ δὲ ..., 36.15) any very serious consequences after all. At any rate (if we read ὥ[ϲτε, "so that, therefore," as the text resumes at 36.17), we have lost the excuse Philodemus made, but we have the conclusion: "just as some sages will present the impression of being irascible more than others, (namely,) those in whom there is more natural (sc. anger) present, as we said before, or who are more given to frank criticism for the reasons we listed at length in our *On Frank Criticism*, or because such things" (as provoke anger) "happen to them more often" (36.17–26). On Philodemus's arguments that the Epicurean sage need not always appear unmoved by emotion, see Armstrong 2008, 111–12, 114–15).

158. We are grateful to Ben Henry, who is reediting the text, for giving us his texts and notes on these fragments, which take account of the rearrangement of the order of the fragments arrived at by White 2009. See also Delattre 2010 and 2015 for another understanding of the ordering and Ghisu's 2015 Italian translation and commentary. For convenience's sake, we retain Olivieri's numeration, as do Konstan et al. 1988.

Philodemus, *Lib.* 3b (Olivieri 1914)

1 καὶ κ]αθάπερ ἐντ[έχνως χοροδ[ι]δασκαλούντ[ω]ν, ἐν φιλοcοφίαι· καὶ τὸ[ν] μὲν ἀκράχολον εἶναι κα[ὶ] κυνώ- 5 δη πρὸc ἅπανταc, ὡc πάλιν ἄλλοι [τ]ινέc εἰcιν· τ[ὸ]ν δ' ἀ- εὶ βληχρόν· καὶ τὸν μὲν εὖ κατὰ πᾶν, τὸν δ' ἐλλε[ί]πόν- τως κατά τι παρρηcιάζε- 10 cθαι. πάντεc γὰρ ὁμοίωc καὶ φιλοῦcι κατ' ἀξίαν ἑκά- cτου καὶ τὰc ἁμαρτίαc 13 βλέπουcι καὶ τὰc διὰ παρ-|| [ρηcίαc …	[And] just as in the case of those who train choruses [skillfully], (so also) in philosophy: and one [sc. teacher] is sharp-tempered and cynical toward everyone, as certain others are in turn, while another is always mild; and the one speaks frankly about everything in a good way, but another does so deficiently in some respect. For all [sc. the sages] both love[159] [sc. their students] alike in accord with the worth of each and see their faults alike and, through [frankness], the …

Epicurean teachers have their own personal styles. For an Epicurean, this is at least partly a function of their disposition, which Philodemus admits might have flaws. What unifies them is a love for their students, which does not prevent them from seeing the students' faults and rebuking them.

Philodemus warns his students to expect harsh rebukes and impatient behavior from some of their teachers.

Philodemus, *Lib.* 5a (Angeli 1988b)

οἱ δ' [ἀκρι- 5 βέcτεροί πωc ὑπάρ[ξουcιν ἐν cπάνει τῶν πρὸc [εὔνοι- αν καὶ φιλίαν εὐθέτων γενηθέντες καὶ παρ[ὰ τὴν ἀπομίμ[υ]ηcιν δὲ τὴν πο-	… and other (teachers) will be all the more exacting, if born in want of things that make for goodwill and friendliness and because of their long-term imitation of their own teachers, whether these were

---

159. φιλοῦcι: this supports the supplement of Mewaldt, διὰ τὸ φ[ιλεῖν], at *Ir.* 35.18: the sage rebukes his students for love.

10 λυχρόνιον τῶν καθηγηcα-
   μένων, ἢ cφοδρ[ῶ]ν κατὰ
12 τὸ [γέ]νοc ὄντων ἤ πω[c.]ϲ

vehement in the usual way of their kind, or somehow ...

This is another indication that harshness on the part of teachers is not out of place in Epicurean schools. Philodemus may even be hinting that he was himself a faithful imitator of his famously sharp-tempered teacher Zeno of Sidon.[160]

At *Lib.* fragment 45 Philodemus says:

Philodemus, *Lib.* frag 45 (Henry)

```
1   .....  .....]επι[....
    τονοιπ[.....  .....]με-
    τὰ πολλῆc πεποιθήcεωc
    ἄλλουc νουθετήcομεν
5   καὶ νῦν καὶ διαπρέψαν-
    τεc οἱ καθ' [α]ὑτῶν οὕτωc
    ἀπότομοι γενηθέντεc.
    κα[ὶ] τὸ cυνέχον καὶ κυ[ρι-
    ώτατον, Ἐπικούρωι, κα-
10  θ' ὃν ζῆν ἡ⟨ι⟩ρήμ[ε]θα, πει-
    θαρχήcομεν, ὡc καὶ παρ-||
    [ρηc-
```

... with great confidence we shall admonish others, both now and when we have become eminent, we who have been so severe against ourselves. And—the principal and most important thing—we shall obey Epicurus, according to whom we have chosen to live, as also frank ...

The teachers were rigorous in self-criticism (Henry's new reading of line 6 is important here) and therefore earned the right to criticize others (their students) harshly, in full knowledge of what they were doing and why: this is what obedience to Epicurus means.

But as the Epicurean sage is neither without emotion nor infallible, the students are usually wrong to resent his rebukes—but sometimes not! As Philodemus puts it in *On Frank Speech*: "now and then, the sage applies his frank speaking (παρρηcία) when they have done no wrong, because he

---

160. Zeno was famously called *acriculus senex* (Cicero, *Tusc.* 3.28 = frag. 8 Angeli and Colaizzo 1979), with a delightful pun on the Greek word ἀκράχολοc, used here by Philodemus himself of the worse-tempered sages at *Ir.* 36.3 and *Lib.* 3b.4 (quoted just above).

has himself reckoned wrongly and [offered] frank criticism [out of place], [for various] reasons" (frag. 62.7–13 Olivieri). Compare the sage's rebuking people before fully realizing that their bad behavior was accidental (*Ir.* 34.24.26). Obviously, Philodemus learned from Zeno that humility is a great thing even for teachers. Epicurean therapy, like all ancient medicine, is a stochastic art: the sage can apply harsh criticism and be wrong, though that will not happen often.

Finally, there is new evidence for Philodemus's theory of how to deal with anger manifested by a student, which is important for the interpretation of columns 34–37. We give parts of fragments 70 and 87, now known to come in sequence, though we omit the fragmentary lines at their beginnings.[161]

Philodemus, *Lib.* frag. 70 (Henry)

6	πῶc χρήcεται τοῖc διὰ	How will (the sage) deal with
	τὴν παρρηcίαν ὀργίλωc	people who have become angry
	πρὸc αὐτὸν ἐcχηκόcιν;	with him because of his frank
	ἐπεὶ δ' ἐνίουc cυνβαίνε[ι	speech? Since it happens that some,
10	πα[ρ]ρηcιαcαμένου τοῦ	when the sage exercises frank
	co[φ]οῦ [δι]ατί[θεc]θαι πρὸc	speech on them, are made angry in
	αὐτὸν ὀργίλωc, ἐὰν μὲν	their disposition to him, if, on the
13	ἔνμονον ἔχωcι τὴν [ὀ]ρ‖[γήν	one hand, the anger they have is persistent ...

Philodemus, *Lib.* frag. 87 (Henry)

3	... διότι	... because [one?] man who keeps
	τὸν .[........]c [ἀ]νὴρ ἀ-	company with true ... is worth
5	ληθινῶι cυνουcιάζων	far more than a flock of winged
	π[ολ]ὺ κρείττων ἀγέλης	disciples. But if, on the other hand,
	πτηνῶν μαθητῶν. ἐ-	the anger is endurable and can be
	ὰν δ' ἀνεκτ[ὴ]ν καὶ λήξειν	expected to cease, the anger with
	προcδοκωμένην, οὐκ ἀν-	which he responds will

---

161. White 2009 showed that frags. 70 and 87 are the bottom of one column and the top of the next.

10 τοργιεῖτα[ι τ]ὴν μισοῦcαν   not be the kind that hates but the
ὀργὴν ἀλλὰ τὴν μεμφο-   kind that blames the person's follies
μ]έ[νην] τὰ[c] ἀβελτερία[c...   ...

Philodemus's response to irascible students is largely lost in a gap in the papyrus, but perhaps he consoled himself with the thought that one good one of this kind is a much better pupil than a flock of (placid?) birds (i.e., mere parrots?). But if the anger is not excessive and is likely to be transient, the philosopher simply uses anger in response to blame his follies and, he hopes, correct the student. The distinction that Philodemus draws here between hating anger and blaming anger is that between simple alienation, shunning, dismissing the student from the school, on the one hand, and the kind of anger that aims at changing the student's disposition, on the other. As we will see in the passages from *Nat.* 25 discussed at excursus 4 below, blame and praise are essential to moral education, even physically essential. "Blaming anger" is for the students' good, to spur them to improve.

Nothing in these passages, except perhaps the last, concerns anger in the fullest sense: the teacher acts and is in fact angry but dislikes the experience, which is painful to her and the students. She rebukes them without pleasure and only under the compulsion that results from her analysis of the situation. But her object is to correct the students by frightening them into reconsidering and correcting their actions and *diatheseis*. This is a milder manifestation of natural anger, it would seem. These passages of *On Frank Speech* help to illuminate not only columns 34–37 but also the description of angry students in the classroom address section of the diatribe, columns 18–21. There the students' anger is empty and comes from an immature disposition.

In column 36, Philodemus says that some Epicureans are bitter, censorious, and severe in their talk or portray themselves as haters of bad behavior or profess to believe that most men are no good. Sometimes these people, who are not sages and do not pretend to be, do themselves harm by such behavior.[162] It does not seem that the harm in this case can be very great.

---

162. There is no reason the sage should be incapable of doing himself *any* harm; Philodemus is only concerned to show that he never suffers *great* harm (41.39–42.7) and thus never feels great or intense anger.

Excursus 2: Nicasicrates[163]

Nicasicrates is, to all appearances, an Epicurean who believed that even the natural anger of the sage, let alone empty anger, is dangerous and only to be allowed with great caution and reserve. The decisive passage is 39.21–25: if the sage's natural anger is so great an evil as Nicasicrates claims, Philodemus asks, "how could we still say anything frankly against the arguments of those who take away anger entirely from the sage?" It seems that these must be the Stoics and that Nicasicrates must therefore be an Epicurean who disagrees with the Stoics and believes the sage can indeed feel anger but comes so close to their position that he damages his own side's case.

Philodemus says that Nicasicrates believed in the existence of natural anger and quotes from him to that effect:

> Now, in Nicasicrates, it is said that "the natural kind of anger is painful not only in its own nature, but also it darkens one's reasonings, to the extent that is in its power," and "impairs the perfect tolerability and untroubled character of one's communal life with friends" and brings with it many of the disadvantages that have been e[nu]merated [i.e., by Philodemus earlier]. But since he did not compare it (natural anger) with empty (anger)…." (38.34–39.9)

It is not certain whether Nicasicrates distinguished empty and natural anger, at least in the way that Philodemus advocates. Philodemus agrees that natural anger is painful per se and therefore an evil, even if it can be a good in certain circumstances (see, e.g., 37.39–38.34), but he disagrees that it darkens the sage's reasonings. However, Nicasicrates thinks that natural anger is an enemy of Epicurean *ataraxia* (roughly "imperturbability") and damages "one's communal life with friends." As Ringeltaube saw, this seems to identify him as an Epicurean who believes in *ataraxia* and communal life with friends. Most of all, Nicasicrates held that sages sometimes do themselves harm in their fits of anger (37.4–7). Thus, Nicasicrates's natural anger would bring in its wake at least some of the negative consequences that Philodemus attributes to empty anger.

---

163. For Nicasicrates, see in general *DPA* N34 (Dorandi). Mention of his name at frag. 15.15 shows that Nicasicrates had been treated earlier in the text, though all context there is lost.

Philodemus also argues that anger, as Nicasicrates saw it, was not consistent with "being called a sage and keeping away from futile things, nor could it ever be given this appellation (sc. natural), if it is so great an evil" (39.17–21). The topic, as shown by the mention of anger's appellation, is in what sense anger can be said to be natural. That this was the general thrust of Philodemus's objection to Nicasicrates is shown by the rest of the discussion, in which Philodemus asks and answers a series of rhetorical questions:

> How can that which impedes such important things and causes so many evils be natural? If it is inescapable, and therefore called natural, then how is it not a great evil that must be endured even by sages? Or how are there not outbursts of anger manifested even in the case of good men? Because [sc. these outbursts] are free from everything that is attached to them by those [sc. other philosophers] and they bring only some little amount of embarrassment upon those who will make out that it (the emotion) is both natural and, in the case of the sage, brief. (39.26–40.2)

Nicasicrates is only dismissed at 40.22–26: sages do indeed fall into natural anger, which is inescapable for human nature, and in fact "even this man (sc. Nicasicrates), I suppose, since he shares in it (human nature), could not escape all anger but would as a matter of course be receptive to some of it."

6.6. On the Painfulness of Natural Anger (Cols. 37.16–44.35)

We return to a brief description of what survives of Philodemus's own theory. Here he lays out an argument, against the Peripatetics, the Stoics, and Nicasicrates at once, that, properly defined, natural anger is painful rather than pleasurable and thus an evil per se. But despite being painful, it is to be accepted and acted on in certain circumstances, which are determined by the hedonic calculus. Thus natural anger is limited to good people with good dispositions, not only to Epicurean sages.[164] Its aim is deterrence of further harm by punishment, not vengeance. Here we need only indicate the principal texts from which Philodemus's own theories about anger are to be learned.

---

164. Epicurean sagehood may be the best disposition, but it is not the only good one, since, e.g., *technai* and liabilities to emotions are also dispositions.

37.16–38.34: natural anger taken in isolation and by itself is an evil, like all painful things, but in conjunction, or literally interwoven, with a good *diathesis*, it can even be called a good thing because it comes from seeing "what the nature of states of affairs is and from not having any false beliefs in our comparative calculations (*symmetrēseis*) of our losses and in our punishments of those who harm us."[165]

Or perhaps—Philodemus pretends to hesitate over the right formula here—it is a nonevil (οὐ κακόν, 38.5–6)? He quotes Menander, correcting him twice, and finally arrives at the true formula: even natural anger is not a good, but accepting it is a good (ἀγαθὸν δὲ τὸ ἀναδέχεσθαι, 38.33–34; cf. 38.18–22). Empty anger comes from a bad *diathesis* and entails countless troubles; natural anger limits itself, because it is a painful thing, to dealing with as few things as possible (38.7–9).[166] It is good to submit to natural anger, therefore, but only if those conditions are fulfilled.[167]

39.29–40.32: natural anger is inescapable for everyone, and that is one reason why it is natural. It is inescapable even for Nicasicrates, who is now dismissed from consideration (40.2–25). Experiencing natural anger is simply a fact of human nature, and it does not bring the consequences that Timasagoras and Nicasicrates attach to it. That is, they attach further false beliefs to the *prolēpsis* of natural anger that confuse the issue.

40.32–40: "when he [the sage] has been intentionally harmed by someone or has received the impression he will be harmed, will he experience an indifferent feeling, as if someone looked at him, or a painful one (ἀλλότριον, *allotrion*), since calling it attractive (οἰκεῖον, *oikeion*) to him is senseless?"[168] The use of Epicurean technical terms here is interesting. *Oikeion* means "what is naturally attractive to our nature," that is, "what is pleasant," and *allotrion* means "what is foreign to our nature," that is, "what is painful." We also note that the word *pathos* here suggests the basic Epicurean usage of the word to refer to the basic *pathē* of pleasure and pain,

---

165. On *symmetrēsis*, see above, p. 21.
166. See 38.8: περὶ ἐλάχιστα γίνεται (περί + acc. "concerned practically with," LSJ s.v. "περί," C.I.3).
167. See *On Epicurus* cols. 24 and 26, quoted below.
168. Here first, the need for the harm to be perceived as "intentional" to provoke anger is mentioned, but from the final columns of the text it is obvious that it was always an integral part of it. Most of what we summarize in this section, similarly, will have been known to readers of the treatise, either from an initial summary or from other works.

as opposed to the general meaning of affect or emotion.[169] Here we have a third meaning for *pathos*, which refers to a neutral "experience" such as the feeling when "someone looked" at me, which causes neither pain nor pleasure.

The answer to Philodemus's question follows immediately (41.2-9): if the sage has an *allotrion* feeling but knows that, when her enemy has experienced punishment, he will not inflict further harm and others who might want to imitate the offender will be also stopped, then the sage would be insane not to grit her teeth and accept that she must punish him. So here we have another element for inclusion in the *symmetrēsis*: if punishment can be expected to deter the offender and others from doing any further harm, anger is likely to be natural.

Philodemus then (41.39) imagines an objector asking, "But if he (sc. the sage) is angered because he is harmed intentionally and he is harmed by certain people to the greatest extent, how will he not experience a great anger and have a violent desire for revenge?" The question assumes that intense anger and an eager desire for vengeance are the same thing, or at least occur together. The answer is that he will certainly feel great alienation from the person who harms him to such a degree, or clearly intends to, and will hate and avoid him to the greatest extent possible (*akrōs*), but he will not experience any comparably great disturbance. The sage does not experience that kind of disturbance even in the case of great physical pain, certainly not from anger (41.39–42.12). Empty anger can be great, amounting to rage, and it can cause numberless entailments and consequences that are invisible to fools, as Philodemus repeatedly claimed throughout the first thirty columns of *On Anger*. But the sage sees all these entanglements and consequences coming and does not fall into any of them (42.15–20).

---

169. For discussion of and bibliography on the terms *allotrios* and *oikeios*, see Obbink's (1996, 472-73) note to *On Piety* part 1, ll. 1051–1054. For the technical meaning of *pathos*, see *Men.* 124 (*ad fin.*) and frag. 260 (Usener 1887, 190) = [1].34 Arr., *apud* Diogenes Laertius, *Vit. phil.* 10.34: the Epicureans "say that there are two *pathē*, pleasure and pain, that every living creature has and that the former is welcome and the later foreign; through these choices and avoidances are decided" (πάθη δὲ λέγουσιν εἶναι δύο, ἡδονὴν καὶ ἀλγηδόνα, ἱστάμενα περὶ πᾶν ζῷον, καὶ τὴν μὲν οἰκεῖον, τὴν δὲ ἀλλότριον· δι' ὧν κρίνεσθαι τὰς αἱρέσεις καὶ φυγάς); see Konstan 2008, 1–25; Verde 2018.

Again, it is empty and foolish to think that inflicting punishment is desirable and enjoyable, as always happens when people feel "great" anger: they think it is the greatest good, turn to it as something to be chosen for itself, and believe that one cannot effectively punish otherwise. That is involved in having a merciless disposition. But the sage knows that the sort of person who enjoys inflicting punishment is inflicting a still greater punishment on himself (42.21–39). It makes no difference whether you call your object vengeance or punishment: desire and enjoyment must be absent, or your anger is empty.

At 43.19–41 we find an interesting mention of what may have been a treatise entitled *Against the Kyriai Doxai of the Epicureans*. In this work, Philodemus says, the authors attack the first *Kyria Doxa*, with its assertion that feelings and acts of anger and gratitude are impossible for the gods but are signs of the weakness of human nature. They ask whether that means Alexander the Great was "weak" in conferring such enormous favors on so many and going into such tremendous fits of anger. The numberless panegyrics to Alexander will have suggested this objection to whoever wrote the treatise Philodemus has in mind. Philodemus replies that his fits of generosity and rage made Alexander all the more human, *ergo* more weak, not less.[170]

At 43.41–35, Philodemus engages in a discussion of technical terminology, specifically *orgē* and *thymos*. The sage is certainly capable of *thymos*, in the word's commonest meaning, that is, synonymous with *orgē*, but not in the sense of rage or intense anger. The sage does not experience intense emotions and cannot have an impulse even to *kolasis* (punishment) as if it were something enjoyable.[171] In fact, anger has no pleasure to offer; one approaches it as something compulsory and most unpleasurable, like a drink of wormwood or the surgeon's knife (44.20–23), as also in *Lib.* 2b.4–8: "obviously the sage praises with great pleasure and merely

---

170. See Stoneman 2003. What Stoneman calls the "legacy of Alexander in ancient philosophy" is as much a legacy in rhetoric as in philosophy; Nachstädt (1895) is more realistic: there was also a tradition of the *psogos Alexandrou*, vituperation of Alexander, and Philodemus's reply is no more original than his opponents' efforts at panegyric. For Seneca's differing treatments of Alexander, see Nachstädt 1895.

171. Philodemus, by putting it this way, suggests that it does no good to call one's action "punishment" if it gives one some kind of violent pleasure and presents itself as desirable. In that case, it is just revenge under another name. He needs to specify that pleasurable punishment is to be avoided because usage does not allow that venting anger on slaves or children is to be called vengeance (see frag. 24.19–20, of slaves).

endures blaming, without pleasure, and like a drink of wormwood."[172] The Epicurean teacher's frank speaking is needed for effective admonition, "as when they call in wise doctors for an operation, when they apply the scalpel to the sick" (*Lib.* 17a.4–8). This makes acceptance of anger a deliberate choice, which must be made on what the agent reasonably believe are good grounds, such as the Epicurean teacher's resigning himself to the hard work of blame. As Philodemus had argued in the fragments, anger is never compulsory on the mere supposition one has been intentionally harmed. What he calls natural anger is a feeling that one accepts after careful consideration, in full acceptance of moral responsibility. In some cases, when one can expect to succeed in punishing the offense, the choice of anger will be nearly inescapable. He emphasizes again: "it is insanity even to imagine a sage being inclined to punishment as if it were such a thing (sc. a pleasure)" (44.33–35). The hard work of punishment and deterrence is the sign of natural anger, but the desire for and enjoyment of vengeance is the sign of empty anger.

6.7. The Maximalists (Cols. 44.35–50.8)

Philodemus now concludes the treatise as a whole by dealing with some people (46.13) who claim that the sage will become "enraged" (θυμωθήcεcθαι), a word that they understand to indicate a particularly intense degree of anger rather than as a synonym of ὀργιcθήcεcθαι (see also 43.41–44.5). Because of this maximizing of the sage's anger, we call them the maximalists, and they form an interesting contrast to Timasagoras and Nicasicrates, who try to minimize the role of anger in the Epicurean life. First, Philodemus cites phrases from Epicurus, Metrodorus, and Hermarchus: they all spoke of the *thymos* of the sage, but all three characterized it as mild and brief, as the context showed. Thus, Philodemus argues, in their usage *thymos* corresponds to the broader *prolēpsis* by which *thymos* and *orgē* mean the same thing, normal anger, not intense anger or rage. He seems to be right, but he clearly does not have any more explicit evidence from the Founders than this. Next he discusses three *epilogismoi* (here, by a slight extension from the usual meaning, "arguments

---

172. Not by accident does this repeat comparisons from *On Frank Speech* about the sage's attitude toward praise and blame, which we now know is a topic that goes to the roots of Epicurean psychology in *Nat.* 25. See excursus 4 below.

from experience"[173]), which these heterodox Epicureans use to prove that rage, which they include in natural anger, is appropriate.[174] They are as follows: (1) by analogy to natural gratitude; (2) by analogy to the fact that sages may drink wine and become tipsy if they wish; and (3) by arguing that anger is inevitable as the response to the supposition that "one is being intentionally harmed" and that, the more serious the provoking harm is, the more intense the resulting anger will be. These *epilogismoi* are used by "some" or "certain" people to justify the further proposition that sages can appropriately feel not only anger but rage.[175] Philodemus accepts, at least hypothetically, the premises of the three *epilogismoi* as stated but denies on empirical grounds that the conclusions are correctly drawn from them. Philodemus groups their arguments together, then follows with his criticisms; we have treated each argument and counterargument together in the following.

A (46.18–40; 48.3–32). Just as we feel gratitude for good done to us intentionally, we feel anger at harm done to us intentionally; that is, the two emotions correspond to each other. Here again, it is assumed by both sides that mutual obligation and anger are compulsory for human beings, as *Kyr. dox.* 1 implies.[176] It seems that Philodemus has no quarrel with this formulation. If so, he and the opponents agreed that anger requires the supposition of intentional harm and that gratitude, its mirror emotion, requires the supposition of being intentionally benefited.[177] The beginning

---

173. For the specific meaning of *epilogismos* suggested here, see n. 60 above and Sedley 1973, 27–34, esp. 28–29.

174. In Philodemus's technical language, *thymos* is usually a synonym for, or a type of, empty anger, but he recognizes that it was synonymous with *orgē* in normal usage; see 44.41–46.16 for a lengthy terminological discussion with doctrinal importance. For other treatments of this passage, see Asmis 2011, 154–58; and Tsouna 2007, 230–38.

175. They are called ἔνιοι at 47.41 and τινες at 46.13.

176. *Kyr. dox.* 1: "What is blessed and indestructible neither has troubles itself nor troubles another, so that it is liable neither to feelings of anger nor of gratitude, for all that sort of thing is only in the weak" (τὸ μακάριον καὶ ἄφθαρτον οὔτε αὐτὸ πράγματα ἔχει οὔτε ἄλλωι παρέχει· ὥστε οὔτε ὀργαῖς οὔτε χάριcι cυνέχεται· ἐν ἀcθενεῖ γὰρ πᾶν τὸ τοιοῦτον).

177. These formulations were evidently common ground at this period for Epicureans of different stripes, part of the accepted interpretation of *Kyr. dox.* 1. It is interesting that Philodemus and the maximalists agree on parallel formulations for anger and gratitude: that anger comes from a supposition of intentional harm inflicted and gratitude (*kharis, eukharistia*) from a supposition of benefit intentionally conferred.

of Philodemus's response is lost in a lacuna, but he seems to argue that external goods, like external evils, are not that important to the sage.[178] He appears to share the maximalists' assumption that great good can be done for us by those who make us wise but to deny that there is any other great good that can make us feel intensely obliged to our benefactors, apart from what we feel for them as friends. Even the intensity of our gratitude to those who made us sages, he adds, does not depend on our assessment of their intentions; the effect of their action plays a role, too. Thus the great harm that would be required to provoke natural rage, as opposed to natural anger, can never occur, whether or not we feel great gratitude to our teachers in philosophy.

B (46.40–47.18; 48.33–49.26). Sages can drink and become tipsy—so Aristotle and all the Hellenistic schools agreed—but the maximalists claim that the sage can even become drunk rationally and naturally, and thus a sage can become intemperately angry.[179] In response, Philodemus simply denies that the sage ever gets profoundly drunk and calls the suggestion shameful. Perhaps, he sarcastically adds, his opponents were inappropriately basing their argument on their own practice.

C (47.18–48.3; 49.27–50.8). The third argument, that anger cannot happen without a supposition of intentional harm, is true enough—if one adds, as Philodemus does, that great anger will never be felt by the sage because the sage cannot be greatly harmed. But in a second and final reply to their claim, Philodemus points out another fatal misunderstanding on their part: they take this supposition for a sufficient condition, but it is only a necessary one. So their argument is doubly futile: it concludes from the propositions that "anger cannot occur without a supposition of having been harmed" and that "the sage is intentionally harmed" that "he is angered." Just as an illiterate person cannot become a sage, but a literate person is not necessarily a sage—that is, literacy is a necessary but not sufficient condition for sagehood—they cannot conclude that "he who has received an impression of being harmed will as a matter of course [πά]ντως[180]] be angered," unless the maximalists also demonstrate that the supposition of harm is a sufficient (*drastikon*, i.e., efficient) cause of anger. Philodemus leaves this last sentence hanging in the air, a question to his

---

178. This is just a restatement of his view that the sage cannot be greatly harmed.
179. On the question of whether the sages of any given school should drink and become tipsy, or even drunk, see Fitzgerald (2015, esp. 347–51).
180. Or "in every case."

audience or to the class: How have we shown, and in how many ways, that the mere supposition of intentional harm is never enough to make sages, or even ordinary intelligent people, angry?

7. The Epicurean Context of *On Anger* and the History of Philodemus's Theory

Much of our surviving text of *On Anger* is taken up with criticism of other Epicureans, and the obvious inference is that it was written for an Epicurean audience. Timasagoras wrote against Basilides and Thespis and was refuted by them; accordingly, he was their contemporary and wrote late in the third or early second century BCE. Nicasicrates and the "maximalists" may have been even later, for all we know, contemporaries of Philodemus or his teacher, Zeno of Sidon (ca. 160–75 BCE). Philodemus treats their arguments as still influential and worth answering.

We know that competing interpretations were not just a theoretical but a live issue in the school during the first century BCE and apparently had been since the death of Epicurus's last direct students.[181] Even Diogenes Laertius bears testimony to the division within the school in his list of famous Epicureans, which ends with "and those whom the legitimate Epicureans call 'sophists'" (*Vit. phil.* 10.26). Beyond the debate over rhetoric (discussed just below), Cicero, via "Torquatus," claims in *Fin.* 1 that there were three different views current on pleasure as the chief good and pain as the chief evil. Epicurus thought that this was obvious without further discussion, even from the evidence of the senses, but some contemporary Epicureans argued that the intellect and reason were also needed to establish this, and others felt that theoretical argument and defense were now indispensable (*Fin.* 1.29–31; cf. 1.55). Similarly, differing views were current in the school about whether friendship entails loving our friends as much as or more than ourselves (1.66–70). Beyond debates over philosophical interpretation, there were works of Epicurean textual explication and criticism exploring issues of corruption in the transmission as well as identifying whole works as inauthentic.[182] If a work's authenticity could be

---

181. Cf. frags. 90 and 117 of P.Herc. 1005 (Angeli 1988a) of *Against Those Who Claim to be Literalists*.

182. Demetrius Laco's *Aporie testuali* both discusses corruptions and explains various passages. Zeno of Sidon argued that some works attributed to Epicurus were inauthentic: P.Herc. 1005 col. 11 Angeli = frag. 25 Angeli-Colaizzo. See Erler 1993.

questioned, or if the Founders' treatment was insufficiently detailed, confusion could, and often did, arise. In a well-known passage, Philodemus clearly implies that disputes over the interpretation of doctrine began as soon as the last of the first-generation students died.[183]

On Anger is one of several treatises that show a lively interest in rival Epicurean interpretations. Philodemus's *On Rhetoric* begins with a three-book-long attempt to establish his doctrine about rhetoric against that of rival Epicureans, backed up by extensive quotations from Epicurus, Hermarchus, and Metrodorus, and only then turns to rebut the positions of other, non-Epicurean philosophers, such as Aristotle and Nausiphanes in book 8 (P.Herc. 1015/832) In this case, for Philodemus, a grasp of the correct Epicurean position was required before arguments against other schools could be undertaken. It was not so in other of his works: Philodemus's *On Poems*, in five reasonably complete books, shows no sign of intraschool argumentation, nor do the surviving parts of *On the Gods*.

Philodemus understood himself to be a faithful Epicurean and an heir to Zeno of Sidon's teaching. This emerges clearly from his references to older Epicureans: he finds those who disagree with Epicurus, Metrodorus, and Hermarchus guilty of beating their own fathers at *Rhet*. 1.238.18–29 (Nicolardi 2018), and he strongly asserts his own loyalty as Zeno's faithful admirer while he was still alive and now as his untiring praise-singer in his oddly titled *Against Those Who Claim to Be Literalists* (P.Herc. 1005, col. 14.6–13 Angeli), whose title suggests that it was dedicated to intraschool argument.[184] Philodemus also used Zeno's lectures as the basis for his *On Frank Speech*, which shows that he agreed with their doctrines.[185] Inculcating correct doctrine is an obvious concern of philosophical education, though there are no polemics of this kind in *On Frank Speech* itself.

---

183. P.Herc. 1005, frag. 107.9–17 Angeli: cυγκ]ρίνομεν τρόπους, τῶ[ν] μετὰ τὴν Ἑρμάρχου τελευτὴν cυντάξεις ἐγδεδωκότων, εἰ δέ τις βούλεται, καὶ μετὰ τὴν ἔγλειψιν τῶν Ἐπικούρου διακηκοότων ἁπάντων, ἵν', ἐὰν ἦ[ι] τοιαῦθ' ὁποῖα... ("we compare the characters of those who published treatises after the death of Hermarchus or, if someone wishes, even after the passing of all those who were students of Epicurus, so that, if such things should be..."). See also Erler 1992a, esp. 178.

184. For the title, Πρὸς τοὺς φαςκοβυβλιακούς, see Del Mastro 2014, 184–87.

185. The *subscriptio* of *On Frank Speech* bears the note ἐκ τῶν τοῦ Ζήνωνος cχολῶν, but its interpretation is not clear: perhaps nothing stronger than "based on Zeno's lectures" but potentially "my lightly edited transcript of Zeno's lectures" (though Philodemus's claim to authorship is hard to square with the strongest interpretation).

The focus on heterodox Epicurean opponents (the Peripatetics are a minor target, and the Stoics are barely mentioned) and the cultural context in which such debates were common suggests that *On Anger* was a "teaching treatise" intended for use within the school to warn students away from heterodox views, while also teaching the correct one, rather than a treatise primarily intended for wider circulation among the educated public.

Did the analysis of anger that Philodemus reports originate with Epicurus, either whole or in part? We have little direct evidence of an explicit theory of anger from Epicurus and his circle's writings, though there was at least one work that probably discussed anger in the early stages of the school. Epicurus wrote *Opinions about the Pathē: Against* (or "*To*") *Timocrates* (Περὶ παθῶν δόξαι πρὸς Τιμοκράτην, Diogenes Laertius, *Vit. phil.* 10.28), and several dicta survive as well. There is no question that, after Aristotle, the question of how to describe and discipline the emotions was an important issue in ethical philosophy, and such debates, especially with a nascent Stoic school, would provide a suitable context for developing a detailed theory.

An anonymous Epicurean at *Gnomologium Vaticanum* 62, perhaps Epicurus, discusses how people should behave when fits of anger break out in families: "for if fits of anger (*orgai*) occur between parents and their offspring by necessity, it is clearly foolish to resist and not beg forgiveness. But if the fits happen not by necessity but instead irrationally, it is completely ridiculous to inflame their irrationality further by holding fast to one's anger (*thymokatokhounta*) and not to seek in various ways to alter the other person to a better mood by showing goodwill."[186] Not much can be drawn from this passage; we do not even know how severe the fits of anger are supposed to be in this case. But we can see that *orgē* and a word related to *thymos* are used indifferently to refer to the same kind of anger (Philodemus could have cited this against the maximalists), that some fits of anger come about "by necessity" and others "irrationally," and that "necessary" fits of anger can (sometimes?) be resolved by an apology. Some irrational fits simply require humoring the other party, presumably until the anger fades and one can reason with him or her. Seneca quotes Epicu-

---

186. Epicurus, *Gnom. vat.* 62: εἰ γὰρ κατὰ τὸ δέον ὀργαὶ γίνονται τοῖς γεννήσασι πρὸς τὰ ἔκγονα, μάταιον δήπουθέν ἐστι τὸ ἀντιτείνειν καὶ μὴ παραιτεῖσθαι συγγνώμης τυχεῖν· εἰ δὲ μὴ κατὰ τὸ δέον ἀλλὰ ἀλογώτερον, γελοῖον πάν(τως) (add. von der Muehll) τὸ προσεκκαίειν τὴν ἀλογίαν θυμοκατοχοῦντα καὶ μὴ ζητεῖν μεταθεῖναι κατ' ἄλλους τρόπους εὐγνωμονοῦντα.

rus in a letter (*EM* 18.14 = 484 Usener = [246] Arrighetti) to the effect that "unmoderated anger produces insanity" (*immodica ira gignit insaniam*); evidently too much anger habituates a person and makes one irrational. This distinction between necessary and irrational anger is not obviously the same as Philodemus's distinction between empty and natural anger, which may have been invented by a later generation of Epicureans.

The apparently synonymous use of *orgē* and *thymos* is characteristic of this period of the school, and we see further examples in *On Anger*, where, in his argument with the maximalists, Philodemus cites Epicurus's *First Appellations* (*Anaphōnēseis*, col. 45.5–8) as well as Metrodorus (ll. 8–12) and Hermarchus (l. 12). Three of the most important of the Founders had said that the sage will feel *thymos*, and Philodemus must explain the Founders' use of the term by citing passages in which *thymos* is conjoined with "moderately" or "very briefly" or such expressions to prove that it was there, as frequently, simply a synonym for *orgē*.[187] Philodemus and the maximalists reserve *thymos* for rage, an attack of empty anger, where *orgē* is just the general word for anger (though they have very different views about the appropriateness of *thymos*).[188] All these passages show that Philodemus is probably right to interpret *thymos* as he does, but the general tenor of the argument shows that these texts did not offer such final evidence against the maximalists as Philodemus must have wanted. Another evidently shared element is the reconstructed *hypographē*, "supposition of intentional harm."[189] Nonetheless, their agreement in these matters may reflect a shared, later innovation in the school, but we have no evidence to suggest when the developments could have been introduced.

As previously discussed, Epicurus presents anger and gratitude as a pair in *Kyr. dox.* 1 and *Hdt.* 77.[190] These statements discuss the life of the gods but contrast it with human life, specifically with human liability to

---

187. Certainly *thymos* and *orgē* appear to be treated as mere synonyms throughout the argument with the Peripatetics (the last three instances are quoted from Antipater, a Stoic).

188. See his mentions of the two *prolēpseis* at cols. 44.41–45.5.

189. See the maximalists' third argument, discussed above at §6.7.

190. For *Kyr. dox.* 1, see above n. 176. *Hdt.* 77: "For troubles and worries and feelings of anger and gratitude do not fit in with blessedness, but these things come about in weakness and fear and dependence on one's neighbors (sc. to survive)" (οὐ γὰρ cυμφωνοῦcι πραγματεῖαι καὶ φροντίδεc καὶ ὀργαὶ καὶ χάριτεc μακαριότητι, ἀλλ' ἐν ἀcθενείαι καὶ φόβωι καὶ προcδεήcει τῶν πληcίον ταῦτα γίνεται).

anger and gratitude, which in turn implies the existence of an analysis of these emotions. Anger and gratitude are associated with weakness, fear, and need of others' help to live, along with cares and worries; the gods need never feel them, but human beings, including sages, must do so. The use of these two terms requires some kind of analysis as support, but we have no details.

This doctrine was developed at some point in school history, as shown by Philodemus's argument with the maximalists' first *epilogismos*.[191] There the two emotions are presented as equal and opposite to each other: anger is caused by a supposition that someone is harming you intentionally; gratitude is caused by a supposition that someone does or has done something good for you intentionally.[192] Philodemus and the maximalists part ways over the question of the magnitude of the emotional impact that outside events can actually have on the sage: the maximalists allow the impact to be quite great and the emotion to be intense, but Philodemus limits it rather strictly. But it is clear that they agree on a basic definition of anger and gratitude, as caused by a supposition of intentional harm or benefit.[193] This agreement might have the same origin as their agreement in the use of *orgē* and *thymos*.

Beyond all this, there is some slight evidence from the second book of Philodemus's treatise *On Epicurus*, apparently Philodemus's biography of Epicurus or an *apologia* for his life and actions.[194] The text is in poor shape, and the connections between columns are lost, but there are signs that Philodemus is trying to promote his own view of anger. The general thrust of the passages is that Epicurus was slow to anger, did not engage in behavior that would provoke enmity, and generally avoided conflict.

---

191. See above, pp. 79–80.
192. We can write a second definition for gratitude as a mirror image of that of anger that we have reconstructed: ὑπόληψιc ἑκουcίαc εὐεργηcίαc vel sim.
193. The maximalists' understanding of the life of the sage is quite different from Philodemus's, as their belief that the sage will get drunk shows. See above, p. 79.
194. We thank Enrico Piergiacomi for calling these passages to our attention and Gaia Barbieri for making her draft edition available to us; her column numeration is still provisional. The previous edition is Tepedino Guerra 1994.

Philodemus, *Epic.* 2, col. 19.1–14 Barbieri = 24 Tepedino Guerra[195]

1 . . . .] ἀνεϲταλ[κέ]ναι τινῶν ἀδικίαϲ, κα- τὰ [δὲ τ]ο[ὐ]ϲ τρόπουϲ ὅμω[ϲ χωρεῖν πρὸϲ τὰϲ τιμω- 5 ρ]ίαϲ οὐ κατὰ τὸν φιλό- ϲ]οφον ἡγ[ε]ῖτο, καθ[ά]περ ἥ τε γραφὴ παρέϲτηϲεν α]ὐτοῦ καὶ πᾶϲ ὁ βίο[ϲ ἐ]μαρ- τύρηϲεν· [ο]ὔτε γὰρ ὑπ' ἐ- 10 ξουϲίαϲ ὄχλων ἢ μοναρ- χ]οῦντοϲ ἢ γυμνα[ϲι]αρ- χοῦντο[ϲ ἀ]νδρὸϲ ἄ[λ]λωϲ πι]εϲθε[ὶϲ] ϲυνεκρ[ί]θη 14 ϲ]οφιϲτῶ[ν τιϲ]ι̣ν αν [. . . .	[perhaps: *although Epicurus thought it right*] to put a stop to the wrongdoings of some [people?], nonetheless he thought that habitually resorting to acts of vengeance does not become a philosopher, as both his writings established and his entire life bore witness. For, repressed neither by the power of crowds nor of a monarch nor of a gymnasiarch, he was compared to certain sophists (?) …

Without context, it is difficult to be certain, but it appears that Epicurus deprecated revenge as a motive by calling it unsuitable as a habit for the philosopher, whereas putting a stop to some people's wrongdoings was recommended. This suggests he approved of punishment, for in the definition of anger at 41.2–8 the sage goes after punishment only if, "having been punished, the offender will be brought to a halt." The verbal coincidence cannot be accidental, but it may be Philodemus's own attempt to link his theory to Epicurus's statements. Depending on how *habitually* is

---

195. If δέ is correctly restored in line 3, it is worth noting that δέ … ὅμωϲ ("but nonetheless") is often preceded by the protasis of a condition or by καίπερ, as at col. 7.9–13; cf. LSJ s.v. "ὅμωϲ," II.1–3. For ll. 9–14, see Epicurus, *Gnom. vat.* 67: "the free life cannot own many possessions because that is no easy thing without being servile to crowds or dynasts" (ἐλεύθεροϲ βίοϲ οὐ δύναται κτήϲαϲθαι χρήματα πολλὰ διὰ τὸ τὸ πρᾶγμα μὴ ῥάιδιον εἶναι χωρὶϲ θητείαϲ ὄχλων ἢ δυναϲτῶν). For ἀναϲτέλλω, "to suppress" or "restrain" an offense, cf. *Ir.* 41.4 and *Piet.* col. 42.1202–1216 (Obbink 1996), where it is closely associated with punishment: "Consequently that was what those of the theologians and philosophers who were just did. For the truth did not escape them [the earliest theologians and philosophers], but since they observed that evil deeds were held in check (ἀναϲτελλομέναϲ) by the tales" (or myths) "because they made foreboding hang over the more foolish of mankind." See also the discussion of Plato's *Protagoras* at §3. The end of the column suggests politics as a context (Epicurus's initial difficulty establishing a school?). The gymnasiarch, prima facie out of place in the list, was a much more important government official throughout the Greek-speaking world in the Hellenistic period than he had been in the classical period.

understood, Philodemus might even be saying that Epicurus thought it was acceptable for a philosopher to pursue vengeance occasionally, which would contradict Philodemus's strong ban on vengeance throughout *On Anger*. If Epicurus himself actually even punished anyone publicly, let alone sought vengeance, there is no record of it.[196] A distinction between vengeance and punishment seems coherent with Epicurus's philosophy in general, but we do not find it in the surviving remains of Epicurus.

The rest of the surviving text shows that Philodemus went on to give actual examples from Epicurus's "whole life," and it seems probable that he had already given examples from the writings just before this passage.[197] But his quotations from the writings evidently did not prove that Epicurus categorically rejected all vengeance, as Philodemus himself does, or the summary of them would not be so cautious.

Philodemus, *Epic.* 2, col. 21.1–14 Barbieri = 26 Tepedino Guerra

1	πᾶcιν †ἐξειεicιν· οὐ γὰρ εἰc cάρκα πημα[ί]νειν, ἀλλ' [ο]ὐδὲ μελή[cε]ιν· οὐδ' ἀπὸ τα[ρ]αχῆc ἰδί- 5 αc οὐ[δ]ὲ cυνμολ[υ]νούcηc ἑαυτ[ό]ν τε καὶ τ[ὴ]ν αἵ- ρ[ε]⌈cιν⌉ ὅλην βλαcφημί- ⌈αc μ⌉[ε]τῆλθεν αὐτούc, ⌈ἀλλ'⌉ οἷc μεθώδευεν λό- 10 ⌈γοιc τ⌉ὴν ἀλ[ο]γίαν, μᾶλ- λ]⌈ον δ⌉[ὲ] μαν[ία]ν ἐπεκά- λεc]⌈αν⌉, [ο]ἳ cυνήιc[θ]οντο [τῆ]c κατεχ]ούcηc α[ὐ]τοὺc λ[υ]τ- 14 τῆc ....]π⌈ν⌉ε[..] ... [..	... to all going out (?), for (he said?) that it (?) was not afflicting (them?) corporally, but was not even going to matter; nor even because of the disturbance to himself nor because of slander that damaged at once himself and his whole sect did he go after them (for vengeance),[198] but, using the arguments he was creating, those who charged them with unreasonableness, or rather madness, who perceived the insanity that had hold of them ...

---

196. Philodemus claims (*Piet.* col. 53) that Epicurus never entered into any lawsuit or even legal quarrel with his fellow citizens, diverse as they were in their lifestyle from each other and from him, and lived in perfect peace with them, so that "even the virtue-hating and all-harassing mouth of Comedy" left him alone (which is not quite true; see Obbink 1996 ad loc. and Gordon 2012, 14–37).

197. τε ... καὶ can mean "not only ... but also"; see Denniston 1950, 511–13.

198. The term μετελθεῖν quite often means "to go after (vengeance)" in *On Anger* and elsewhere.

Despite difficulties with the first two words and with lines 10–14, the general thrust of the column is clear. Personal attacks, as well as slander against the school, did not motivate Epicurus to respond with vengeance, even when no one would have criticized him for doing so, but rather to answer with arguments aimed at correcting the attacker's mistakes and irrationality. The reference is evidently to Timocrates's slanders against Epicurus in his *Euphranta*, and it is of a piece with column 19 (24): Epicurus is presented as calm and unflappable.[199] However, Cicero has Cotta report that Epicurus "slaughtered him (Timocrates) in whole volumes because he disagreed about some philosophical point" (*quia nescioquid in philosophia dissentiret, totis voluminibus conciderit, Nat. d.* 1.93), which is itself obviously a polemical move on Cicero's part.[200] The same account of Timocrates's *Euphranta* is given by Diogenes Laertius (*Vit. phil.* 10.6–8) and dismissed as the work of a madman. It seems that, in Philodemus's account, Epicurus merely responded to Timocrates's mix of malicious slander and philosophical criticism with a reasoned defense of his own positions.[201] Metrodorus may have been less restrained in his response and written savage mockery of his brother's treatise in his own *Against Timocrates*. In this case, Epicurus did not respond intemperately to a provocation, even a severe one, but instead set out the facts without descending to the level of his adversary. This is certainly good evidence for (how he presented) his attitude, though less good for doctrine.

This is the sum of our direct evidence for what the Founders thought about anger. We can confidently attribute to them the doctrines that anger and gratitude are mirror emotions and that anger could be necessary or irrational. This last is surely at least ancestral to Philodemus's distinction between natural and empty anger, though what, if anything, hangs on the difference in terminology is not clear.

---

199. The following column, the last surviving, goes into detail about Timocrates's education and seems to show that Philodemus gave a fuller characterization of him here than at col. 12.

200. Sedley (1976a, 128–29) sees Timocrates himself behind this report in Cicero; see also Diogenes Laertius, *Vit. phil.* 10.6–7, which makes clear that there was a philosophical component to Timocrates's work. Besides Epicurus's work, Metrodorus is credited with both a *Timocrates* and an *Against* (or *To*) *Timocrates*. See also Verde 2017.

201. For this and the next sentence, see *DPA* T156 (Angeli) and Pease 1955 on Cicero, *Nat. d.* 1.93 and 113.

It is also perfectly possible that the analysis of anger in terms of natural justice and the social contract is also due to Epicurus or another first-generation Epicurean. Surely the developed doctrine of natural justice included discussion of what counted as breaking the agreement not to harm and how to punish and deter those who did break the agreement.

Unfortunately, little discussion is still extant, which leaves open the possibility that later Epicureans developed the doctrine of anger and punishment to fit (or fill out a gap in or answer criticism of) Epicurus's doctrine of natural justice. A necessary feeling of natural anger could have been appropriate in response to a violation of natural justice as defined by the social contract, and an irrational fit of empty anger could have been inappropriate because it was marred by a desire for the pleasure of vengeance, but we do not have the textual evidence necessary to attribute this doctrine to the Founders. If we could say for certain that this is all Epicurus's or the Founders' work, it would provide a very striking context for Philodemus's analysis of anger.

We feel more comfortable attributing the innovation of using therapeutic diatribe and encomium, a practice begun by Chrysippus and Bion, to Basilides and Thespis. The basis for this is Philodemus's note that Timasagoras's anger at them over this apparently minor issue was unrestrained (col. 5.17–25). From this we infer that Basilides and Thespis were responsible for the innovation and that Timasagoras reacted badly to what he understood as an abandonment of school doctrine.[202] Or possibly, Basilides and Thespis changed or increased the use of tactics that already existed in the school, which could have led to the same reaction from Timasagoras.[203] If they developed school doctrine on the treatment of anger, it is certainly possible that they developed it about other aspects of anger as well, though evidence is, as usual, lacking. They may have connected the therapeutic diatribe with Epicurus's analysis of the soul's atomic constitution and its dispositions. If so, they might have been following a hint in Epicurus himself: Seneca's statement that "unmoderated anger produces insanity" can

---

202. Borrowing useful material from other schools was reasonably common in the Hellenistic schools; for the Epicureans' attitude, see Erler 2011. At *Sup.* 10.11–31, Philodemus admits summarizing Ariston (probably of Ceos, the Peripatetic), since his epistolary treatise *On Lightening Arrogance* contains some potentially useful material; cf. Seneca's famous statement that the good sayings of philosophers are common property at *Ep.* 1.8.8.

203. David Kaufman suggested this possibility to us.

be understood as a statement about habituation and the production of a new disposition to anger. It would certainly be convenient to attribute to Basilides and Thespis whatever other developments are needed to bridge the gap from Epicurus to Philodemus, such as the terminological strictness with *orgē* and *thymos* and the reconstructed definition, but, without further evidence, we refrain from doing so.

As for the other elements of his theory, the broad disagreement between Philodemus and his Epicurean opponents prevents certainty.[204] Several fundamental questions—whether natural anger is purely an evil or to what extent it is evil and the duration and intensity of the sage's anger—were still a matter of debate between Philodemus and his Epicurean opponents. It appears that none of them saw anger as a pleasure, recommended revenge, failed to encourage contextualizing anger by *logismos* or *epilogismos*, or forbade the sage to feel anger at all, though the paucity of direct citations of their work does not inspire confidence that we are characterizing their doctrines accurately. The situation appears similar to the debate over the status of rhetoric among various Epicurean groups in the first century BCE: three views were current, and a fourth view was found in a treatise whose authenticity had been denied by Zeno of Sidon.[205] Sedley has cogently suggested that no explicit word was to be found in the works of the Founders and that each group was developing the various hints and references by their own lights.[206] It is worth emphasizing that Epicurus himself wrote an *On Rhetoric* that somehow failed to settle the question. Elsewhere McOsker has suggested that Epicurus and Philodemus had different priorities in their discussions of poetry: Epicurus and the early school were primarily concerned to deny the poets' educational authority, whereas Philodemus was free to discuss theories of poetic interpretation.[207] Something similar may have happened in the cases of rhetoric and anger: the interests of the early school may have been dedicated to countering false but common beliefs, but this meant that some points of doctrine were not developed in detail. If the parallel holds, then Epicurus may have been concerned with precisely the sort of attitude adjusting we see implied in

---

204. Nothing is known about the dates of Nicasicrates and the maximalists that could help us pinpoint stages in the history of the argument.
205. See Sedley 1997, 103–17.
206. For more on these groups, see Sedley 1997 and the next section.
207. McOsker 2020b.

Philodemus's *On Epicurus* and not the finer-grained argumentation in *On Anger*. But this, too, is only a conjecture.

In sum, the evidence does not establish much. We consider it more likely than not that Epicurus, or at least the first generation or two of the school, developed the doctrine of "supposition of intentional harm" in debates with Academics, Aristotle, and the Peripatetics, as well as, perhaps, the early Stoa. The connection with Epicurus's definition of natural justice implied by the word *harm* could then belong to this phase as well. Also, since Philodemus and the maximalists agree on this formula for the cause of anger and argue elaborately from its terms, there is more reason to suppose it was a common formula in the school. It seems certain that no Hellenistic school of philosophy failed to require its students to investigate and secure the truth or at least probability of "suppositions." The distinction between necessary and irrational anger found in *Gnom. vat.* 62 is at least ancestral to Philodemus's natural and empty anger. The terminology definitely developed over time, but this may obscure the fact that the doctrines remained constant. Finally, Epicurus's attitude toward anger matches Philodemus's: anger is not highly valued, though it is not forbidden, and it is in some circumstances unavoidable (as seen in *Gnom. vat.* 62).

A second stage in the development of school doctrine is probably represented by Basilides and Thespis, who appear to have adapted therapeutic techniques from Bion and Chrysippus to Epicurean use. They could well be responsible for developing the incomplete discussions left by Epicurus and the other Founders into the coherent doctrine that was eventually inherited by Philodemus.

It is likely, given that *On Anger* cross-references *On Frank Speech* and that *On Frank Speech* had Zeno as its main source, that the views on anger that Philodemus defends here were also held by Zeno, but Zeno need not have originated them. It is possible, though unlikely, that they are Philodemus's innovations that he intended to harmonize with Zeno's doctrine on a similar topic. Unfortunately, as it stands, we know little about the history of the theory that we find in Philodemus.

Excursus 3: *Diatheseis*: Physical and Moral Dispositions in Epicureanism

Disposition (διάθεcιc, *diathesis*) is a fairly straightforward concept when applied to moral character in general.[208] From Hippocrates onward, doctors used it to denote patients' bodily disposition or state (ἕξιc), which gives a larger context to their health problems and can be improved by diet, exercise, or better climate to make them less liable to disease. Because *diathesis* means, literally, "arrangement" or "disposition" of parts, it suggests that there is a physical context for mental events and moral characters. Any change in our thoughts or emotions is also a change, even if only a momentary one, in our physical structure. A change in habit, in how we deal with our thoughts or emotions, is the same sort of change but more durable. For anger, the conjunction of physical state and mental experience is articulated first by Aristotle in his *On the Soul*: "a physicist would define an emotion in the soul differently from a dialectician; the latter would define, for example, anger as 'the appetite for returning pain for pain' or something like that, while the former would define it as 'a boiling of the blood or warm substance surrounding the heart'" (1.1, 403a27–3b1).[209] An Epicurean will view bodily and mental states both as characteristics of individual conscious beings and as arrangements of groups of atoms spread through the bodies of those individuals.

In Lucretius's discussion of the constituent atomic parts of the soul (*Rer. nat.* 3.288–322), he treats irascibility, cowardice, and apathy as dispositions in animals and human beings. Three parts of the soul, those made of fiery atoms, a colder element, and tranquil air, if predominant, produce anger, fear, and indifference respectively (3.288–295). Lions serve as the example of an animal with a predominance of the fiery element, who cannot restrain their anger; deer, with a predominance of the colder ele-

---

208. The Epicureans call the purely physical makeup of human beings their constitution (cύcταcιc). Like Plato, they sometimes use ἕξιc to mean the same thing as διάθεcιc; cf., e.g., *Rhet.* 2 (P.Herc. 1674, col. 38.5 Longo Auricchio) ἕ]ξιc ἢ διάθ[ε]cι[c. On dispositions in Epicureanism, see Diano 1974 and Grilli 1983. On the Stoics and their inheritance from Aristotle, see Rabel 1981. Grilli overlooks the facts that, for Epicureans, people have multiple dispositions and that the disposition of sagehood is merely one among several. This means that Epicurean sages are more individual and more affected by their pasts than Stoic sages. McOsker intends to treat this topic in greater detail elsewhere. The connection between physics and ethics was important to Democritus as well; see Vlastos 1945 and 1946.

209. On the physical basis of anger in Aristotle, see Viano 2016.

ment, are more liable to fear; cattle, with their placid temperament, have a predominance of the airy element (3.296–306). Lucretius continues:

> sic hominum genus est: quamvis doctrina politos
> constituat pariter quosdam, tamen illa relinquit
> naturae cuiusque animi vestigia prima.
> ³¹⁰ nec radicitus evelli mala posse putandumst,
> quin proclivius hic iras decurrat ad acris,
> ille metu citius paulo temptetur, at ille
> tertius accipiat quaedam clementius aequo.
> inque aliis rebus multis differre necessest
> ³¹⁵ naturas hominum varias moresque sequacis;
> quorum ego nunc nequeo caecas exponere causas
> nec reperire figurarum tot nomina quot sunt
> principiis, unde haec oritur variantia rerum.
> illud in his rebus video firmare potesse,
> ³²⁰ usque adeo naturarum vestigia linqui
> parvola, quae nequeat ratio depellere nobis,
> ut nihil inpediat dignam dis degere vitam.

> And the human race is like that. For however much teaching can polish some persons and make them more equable, it still leaves in place vestiges of the earlier nature of each one's soul. And these evils, one must believe, cannot be uprooted entirely. No, one person still keeps a proclivity to acrid fits of anger; another is still a little too easy prey to fear; a third will still take this and that more placidly than one should. And in many other ways the nature of humans must vary and differ, and the habits that result from it, ways whose invisible causes I cannot now expound, nor can I give all the names of the atomic arrangements that are the principles from which all these variances arise. But for all that, this I know can be affirmed for certain in these matters: the vestiges of these natures that must remain in us and that cannot be dispelled by reasoning are trivial to such a degree that nothing can keep us from leading a life worthy of the gods. (3.307–322, our translation).

Unlike animals, our initial constitutions can be shaped first by *doctrina* and then by *ratio*. First we are taught by others, then we go on to reason for ourselves. Irascibility, cowardice, and habitual indifference are used as paradigm cases of imbalances that can be rectified by the therapy of teaching and reasoning, since they come from one or another of the three namable elements of the soul and can be dominated by the fourth, "unnamable" part, the intellect, if we train it well. For Philodemus, natural anger is associated with a good disposition (37.29-39). By contrast, in 2.15-21 we see that a bad *diathesis* is associated with empty anger.[210] The associations are probably quite firm but not absolute; it is possible that someone with a good *diathesis* may nonetheless fall prey to empty anger on occasion, and someone with a bad *diathesis* may not be subject to empty anger in every case. Faulty dispositions can be improved (though not completely eradicated) by education and reasoning for oneself (*ratio, logismos, epilogismos*). The sage, we assume, cannot have an irascible disposition, though she may once have had one.[211] A sage who is completely without anger (see 34.32-35) might give the impression of being angry on occasion or even irascible. Some sages give the impression of being more irascible than others, if there is "more natural [anger] present, as we said before" (36.17-22). If this is a reference to the physical constitution of the soul (as it appears to be), it is the only surviving reference to the physical nature of dispositions in *On Anger*. The sage's angry moments as Philodemus describes them are like Lucretius's *naturarum vestigia parvola*, the small vestiges of originally much more anger-prone natures.

As this account suggests, our own *diatheseis* are a result not just of nature but of training. They are our own responsibility; that is, they and the actions that come from them are "up to us."[212] To explain Philodemus's meaning, we refer again to the passage of the *Letter to Menoeceus* that we explained earlier, apropos of fragment 24: "What is compulsory is unaccountable; chance is unstable; only what is up to us (παρ' ἡμᾶς) is free, and only on that which is up to us do blame, and its opposite (i.e., praise), naturally follow" (*Men.* 133). This is a principle both of freedom

---

210. Compare the tremendous malediction on the evils created by the bad *diathesis* toward anger, later in the diatribe, at col. 27.19-39, echoed later at 38.2-5.

211. This is different from the cases where a sage appears angry or irascible, but is not really so. Philodemus says (34.16-24) that a sage can look similar to an angry person without being one, "without the emotion itself, the disposition, and all the things that are up to them personally because of those things." They may appear angry for short periods "even when their disposition is quite opposite" (34.39-35.1). These fits of apparent anger, perhaps usually intended to motivate students, do not keep them from leading a good Epicurean life.

212. The idea in Plato, Aristotle, and the Stoics is more frequently expressed with ἐφ' ἡμῖν, whose history as the common marker of personal responsibility from Plato to Plotinus is well covered by Eliasson (2013, 45-167), who surveys its occurrence in Aristotle, the Stoics, and the Middle Platonists; he notes that the expression is less common in Epicurean texts (20). In *On Anger* we see only παρ' ἡμᾶς.

from compulsion and of moral responsibility. Philosophical study, including diatribes against anger and praises of those who only show natural anger, brings with it habituation to correct actions; that is, it improves the *diathesis* of the student.

Excursus 4: Epicurus, *On Nature* 25[213]

Texts such as *Men.* 132–133 and *Kyr. dox.* 16 served as protreptics or mnemonic aids, but they draw on the language and arguments of a more esoteric and difficult text, Epicurus's *Nat.* 25, whose centrality to Epicurean ethical thought has been properly emphasized by Furley (1967), Sedley (1973), and many others since. Much of the extant text of this book focuses on the question of the development of moral responsibility in humans. Epicurus opposes "compulsion" to "what is up to us," or what counts as "a cause from within ourselves," and discusses how people can be responsible for their voluntary actions and merit praise and blame, even in an atomic world. Because we can reflect and reason before acting, we are liable to praise and blame for acting (e.g., for acting in anger) whether we actually reflect and reason before acting or not. We have shown that the concepts of necessity and compulsion, and the question of how one gets free of them by reasoning and reflection, are important to the later fragments and colums 1–7, and here we cite some passages from *Nat.* 25 to illustrate how Philodemus's moral vocabulary in *On Anger* reflects it. The text is very difficult and in need of a new edition; *caveat lector*.[214]

---

213. For the secondary literature on *Nat.* 25 and the problem of Epicurean free will, see, in addition to the editions, Sedley 1983; Long and Sedley 1987, §20; Annas 1992, 123–56; Purinton 1999; O'Keefe 2005, summarized in 2009; Masi 2006a and 2006b; and now Németh 2017.

214. The editorial situation of *Nat.* 25 is complex because there are three extant copies of the book. The best and most complete edition currently available is Laursen 1995 and 1997; a number of key passages have been reedited by Hammerstaedt 2003. Parts of the book had been previously published with brief commentary by Arrighetti 1972, 322–58, where it is [34]. A new edition is promised by Hammerstaedt 2003. Some of the fragments from the exterior of one of the rolls are available in Corti 2016, which supplements Laursen's work.

In all the quotations from *Nat.* 25, we have printed a composite text with normalized spelling that combines all three extant papyrus rolls. Because of damage to each roll, they all preserve different material, and a continuous text can be achieved only by combining their texts. Sublinear dots are used when a letter is genuinely in

Epicurus here made praise and blame indispensable for our education: they shape us and lead us to internalize choices that are up to us and free us from necessity as much as possible. These choices make us moral agents acting in our own interest and not simply a concatenation of atoms moving in void and impelled by forces impinging on us from outside.

Epicurus, *Nat.* 25[215]

. (.)] νουθε[τ]εῖν τ' ἀλλήλους καὶ μάχε[c]θαι καὶ μεταρυθμίζειν ὡς ἔχοντας καὶ ἐν ἑα[υ]τοῖς τὴν αἰτίαν καὶ οὐχὶ ἐν τῆι [ἐ]ξ ἀρχῆς μόνον cυcτάcει καὶ ἐν τῆι τοῦ περιέχοντος καὶ ἐπειcιόντος κατὰ τὸ αὐτόματον ἀνάγκῃ. εἰ γάρ τις καὶ τῶι νουθετεῖν καὶ τῶι νουθετεῖcθαι τὴν κατὰ τὸ αὐ[τό]ματον ἀνάγκην προcτιθ[εί]η καὶ (ἀεὶ) τοῦ (πο]θ' ἑαυτῶ[ι]) ὑπάρχο[ντος [ca. one line illegible] [cυ]νιέναι [μεμ]φόμενος ἢ ἐπαινῶν, ἀλλ' ε[ἰ] μὲν τοῦτο πράττοι, τὸ μὲ[ν] ἔργ[ο]ν ἂν εἴη καταλείπων ὃ ἐφ' ἡμῶν αὐτῶ[ν κατ]ὰ τὴν τῆς αἰτίας πρόληψιν ἐννοοῦμεν, τὸ δ' ὄ[νο]μ[α] μετατε[θει]μένο[ς...

... to admonish, contradict, and reform each other, as if we were people who have the cause (of action) also in themselves, not just in their original constitution by itself and in the automatic compulsion from its environment and enters it. For if a person were to ascribe to admonishing and being admonished this "automatic compulsion," and though (?) there is always something in oneself (?) ... to understand ... blaming or praising ... but if were he to do that, then he would, on the one hand, be abandoning the thing that we notice in ourselves that fits the *prolēpsis* of "a cause" and, on the other hand, having changed the name...

We find that automatic necessity does not rule our natures once they have reached a certain stage of development, because our good or bad *diatheseis* are themselves causes, according to the *prolēpsis* of "a cause." They are causes coming out of our own selves and are amenable to correction

---

doubt (i.e., it is not securely legible in any text), and brackets are used when the letter is not preserved in any text. We have not marked when the text depends on only one or two of the manuscripts. Words in parentheses are not found in all the extant witnesses at that point. Translations are ours throughout, though indebted at points to predecessors.

215. Laursen 1997, 35 = [34] [27] Arrighetti 1972, 347 = Németh 2017, text P = Masi 2006a, 8c. See also Furley 1967, 187. In this passage, one witness reads καταλεῖπον for καταλείπων.

and encouragement by praise and blame.[216] By praise and blame, Epicurean therapists hope to change their subjects' physical and moral *diatheseis* and to prove to the subjects that they are not victims of necessity but free to choose.

Another text from *Nat.* 25 discusses "products," which are probably to be understood as emergent properties.

Epicurus, *Nat.* 25[217]

> ἐπειδὰν ἀπογεννηθῆι τι λαμβάνον τινὰ ἑτερότητα τῶν ἀτόμων ... ἰϲχάνε[ι] τὴν ἐξ [ἑ]αυτοῦ αἰτίαν· εἶτα ἀναδίδωϲιν εὐθὺϲ μέχρι τῶν πρώτων φύϲεων καὶ μίαν πωϲ ἅπαϲαν αὐτὴ[ν] ποιεῖ.

> whenever something is developed (in us) that takes on a difference of some kind from its atoms ... it acquires the character of a cause from within oneself, and immediately spreads that down as far as the first natures [i.e. the systems of our atoms] and makes all this into one and the same cause.

As Hammerstaedt explains, "For Epicurus the new cause, which consists in a difference of the product (*prodotto*) from the original motion of the atoms, is spread down immediately to the first natures to flow together in their sphere of action into a single cause. And thus the first natures

---

216. For the educational value of praise and blame in Epicurean teaching, see above and compare *Lib.* cols. 2a–2b. Ben Henry has confirmed our suspicion that at *Lib.* 2a.12, Philippson's supplement πρὸϲ ψό]γου[ϲ ἢ ἐπαί]νουϲ is impossible, but something like that must have occurred in the lacuna that follows. So that does not change the fact that 2a fin.–2b are about the educational value of praise and blame and that "the one" (i.e., blame) is as bitter for the teacher as the pupil: "If one asks whether (the teacher) is more prone..." (2a.9–12; lacuna follows, then 2b): "... (more) strongly. Or if he should ask which he does with more pleasure, the answer he seeks is obvious, for it is obvious that he does the one (i.e., praise) with very great pleasure and merely endures the other (i.e., blame) without pleasure and like a draught of wormwood. Or if he asks which the teacher does more of, we will say, neither, nor is it necessary to employ frank speaking (i.e., blame) in every case" (2b, our translation). As for νουθετεῖν, νουθέτηϲιϲ, "admonish, admonishing," this is prominent as a theme word of the theory of teaching and therapy in *On Frank Speech* as a whole and occurs at least two dozen times in the text, though only once in *On Anger* (frag. 27.29–30).

217. Laursen 1997, 22 = [34] [22] Arrighetti 1972, 338–39 = Németh 2017, frag. 13 = Masi 2006a, 7c = Hammerstaedt 2003, 157. Our text follows Hammerstaedt's edition.

undergo a change produced by that emergent character (*prodotto*), which is nothing else than our own free-will."[218]

Another passage will suffice to show how its teaching is reflected in the language of *On Anger*.

Epicurus, *Nat.* 25[219]

> ... ἀπ[ὸ τῆc πρ]ώτηc ἀρχῆc cπέρμ[ατα ἡμῖν ἀγ]ωγά, τὰ μὲν εἰc ταδ[ί], τὰ δ' εἰc ταδί, τὰ δ' εἰc ἄμφ[ω ταῦ]τά [ἐ]cτιν ἀεὶ [καὶ] πράξεων κ[αὶ] διανοήcεων καὶ διαθέ[cε]ων καὶ πλεί[ω] καὶ ἐλάττω, ὥcτε παρ' ἡμᾶc π[οθ]' ἁπλῶc τὸ ἀπογεγεννημένον ἤδη γίνεcθαι τοῖα ἢ τοῖα καὶ τὰ ἐκ τοῦ περιέχοντοc κ[α]τ' ἀνάγκην διὰ τοὺc πό[ρο]υc εἰcρέο[ν]τα παρ' ἡμᾶc π[ο]τε γίγ[νε]cθαι καὶ παρὰ τὰc ἡμετέραc [ἐ]ξ ἡμῶν αὐτῶν δόξ[αc], καὶ εἰ παρὰ τὴν φύ[cιν...

> ... from the first beginning, there are seeds that lead us, some to one kind of things and some to another, some to both these, seeds that are always there, both of deeds and of thoughts and of disposition, seeds lesser and greater, so that it is up to us, then, for the resultant character to become at that point of one kind or another. And also the influences that flow in through our pores by necessity from the environment are up to us to (see that they) become of one kind or another, that is, up to our own opinions that we form out of our own selves, and if ... against his (?) nature...

Thus mere necessity, in the more mechanical world of wild animals' reactions, is supplemented by our ability to make decisions that are up to us. Praise and blame, in turn, encourage good decisions and discourage bad ones by building good *diatheseis*. Diatribe is one of many methods that a teacher can use to admonish us and turn us away from harm. Eventually, we internalize this education, identify examples of natural and empty

---

218. Cf. the passages from Laursen 1997, 18–21, which Hammerstaedt translates and reedits (2003,154). Hammerstaedt keeps for the moment Laursen's unhelpful translation "product" ("prodotto") for ἀπογεγεννημένον. Earlier, Sedley (1983) suggested "that which we develop," which is the translation found in Long and Sedley 1987, 20C. See also Masi 2005.

219. Laursen 1997, 32 = [34] [26] Arrighetti 1972, 345–46 = Németh 2017, frag. 17 = Masi 2006a, 8a. For διὰ τοὺc πόρουc, one witness apparently reads δι]ὰ τ[ῶ]ν πό[ρων, which is possibly correct (διά + acc. in the meaning "through" a space or place is usually poetic).

anger for ourselves, and come to good decisions on our own by using *logismos* and *epilogismos*. Thus diatribe, with its relentless parade of examples of how empty anger can ruin us, is not a mere rhetorical exercise but has its legitimate place in philosophical education.

8. The Papyrus and the *Disegni*

The papyrus P.Herc. 182 was unrolled in 1802–1803 by Giambattista Casanova under the supervision of John Hayter and is conserved in twenty *cornici* ("frames," on which see the next section). The better-preserved parts were hung on display for some time in the museum and underwent remounting (*cornici* 1–16; see below §9). The papyrus unrolled reasonably well but broke into two parts: a small upper section containing about the top fifth to a quarter of each column and a much larger lower portion containing the majority of the text. The outer parts of the scroll, containing the beginning of the text, are either missing, were destroyed before unrolling, or came off the roll many layers at a time and are conserved in the damaged and nearly unworkable chunks of papyrus among the first several *cornici*. The upper quarter of the text is missing for much of the papyrus, and it is clear that there were difficulties in unrolling it here. It is fully separated from the lower portion in *cornici* 12–16, but parts are attached and others fully detached in *cornici* 4–11. Further, some of the pieces that are (or appear to be) attached to the main body of papyrus are manifestly out of place (see below, §10). The papyrus itself is now dark black from the charring, but the ink provides enough contrast to make it legible under natural light. It has been damaged by mold in parts and has deteriorated noticeably over the course of its history. Originally, it was well made and probably of normal quality. The *kollemata*, or sheets of papyrus affixed to each other to form the roll, are each 9–11 cm wide, which is the norm among the Herculaneum papyri. This fact is important for placing some fragments (see below §10).

Two sets of *disegni*, or sketches, of the papyrus were drawn. The first set was made by Carlo Orazî (also spelled Orazij and Orazii) during and shortly after the unrolling of the papyrus in 1802–1803; these were taken by John Hayter first with the court in exile to Palermo in 1806, then back to England in 1807, on the pretext that, since the British Crown paid for them to be made, they were Crown property. They are now kept in the Bodleian Library at Oxford and were first partially published in *Herculanensium voluminum pars 1* (Oxford, 1824; *pars 2* followed in 1825). Digital photographs are now available online.[220] They are called the Oxford *disegni*, and their siglum is conventionally O. After Hayter took this set of *disegni* to Britain, Rosini, then the director of the Officina, arranged for another set to be made of all the papyri unrolled to that point. The second set of drawings for P.Herc. 182 was drawn in 1806, again by Carlo Orazî, and is now preserved in the Officina dei papiri in Naples. They are called the Neapolitan *disegni* and have the siglum N.[221] They preserve a different selection of fragments from O, as well as different readings throughout the text. These were corrected in pen, usually poorly, and it is these corrected readings that are printed in *Herculanensium Voluminum Quae Supersunt Collectio Altera*. At no point have we found it necessary to cite the corrected readings.

9. The Order and Contents of the *Cornici*

The order of the *cornici* has never really been in doubt, and the only difficulty is with the very fragmentary early part of the roll. That the current order is mostly correct is shown by Hayter's numeration, which is extant on the Oxford *disegni*. This guarantees the order of the current *cornici* 2–16, which were Hayter's F–V; that is to say, they were originally numbered 6–20.[222] *Cornici* 1–16 were remounted from Hayter's original beige *cartoncino* onto blue-green *cartoncino* and were displayed on the walls of the Officina from before 1825 until sometime in the period 1906–1908, when Bassi, the superintendent, had all of the papyri displayed on the walls taken down.[223] (*Cornici* 17–20 were not so displayed.)

---

220. The *disegni* are now MS Gr. class. c. 1 (vol. 1:178–234 in the bound drawings) and are available online at https://www.herculaneum.ox.ac.uk/papyri/online-resources under "The Oxford Facsimiles of the Herculaneum Papyri."

221. Two fragments, 1 and 2 Indelli, were drawn in 1913 by M. Arman, presumably in preparation for Wilke's visit and edition.

222. We thank Sarah Hendriks for supplying us with the numerations of the *disegni*. On Hayter's numeration, see Essler 2006, 106–7.

223. The 1823 *Inventario* (call number AOP Busta XVII.11) has the notice "Avvertasi che sette fram(men)ti di questo Papiro si ritrovano sulla tavoletta 212" (i.e., those fragments that are now in *cornici* 17–20) "ed il rimanente a [*sic*: *lege* è] posto in 16 quadretti nella prima stanza attaccata [*sic*: *lege* attaccati] al muro." The same notice is found in the 1824 *Inventario* (AOP Busta XVII.12). I would like to thank the personnel of the Officina for calling this to my attention and for their assistance in decipher-

Cornici 17–20 were pasted down onto *cartoncino* (stiff paper) during the process of unrolling; due to their ugly appearance and poor legibility, they were mostly ignored and left in storage over the years. Because they were never displayed, they remain on their original *cartoncino*, which still bears Hayter's numeration, A–D (i.e., 1–4), as well as the papyrus number. This guarantees both their order and that they belong to the same roll as *cornici* 1–16. They were mounted on wooden boards by Scognamiglio, who worked in the Officina under Domenico Bassi, and almost certainly were put into *cornici* at that same time, probably in preparation for Wilke's second visit in 1911.[224] So *cornice* 1 was originally 5.

Dürr (followed by Capasso and Travaglione) mistakenly states that the hand of *cornici* 17–20 is different from that of *cornici* 1–16.[225] In fact, the hand is simply less hurried and cramped earlier in the roll than it is at the end, and this is of a piece with the increasing number of letters per line and a possibly increasing number of lines per column toward the end of the roll, as Wilke had already seen.[226] Dürr also was unaware of the evidence of the *cartoncini* of *cornici* 17–20.[227] Lastly, the *inventarii* compiled in 1823 and 1824 record the existence of the seven *pezzi* of 17–20 and their location in the Officina. Bassi had good information and did not err in this instance.

All the early pieces are heavily stratified, which led the Neapolitan *disegnatore* to label them "fragments." The designation "columns" takes over in *cornice* 4. Bassi estimated that *cornici* 17–20 represented about fifteen columns; we suggest at least twenty columns, perhaps as many as twenty-five, most of which would be represented by only a few letters rather than any connected text.[228] (Further, many more layers are hiding underneath the visible surfaces.) Certainty is impossible, given the state of the papyrus.

Physical descriptions of the contents of each *cornice* follow, in their real (rather than numerical) order. Measurements are in millimeters.

---

ing the text. For the removal of this papyrus from the walls of the Officina, see Essler 2006, 126–27 and 133.

224. See Wilke 1914, ii; see §2 above and §15 below.

225. Dürr 1988, 215–17; Essler (2006, 133) silently corrects her error. See also Capasso 1989, 216; Travaglione 2008, 45–46.

226. Wilke 1914, iii.

227. Essler 2006, 103–43, esp. 125, 130, 133, and 136.

228. Bassi 1909, 514.

cornice 17 (labeled: no 182 | A)
   pezzo 1: 142 h x 134.5 w (labeled 1 on the *cartoncino*)
   pezzo 2: 141 h x 184 w (labeled 2)

This *cornice* (Hayter's A, i.e., the first one) contains on the *cartoncino* itself the legend "Frammenti del Papiro No 182 cominciato a svolgere il dì 15 Sett(embr)e 1802 da D. Giambattista Casanova," which conveniently informs us of the date and *svolgitore* ("unroller") and guarantees the identity of this piece of the roll. The *pezzi* in this and the following *cornice* were taken off the roll backwards; that is, the roll was on the *macchina* "upside down," as it were. After the second set of fragments was taken off (i.e., after *cornice* B), the roll was mounted on the *macchina* correctly. The *pezzi* in *cornici* 17 and 18 are probably in the correct order, but because the *macchina* was pulling against the spiral of the papyrus roll, it was impossible to unroll it continuously. After the roll was mounted correctly, the papyrus could be unrolled continuously (though it was not until further on in the roll).

The first piece probably contains the remains of three columns, the second four. How they relate to each other is unknown (a join between columns across pieces is conceivable but unlikely). There are thus probably remains of seven columns visible in this *cornice*. This *cornice* contains our fragments 1–2 on *pezzi* 1 and 2, respectively.

cornice 18 (No 182 | B)
   pezzo 1: 112 h x 216 w (labeled 3)
   pezzo 2: 126 h x 99 w (labeled 4)
   sovrapposto: 49 h x 27 w

There are three pieces, two labeled 3 and 4 and another one labeled in pencil by a later hand "A *sovrapposto* su A1 = Fr. A Wilke." The two pieces are next to each other toward the top of the *cartoncino*; the *sovrapposto* is located under *pezzo* 4. It is not clear to what A and A1 refer; it is possible that they mean *pezzo* 1 in cornice A, but there is no obvious reason why the *sovrapposto* would be placed in *cornice* B. Travaglione states that the *sovrapposto* was removed during the unrolling, but it is not clear on what she bases her comment.[229] Neither goldbeater's skin nor the unroll-

---

229. She remarks in her entry for 182 (2008, s.n.): "Sul supporto della cr. 18, in basso, è fissato un sovrapposto (l 3, h 5) sollevato al tempo di svolgimento."

ing threads are in evidence. Wilke implies that the *sovrapposto* was still in place on the second *pezzo* in *cornice* 17 (i.e., on *pezzo* 4 in Hayter's *cornice* B) when he saw it: "extant *haec* fragmenta" (his A and B, emphasis added) "in tabula B 'pezzo' 4" (1914, ii n. 5). But it had come off by the time Indelli edited the papyrus.[230] It was preserved nearby and labeled to prevent confusion. The pencil annotation must postdate Wilke's 1914 edition and seems to date from the latter half of the twentieth century; it is not in either Bassi or Scognamiglio's hand.

The *sovrapposto* and the upper right corner on *pezzo* 2 are fairly easily legible; the former is our fragment 7 (frag. 1 Indelli = A Wilke), and the latter is our fragment 5 (frag. 2 Indelli = B Wilke). The lower left section that extends out from the rest of *pezzo* 2 is also fairly easily legible. If the *sovrapposto* originally stood at the bottom left of the second piece, the order of the fragments is the unnumbered fragment at the bottom left of the second piece, then 2, and then 1.

Pezzo 1 contains remains of about five or six columns, our fragments 3 and 4; *pezzo* 2 has about two, our fragments 5 and 6. The *sovrapposto* represents another column, our fragment 7, for a total of approximately eight columns. Since the *sovrapposto* was originally on top of fragment 6, it is to be placed after fragments 5 (frag. 2 Indelli) and 6, since it came from later in the roll.

cornice 19 (No. 182 | C)
　pezzo 1: 126 h x 228 w (labeled 5)
　pezzo 2: 107 h x 81 w (labeled 6)

Pezzo 1 contains remains of four columns, perhaps five, and contains our fragments 8–10; *pezzo* 2 has perhaps two columns, in which we can read nothing, for a total of about six in this cornice.

cornice 20 (No 182 | D)
　135 h x 103 w

This *cornice* contains only one piece, not labeled or numbered, that is somewhat to very stratified (perhaps cut from the roll?). There were two or

---

230. Indelli 1988, 108: "hoc fragmentum subpositum erat fr(agmento) A Wilke (= fr. 1 huius editionis)" to his "Tabula B, 'Pezzo' 4 (pars sinistra)."

perhaps three columns' worth of text originally represented on this piece, of which we publish only fragment 11.

There was obviously a second piece that has been removed (there are bits of the *battiloro*, or goldbeaters' skin used to hold pieces to the card and threads around a less-faded area). This "missing piece" is a mystery, since the various inventories mention only seven pieces, and all these are accounted for. It is therefore not clear that anything is really missing from the papyrus, and the remains might simply be the result of an imperfect attempt to glue down the piece or a piece that was mistakenly placed here but then moved when the mistake was noticed.

At this point, we turn to *cornici* 1–3. The papyrus contained in them is still very stratified and difficult to manage as a result of the unrolling, since the outer parts of the roll were more damaged by the eruption, more exposed to incidental damage after discovery, and, perhaps because of their brittleness, did not unroll as cleanly as the inner part. They do not yield much text, but the situation improves rapidly.

Cornice 1 contains fragments 12–20 (frags. 3–9 Indelli = C–E, 1, F, 2, and G Wilke). This *cornice* contains three pieces of papyrus, but they were placed close together on the *cartoncino*, so they appear to be one piece connected by the goldbeater's skin and unrolling threads. In fact, the goldbeater's skin nowhere connects across a break, and, it becomes clear under the microscope that the threads lie *on top of* the papyrus to their left, which means they were pasted in place later instead of being in their original position.

Following are the measurements (in mm) and fragments contained on each piece, of which *pezzo* 3 is in the best condition:

pezzo 1: 144.5 w x 139 h; frags. 12–14
pezzo 2: 110.5 w x 132 h; frags. 15–18
pezzo 3: 75.5 w x 109 h; frags. 19–20

N was able to read and draw two fragments in this *cornice* that O did not. These are our fragments 18 and 19 (frags. 1 and 2 in N [= Gomperz 1864 and Wilke 1914] and 6 and 8 in Indelli).

Fragment 13 is cohesive, but the papyrus on which fragments 12–20 (frags. 4–9 Indelli) rest is quite broken and is, in fact, a mess of *sovrapposti*. Three, perhaps four, layers are visible at parts. This has led to confused readings. Fragment 18, for example, is about half flaked away; the line that Indelli prints as |γαιc ἔχει τοὺc ὀφθαλμούc| now reads |γα̣[. .]εχειτου[.

The same thing happened in the case of our fragments 16 and 17 (frag. 5 Indelli = frag. E Wilke), in the apparatus to which Indelli admits that "the letters that Wilke read are completely dissimilar" ("litterae, quas Wilke legit, omnino dissimiles sunt") to what Indelli read. In all likelihood, a layer of papyrus flaked off and left different readings in its wake. This has been known to happen elsewhere in the Herculaneum papyri.

An absolute ordering of the fragments in this cornice may be impossible. Fragments 19 and 20 are on the same layer and seem to be separated by the correct intercolumnium (curvature of the papyrus makes it impossible to measure directly). In the early sections of the papyrus, relative orders can be hypothesized. Because the fibers do not match over the breaks in the papyrus (therefore, the highest layers are not from the same stratum), an order of fragments across all three sections cannot be securely established.

Fragment 13 (frag. 3 Indelli) seems to stand on a *sovrapposto* and so should follow fragment 12 (frag. 4 Indelli); however, the surface of this piece is very broken, and the top part of fragment 12 may belong to several layers. The bulk of fragment 12 (ll. 13–18) is all on the same level, which may possibly be a *sovrapposto*. Fragments 12 and 13 might be inverted in order.

Fragment 16 (frag. 5 Indelli) is on a lower layer than fragment 18 (frag. 6 Indelli).

Fragment 17 (frag. E Wilke) will have been on top of fragment 16 and so probably on the same layer and to the left of fragment 6.

Fragment 17 is to the right of fragment 18 but at least one layer down. In fact, it seems to be one of the lower layers, based on the amount of goldbeater's skin that shows through the papyrus, but this is uncertain. We propose the order 15, 16, 17, 18. An uncertain amount of text is missing between fragments 15 and 16 and between 16 and 17. If 15 and 16 are on the same layer, the order would be 16, 15, 17, 18, with the major discontinuity between 15 and 17. Fragments 19 and 20 (frags. 8 and 9 Indelli) stand in sequence, but it is not clear how they related to the rest of the columns in this *cornice*. There were, including Wilke fragment E (our frag. 17), probably twenty-one columns, of which various amounts survive. Here a sentence or two of fragment 13, a good bit of fragment 18, and tantalizing bits of fragment 19 can be read, while 12, 15, 16, and 20 offer only a few words.

Cornice 2 contains fragments 21–28 (frags. 10–14 Indelli; frags. 3, H, 4–6 Wilke). The three pieces of papyrus include two small ones to the right (about a third of the material), then a larger piece taking up the center and left part (ca. two-thirds of the material). The measurements (in mm) and fragments contained on each piece are as follows:

pezzo 1: 108 h x 73 w (frag. 21)
pezzo 2: 52 h x 39 w (frag. 22)
pezzo 3: 122 h x 225 w (frags. 23–27)

The original distances between the pieces are not certain, but it is unlikely that much papyrus has been lost.

The third piece contains fragments 23–27; fragment 24 is preceded by the end of the previous column (23) at the correct distance. Fragment 24 is itself a complete column, and a slightly shorter than usual intercolumnium separates it from 25. Fragment 27 is a complete column; 28 is nearly complete, and they are separated by the correct intercolumnium, but 27 is preceded by several traces (26) that stand at the correct distance to be the end of the previous column. Fragments 22 and 23 apparently cannot be joined and are most probably adjacent columns rather than left and right parts of the same column. Fragments 25 and 26 are not wide enough together to constitute a column.

The solution is that fragments 26–28 stand on a *sovrapposto* and are to be moved to the right. If we assume that 21 and 22 are in the correct order and simply need to be placed further apart to allow space for full columns, the order of the eight columns is as follows: 21, 22, 23, 34, 25, 26 (mere traces), 27, 28. Here tantalizing fragments of 21, nearly nothing of 22–23 and 25–26, and interesting pieces of 24, 27, and 28 can be read.

Cornice 3 contains fragments 29–33 (frags. 15–17 Indelli; frags. J, 7–8 Wilke). The measurements (in mm) and contents are:

pezzo 1: 73 h x 39 w (frag. 29)
pezzo 2: 124 h x 174 w (frags. 30–33)

The two pieces, though placed close together on the *cartoncino*, are not connected in any way. This fact provides an easy solution to the problem of the "*altera columna*" that Indelli mentions in the apparatus to his fragment 15 (our 29): the piece of papyrus containing fragment 29 was simply placed too close to the other piece, and the columns are sequential. However, it is possible that the fragment is more out of place than it appears to be: it could have originally been placed after the larger piece rather than before it. However, we have retained the order on the *cornice* in the absence of any indication that it is wrong.

Fragments 32 and 33 are separated by the correct intercolumnium, though both are cut off, on the left and right edges, respectively. However, there is not enough room between fragments 39 and 32 for the supplements necessary, and 33 is too close to 31 to supplement the right half of 17a, an intercolumnium, and the left part of 17a. The solution here is that fragments 32 and 33 lie on a large *sovrapposto* (ca. 9 cm wide) and are to be placed after 31.[231]

Top and bottom margins are nowhere extant, but it is clear from the general condition of the roll that the pieces are from the bottom; not much is lost below the extant text.

We arrive at the following order of columns for *cornice* 3:

29 (after which there is a gap of unknown size containing at least the right part of 29, an intercolumnium, and the left part of 30)
30 (missing column under *sovrapposto*; some letters are visible in a *sottoposto* in frag. 32.13–14])
31 (very fragmentary, left margin only, but with the important citation of *Od.* 20.19)
32
33

Here, next to nothing of 29, tantalizing fragments of 32 and 33, and almost nothing of 30 and 31 can be read.

To summarize, between fragments 6–7 at the end of *cornice* 18 and fragments 12–20 in *cornice* 1, there may have been, in *cornici* 19–20, as many as fifteen columns visible and in *cornici* 17–20 as a whole as many as twenty-nine, instead of the circa fifteen estimated by Bassi. But nothing like connected text can be read anywhere in *cornici* 17–20 except for our fragment 7 (frag. 1 Indelli = frag. A Wilke), and there only by frankly *exempli gratia* supplementation.

In total, then, circa forty to forty-two columns are represented somehow in *cornici* 17–20 and 1–3. About eight or nine columns separate

---

231. Wilke (1914, viii) had already noticed the problematic relationship between fragments 17 and 17a (frags. 8a and 8b in his edition).

fragments 5–7 from fragment 12. *Cornici* 17–20 contain around twenty-three to twenty-five visible columns. However, all of these pieces are badly stratified, and it is all but certain that a substantial amount of text lies on strata underneath the visible layers, making the total number of columns really preserved in these seven *cornici* perhaps much greater (and making any attempt at ordering the fragments a risky operation).

From *cornice* 4 to 16, the *cornici* contain the principal (columnar) text, columns 1–50, in a regular succession of four columns per *cornice* (*cornice* 4 = cols. 1–4; *cornice* 2 = cols. 5–8, etc., until *cornice* 16, which has cols. 49–50 and the *subscriptio*). From the beginning until column 16, the top margin and a progressively smaller number of lines below it are missing (beginning with an average of fourteen and a half missing lines in cols. 1–4 and ending with an average of eight in cols. 13–16). But tops of columns are occasionally missing here and there all the way to column 31. Throughout the papyrus, there is at least a small lacuna between the top and bottom parts of the papyrus.

10. Column Tops in Columns 1–50

From *cornice* 4 onward, the top of the papyrus is sporadically preserved; by the end, it is almost fully preserved with a minimal lacuna (usually a line or so) between the top and bottom parts. It is clear that it did not unroll easily, however. In the *cornici* in question (8–12), some of the tops are well attached to the papyrus (these do not generally present problems), while others are either barely attached by a sliver of papyrus or goldbeater's skin or else are not attached at all. Wilke already identified several fragments of the upper portion as being located out of place in the *cornici*, and several others present improbable or impossible text if allowed to stand as they are. In only one case, a move of a column top creates a secure textual join (the piece found at the top of col. 32 in fact belongs at the top of col. 28); the rest are dubious. Wilke's version is put forward on 1914, viii–xi; Philippson invented a different version in his review and article.[232] Indelli combined Wilke and Philippson's suggestions.

Column tops are glued in above and between columns 1–2, 3–4, 7–8, and directly above 18, 20, 21, 23–27, and from 32 to the end of the roll (these last, 32–50, do not present any problems). Wilke suggested moving

---

232. See Philippson 1915, col. 647; 1916, 443–44.

"28 *supra*" (i.e., the piece of papyrus glued onto the *cartoncino* above col. 28) to join with column 32; this results in a secure textual join. He also moved 26 *supra* to 31 because he thought it formed a lengthy periodic sentence with repeated κἄν and lines of the appropriate length. Column 25 *supra* accordingly goes above 30 and 27 *supra* over 32. Wilke thus thinks the order of 25–27 *supra* was preserved correctly, but they were misplaced during the unrolling (1914, ix). He thinks that the break in continuity between columns 23 and 24 is due to the copyist, not the *svolgitori*, and that columns 18, 20, 21, 23–24, 28, and 30–50 are all correctly placed, but he moves the tops of columns 1–2, 3–4, and 7–8 to his *fragmenta incerta*.

There are problems with this, as is clear from inspection of the papyrus. Some of what Wilke thought were joins turn out to be mere adjacent placements of fragments. In other cases, the appearance of a connection caused by two pieces of disconnected goldbeater's skin overlaying each other misled him.

Philippson suggested moving the tops of columns 25–27 to stand above columns 6–8, which also is not convincing. The mistakes that must be assumed on the part of the *svolgitori* or those who remounted the papyrus later on are even harder to explain. Indelli adopted a compromise position between Wilke and Philippson.[233]

We ourselves have not been able to place many of these fragments, nor are we convinced by the supplements that Wilke and Philippson proposed to make joins. Therefore we have pulled them out of their hypothetical sequence and edited them in the position that they hold in the *cornice* itself, even though we do not believe that they join with adjacent text. (In fact, we have pulled out two additional fragments that previous editors were content to leave in place despite serious problems of continuity: fragment E, from the top of col. 23; and fragment F, from the top of col. 24.)

Descriptions of the unplaced fragments are as follows. As noted above in §9, the *kolleses* can be used to disconfirm placements of fragments. If the *kolleseis* on a fragment and in the column do not match, then they cannot be joined.

A (above and between cols. 1 and 2). This seven-line fragment is placed at the top of the *cornice* between columns 1 and 2 and has no identifiable margins or words except ὥστε in line 4. See Indelli's apparatus at

---

233. Indelli printed the top of col. 25 at the end of that column's apparatus, moved the top of 26 over col. 8 and moved the top of 27 over 32. See his apparatus entries and commentaries to cols. 8, 25, and 27 for details.

1988, 63; and Wilke 1914, 99, frag. incerta a. Neither column nor this fragment shows a *kollesis*.

B (above and between cols. 3 and 4). This five-line fragment is found at the top of the cornice between columns 3 and 4 and has no identifiable margins or words except παθεῖν in line 3. See Indelli's apparatus to col. 4 at 1988, 65; Wilke 1914, 99. There is a *kollesis* after the first letter in column 4, and none is visible in the fragment, which forbids a position in the left of column 4.

C (7 *supra*). This fragment and Fragment D are on a single piece of papyrus that is placed in the *cornice* above the right half of column 7 in *cornice* 5; it does not seem to belong there because its left and right margins do not line up with those in the main text. See Wilke 1914, 99; and Indelli 1988, 67–68 (in the apparatus to col. 7). Fragment C has a *kollesis* circa 3.5 cm from the start of the column, which aligns with the *kollesis* in column 5; unfortunately, the text at the end of column 4 and in this fragment do not join.

D (8 *supra*). See C. Fragment D has a *kollesis* only 6 cm from the last, which is an indication of stratigraphic problems rather than a short *kollema*.

E (23 *supra*). This fragment is found at the top of column 23, but its placement there is doubtful, in large part because of the need to supplement ⟨λ⟩ύμης and the unusual syntax, especially the preposition, of the resulting phrase τ[ῆι] ˋγυναι´κὶ π[ερὶ] | ⟨λ⟩ύμης ἐγκαλο[ῦντας.[234] We think it more likely that the fragment is out of place and that the poor syntax has been restored in an attempt to make it fit. Neither this fragment nor column 23 has a *kollesis*; column 24 has a *kollesis* near the right edge of the column, which would allow this fragment to stand above that column, but no textual join can be discerned.

F (24 *supra*). This fragment is placed above column 24 in the *cornice*, but the grammar does not continue from the end of the previous column (there is a serious anacoluthon right at the column end: παρέ|[πεται δ'] αὐτοῖς καὶ τὸ ⟨***⟩ || [ἀη δ]εῖς δὲ γίνονται καὶ | γονεῦ]ςι καὶ ἀ[δ]ελφοῖς κτλ), nor does the sense follow very well. Previous editors were willing to accept this as a scribal error rather than a papyrological problem because they believed that the piece was attached by goldbeater's skin to the main body

---

234. Bücheler 1864 changed εκκ- to εγκ-, and Schoene is responsible for the conjecture π[ρὸς] | ⟨λ⟩ύμης. See the apparatus for other attempts to force a connection.

of text, but this does not appear to be the case. This fragment does not have a *kollesis*, which proves that it did not originally stand over column 24, which does have a *kollesis* in its right half. Richard Janko (pers. comm.) suggests that it belonged above column 26. The sense matches well, but this would produce a forty-two-line column, which might be too long (the longest column is forty-one lines). This fragment might also belong above column 31, but, given the damage to the bottom of column 30 and the middle of column 31, it is hard to tell.

G (25 *supra*). This fragment stands on the same piece of papyrus as Fragment H (col. 26 *supra*), and it appears to be attached to the main body of papyrus, but the margins do not line up, and the fragment seems out of place. Attempts to place it correctly have not been convincing. Wilke moved fragments G and H to the tops of columns 30 and 31 because the top of column 28 joins at the top of column 32; however, the text at the top of column 31 that results from this join does not show any promise of making sense. The right and top margins of this fragment survives; the estimated number of letters missing is very approximate.

H (26 *supra*). See the description of Fragment G. The left and top margins are preserved, so we can calculate the number of letters missing on the left side with some confidence. The same cannot be said for the right side, however.

All these are printed among the columns of the text where the actual fragment is placed in the *cornici*. That is, we print the tops of columns 25 and 26 as Fragments G and H, though they appear "above" those columns in our text, because that is how the papyrus is physically laid out. We are confident that the reader who compares our text with Wilke's and Indelli's will see that no convincingly restorable text has been lost by this decision. The column 28 *supra* has simply been integrated into column 32, where we believe, with Wilke and Indelli, that it should go.

11. Stichometry and the Length of the Roll

In the best circumstances, the *subscriptio* of a Herculaneum papyrus contains a complete, legible number of *stichoi* and marginal stichometric dots and numbers, which would allow easier placement of fragments and the determination of whether there were two lines per *stichos* or 1.8.[235] Addi-

---

235. A *stichos* is the length of a dactylic hexameter, but actual lines were about half this long, or a little more, so the *stichos* count is as much as twice the actual line

tionally, the number of lines per column would be consistent throughout the treatise. But P.Herc. 182's *subscriptio* is damaged, and the scribe has not used stichometric numbers in his text.

The *subscriptio* reads]ΧΧΓ̄ΗḤΔΔΔΙ̣Ι̣ (i.e., 2,735 *stichoi* of text), with an additional numeral potentially cut off at the beginning. Bassi, followed by Wilke, conjectured another Χ, to read Χ]ΧΧΓ̄ΗḤΔΔΔΙ̣Ι̣ (3,735 *stichoi*). Until recently, each line in a papyrus was taken to be one *stichos*, but this led to confusing and impossible results in some cases. In 1924, Kurt Ohly sorted out the problem and made it clear that each *stichos* was the length of a hexameter verse, that is, more than one physical line in the papyrus.[236] Now we know that each *stichos* was 1.8 or 2.0 lines. Bassi, followed by Wilke, believed that 3,735 *stichoi* could make 90 columns; 2,735 *stichoi* would yield 68.4 columns, which is clearly too few (since it is fewer than the total of columns and fragments).[237] This prompted Bassi's conjecture.

We assume that the number of lines per column was consistently 40, even though we know some had more or fewer.[238] The longest-preserved column is 41 lines long. We use Indelli's assumptions of 36 as the usual number of letters in a *stichos* and 20 as the average number of letters in a line of this papyrus when summarizing his calculations. The "unit," column + intercolumnium, is circa 6.5 cm (i.e., it is 6.5 cm from the left edge of one column to the left edge of the next); thus 50 columns of text require 3.25 meters of papyrus to account for the writing and spaces between the columns. Blank papyrus was left at the start to wrap around the roll to protect it, and some space was left over at the end (ca. 14 cm in our case), so we have added the range "circa 0.5–1.0 meter" to the calculated amount of text in order to account for the initial and final *agrapha*. All lengths are accordingly very approximate.

Indelli takes 20 letters/line and 40 lines/column to get 800 letters/column, then divides by 36 letters/*stichos* to get 22.22 *stichoi*/column. At

---

count of the treatise. Some *subscriptiones* include numbers of columns as well and other bibliographic data, about which see Del Mastro 2014.

236. Cf. Cavallo 1983, 20–22; and Janko 2011, 48–9 and 198–207.

237. Bassi 1909, 513; Wilke 1914, vi. The figure of 90 columns is a little imprecise; it actually works out to be 93.4 columns, which is plausible, given the fact that the last column was not filled. It is also always possible that the scribe miscounted *stichoi*.

238. See also §13.

2,735 *stichoi*, this yields circa 124 columns and circa 8–9 meters for the total length, or 168 columns in circa 11 meters, if 3,735 is read.[239]

If we use Janko's method[240] and assume either 1.8 or 2.0 lines per *stichos*, we again get different figures: 1.8 lines/*stichos* at 2,735 *stichoi* yields 123.08 columns, or 8.5–9.0 meters; at 3,735 *stichoi*, it yields 168.08 columns, or 11.4–11.9 meters. If we posit 2 lines/stichos and 2,735 *stichoi*, we arrive at 136.75 columns (9.4–9.9 meters); if 3,735 *stichoi*, then 186.75 columns (12.6–13.1 meters). Note that 1.8 lines per stichos at 2,735 is substantially in accord with Indelli's version of the calculation.

If we accept the preserved number (as Indelli did, and as we think we should), and consequently the figure of 123–24 columns, then circa 37 columns are lost, or a bit less than 30 percent of the text. If we accept Bassi's larger number, we are missing a bit less than half the text.[241] Even with our somewhat larger estimate of how many columns are contained in *cornici* 17–20 and 1–3, either number remains possible: 50 columns + 40 or 42 + 21 columns in *cornici* 17–20 and 1–3 gives 90 or 92 columns attested, so 32–34 missing (ca. 26 percent) on Indelli's calculation and 76–78 missing (ca. 45 percent) on Bassi's reading. We prefer Indelli's figure.

Our figures for the fragmentary early *cornici* are a minimum, and since the initial pieces are badly stratified, it is possible that many missing columns are on *sottoposto* layers.[242] If so, and if Indelli's reading is correct, P.Herc. 182 may even represent the entire roll of the *De Ira*; that is, no *scorze* were cut away before unrolling. In fact, this seems most likely to us.

12. The Subscription

Although today the subscription is illegible, the *disegni* report part of it clearly enough. All that survives of the author's name is a damaged *eta*, but that the author was Philodemus is not in doubt.[243] Further, ὀργῆϲ was

---

239. Indelli 1988, 37–39.

240. See n. 236.

241. Indelli takes into account the fragments in *cornici* 17–20 and 1–3; see 1988, 39 with n. 28.

242. Even four additional columns per *cornice*, that is, only about one *sottoposto* layer per cornice, would give twenty-eight columns missing over the course of the seven initial *cornici*. This line of reasoning lessens the possibilities that the outer layers burned away during the eruption, decayed during the centuries it was buried, or destroyed after excavation.

243. Style and a cross-reference to *On Frank Speech* at col. 36.24–26 secure

clearly legible, but its position in the line—far to the right rather than centered underneath the author's name—indicates that a word or two are missing before it. Minervini (see n. 281) thought that the *On Anger* was part of the Περὶ κακιῶν ("On Vices"), but Scott (1885, 74 n. 1) noted that anger was not a vice for the Epicureans. He suggested that it belonged to the Περὶ ἠθῶν καὶ βιῶν ἐκ τῶν Ζήνωνος σχολῶν, and Wilke followed him in this, noting that the work showed many points of contact with the *On Frank Speech*, though he shorted the title to Περὶ ἠθῶν ὅ ἐστι (with a book number). Indelli suggested περὶ παθῶν, and the nontechnical use of πάθος to mean "emotion" rather than "feeling of pleasure or pain" is sufficiently common in Philodemus and his contemporaries to make this plausible. The early scholar Genovesi wrote a note in the margin of his edition of column 10 of P.Herc. 1676 (Philodemus's *On Poems* 2) in which he reports the subscription as follows: φιλοδημου | ὑπομνημα περι οργης | Α. ΧΧΓHHΔΔΔ αριθμος 2730. Del Mastro suggests that, because the stichometric number is included, the whole is more likely to be a note about a reading rather than a conjecture.[244] Ὑπόμνημα and related terms are very slippery, and their meanings may have changed over time or never have been very precise in the first place.[245] Here it would mean something like "Notes on Anger," which is plausible. Unfortunately, *On Gratitude* (P.Herc. 1414), presumably *On Anger*'s sister treatise, left out any notice of the ensemble to which the work belonged, although it has a well-preserved

---

Philodemus's authorship, which was suggested by the first *accademici* to study the treatise and has never been questioned.

244. Del Mastro also reads a trace that is possibly, but not necessarily, interpretable as a *mu* and notes that Scott suggested that twelve letters are necessary to restore symmetry with the other lines (2014, 84–87). The Neapolitan *disegno* of the *subscriptio*, which simply reads ὀργῆς with the *stichos* numeral (but not αριθ vel sim.), carries Peyseti's *visto buono* and is hard to imagine that the *disegno* would have been approved if so much more were legible. Indelli's suggestion can be lightly modified to περὶ τῶν παθῶν to fit the letter count.

245. For Herculaneum titles in general, and especially that of this treatise, see Del Mastro 2014, 30–34 with bibliography, reviewed by Puglia 2013 and Dorandi 2015 and 2016; see also Puglia 2016. See further Larsen 2018, 69–75; Tieleman 2003, 51–57; and note that Van den Hoek (1996, 225) argues that Clement explicitly thought the "hypomnematic" style better suited to his subject matter, namely, "philosophical contemplation." Note that Philodemus calls his five books *On Poems* ὑπομνήματα but then refers to the fifth book as a σύγγραμμα in the same passage, at *On Poems* 5.29.13–22.

subscription.[246] It is by no means certain that *On Anger* belonged to a named group of texts in the first place. Because of the uncertainty, we have left the title unsupplemented.

13. Paleography, the Scribe, Errors, and Corrections

Cavallo describes the hand as follows:

> the writing is shown to be written with a quite rapid *ductus*, with uniform strokes that lean to the right to a variable degree. The general aspect that results is hardly calligraphic, almost coarse. *Delta* has a slightly concave base line, *epsilon* has its middle line notably detached from the body, *zeta* shows an oblique middle line, *kappa* is often drawn with its lower oblique descending stroke curving outward and grafted onto the upper ascending stroke, *mu* shows curved external strokes (especially the right one), *xi* is written in three strokes with the middle one written quickly.[247]

To this we add that the middle stroke of *theta* sometimes does not fully cross the diameter (it can be detached on both sides or only on the left). *Epsilon* sometimes connects the top curve down to the middle stroke. *Tau* and *upsilon* can be confused. Serifs are common but not obligatory. Because of the speed with which the scribe worked, letters are sometimes ligatured together. Giuliano observed that, when either *tau* or *gamma* connect with an *omicron* or an *omega*, the vowel does not rest on the notional bottom line (2005, 136). Letters with tails or horizontals are especially liable to ligaturing.

Cavallo assigned the hand to the scribe "anonimo IX" (belonging to his *gruppo* F), assigned it to the middle of the first century BCE, and compares P.Oxy. 24 2399 and P.Tebt. 1 3. The same scribe also copied P.Herc. 1506 and 1674. He puts the work in the first phase of Philodemus's work on the basis of his dating of the hand; this need not be the case.[248]

Columns are usually forty lines long, though thirty-nine- and forty-one-line columns are found. There may have been longer columns; due to the loss of column tops at the beginning of the roll and the lacuna between

---

246. See above §6.7 and Philodemus's brief discussion in col. 46.

247. Cavallo 1983, 33, our translation; see also Indelli 1988, 39–41; Giuliano 2005, 136–37; and Wilke 1914, iii–iv.

248. Cavallo 1983, 45; see Parsons's 1989 review for criticism of Cavallo's method for assigning dates to Philodemus's works.

top and bottom portions at the end, certainty is impossible. The writing became more cramped as the scribe went on, beginning at about seventeen letter widths per line and increasing to twenty near the end of the treatise. The line of writing is 5.4–5.5 cm, and the intercolumnium is 1.1–1.2; that is, the unit from column edge to column edge is consistently 6.5 cm.

The scribe's handwriting is faultless, though unbeautiful, but his attention to his work was seriously lacking. An insertion at 1.5 and a misreading at 43.3 reveals that he worked visually from another copy of the text rather than taking notes or dictation.[249] No column is completely free from error. Most of these are simply spelling errors (many of them common in the Hellenistic period). Another common error is attempting to fit too much text in at the end of a line and having to delete a letter and start over at the beginning of the next line. This may betray inexperience, but confusion of cases seems to betray either careless reading or even the possibility that the scribe was not a Greek. Other, more serious, errors involve the omission of syllables, words, and even whole phrases.

The papyrus departs somewhat from the modern canons of orthography. For instance, the scribe occasionally writes ει for ῑ, regularly writes κ before θ in ἐχθρός and ἔχθρα (as if they were compound words), once writes ἐκκακχάζοντες for ἐκκαγχάζω in 22.20–21, does not assimilate ν before a labial, and once drops the gamma in ὀλιγάκις at 10.19 (but writes ὀλιγ- in all other instances). He probably wrote μυριάκι in 12.35; there are no other instances of this spelling in TLG (cf. Crönert 1903, 143 with n. 3). The scribe also writes ἐπιγένημα for ἐπιγέννημα; this may have been Philodemus's own spelling, since it also appears three times in his *On Death* and twice in *On Poems* 2. The scribe rather than Philodemus might be responsible for μιγνύωσι (instead of μειγ-) at 18.17 and μεισοπόνηρον at 36.39. In compound words, he varies between writing one *rho* (διαρίπτει, frag. 19.10) and two (ἄρρητον, 23.27). The varyingly aspirated αθρόος is clearly felt to have a smooth breathing at 3.12 in the phrase οὐκ ἀθρόως.

As for punctuation, the scribe most commonly uses *paragraphoi* and blank spaces (*spatia*), usually together but sometimes separately, to mark punctuation. There are five instances of other punctuation, which we have

---

249. At 1.5, the scribe left out the sequence μαιτουτοπαςιγαρωςεκεινο in the middle of a line without any obvious paleographic reason; Giuliano (2005, 137) suggests that this was a line in the manuscript from which our scribe was copying (if so, the exemplar would have had longer lines than this manuscript). At 43.3, the scribe misread ΟΥΜΑΔΙΑ and wrote ΟΥΜΑΛΙϹΤΑ, which was subsequently corrected.

not marked in our text.[250] The *paragraphoi* take three forms: the usual, in which it is mostly under the first letter of the line; a "reinforced" *paragraphos* (one with a small additional stroke on the left) in a few instances; and in six instances the *paragraphos* extends almost fully out into the margin.[251] There does not seem to be any important difference in the use of these; all are usually used to mark strong breaks, such as a full stop, semicolon, or beginnings and ends of quotations, though sometimes we punctuate only with a comma. There are a few *diplai* and *diplai obelismenai*, which are of uncertain use, and one mysterious, badly damaged sign in the margin at 41.31.[252] The blank spaces (marked with ᵛ for *vacat* in our text) are usually about a letter's width in size, perhaps a little less or rarely more.

The corrector, who seems to have been the original scribe, corrected most of the errors but was not perfect. The scribe made some corrections as he wrote (e.g., false start errors; see below) during the initial copying, but most were probably made later.[253] Letters are usually deleted with supralinear dots, though they are also deleted with a slash through the letter at 29.24, 43.33, and probably 20.40, and additions are usually supralinear as well (a long one spills over into the margin at 1.5). The corrector tried to correct a letter shape instead of writing a supralinear letter if he thought it was possible.[254] The corrector left serious corruptions in at least three places in the surviving text, especially the one at 11.4–5; the difficulties are compounded by damage to the papyrus (e.g., 30.34 and 33.35).

The scribe typically follows the usual rules for dividing words over two lines in papyri, though he sometimes makes false-start errors (see

---

250. A double *stigme* at 13.11 and 40.19; upper *stigme* at 17.15; lower *stigme* at 7.6; and an odd triple *stigme* (double followed by middle) at 23.19. There is an odd sort of internal space filler at 42.17. All these marks were possibly added by the corrector; see Giuliano 2005, 140.

251. For discussion of the punctuation, see Giuliano 2005, 138–44. In many cases in her *tabella* (144–58), she notes traces of marginal notes. We have printed these as *paragraphoi* in the cases where that seems likely.

252. The *diplai* are found at 2.12, 29.33, 37.9, 39.29, 43.21; the *diplai obelismenai* are at 38.34, 40.26, 44.41, 48.36 and are marked in the text. Giuliano (2005, 141) thinks that in some cases these seem to be used to distinguish the adversaries' theses from Philodemus's argumentation. At 41.31, Giuliano (2005, 143 n. 74) thinks of an *antisigma* marking an argument of interest.

253. See Giuliano 2005, 138.

254. Instances at 8.3, 8.28, 23.34, 25.15, 27.23 according to Giuliano 2005, 138.

above).²⁵⁵ In words with prefixes, both breaks after the prefix and within it are found (e.g., προc|τιθέαcιν at 3.18–19 and δι|ατίθηcι at 12.17–18). The letters ππ are always on the second line. Double consonants—most commonly λλ and ττ—are usually split in the middle, and the scribe breaks ρ + consonant and ν + consonant in the middle as well. A c + consonant is usually but not always broken in the middle, and other consonant clusters are treated inconsistently, with an apparent preference for putting the whole cluster on the second line, as the correction at 16.23–24 (Κά⟦δ⟧|δμον) shows, especially when taken with spellings such as ἐ|χθρούc (26.21–22), ὑπε|μνήcαμεν (29.32–33), πολυ|χρονίοιc 30.16–17, and περιπί|[π]τει (44.9–10).

Two peculiarities should be noted: οὐ|[κ (frag. 32.26–27) and μὲ|ν οὖν (col. 1.12–13). Apparently the phrases cohered closely enough to be treated as single words for the purposes of line division.

Errors

The following is a list of the errors the original scribe made (whether corrected by the corrector or modern critics). By "false starts," we mean instances when the scribe tried to fit too much onto a line and had to delete a letter at the end of a line. "Mistaken words or grammar" means that we suspect that the scribe misunderstood the text; "miscellaneous spelling errors or skipped words" is the catch-all category, including mistakes with *iota*. Some of these perhaps do not warrant inclusion in a list of errors. For instance, οὕτωι was an extremely common spelling in the Herculaneum papyri and other papyri of the period.

> **false starts** (16 total): fragments 18.10, 21.25; columns 16.23, 21.37, 22.22, 22.31, 29.19, 29.29, 30.23, 30.27, 36.24, 43.16, 45.39, 46.25, 46.41, 47.30
> **mistaken word or grammar** (47 total): columns 3.16–17, 5.27, 5.28, 7.15, 8.39, 9.38, 10.25, 11.3, 11.20–21, 14.31, 16.35, 17.9–10, 17.20, 17.29, 18.22, 18.33, 20.27, 23.34, 24.21, 24.22, 25.13, 25.15, 25.20, 27.15, 27.22, 28.39, 29.13, 29.27 (κα⟦τ⟧`κ´ἀ), 31.31, 33.28, 36.35, 37.19–20, 39.24, 39.25, 39.37, 40.21, 41.11, 41.30, 41.36, 42.30, 43.3, 43.33, 46.21, 46.33, 47.24–5, 49.33, 49.38

---

255. For the rules of word division in papyri, see Crönert 1903, 10–19; Turner 1987, 17; for the epigraphic forerunners to this practice, see Threatte 1980–1996, 1:64–73.

miscellaneous spelling errors or skipped words (74 total): fragments 15 (apparatus), 18.7, 19.16, 22.5, 22.10, 24.14–15, 24.15, 24.24, columns 1.5 (twice), 1.13, 3.23, 4.9, 5.7, 5.18, 5.25, 6.26, 6.30 (apparatus), 7.7, 8.39, 9.35, 10.24, 13.14, 13.26, 15.14, 15.27, 16.21, 16.28, 16.37, 18.1, 20.20, 20.23 (two), 20.29, 20.40, 21.22, 22.18, 22.32, 23.22, 23.24, 23.39, 26.5, 26.32, 27.31, 28.2, 28.21, 28.35, 29.22, 29.24, 29.27 (Δημόκρ[η]`ι´τον), 31.29, 32.31, 33.25, 33.35, 33.36, 33.37, 34.25, 35.26, 39.19, 40.22 (two), 40.24, 42.32, 42.37, 43.5, 43.6, 44.2, 44.8, 44.29, 45.17, 46.3, 48.2, 49.10 (repetition from two lines above), 49.35 (repetition from previous line)

The total of known or suspected errors is 137, an average of 2.54 per column throughout the columnar text (127 errors in 50 columns). The corrected misspelling of Timasagoras's name at 7.7 indicates that the original scribe was probably not paying attention to the contents of what he was copying, as do the errors in 20.23: τὰ μηδενὸ[θ]`c´ ἄξι[ο]`α´ λόγου. These probably indicate that the scribe was simply copying the letters he thought he saw without trying to understand the text. The errors at 31.29 (ὀρ[ι]`γ´ἠν) and the dropped gamma in ὀλιγάκις at 10.1 may indicate a weakened pronunciation of this letter, or else they are another indication of carelessness aided by the vertical lines in Γ and Ι. Identical misspellings of ἐν`ί´οτε in 13.14 and 15.14, as well as ἐν`ί´οις at 21.22, are a curiosity. The number of false-start errors probably indicates an inexperienced scribe who was bad at judging the space he had left in each line, and this may help explain the large number of errors overall.

There are a number of marginal slashes or tick marks found mostly toward the end of the treatise (the first in frag. 22.5, the next in col. 8.39), which may mark passages for checking.[256] We reproduced these in our text. In many cases there are corrections in the lines so marked. In the following list, C indicates that there is a scribal correction or known corruption in that line: fragment 22.5 C, columns 8.39 C, 11.5 C, 20.20 C, 20.27 C, 26.32 C, 27.12, 27.29, 27.32, 30.29 C, 31.24 (caused by a rare word?), 31.31 C, 32.39, 35.26 (?), 42.1, 48.2, 48.32.

---

256. See Giuliano 2005, summarizing Cavallo 1983, 24, who thought it was associated with alterations and errors, followed by McNamee 1992, 24; Wilke (1914, vi) and Indelli (1988, 41) think it is intended to attract the reader's attention.

14. Philodemus's Style

14.1. Grammar and Vocabulary

We can characterize Philodemus's language as good, correct Koine with some Attic features, perhaps left over from his education in that city. The most obvious difference between Classical Attic grammar and Philodemus's educated Koine is that μή is used with participles generally rather than only with conditional participles and generally shows its tendency to encroach on the territory of οὐ, though our impression is that he is still fairly strict.[257] The optative is used correctly, though rarely. In our treatise, the conditional particle is consistently written ἄν rather than ἐάν; this is probably scribal, given that spelling is inconsistent across Philodemus's corpus. The modal particle ἄν is used in all the expected cases, as well as with future infinitive (at 37.31–32 and 39.19; cf. its use with a future participle in *Poem.* 5.17.23) to add a potential flavor to the future.[258] In this treatise, κἄν is not used in the sense of "even" (as if καί). Notable also is the use of κατά with the neuter accusative of an adjective in an adverbial sense; examples are κατὰ πυκνόν (23.22) and κατ' ἄκριτον (33.31).

Philodemus is willing to omit forms of εἰμί, even in cases where this impedes understanding, notably with participles where a finite verb seems normal, as in 39.26–31: πῶς φυσικὸν τὸ πρὸς τὰ τηλικαῦτα ἐμποδίζον καὶ τοσούτων αἴτιον κακῶν; εἰ δὲ ἀνέκφευκτον καὶ διὰ τοῦτο φυσικὸν λεγόμενον.... The repeated rhetorical questions show that the tone is indignant (and therefore abrupt). An ἐcτι must be understood three times: once in the first question, then with ἀνέκφευκτον, and again with λεγόμενον. The nuance of the last is perhaps "if there is something inescapable and therefore called 'natural'...." An εἰcι is also missing cυνεχόμ[ενοι in 2.18 (and the μ is securely read, ruling out cυνέχονται).

Philodemus uses the late/Ionic forms of εἶπον (and of οἶδα, but these do not appear in this treatise[259]), as in 40.16: οἷc οὐκ ἂν εἴπαιμεν (Attic

---

257. Cf. e.g. Smyth §2689, esp. c.

258. This usage is attested for classical authors, but seems to have been avoided; perhaps it was felt to be a grammatical error or too colloquial; cf. *GMT* §§197, 208, and 216, Moorhouse (1946 and 1959), the latter in reply to Hulton (1957), and Macleod (1956) on Lucian's usage.

259. For οἶδα, see Philodemus, *Lib.* frag. 75.5 (οἴδαcι for ἴcαcι) and col. 8b.13 ε⟨ἰ⟩δήcουc[ι for εἴcονται.

εἴποιμεν). On the other hand, he consistently uses spellings in -ττ- rather than -σσ- (e.g., he writes πράττειν, not πράσσειν). Similarly, note χάριτα (43.24) as the accusative of χάρις instead of Attic χάριν. This was apparently the usual form in Koine (e.g., Polybius, *Hist.* 22.20.4, as well as the LXX, New Testament, and Philo), and was inherited from Ionic (cf. Herodotus, *Hist.* 6.41 and 9.107). The word ἀλογιστία (47.7) is uncommon and probably Koine. Similarly, Philodemus prefers ὑπομενητός (29.33) to the equally Koine form in -νετός.

Philodemus usually prefers thematic verbs to athematics, such as κιρνάω (26.12) for κεράννυμι, παραμίσγω (25.29–30) for παραμείγνυμι, and ἐπιδεικνύειν (7.10) for ἐπιδεικνύναι. The thematics ἐφιστάνειν (19.1) for ἐφιστάναι and παριστάνουσι (45.33) for παρίστασι are particularly surprising, since he uses the athematic forms of the simplex ἵστημι. Note also Koine κατασφάττω for the older κατασφάζω (15.15).

Philodemus's vocabulary (and other elements of his style, for that matter) shows the greatest affinity to that of Polybius, though parallels to his usage can be found in authors from Xenophon, who is sometimes called "the first Hellenistic author," to Galen and Plutarch. Greek later than that has not generally been of any use to us in looking for parallels. Since Philodemus was a contemporary of Cicero's, it is significant that his vocabulary sometimes corresponds with the Greek words that Cicero uses in his letters; see our notes on βαθύς (34.37), βαθύτης (28.40), and μυστικός (20.26). The diatribe shows a wide array of medical terminology and more colloquial vocabulary, both of which are appropriate to the topic and genre.

Philodemus also has a fondness for compound words, often ones not attested elsewhere. In our text, for instance, ἀνεπιλογιστούμενα (3.19–20), εὐανάσειστος (16.27–28), ἀνευδόκητος (25.6), ἀνευδοκησία (39.39), and προκινησία (38.28) are *hapax legomena*. The last might be a technical term from psychiatry, and the first is built on an Epicurean technical term (ἐπιλογίζομαι). If rightly conjectured, προσπαροινέω (frag. 19.2–3) is found only once elsewhere, while ἀπρόβατος is found only in Philodemus, in this treatise, at 19.12 and twice in his *On Signs*, but belongs to a group of Epicurean technical terms (see our note). If correctly read at fragment 21.5, ἔνοχλος is an *addendum lexicis*.[260] At 28.30 and 36.38, καχυπόνοος is a rare

---

260. Cf. ἐνοχλής with the same meaning, attested at *SB* 14587.17 (fourth century CE).

by-form of καχύποπτος; at 30.18, δυςαποκατάςτατος is also rare. Additionally, Delattre and Monet suggested προςενδύω at 23.22–23, a further compound of ἐνδύω that would be an *addendum lexicis*. In general, though, it seems that Philodemus used correct Koine and the technical language of philosophy rather than inventing new terms; it is probably due to the accidents of transmission that so many *hapax legomena* appear in his texts.

Philodemus's philosophical terminology is generally in line with Epicurus's, but he does show occasional creations and innovations in meaning. He will use opponents' terminology when discussing their arguments but does not normally use non-Epicurean technical terminology to carry his own positive arguments. In at least one case (προκόπτω and related words), an originally Stoic technical term has passed into common usage, and other instances of this are possible. The technical senses of ἐπιλογιςμός and related words remain (see below). Philodemus keeps ὀργή (anger, fit of anger) carefully distinct from θυμός (rage, fit of rage), but he does not alter other writers' text to conform to his own usage and even argues that they were virtual synonyms for the Founders.

14.2. Hiatus

Philodemus avoids hiatus with roughly the same strictness as Demosthenes.[261] The main lines of his practice are as follows:

1. Any short vowel, including "short" -αι in verb endings such as -εται, is presumed to be elided in pronunciation before any other vowel (i.e., *scriptio plena* is irrelevant), but υ and many instances of ι (as in ὅτι or in the datives of third-declension nouns) are not elided.
2. Punctuation excuses hiatus (this includes pauses before quotations, conjunctions, and the words before μέν/δέ).[262]
3. Hiatus is excused when the words are part of a "chain of concordant nouns"; for example, in the phrase τῶι ἀξίωι ἀνδρί the

---

261. This section largely summarizes the results of McOsker 2017, who builds on Strathmann 1892. Relevant to specific issues are Reeve 1971 on punctuation and Radt 1980 on *scriptio plena* and pronunciation. Cirillo 2008 updates Strathmann for certain works.

262. Consequently, hiatus before (and after) ὅτι, ἤ, ἐπεί, and similar words is permitted.

hiatus between each pair of words is acceptable because all the words belong to the same phrase. All the words need not be in the same case, though they must stand in some close relationship to each other.²⁶³

4. There are other miscellaneous exceptions: monosyllables or disyllables that end with a long or unelidible vowel (e.g., μή, ἐπεί, που, ὅτι, unelidible prepositions) often admit hiatus (a complete list can be compiled from Strathmann 1892 or McOsker 2017). Some words allow hiatus between themselves and the *preceding* word (or, perhaps more accurately, imply punctuation there), and such are ἤ, relative pronouns, and most, if not all, conjunctions.

These principles should explain any apparent cases of hiatus. Philodemus does not correct quotations to match his own stylistic practices, and his paraphrases often retain aspects of the original style.

14.3. Prose Rhythm

Philodemus's avoidance of hiatus was noticed long ago and is basic to establishing a correct text.²⁶⁴ But no one before us has explored the issue of prose rhythm and clausulae in his texts. Recent work, especially by G. O. Hutchinson (2018), has given us convincing models and statistics that are essential to assessing Philodemus's prose style and may well help editors choose between possible readings. Rhythmic clausulae are usually sought at the ends of sentences or at other heavy punctuation, but sentences may be shot through with them to provide a variety of effects.²⁶⁵ The basic system is as follows:

---

263. See McOsker 2017 for details. The possibilities are (1) that hiatus was simply pronounced and tolerated, (2) that there was crasis (τῶξίωνδρί vel sim.), or (3) that there was a glide (τῶy ἀξίωy ἀνδρί) in pronunciation, or a combination of one or more of these, depending on the specifics of the particular case.

264. This section summarizes McOsker forthcoming a, which should be consulted for full details.

265. For more detailed discussion of prose rhythm in general, see Hutchinson 2018, especially the first three chapters. I draw all my figures from him, except those for Philodemus (see 2018, 21–23). For Philodemus's practice, see McOsker forthcoming a. The statistics discussed are always for clausulae at sentence end or heavy punctuation.

1. −⏑− −⏑−   two cretics = 2Cr
2. −−− −⏑−   molossus + cretic = Mo+Cr
3. −⏑ −−   two trochees = 2Tr
4. −⏑− −−   cretic + trochee = Cr+Tr
5. −⏑−⏑−   hypodochmiac = Hd

Final syllables of clausulae are counted as *brevis in longo* (or *anceps*, depending on choice of terminology). Two resolutions of a single long into two shorts are permitted per clausula, which can lead to some ambiguity in the identification of specific clausulae.[266] Philodemus's treatment of diphthongs before vowels (e.g., in ποιεῖν) and of Attic correption (scanning a short vowel short before a plosive and a liquid or nasal) are both uncertain, hence the range in our statistics below.[267] There are unmetrical endings as well: most can be scanned as a sequence of two spondees with one or more resolution (2Sp or simply Sp); this includes most dactylic endings (2Da). The sequences −⏑−−−⏑− (an E in West's notation), −⏑−⏑⏑⏑− (an E with the middle *longum* resolved), and −⏑⏑−⏑⏑− (the second half of an elegiac pentameter) are also unmetrical. The scansions shown below provide examples of most of these.

On Anger shows an overall percentage of rhythmic clausulae at sentence end and other heavy punctuation of 72–76 percent, which probably qualifies it as rhythmic according to Hutchinson's method.[268] But this figure is somewhat deceptive: the diatribe (cols. 8–31.24) shows a higher percentage of rhythmic endings than the treatise as whole: somewhere between 75–80 percent of the sentence ends or heavy punctuation are marked by a rhythmic clausula, which makes it clearly rhythmic by Hutchinson's standard. The same can be said of other stylistically elevated passages in Philodemus, for example, the peroration of *On Death* (cols. 37–39). By contrast, the percentage of rhythmic clausulae in purely argumentative

---

266. E.g., resolved trochees are not very different from resolved cretic + trochee: ⏑⏑⏑⏑− against −⏑⏑⏑⏑−.

267. In poetry, such diphthongs are usually scanned long, but they are scanned short with increasing frequency as time passes, and there also seems to be variation between dialects; see West 1982, 11–12. For Attic correption, see West 1982, 16–17.

268. Hutchinson (2018, 23) places the cutoff at 73.75 percent rhythmic at heavy punctuation. The endings identified as rhythmic have a predicted percentage of 60.5 percent, so a rate of 73.75 percent is certainly intentional on the part of the author. Other treatises by Philodemus have still higher percentages of rhythmic endings, such as *On Signs* at 71–79 percent and *On Death* at 90–94 percent!

passages is markedly lower. The argumentative part of the treatise (i.e., the rest of it) has a rate of only 70–73 percent; that is, it is not rhythmic by Hutchinson's standard.[269] Comparable authors for this part are Iamblichus in his *Mysteries of Egypt* (70.75 percent), Pausanias (72 percent), and Lucian and Dionysius of Halicarnassus (both 73.5 percent). The diatribe is clearly marked out stylistically by its rhythms and is comparable with Xenophon of Ephesus (75.75 percent), Aristides's *Hymn to Sarapis* (77.78 percent), Heraclitus the Allegorist[270] (78.50 percent), and Musonius Rufus (80.05 percent). That is, the difference between the argumentative part and the diatribe is comparable to the difference between unfussy but correct prose and formal, polished prose. In fact, as a few sample passages below show, the diatribe is much more thoroughly rhythmic even within the sentences, not only at sentence end.

Philodemus's rhythmic practice gives us grounds for doubt when the papyrus presents an unmetrical clausula or when an emendation produces one. No author is completely rhythmic—according to Hutchinson's figures, Chariton is the most rhythmic at 89.75 percent—so unrhythmic clausulae are not necessarily wrong, but such readings and restorations do invite greater skepticism than they might otherwise. McOsker has suggested three emendations on the grounds of rhythm: (1) ἀπ[ο]φ{ε}υγεῖν at 6.26, where the aorist infinitive could be preferable as connoting success; (2) retaining τοῖc at 10.25, where the article is idiomatic, and (3) reading αὐτῶν at 46.22, a partitive genitive. Other cases will almost certainly present themselves when the rhythmic aspects of Philodemus's prose have been more fully studied. For instance, Gomperz's conjecture at 35.4–5 (τοιούτου [φαντac]ίαν·) gives a unrhythmic clausula, though the sense is appropriate; perhaps we should find a synonym.

By way of example, we provide three columns from the diatribe (the first [8], the last [31], and one from the middle [18]) and two from the argumentative portion, the first well-preserved column and the last complete column run together with the final column, for comparison. We have scanned (as well as McOsker's word processor permits) and identified the basic form of the clausulae (without noting resolutions) throughout the passage. Beyond the abbreviations above, Sp stands for a spondaic ending (with or without resolutions), and an * prefixed to the notation means

---

269. Whether more or more secure text would improve the figures is an open question.

270. Note Russell and Konstan's 2005 edition.

that it includes the final syllable of the previous clausula, a phenomenon that Hutchinson calls "overlap."[271] Unrhythmic endings have been noted before punctuation but not elsewhere. Note that some analyses depend on resolutions.

Diatribe

Column 8.20–9.1

ὡσπερεὶ συνκείμενον ἐξ ἐκπυρώcεωc (Hd) καὶ διοιδή[c]εωc (2Cr) καὶ διερεθιcμοῦ (Cr+Tr) καὶ βριμώcεωc (*Mo+Cr) καὶ δεινῆc |25 ἐπιθυμίαc (Mo+Cr) τοῦ μετελθεῖν (2Tr) κ(αὶ) ἀγωνίαc (*Mo+Cr), εἰ δυνήcεται (Hd), καθάπερ ἀποδείξου[c]ιν αἱ φωναί, (Cr+Tr) τοτὲ μὲν εὐχομένων (Cr+Tr) περιζώ|30cαcθαι τοῖc ἐντέροιc (Mo+Cr) τοῦ λυπήcαντοc (Cr+Tr), τοτὲ δ' "ὠμὰ δάcαcθαι." (quotation) εἶτ' ἐπὶ τὰc διαδιδομέναc (Cr+Tr) τῶι cώματι κεινήcειc ἀcταθεῖc (Mo+Cr), οἷον λέ|35γω τὴν ὑπὸ τῆc κ[ρ]αυγῆc διάcταcιν (Hd) [τ]οῦ πλεύμονοc cὺν αὐταῖc πλευραῖc (2Sp), τὸ μετεωρότερον ἄcθμα (Cr+Tr) τῶν χίλια δεδρα|40μηκότων cτάδια (Cr+Tr) καὶ τὴν πήδ[ηcι]ν τῆc [κ]αρδί||[αc (Mo+Cr)

Column 18.14–40

πα|15ρὰ χαλκοῦν ἐc[τιν ἀνυ]πέρβατοc (2Cr), ἐπ[ειδὰν τὴν γῆν οὐρ]ανῶι μιγνύωcι (2Tr) [π]αραπεμφθέντεc ὑπό [τ]ινοc ἑcτιῶντοc (2Tr), ὥcπερ |20 [ὁ] Cοφοκλέουc Ἀχιλλεύc (2Tr), [ἢ] κατά τι τοιοῦτο παρολιγωρηθέντεc (2Sp)· οὔπω γὰρ "ἀδικηθέντεc" λέγω (Mo+Cr). καὶ τῶν μὲν κυνῶν (*Mo+Cr) |25 οἱ πρὸc τὰc θήραc (2Sp), ἂν οἰκουρὸc αὐτοὺc (2Tr) ὑλακτῇ παριόνταc (2Da), οὐκ ἐπιcτρέφονται (2Tr), ᵛ τὸν δ' Ἀλεξάνδρου φαcὶ (2Sp) μηδ' [ὅ]ταν ἄλ|30λο κινηθῇ θηρίον (Mo+Cr) ἀλλ' ὅταν λέων (Hd)—οἱ δὲ τῶν ποιητῶν θεοὶ (2Cr[272]) μικροῦ καὶ τα[ῖ]c ὑcὶν (Mo+Cr) ὀργίλωc διατίθενται (Cr+Tr). ᵛ τί γὰρ δεῖ |35 το[ὺc β]αcιλεῖc λέγειν (Mo+Cr); ἐμπο[δίζ]ονται (Cr+Tr) δὲ καὶ πρὸc τὴν ἐν φιλοcοφίαι cυναύξηcιν (Cr+Tr), οἷc μεταδιώκεται τοῦτο (Cr+Tr), διὰ πολλὰc |40 αἰτία[c (Mo+Cr)

---

271. For discussion, see Hutchinson 2018, 62–63.
272. If the -οι- is scanned long, then we have the equally rhythmic Mo+Cr.

Column 31.10–24

πλὴν τ[οῦ] καν[ονικοῦ] λόγου (2Cr). ᵛ τοὐναντίον δὲ πᾶς ἀντίδικος (Sp), ὁ μὲν ἔξωθεν καὶ διερεθίζων παντοδαπῶς (Sp), γονεῖς δὲ |¹⁵ καὶ πᾶς προσήκων τὰ πολλὰ (2Tr) καὶ συνχαίροντες ὡς ἐπάνδροις (2Tr), τῶν δὲ φιλοσόφων (Hd) οἱ μὲν φλυαροῦντες (Cr+Tr) ἐν ταῖς παραμυθίαις (Mo+Cr), οἱ δὲ |²⁰ καὶ μετὰ ϲυνηγορίας (Cr+Tr) ἐπιρρωννύντες (2Sp)· ἀφ[ί]ημ[ι] μὲν ῥήτορας (2Cr) καὶ ποιητὰς (2Tr) καὶ πᾶσαν τὴν τοιαύτην γρυμέαν (E!²⁷³).

The "demo" diatribe is a carefully composed and stylistically elevated piece of writing, and it shows in the sentence rhythms.

Argumentative Columns

Column 1.5–27

. . . . οὐ]δ' [ἀνα]ίνομαι τοῦτο (Cr+Tr). πᾶσι γὰρ ὡς ἐκεῖνο φα[νερόν ἐστιν] (2Tr) ὅτι κα[κόν, ο[ὔ]τω κ[αὶ] τοῦτο (Sp). διὰ [μ]ὲν δὴ τοιούτων (2Tr²⁷⁴), ᵛ ὅτι ληρῶδές ἐστι (2Tr) τὸ ψέ|¹⁰γειν ἐγκεχείρηκεν (Cr+Tr), ἀδολέσχως δὲ καὶ καθάπερ εἴωθεν (2Tr²⁷⁵). ᵛ εἰ μὲν οὖν ἐπετίμα τοῖς ψέγουσι μ[ό]νον (Cr+Tr), ἄλλο |¹⁵ δὲ μηδὲ ἓν ποιοῦσιν ἢ βαι[ό]ν (Hd²⁷⁶), ὡς Βίων ἐν τῶι Περὶ τῆς ὀργῆς καὶ Χρύσιππος ἐν τ[ῶ]ι Πε[ρὶ] παθῶν Θεραπευ[τι]κῶι (Mo+Cr), κἂν |²⁰ μετρίως ἵστατο (2Cr). νῦν δὲ τ[ὸ] καθόλ[ο]υ (Hd) τὰ παρακολουθοῦν[τ]α κακὰ τιθέναι πρὸ ὀμμάτων καταγέλαστ[ο]ν εἶναι (2Tr) |²⁵ καὶ ληρῶδες ὑπολαμβάνων (2Cr), αὐ[τός ἐστι ληρώδης (Cr+Tr) καὶ κα[ταγέλαστος... (Cr+Tr?)

Columns 49.1–50.8

τῶι καὶ τοὺς χα[ρ]ίεν[τας (2Da), φλ]υαροῦσιν (*Cr+Tr)· ᵛ εἰ δ' ἑα[υ]τούς (2Tr), ἀτόπως περὶ ἐκείνου φ[ανερὸ]ν ἐκ τούτων (Cr+Tr) ϲυλλογίζ[ε]ϲ[θ]αι (Cr+Tr)· ᵛ τῶι τε |⁵ παραπλησίωι τρόπωι (Hd) πορευόμενός τις ἀποδ[εί]ξει (Cr+Tr) τὸ καὶ φ[ιλ]οδοξ[ή]σει[ν ἢ ἐρας]θήσε[σθ]αι τὸ[ν σο]φὸν (Mo+Cr) [καὶ μυ]ρίοι[ς ἄ]λλοις (Cr+Tr) ϲ[υϲ]χεθήϲ[εϲθαι] |¹⁰ π[άθ]εϲιν (2Sp), εἴ[περ

---

273. If the -οι- is scanned long, we have Mo+Cr, which is better; this is probably a sign that the treatment of diphthongs before other vowels was inconsistent.

274. If the -οι- is scanned long, we have the nonrhythmic 2Sp.

275. If the -ει- is scanned long, we have the equally rhythmic Cr+Tr.

276. If the -αι- is scanned long, we have the equally rhythmic Cr+Tr.

ἄλ]λο[ι (2Tr) κ]αὶ τῶν [πά]νυ χα[ριέν]τω[ν (2Tr) cυ]νεχ[ῶc πό]νους ἔ[χου]|¹³cιν (2Tr)...|¹⁹...θαι πρόχειρό[ν ἐcτ]ι (2Tr), καὶ ⟨τὸ⟩ τὸν co|²⁰φὸν προcδε[κ]τέον εὐεμπτωτότερον ἐνίων ἀλογίcτων εἰc τὰc ὀργὰc ὑπάρχειν (2Tr). ᵛ καὶ τὸ μὴ τῶν ἀφρόνων ἧττον τοῦτο πάcχειν (2Tr), ἐπειδήπερ |²⁵ οὐχ ἧττον αὐτῶν μεθύcκεται (Hd), καθὸ λέ[γ]εται μεθύειν (Sp). ὁ δ[ὲ] τελευταῖοc λόγοc ἀπέραντόc ἐcτιν (2Tr) ἐκ τοῦ τὴν ὀρ[γ]ὴν χωρὶc ὑπολήψεωc (Hd) τοῦ |³⁰ βε[β]λάφθαι μὴ γίνεcθαι καὶ τοῦ τὸν cοφὸν ἑκουcίω[c] βλάπτεcθαι cυνά[γ]ων τὸ καὶ [ὀ]ργίζεc[θ]αι. (Sp) καθάπ[ε]ρ γὰρ χωρὶc τοῦ γράμματα μαθεῖν (2Tr) οὐχ οἷ|³⁵όν τ[ε] γενέcθαι cοφόν (Mo+Cr), ἀλλ' οὐκ, εἰ γράμματά τιc ἔμαθεν (Mo+Cr), ἐποιcθήcεται τὸ καὶ cοφὸν αὐτὸν ὑπάρχειν (2Da), οὕτωc οὐδὲ |⁴⁰ τῶι προcτηcαμέν[ωι τὸ ὑ]πολήψεcιν τοῦ βεβλάφθαι ||¹ τὴν ὀργὴν ἐπακολουθεῖν (2Tr), ἄλλωc δ' ἀδυνατεῖν (2Tr), τὸ [πά]ντωc ὀ[ρ]γιcθήcεc[θ]αι τὸν ἔμφαcιν εἰληφότα |⁵ βλάβηc (2Tr), ἂμ μή τιc ἐπιδείξηι κ[α]ὶ δραcτικὸν αἴ[τι]ον ὀργῆc εἶναι τ[ὴ]ν ὑπόληψιν τ[ῆ] c [βλ]άβηc (Mo+Cr).

The overall impression is that Philodemus sought out rhythmic clausulae much more frequently in the diatribe than in the argumentative passages and did so by writing shorter, more clearly defined phrases that could be artfully arranged into a larger sentence. In his argumentative prose, he uses quite long phrases or even sentences that do not break into easily definable phrases, such as τὸ τὸν cοφὸν προcδεκτέον εὐεμπτωτότερον ἐνίων ἀλογίcτων εἰc τὰc ὀργὰc ὑπάρχεῖν (2Tr). It is difficult to find shorter phrases in this: τὸν cοφὸν is a cretic, and ἐνίων ἀλογίcτων ends with 2Da, but otherwise there is only the final clausula. At twenty-eight syllables, this is much longer than any of the longer word groups in the columns of the diatribe that we surveyed, but it is perhaps only a little out of the ordinary for the argumentative prose in this treatise. The diatribe is made of shorter, more rhythmic parts that were selected with more care.

14.4. Style

Philodemus's prose is much maligned, usually for insufficient reasons. Sudhaus (1895, vi) voiced a defense of Philodemus's prose: faulty emendations and conjectures were the problem. To those can be added misreadings of the papyrus and incorrect joins between fragments. It is true that his Greek is not the correct Attic of several centuries before his birth, nor is it the Atticism of several centuries after his death, but it is grammatically correct and sometimes even succeeds on a comparatively high level as rhetoric (e.g., what survives from the peroration of his mock diatribe,

31.11–24). His avoidance of hiatus and use of prose rhythm are important: he tried to be somewhat stylish, which should inform our judgments.

In general, Philodemus's writing is free from conventional rhetorical features such as balanced clauses and antithesis: the real goal was clarity of argumentation, not beauty of expression.[277] His sentences can be long and occasionally difficult to follow, but they always turn out to be correct when completely preserved.[278] His taste for long sentences is particularly damaging to understanding him given the state of the papyri.

Adjectives and other modifiers are rarely far from their nouns. He is fond of participles and articular infinitives, particularly chains of infinitives. As for particle usage, he occupies an intermediate position: the full range of particles is not found, but his usage is not so stereotyped and bland as that of later authors.[279] The neuter article carries a lot of weight, since it serves to introduce quotations from other authors (e.g., 44.41–45.34) as well as to introduce propositions for discussion, in addition to its more common uses. The phrase εἰc τοὺc οἷc ὀργίζεται (frag. 18.11–12) is noteworthy: "at those with whom he is angry," where the relative clause is treated like the noun that goes with the article. This may be an extension from his use of the neuter article to mark phrases treated like nouns.

Obbink's characterization of the style of *On Piety* holds for *On Anger* as well: "Sentences gravitate to the longish side.... they are made to seem even longer by the lack of the antithesis, parallelism, and periodicity familiar from classical Attic prose. There is no postponement of the verb till the period is complete; often the main verb falls early, with subordinate clauses straying on. The writer avoids giving the impression of having

---

277. We must always remember that Philodemus's treatises are not merely explications of doctrine but argumentation against other philosophers' views, which had probably been summarized at the start of the work. No certain example of an initial summary of Epicurean views survives, but this may be due to poor preservation of beginnings of rolls rather than his compositional practice. However they did, his audience knows the Epicurean position and has been made familiar with the adversary's views. If his prose seems obscure, it is probably the fault of the conservation of the papyrus rolls, in which many of the opening pages of a roll had to be destroyed to open the rest, and our ignorance of the details of the argument, rather than Philodemus's obscurity.

278. We have tried to analyze the grammatical complications of one or two difficult sentences in the notes to our translation (e.g., n. 86 on col. 7 and n. 123 on col. 19).

279. Beyond Denniston 1950, see Blomqvist 1969. Both are useful for Philodemus.

cast the whole thought in his head before writing, as though the sentence were 'merely built up in the course of composition, as new thoughts and modifications occurred to the writer'" (1996, 86–88, quoting Bailey 1926, 173, on Epicurus's *Letter to Herodotus*). Additionally, the main verb usually comes early, with prepositional phrases and subordinate clauses piled up afterward. Rather than obeying any rhetorical practice, they seem to be organized by the steps in Philodemus's line of thought. Philodemus likes contradicting false assertions as soon as possible, rather than waiting for a more artistic point in the sentence.

Monet (1996, 62–64) adds perceptive comments on several specific points. She notes Philodemus's willingness to repeat nouns out of a concern for clarity, his Atticism (or "proto-Atticism"; see above), his fondness for hyperbaton, use of the article (repeated if necessary) to clarify long noun phrases, occasional ellipse of verbs of saying, and fondness for chains of infinitives, especially articular infinitives. She also notes that his sentences often begin with a subordinate clause.

Hyperbata, as both Monet and Obbink note, are common, especially separation of an article-adjective from their noun by a verb, commonly at the end of a sentence, and separation of genitives from the nouns on which they depend. In some cases, this may have to do with avoiding hiatus; in others, it seems to be used to distribute emphasis within the sentence.

In general, when the text is well preserved, Philodemus succeeds in being clear. His allusions are occasionally opaque to us but probably were not so to his contemporaries. His long sentences can be challenging in isolation but not when we have sufficient context, and they are often alternated with shorter sentences for variety. This usually impedes our understanding of his and his opponents' arguments, and the loss of the first part of the roll exacerbates this problem.[280] He uses biting sarcasm, rhetorical questions, and even direct insults to show contempt for opponents and their arguments—and to enliven his prose. He is fond of describing opponents as blind, insane, or stupid when they do not understand an argument or make an assertion that does not reflect reality. All this makes for a somewhat livelier style than is commonly attributed to him, with traces of the seminar room or lecture hall. On the whole, he is correct and fairly polished but not fussy or grand.

---

280. When scholars have succeeded in reconstructing entire book rolls of Philodemus, this seems to be his procedure, as in *Mus.* 4 and *Poem.* 1–2, where a lengthy initial summary in book 1 is the subject of discussion throughout book 2.

The mock diatribe is a tour de force and has several peculiar features. Philodemus uses the diatribe form to put forward arguments in favor of using a diatribe and uses an angry persona to put forward arguments against empty anger. It is therefore highly ironic and stylized. The level of diction is generally high, but clauses are shorter and linked together paratactically. This contributes to its greater proportion of rhythmic clausulae and denser rhythms generally. It abounds in lists, sometimes of medical terminology appropriate to the diagnosis, other times just in general (col. 28), but occasionally Philodemus ironically undercuts himself by trailing off into anticlimax ("and that sort of thing," e.g., cols. 13 and 14). Illustrative examples are common, some drawn from Epicurean literature (col. 12), mythology (14 and perhaps 16), history (18), and apparently New Comedy (15). Diminutives are used for pathetic effect, to highlight the outrageousness of the angry man's wrath (17), and throughout small provocations to anger are juxtaposed with their disproportionate results. The whole rant ends with a majestic *ex cathedra* dismissal of orators and poets as γρύμεα, "trash."

15. Previous Textual Scholarship

John Hayter, who supervised the opening and drawing of the papyrus, made a partial edition and Latin translation that is now preserved in manuscript in the Bodleian library in Oxford. It has never been published, and our knowledge of its readings is drawn from Indelli's edition.

In 1863, Spengel published a partial edition in a Supplement-Band to *Philologus*, but Gomperz's edition of 1864 is the first complete published edition of the text. He worked from the Oxford and Neapolitan *disegni*, taking O as his primary source but recording N's variants and occasionally adopting them. O had been published in *Herculanensium Voluminum Pars Prima* (*HV*, published in 1824; the *Pars Altera* followed in 1825); N, after alterations, in *Voluminum Herculanensium Quae Supersunt Collectio Altera* (*HV²*, 1:16–73), in 1862. In both publications, the papyrus was officially anonymous, but *HV²*'s table of contents suggests Philodemus as the author and the Περὶ κακιῶν καὶ ἀρετῶν as the ensemble to which it belongs; Gomperz was convinced that the author was Philodemus.[281] Both *HV* and *HV²* reproduced the *disegni* by copperplate.

---

281. Giulio Minervini signed the preface to this volume, so the table of contents (or rather *Index Scriptorum Quae in hoc Volumine Continentur*) is probably also his

Gomperz's numeration follows that of N (the pages of O were clearly out of order), with eight fragments and fifty columns. Some of the fragments have a double numeration; the first is his number, the second that of N (so that "IIII [III]" is the fourth in his series but third in N). He promised a commentary, but it never appeared. He never saw the papyrus but was correct about its color: "the original, which I have never seen and believe to be black" (1864, 6: *archetypum, quod nunquam vidi et atrum esse puto*). He did go to Oxford to read O in person and quotes two readings from Hayter's edition.[282] We suspect that the librarian, Henry Octavius Coxe, did not allow him unfettered access. Gomperz and Spengel worked independently and duplicated much basic work on the text, but each also made a number of important contributions of his own. Both were sober, careful editors who did not print adventurous supplements. Given that they were working and publishing so close in time to each other, we have given both scholars credit for their shared supplements and conjectures.

The copy of Gomperz's edition found in the Ghent University library is a curiosity.[283] It contains occasional learned annotation in Latin, as well as much interesting work on the text. Against column 1 is a note that refers to Heinze's article in *Rheinisches Museum* 45 (1890), but we cannot otherwise date it. More than one hand seems to have made annotations, and Ben Henry suggests to us that it was used in a seminar, which might also explain the curious fact that the annotations stop abruptly at the end of column 40—as so often, end of term interrupted. We have only been able to consult the scan on Googlebooks, and autopsy might reveal more details of interest. We have adopted some readings and recorded others in the apparatus; they are marked "Gand." (for Gandavensis).

Karl Wilke (1880–1916) visited Naples twice during his work on this treatise, in 1906 and 1911, where he read the papyrus with the help and encouragement of Domenico Bassi (director of the Officina 1906–1926); his edition appeared in 1914.[284] He was the first editor to inspect the papy-

---

work. On Minervini, an archaeologist and *ispettore* of the numismatic and epigraphic collections in the Museo Nazionale (formerly the Museo Borbonico), see Travaglione 2003, 119–23.

282. Gomperz mistakenly refers to John Hayter as William in his preface, which indicates no great familiarity with the man or his work.

283. We thank Ben Henry for calling it to our attention.

284. He had visited already in 1904 for his 1905 edition of Polystratus's *On Irrational Contempt for Common Opinions*.

rus firsthand, and his text consequently shows great improvements over its predecessors. Not only are his readings of the text better, but he was able to include an additional eight fragments beyond those Gomperz had published, as well as numerous parts of columns that the *disegnatori* had neglected, including the difficult column tops (see §10 above).[285] His apparatus is full (though he does neglect to record authors of easy corrections), and his text is a bit more adventuresome than Gomperz's and Spengel's in accepting supplements into the text. The edition provoked some textual work (especially in reviews) but little philosophical interest.

By far the most prolific author of emendations and supplements was Robert Philippson (1858–1942). He had announced a major project on anger, of which his studies of Philodemus were forerunners, which was never completed. His conjectures, while overbold, are usually at least interesting and thought-provoking. We have retained many in our apparatus for those reasons and because they are occasionally plausible supplements for lengthier lacunae. However, they are often too plausible; that is, they do not add anything to the argument but merely reproduce what we can find elsewhere in the text, and nothing of consequence changes when they are rejected.

Giovanni Indelli published an edition in 1988 in the La scuola di Epicuro series (vol. 5), founded by Marcello Gigante. Indelli completely reread the papyrus with the advantage of good microscopes (resulting in many changes to Wilke's text), though his apparatus is intended as a supplement to Wilke's. He also was able to take advantage of the sparse textual and interpretative work that had appeared in the seventy-four years between his and Wilke's editions. He included a useful Italian translation (the first into a modern language) and a full and still-essential commentary (also the first published), which our notes are intended to supplement rather than replace. These features finally made the text accessible to scholars, since

---

285. His numerations follow those of Gomperz with the addition of eight fragments from the beginning of the text labeled with letters A–H, so as not to disturb Gomperz's numeration. He printed these fragments in their actual locations on the papyrus but warned that this was not necessarily their correct order: *sed quoniam omnia tam lacerata vides, ut sententiarum ordo et conexus certo restitui non possit, in eundem ea ordinem digessi, quo in ipsa papyro agglutinata continuantur* (1914, viii: "But since one sees everything so torn that the order and connection of the contents cannot be certainly restored, I have arranged them in the order that they have been mounted in the original papyrus").

the difficulties of Philodemus (real and apparent) were made manageable, and the translation and commentary provided an excellent starting point for consideration of the philosophical ideas in the treatise.

Indelli's edition spurred a great deal of work on the treatise, most of it philosophical now rather than textual (see §2). Among the textual work, the most important are a series of articles by Indelli and the translation into French and notes by Daniel Delattre and Annick Monet for the volume *Les épicuriens* in the Pléiade series.[286] We have adopted some of these in the text and included others in the apparatus.

16. Principles of Our Edition and Translation

Our text is based on Indelli's 1988 edition, though we have had the benefit of Brigham Young University's infrared images, and Michael McOsker reread the papyrus by autopsy during visits to Naples in 2013–2018. A more intensive autopsy of the papyrus might provide some incremental gains, but this papyrus is one of those whose condition has deteriorated since unrolling, and in many cases much less is legible now than when Wilke read it or even it seems, in some cases, Indelli. Our major contribution has been use of the infrared images taken by the Brigham Young University team, which shed much light on the text.

Our goal is to provide a readable and reliable text that nonetheless does not obscure the difficulties. The major remaining difficulty is that we have left some fragments that we have not been able to place —the series A–H, which can be found in the columnar part of the text—where they are found in the *cornici*. They are certainly out of place where they are printed, as outlined in §10 above. In terms of indicating the origins of the text that we print, we have obeyed "Gigante's Law," according to which the readings of the *disegni* count as readings of the papyrus in cases when the papyrus has been damaged or is otherwise illegible and the *disegni* do not present problematic readings.[287] Thus we have not specially marked text that is

---

286. Delattre and Pigeaud 2010, 571–94 (translation) and 1250–60 (notes). An unpublished list of their conjectures and readings is in private circulation.

287. Gigante formulated the law as follows: "Anche quando non si legge oggi in *P*, una lezione di *O N* o di *O* o di *N*, riconosciuta attendibile e non contraddetta da qualsiasi altra considerazione, è data senz'altro come lezione del papiro" (1983, 115). The theory is that the *disegni* are, in effect, manuscript copies of the papyrus, so they are primary witnesses to the text when the exemplar from which they are copied is dam-

preserved only on the *disegni*. All text that is printed normally is legible in that form on the papyrus, in the infrared photographs, or on at least one of the two *disegni*. In cases where the witnesses disagree about a matter of substance, the apparatus contains their readings. We do not record the readings of the *disegni* when we feel that the text is not in doubt or that their evidence is not useful; in fact, they appear quite infrequently in our apparatus (usually only when the papyrus has deteriorated and they are our primary sources for disputed text).

The handwriting of the text is not difficult, but the scribe was careless (see §13), and, although the papyrus was corrected, almost certainly by the scribe himself, many errors remained. We have used all the normal papyrological conventions for printing corrected text, as well as the under-asterisk (a̱) to indicate that the letter has been changed as the result of a conjecture. Only two complete columns (and the final one, which is much shorter) are free from error, out of the fifty that constitute the text; most columns have multiple errors. We saw no benefit in shielding our readers from the ugly fact that the scribe did a poor job and that not everything was successfully corrected. This text has consequently required greater editorial intervention than many other Herculaneum papyri, and the argument is, at some points, left in darkness because of the scribe's incompetence.

Those familiar with Indelli's text will notice that we have reinserted those fragments that he printed in the apparatus into their places among the columns and have added to their number. The papyrological explanation for this can be found above (§10), and our justification is that this was the most honest means of presentation for these difficult fragments that we cannot place.

Unfortunately, we have had to renumber the initial fragments, due to the fact that we nearly double their number (from Indelli's seventeen to our thirty-three), and they are almost completely rearranged. The first is simply due to our ability to read more text via the infrared photographs; the second is due to the much more complicated matter of correctly collocating *sovrapposti and sottoposti* in their original homes. This is tricky

---

aged or illegible but not of use when their exemplar is extant. Additionally, graphically marking the origin of letter in the text would burden it with nearly useless signs that would distract the reader without adding important information. Accordingly, we note the readings of the *disegni* in the apparatus when there is uncertainty about the text.

business, but we think that the gains in the continuity and intelligibility of the argument make it worthwhile.

Only Wilke's edition, out of the previous three editions of *On Anger*, attempted a reasonably complete *apparatus criticus*; Gomperz's included only the readings of the *disegni* (since he did not see the papyrus), and Indelli's only registered divergences from Wilke's text and apparatus (including new readings, new conjectures, and reassignment of some readings and conjectures to different scholars). Since Wilke's edition is now over a hundred years old and there has been substantial work on the text, we felt it was worth the effort to compile a complete apparatus. As a rule, we have not recorded any suggestion that has been ruled out by a new reading of the papyrus, nor have we usually recorded readings that we think are certainly or almost certainly incorrect for whatever reason. We have made exceptions when we think that knowledge of an early editor's reading may be useful or when a conjecture is suggestive or diagnostic, even though it cannot be correct as proposed.

When we know the first author of an emendation or supplement, we record the fact. Since Spengel and Gomperz worked independently and published within a year of each other, they are credited together for many readings. Hayter's edition was not—*still* is not—published, and, though we give him sole credit when we know him to be the first, we have not been able to collate his edition systematically. Indelli collated this edition and reported everything that he thought was useful; we have used Indelli's reports in our apparatus. Likewise, since we do not know the scholar or scholars responsible for the conjectures in the Ghent library copy of Gomperz's edition, we have had to resort to the siglum "Gand." Not very often, but perhaps more often than is usual in an apparatus, we cite comparanda in support of readings or conjectures. We do not think that this material will be cumbersome or distracting and hope that it might prove useful in the absence of a full textual commentary in which to explain our choices.

In the English translation, our primary goal has been to give a reliable guide to the Greek text for the Greekless and for those without experience of the challenges of the Herculaneum papyri or of Philodemus's sometimes demanding style and vocabulary. Our second goal was to produce something pleasant to read that would reflect Philodemus's occasional rhetorical heights as well as his more straightforward argumentative style. We try to translate every word that we print and can confidently read: parts of words, especially ones that admit of several supplements (e.g., παρα[or -ε]ιναι) are left untranslated.

We have tried to translate the more frequently recurring technical terms in Philodemus's theory of anger the same way every time: μετέρχομαι is "get revenge"; βλάβη and βλάπτω are "harm" and "to harm"; κόλαcιc and κολάζω are "punishment" and "to punish," though the ideas of "retaliation" and "deterrence" are always present or implied; τιμωρία and τιμωρέω are "revenge" or "vengeance" and "get revenge." Epicurean technical terms have been given the same treatment: λογιcμόc is "reasoning," ἐπιλογιcμόc is "(rational) appraisal," ὑπόληψιc and ὑπολαμβάνω are "supposition" and "suppose," ἑκούcιοc is "intentional," and διάθεcιc is "disposition." Our explicit motivations for all these choices are to be found in the introduction or notes.

Our notes do not attempt to replace either Wilke's collection of related passages or Indelli's commentary, one of the finest in La scuola di Epicuro, but we hope that they (with the introduction) suffice to explain at least the main lines and some of the obscurer details of Philodemus's treatise.

17. Concordance of Fragments and Numerations across Editions

The editors before us have renumbered the lines according to their own opinions about how much is lost at what points in the text. All the fragments, and most of columns 1–32, are missing the upper margin and several lines at the top. Wilke set the line numbers by assuming that each column had forty lines and counting up from the bottom. Gomperz and Indelli numbered the first surviving line as one and counted downward. Indelli's edition contains *tavole di concordanza* that include the line-number equivalencies between his text and Wilke's. We have retained Indelli's line numbering for the columns but found too many new fragments (there are now thirty-three instead of seventeen, and the order of some of the older fragments is different because of stratigraphy) to keep Indelli's fragment numbers: these are given in our edition, along with Wilke's, after our own number.

Indelli (1988, 106–8) records several, very exiguous fragments, some of which appear to have since flaked off and disappeared. In the chart of fragments below, "app." means that Indelli records the fragment in the apparatus to the fragment named.

Introduction

This edition	Indelli	Wilke	Gomperz	HV^2
1	p. 106			
2				
3				
4	p. 107	B		
5	2			
6	app. 1			
7	1	A		
8				
9				
10				
11				
12	4	D		
13	3	C		
14	app. 3			
15	7	F		
16	5			
17	v. app. 5	E		
18	6	1	1	1
19	8	2	2	2
20	9			
21	10	3	3	
22	11			
23	app. 11			
24	12	4	4	3
25	app. 12			
26	app. 12			
27	13	5	5	4
28	14	6	6	5

This edition	Indelli	Wilke	Gomperz	*HV*²
29	15	J pars sin.		
30	app. 15	J pars dex.		
31	app. 17	8b	8	7 pars dex.
32	16	7	7	6
33	17	8		7 pars sin.

Sigla

In the translations, parentheses mark our expansion of the text for clarification; square brackets mark damaged and uncertain words in the Greek.

For the Greek text, these are the conventions:

P	Papyrus Herculanensis 182 (I BCE)
MSI	The infrared photographs made by the Brigham Young University team in cooperation with the Biblioteca Nazionale di Napoli
N	The Neapolitan Disegni
N^{ac}	N before correction
N^{pc}	N after correction
O	The Oxford Disegni
⟦α⟧	scribal deletion
\`α´	scribal supplement (above the line, unless otherwise noted in the apparatus)
{α}	editorial deletion
⟨α⟩	editorial supplement
$\overset{*}{\alpha}$	editorially emended letter
$\dot{\alpha}$	uncertainly read letter (i.e. the letter could be read differently; damaged but certainly read letters are not noted)
[.]	one letter missing
[]	perhaps one letter missing
[.(.)]	one to two letters missing
⌜α⌝	a letter preserved on a *sotto-* or *sovrapposto*
⌊α⌋	a letter preserved in a parallel source (e.g., a quotation)
[- - -]	an uncertain number of letters missing in an unknown configuration, usually because the papyrus is no longer extant to

	measure and we do not know where in a column a fragment stood
v	*vacat*: a space left by the scribe in the text
‖	column end

Scholars responsible for conjectures that have not been previously published:

(e.g.)	after a critic's name indicates that we record a reading *exempli gratia* only; before an asterisk or one of our names indicates we propose the reading solely e.g.
Asmis	Elizabeth Asmis, *per litt.*
DA	Armstrong, *suo Marte*
Gand.	the notes of one or more anonymous scholars in a copy of Gomperz' edition in the library of the University of Ghent.
Hayter	reports of Hayter's unpublished edition are taken from Indelli (1988)
Henry	W. Benjamin Henry, *per litt.* (some subsequently published in 2017)
Janko	Richard Janko, *per litt.*
McO	McOsker, *suo Marte*
*	Armstrong and McOsker together

Text, Translation, and Notes

⟨Φιλοδήμου⟩
⟨Περὶ ὀργῆς⟩

Fragment 1

1   ]ντο.λε[
       ] . ἐπῄιει [
       cφ]οδρὸν c[
4   τῆ]c βλάβη[c

2 vel ἐπῄιεν ‖ 3, 4 *

Fragment 2

margo superior exstare videtur
] ἠθικὸν [

Fragment 3

1   ] . ν . νε
            ] τῆc χά-
3   ριτοc . . . . .] . . . τυν-

2–3 * vel χα|[ρᾶc *

⟨Philodemus⟩
⟨On Anger⟩

THE INITIAL FRAGMENTS

Fragment 1[1]

... went[2] ...
... [in]tense ...
... [of the] harm ...

Fragment 2[3]

... ethical ...

Fragment 3[4]

... of fa[vor][5] ...

---

1. For the state of the fragments on *pezzo* 1 in *cornice* 17, see the introduction, p. 101.
2. From ἐπιέναι; "understood" from ἐπαΐω is also possible. βλάβης in line 4 is the first of some thirty occurrences in the treatise of the root βλαβ- ("harm"), which is key to Philodemus's definition of anger.
3. The state of the second *pezzo* of *cornice* 17 is similar to the first; see the introduction, p. 101.
4. From the first *pezzo* in *cornice* 18; see the introduction, pp. 101–2. This fragment is the lower part of the first *sezione* of the first piece; no margins survive.
5. Or "joy."

Fragment 4

|¹ - - -]υτ[. .] . . [- - - | - - -]ττομ[- - - | - - -] . ημ . [- - - | - - -]ουκο . c[- - -
|⁵ - - -] . [- - - | - - -]αφηcι . α[- - -] . ιν παρα . | - - -] . ζο . . [- - - | - - -]τοιc το
. [- - - |¹⁰ - - -]πν . [.]εω[- - - | - - -]αθουχω[- - - | - - -]τη κλε[- - - | - - -]
. τον cε[- - - | - - -] . κα[] . [- - - |¹⁵ - - -]τεμ . [- - - | - - - c]υνβαι[ν- - - - | - - -]
ευ[. .]υο[- - - | - - -]co . ν πον[- - - |¹⁹ - - -] . . χτ[- - -

11 ἀγ]αθοῦ Janko ‖ **16** *, γ: non μ

Fragment 5

desunt ca. 16 lineae

1   ἐ]πιμε[
    ]ρ[.]υc[
    ὅ]cτιc κ[
    ]νουcιν επ[
5   ἄ]λλων εχα[
    ]αι ἐπ[ὶ] το[
    ] ἀδικήcει[ν
    ] μέλλει . [
9   ]α[. .]εινειδ[
    restant vestigia 15 linearum

Frag. 5 = Indelli 2. ‖ **1** Janko ‖ **3, 5, 6, 7** Wilke ‖ **5** ἔχα[cτ- *

Fragment 4[6]

... happen ...

Fragment 5[7]

... whoever ...
... of others...
... to ...
... will commit injustice ...
... about to ...

---

6. This is the upper part of the second *sezione* of the first *pezzo* in *cornice* 18; no margins survive. See the introduction, pp. 101–2; Indelli 1988, 107.

7. *Pezzo* 2 is heavily stratified, as shown by the fact that a layer of it came off in the time between Wilke's edition and Indelli's. The top is very confused, and contiguous letters are not recoverable with any confidence. In the lower part, stratification is bad, but it can be sorted out.

Fragment 6

1   καχλαζ[..........
     τεθ..θ.[..... ...(.) ὀρ-
     γίcαcθαι [..... .....
     εἶναι τ[..... ...(.) ὀρ-
5   γίcαcθ[αι
     ἀλλὰ το[
     αυτὸν ολ[
8   αιτοναυc[
     margo fort. adest

Frag. 6 = Indelli 1 app. ‖ 1 χ vel ϛ; ζ vel ϙ ‖ 2-3, 4-5 Indelli ‖ 8 τὸν αὐc[τηρὸν tempt. Janko

Fragment 7

     desunt ca. 30 lineae
1   τὴ]ν ὀργὴ[ν λέγουcιν εἶ-
     ν]αι λύπην [μεγάλην τοῖc
     ὀ]ργιζομέν[οιc εἰc τὸ
     πᾶν, ὅταν μὴ [κατιcχύω-
5   cι τῆc τιμ[ω]ρί[αc ἅπτεc-
     θαι. μακάριοc ο[ὖν ὅcτιc
     διελάμβανεν, [ὅτι τό-
     τε λυπεῖcθ[αι ....
     ...]ρο[
10   .]οντιπ[
     margo adest

Frag. 7 = Indelli 1. ‖ 0 [χωρὶc δὲ τοῦ τιμωρεῖcθαι] Philippson (e.g.) ‖ 1 τὴ]ν ὀργὴ[ν Wilke ‖ 1-2 λέγουcιν εἶ]ν]αι Indelli : νομιζεc|θ]αι Wilke ‖ 2-4 Delattre-Monet (e.g.) ‖ 3 ὀ]ργιζομέν[ουc Wilke ‖ διὰ]‖ Indelli : περὶ]‖ Wilke ‖ 4-5 κατιcχύω]|cι τῆc τιμ[ω]ρί[αc Wilke ‖ 5-6 ἅπτεc]|θαι Philippson : ἀπέχεc]|θαι Wilke ‖ 6 ο[ὖν ὅcτιc Wilke ‖ 7 ὅτι Wilke ‖ 7-8 τό]|τε λυπεῖcθ[αι Henry (vel τό] | τε Janko) : τό]|τε λυπεῖ cῶ[μά τε καὶ ψυχὴν Wilke (τε eiecit Indelli) : τό]|τ' ἐλύπει cῶ[μα καὶ ψυχὴν * : [ὡc, ὅ]|τε λυπεῖ cῶ[μα ἡ ὀργή Delattre-Monet

Fragment 6[8]

... plash[9] ...
... to get angry ...
... to be ...
... to get angry ...
... but (?) ...
... him(self?) ...

Fragment 7[10]

... [they say[11]], anger is altogether a [great] distress to the angry, whenever they [do not have the power] to [achieve] vengeance. [7] Blessed, th[erefore, is whoever] came to understand clearly, [that[12] at that time] ... was distressed ...

---

8. This fragment is found at the lower left part of the first *sezione* of the second *pezzo;* see Indelli 1988, 108. It is not clear whether the bottom margin is extant, nor how many lines are missing at the top. This piece is a *sovrapposto*, two layers above the main layer.

9. καχλάζω ("bubble, plash") is found only in poets before this instance and another in Philodemus's contemporary Diodorus Siculus (*Bib. hist.* 3.44.2).

10. Cf. 31.24–27 and introduction, §6a. This fragment is on a *sovrapposto* that is no longer connected to the main body of the papyrus.

11. It is likely that something like Philippson's conjecture, "but aside from getting vengeance," preceded. Apparently, (empty) anger is painful until one gets revenge and at last becomes "blessed," as Philodemus sarcastically put it. This fragment, like frag. 13, may have belonged to an earlier attack on the Peripatetics that is mentioned at 31.24–27.

12. For διαλαμβάνω ὅτι, cf. Philodemus, *Sign.* 19.4–5, and see also our note on διειλημμένως (41.22).

Fragment 8

|¹ - - -]να̣[- - - | - - -]ι[.] . . [- - - | - - -]της αδ . . [- - - | - - -] . ρομει̣|⁵ - - -]
γη .(.)ο̣υ[- - - | - - -]κ . . επ̣[- - - |⁷ - - -]λιτων[- - - |vestigia ca. 9 linearum
|¹⁷ - - -]ενο[- - - | - - -]ιcται [- - - | - - -]ο̣[. . .].ο[- - - |²⁰ - - -]λλον . . .
[- - - |vestigia ca. 5 linearum

Fragment 9

desunt 4 lineae vel plures |¹ - - -]θ[- - - | - - -]γκο| - - -]coμε| - - -]υκα|⁵ - - -]νο . [

2 γ vel α̣ι̣

Fragment 10

desunt ca. 29 lineae | vestigia 8 linearum | - - -]νοτερον θ[- - - | vestigia 2 linearum

τερπ]νότερον vel κοι]νότερον Janko ‖ θ vel ε̣

Fragment 11

- - - δι]ασαφεῖν, ἀλλ[- - - | - - -]εν . . ειναι . . [- - - |vestigia duarum linearum

1 δι]ασαφεῖν Henry : ἀσάφεια *

The Initial Fragments (Frags. 1–16)

Fragment 8[13]

[no words legible]

Fragment 9[14]

[no words legible]

Fragment 10[15]

[no words legible]

Fragment 11[16]

… to make clear, but (?) …

---

13. *Pezzo* 1 of *cornice* 19 is very disappointing; little can be read continuously. The second *pezzo* is almost completely illegible; cf. the introduction, p. 102. This fragment is the second *sezione* of the first *pezzo*; no margins are extant.

14. This fragment is on the sixth *sezione* of the first *pezzo*, at the top. It seems that the left margin is extant.

15. This fragment is on the eighth *sezione* of the first *pezzo*, near the bottom, perhaps only two lines from the bottom.

16. *Cornice* 20 contains only one, barely legible *pezzo*. This fragment is at the bottom of the right-most *sezione*; cf. the introduction, 102–3.

Fragment 12

desunt ca. 22 lineae

13 τ[. .]ν[. . . .   .   ἄλ-
    λων οὐδ[. . . .]βα̣λ[. . . . -
15 νων αλ[. . .]cθαι κλ[. . . . -
    τεc π̣ι̣cε[. . . .] φήcε[ι τὴν
    ἕ]ξιν [. . . π]ᾶcιν [. . . . . . .
18   . . . .]cι[

Frag. 12 = Indelli 4. ‖ **13-16** ἀλ|λων οὐδ[ὲν ἐπι]βα̣λ[λομέ]|νων ἀλ[ίcκε]cθαι κλ[αίον]|τεc Wilke ‖ **15-16** κλ[ηθέν]|τεc Janko ‖ **16** π̣ι̣c vel ηχ ‖ **16-17** φήcε[ι τὴν | ἕ]ξιν Wilke in apparatu ‖ **17-18** [τοῖc π]ᾶcιν * : [τῶν π]ᾶcιν [ὀργιζομέ|νων Philippson

Fragment 13

desunt ca. 5 lineae
adsunt reliquiae 18 linearum

24   . . . [. .   . . .]τα cο
25 νονδ[. . . .   .   ]ιcα
    τὰ ποιο[ῦντα . . . .] . . αὐ-
    τοῦ γὰρ ἀλλαγὴν [] †απο δι
    δολην†. ᵛ καὶ και[νὸν] πε-
    ρὶ τῆc ἀπ[ά]cηc τίcεωc
30 ὅλ[ω]c οὐδὲν εἰρήκαcι
    καὶ καθ' ὅλον ω[. . . . .]ον-
    τοc τοῦ μὴ το[. . . . .]ν
     . .]νον ἐπ[ὶ] του[. . .]cι[.
     . . . .]ε[ι]ν ἀλλ' ὅπερ
35   . . . .]μο[. . . . .
    vestigia unius lineae

Frag. 13 = Indelli 5. ‖ **24-25** ὅ|νον possis ‖ **26** χάρ]ι̣ν̣ Janko ‖ **27** ἀλλαγὴν, quod voluit Asmis, legi videtur in MSI : αλλο[.]ην[Indelli ‖ **27-28** ἀποδι|δο[.]ην legit Indelli : αποτε̣ | δ' ὅλην Wilke (δολην P, ut vid.); fortasse ἀποδί|⟨δομεν μέροc τι μόνον, οὐ⟩|δ' ὅλην McO vel ἀποδί|δομεν Janko ‖ **29** καὶ[νὸν] ‖ **29, 30, 33, 34** Wilke ‖ **31** ὡ̣[c *

Fragment 12[17]

... of others, nor (?) ...
... he will say the state (of) ...
... for all ...

Fragment 13[18]

... things making ... for ... a retribution of it (sc. the offense?).[19] [28] And they have said nothing new at all on the whole subject of vengeance, and in general ... of that which ... not ... to ... but that which ...

---

17. *Cornice* 1, *pezzo* 1. Only the left margin of this fragment survives securely, but it is clear from comparison with the adjacent columns that line 18 is the last or perhaps second-to-last line (though we have retained Indelli's numeration).

18. This fragment is on the first *sezione* of the *pezzo*; only the very bottom survives.

19. The grammar is difficult. The easiest correction of the text is ἀποδιδοίην, but there is no way to explain the optative. If it is part of the apodosis of a future less vivid condition, either one should insert ⟨ἄν⟩, or the surviving words restate an apodosis with ⟨ἄν⟩ immediately preceding these words (e.g.,] ἴca | τὰ ποιο[ῦντα ἄν εἴη, αὐ|τοῦ γὰρ...). Another possibility is that a line fell out between lines 27 and 28 (see the apparatus for a suggestion).

Fragment 14

|¹ α[- - - | (deest una linea) | - - -]o[- - - | - - -]τ|⁵ - - -]π| - - -]θυ[- - - |
- - -]o| (desunt 4 lineae) |¹² - - -]α[- - - |ο̣υν̣[- - - |¹⁴ (desunt 5 lineae) |¹⁹ - - -
]τ[- - - | (deest una linea) |²¹ - - -]ο̣[- - - | (desunt 5 lineae) |²⁷ - - -]μ[- - -

Frag. 14 = Indelli 3 app.

Fragment 15

1–5   ]τ̣[- - - | - - -]επῳ[- - - | - - -]ταxα[- - - | - - -]cμη[.]ι[- - - | - - -]ν
      βαρυ[
6   β]αρυνομ[-
      ἐ]λαττ̣ωμ[α
8   .]ωται[
      ca. 5 lineae desunt
14   ]ατοιc διο[
15   ] Νιxαcιx[ράτ-
      ] αὐτῶι προcτιθ[-
      ] τῆι [- - -]επιτα[
18   ]πα[
      margo fortasse adest

Frag. 15 = Indelli 7. ‖ **6, 7** * ‖ **8** ι̣ϲν̣⟦τ⟧ superpositae ad init. ‖ **15** Wilke ‖ **16** προc-
τίθ[εται Wilke

Fragment 14[20]

[*no words legible*]

Fragment 15[21]

... heavy ...
... weighed down ...
... loss ...
... Nicasic[rates][22] ...
... is ascrib[ed?] to him ...

---

20. This column seems to follow on the previous one, but no connected text remains. The left margin survives only in places, and the numeration is relative to frag. 13.
21. This fragment is at the far right edge of *pezzo* 2 in *cornice* 1, just to the right of frag. 18.
22. Nicasicrates appears later as Philodemus's adversary in cols. 37–41. See excursus 2 in the introduction.

Fragment 16

|² - - -]δε[- - - | - - -]αιτο[- - - | - - -]ογι[- - - |⁵ - - -]ρτ[| - - -]επι[- - -|
(deest una linea) |⁸ - - -]θαι εἰς α[- - - | - - -]νκ[- - - |¹⁰ - - -]ε[- - - | - - -]
ω[- - - | - - -]α[- - - | - - -]θ[- - - |¹⁵ - - -]ται̣π[- - - | - - -]μενουτ[- - - |¹⁷
- - -]κα̣[. .]ν[.]ε[- - - | (deest una linea) |¹⁹ - - -]ι̣ντ[. . .]ιc[.]υ̣[- - - |²⁰
- - -]α[. . .]καρε̣δ̣[- - - | - - -]οντο[- - - | - - -]πιε[.]ο[- - - | - - -]ετα[. .]
ων[- - - | - - -]τοc[. . .]ε[- - - |²⁵ - - -]θ[. .]τ[. . .]κα[- - -
26   ]c. εἰ δὲ καὶ με̣ [
         ]αντι δε̣ κ[
         ] ὡc ὀργίλοc ον̣[
29   ]υ[.]ν[- - - |³⁰ - - -]δοπα̣[. .]τα[- - - | - - -]ττειν [. .]α[- - - | - - -]
         λε[- - - |³³ - - -]τη[

Frag. 16 = Indelli 5. ‖ 16 cμεν legit Wilke ‖ 17 κεκα legit Wilke ‖ 26]πε[Wilke
‖ ad fin. τ vel γ ‖ 28 ὄγ[τωc * ‖ 31 πτειν legit Wilke ‖ 32]γο.μεγι[legit Wilke ‖
33]ατηc δ[legit Wilke ‖ 34] . εα. πι[legit Wilke

Fragment 17

desunt ca. 11 lineae
|¹ - - -] . ην̣[- - - | - - -] . αυτον εν[- - - | - - - δι]ακνίζει το[- - - | - - -]
. . φ.αρυπ[- - - |⁵ - - -]c καὶ τὸν μη[- - - | - - -]ι πτωc[- - - | - - -]ν καταρ[
- - - | - - -]π[- - - | - - -]cτ[- - - | (desunt duae lineae)
12   . . . .αλ[
         .γραφε[
         δ' ὁρῶν α[
15   καὶ μητ[
         τὴν γῆ[ν
         τύπτει [
         λέγων [
         __τι[c] καὶ [
|²⁰ γίνεται [- - -]|²¹ κ . . . .[- - -] |γοc ὡc[- - -] | καὶ τολ[- - -] |λειν τρ[- - -]
|²⁵ . .αρατ[- - -] | . .cτρα[- - -] | . .χαι[- - -] | . .ατα[- - -] |²⁹ . .αλ[- - -

6 πτῶc[ιc Wilke dub. ‖ 16, 19 Wilke ‖ 21-22 λό]|γοc* ‖ 23 τολ[μᾶι Wilke

Anger, Reasoning, and Timasagoras (Frags. 17–33, Cols. 1–7)   155

Fragment 16[23]

... and if even ...
... like an irascible man ...

ANGER, REASONING, AND THE CRITIQUE OF TIMASAGORAS

Fragment 17[24]

... tears into pieces ...
... write[...
... seeing ...
... the earth ...
... beats[25] ...
... saying ...
... comes about ...

---

23. The line numeration of this column is borrowed from frag. 18, to which this is a *sottoposto*. Wilke reported some readings from this column in the apparatus to his frag. E. Because the layer covering it is now gone, we can read more, but this fragment was also damaged, so we partially depend on Wilke's readings for a complete report.

24. This fragment, originally a *sovrapposto* on top of frag. 16, is no longer extant in the papyrus, and we depend on Wilke for the readings and the relative position of the parts of the fragment. He reports that it is clear that lines 12–29 are the left part of a column, which we take to mean that the margin was visible.

25. Probably symptoms of foolish anger were listed here, along the lines of those listed by Chrysippus; see n. 31.

Fragment 18

desunt ca. 19 lineae

μοcιν[..]παγ[..... ..
ο̣ὐκ ἔξω[θε]ν ω[....... ...
μαιν]ομ[έ]νων ἐν τ̣[αῖ]c ὀρ-
γαῖc ἔχει τοὺc ὀ̣φθα̣λμούc,
5 ἔcτιν δ' ὅτε καὶ cτιλβηδό-
νac προ[ϊ]εμέν[ο]υc, ὅπερ ἐ-
οίκα⟨cι⟩ᵛ {μηουτονπρωτ̣} οἱ
πρῶτοι τῶν ποιητῶν
ἐπιcεcημάνθαι, καὶ δε-
10 δορκότac καὶ βλέπον-⟦τ⟧
τac [λοξὰ] εἰc τοὺc οἷc ὀργίζεται, καὶ ἰδίωc ἤ̣δ̣η
τὸ πρόcωπον ὡ[c] ἐπὶ τ̣ὸ
πλεῖcτον ἐνερ[ευ]θ[έc· ἔ]-
15 νιοι δὲ [αἰ]μηρό̣γ̣· [ἔ]ν[ιοι δὲ
τὸν τράχηλον ἐντε[τα-
μένον καὶ τὰc φ[λέ]βα̣[c ἀ]γ-
οιδούcac κα[ὶ] τὸ c[ί]α̣[λο]ν
περίπικρον καὶ [ἁλμυ-
20 ρόν, καὶ το[ιοῦτόν τ]ινα
21 τρόπον κ[..... ....
margo adest

Frag. 18 = Indelli 6. ‖ **2** Wilke ‖ ὥ[cπερ τῶν Janko ‖ **3** μαιν]ομ[έ]νων Wilke ‖ τ̣[αῖ]c Gomperz ‖ **6** Gomperz ‖ **7** add. Gomperz ‖ del. Wilke ("an μὴ οὐ recipiendum?") ‖ **11** Bücheler : [ἄγριον] Gomperz in apparatu ‖ ante εις, hasta horizontalis in summa linea cum hasta verticali ad dextram (π vel η?) N ‖ ⟨τού⟩τουc Janko ‖ **13** Wilke ‖ **14** Gomperz **15** αἰ]μηρό[ν Gomperz (]μηροc[N) ‖ ἔ]ν[ιοι Wilke ‖ **16–18** Gomperz ‖ **19, 20** Wilke ‖ **21** κ[ακοπαθοῦcι Indelli

Fragment 18[26]

... (not?) from without ...
... he has the eyes of [madmen] in his outbursts of anger, eyes [5] sometimes even throwing out flashes, a thing that the greatest of the poets appear to have made a distinguishing mark (sc. of anger),[27] and "gazing," [10] that is looking, ["askance"[28]] at those with whom he is angry, and characteristically he has a flushed face in most cases, but some have [15] a blood-red one, and some have their neck stretched tight, and their veins swelling up, and their saliva very bitter and salty, [20] and in some such way ...

---

26. This fragment stands on a high level, near the right of *pezzo* 2 in *cornice* 1.

27. Early poets, such as Homer, used this trope, as the physiognomists were to do later. The topic is how the Epicurean therapist, assimilated to the medical doctor, can recognize the physical signs (cημεῖα; cf. ἐπιcεcημάνθαι, l. 9) and diagnose anger. Fragment 19 makes the point (repeated in the diatribe) that all this physical distress is frequently over mere trifles.

28. For "flashing eyes" in poetry, see Indelli on line 5. LSJ, s.v. "λοξός" (if λοξά is restored), cites Tyrtaeus, Theocritus, and Apollonius Rhodius for various forms of the idea "looking askance." βλέπω does not occur in Homer, but δέδορκα does (e.g., *Od.* 19.446: πῦρ ὀφθαλμοῖcι δεδορκώc) and is glossed in the scholiasts with βλέπω.

Fragment 19

desunt ca. 16 lineae

1   . . . .]πα
       . . . .]ρι προcεπιπο-
       νήcει], εἰ καὶ τὴν κλεῖ-
       δα δάκνων] τιc θυμοῦτα[ι
5   θύραc κεκλει]μένηc, κα[.
       . . . .]ν μὴ πρὸc
       δη[. . . . .   . . ἀποδ]ηλοῖ
       πολ[λοῖc], πολλάκιc δὲ
       βαθ[εῖαι] βριμώcειc, εἰ
10   καὶ [λίθον] διαρίπτει καὶ
       απο[. . .]τηνου χαν αμα
       αρα[. . . . .]ωcεc αὐτὴν
       ων[. . κατ]ατέμοι θύρα[ν
       πωc [. . . .] δὲ καὶ τῶν πρ[.
15   .]αcι[. . . .]τωc καθεώρ[α-
       κ[ε]ν [. . . .]ε̣καc⟦το⟧cπο[. .] . . .
       δρωι[. . . .]κιc εριων βλα
       τωcο[. . .]υcευματαc καὶ τὰ
       παρεγ[τι]θέμενα δὲ ἐπὶ
20   δόξα[ν] απε[. . .]cαν[.]πο
       λειν[. .] κατὰ τοὺc cο[φούc
       θη[. . . .]λημενουc[. . .
       ον[. . . .]νει δοξα[. . . .
24   ο[. . . . .   . .]υτον[. . . . .
       margo adest

Frag. 19 = Indelli 8. ‖ 2-3 προcεπιπο|[νήcει] * : προcεπιπο|[λεμεῖν] Wilke ‖ 3-4 κλεῖ|[-δα Wilke ‖ 4 [δάκνων] (vel [ἐνθεὶc]) Castiglioni ‖ θυμοῦτα[ι Wilke ‖ 5 Philippson ‖ 6 ἂ]ν Janko ‖ 7, 8 Wilke ‖ 9 Wilke post Gomperz (βαθεί[αc β]ριμώcεωc) ‖].ριμ N ‖ 10 Wilke ‖ 11 χ vel ι̣, γ ‖ 12 ἀρά[ττοι Janko ‖ c vel μ ‖ 13 Wilke ‖ 14 ad fin πρ[N ‖ 15-16 Wilke ‖ 16 το[potius quam το[‖ cπό[γγ]ο̣ν McO ‖ 17 ἐρίων vel ἔριο̣ν Wilke, εργων N ‖ 19, 20 Bücheler ‖ 21 Wilke

Fragment 19[29]

... [will be] yet more [troubled][30] ...

... even though someone [bites] his key[31] in a fit of rage [when the door stays cl]osed ...

... [7] he shows to ma[ny], and often pro[found] bursts of indignation,[32] if he even throws [a rock] and ...[33]

... [13] might cut down the door ...

... has seen ...

... [17] balls of wool (?)[34] ...

... and also the things added ... to opinion ...

... [21] according to the sa[ges] ...

---

29. This column is in the first *sezione* of the third *pezzo* in *cornice* 1. The left part survives only in N, and there maybe be stratigraphical problems we cannot now see.

30. The word προcεπιπονέω is found only at Aesch. *Fals. Leg.* 44.5; ΣF *ad loc.* glosses it as πρὸc τῶι ἤδη πόνωι ἔτι πονῆcαι ("to become troubled above and beyond the trouble one has already").

31. See Chrysippus in *SVF* 3:129,19–30 (from Galen, *Plac.* 4.6 44.5; echoed at *Aff. dig.* 12.12–13), where biting door keys that do not work is given as an example of things the angry man does in a fit of irrational rage over trifles: "We become so insane and so beside ourselves and are so completely blinded in our errors that, sometimes if we have a sponge or a ball of wool in our hands, we throw it at someone (cπόγγον ἔχοντες ἢ ἔριον ἐν ταῖc χερcὶν τοῦτο διαράμενοι βάλλομεν), cursing them, as if we could do some damage by these means, and if we happened to have a sword or something else, we would have used it similarly.... Often in this sort of blindness we bite the keys and beat the doors (τὰc κλεῖc δάκνομεν καὶ τὰc θύραc τύπτομεν) if they will not open quickly enough, and if we trip on rocks, we break them or throw them about and uttering the vilest curses against them as if we were getting vengeance on them (πρόc τε τοὺc λίθουc, ἐὰν προcπταίcωμεν, τιμωρητικῶc προcφερόμεθα καταγνύντεc καὶ ῥίπτοντεc αὐτοὺc εἴc τιναc τόπουc ἐπιλέγοντεc καθ' ἕκαcτα τούτων ἀτοπώτατα)." This passage is probably from the *Therapeutikos Logos* (*Aff.* 4), which Philodemus cites at 1.16–19 as a key text for the genre of the diatribe against anger.

32. See note on 8.24 below.

33. After this point, it is very difficult to join the two parts of the column across the vertical lacuna in the center; some sense can be made below at lines 19–20. It is possible that the left part, which only survives in the Neapolitan *disegno*, belonged originally to a different layer.

34. Thrown for lack of a better missile in impotent anger, if the conjecture is right. This is another allusion to Chrysippus; see n. 31. "Sponge" may be legible in line 16, in which case there is a third allusion to the same famous passage.

Fragment 20

desunt ca. 18 lineae |¹ φα[- - -]|απο̣θ[- - - |πεπρα̣ .[- - -]| . . ₍.₎]α̣ καὶ η[- - -]|⁵ ϲτεπα[- - -] | . ₍.₎]τ̣[- - -]|δετο̣[- - -]|.] ἢ καὶ [- - -]|προϊον ϲ[- - -] |¹⁰ ταῦτα δε[- - -]|γεϲ ἢ τουτ[- - -] |το[ῦ]το μαλ[- - -] | (deest una linea) |τιζομεν[- - -] |¹⁵ ται λαλοῦ[ϲι - - -]| (desunt duae lineae) |μ[ό]νον, ἀλλὰ [- - -]|ηκουϲιν καὶ τ̣[- - -]|²⁰ καιπ̣οαυαν[- - -] | . . . . .]ελαρι[- - -]| . . . .]ωνελϲ[

Frag. 20 = Indelli 9. ‖ 3 πεπραγ[μέν- * ‖ 4–5 ὥ]|ϲτε Janko ‖ 12 Wilke ‖ 13–14 τραυμα]|τίζομεν[- e.g. * ‖ 15 Wilke ‖ 18 Philippson ‖ 18–19 προϲ]|ήκουϲιν Janko ‖ 20 καιπ̣ο[vel fort. καπ̣ιο[legit McO : κλητοαυαν leg. Wilke

Fragment 21

desunt ca. 14 lineae

1   . . . .]ον[. . . . .
    . . . .]νυϲ[. . . . .
    . . .]ϲεφεν[. . . . .   . .]γ[.
    . .]ο̣θαϲγ[. . . .]τ[. .]ν ἢ
5   . . .]λλον, ὀ[δύρ]ονται δέ,
    ἐὰν] ϲτάϲιμο[ν] ἀνάγη-
    ται· καὶ μὰ τ̣ὸν Δία τὸ το[.
    . . . .]ϲυ[.]ν[. . . . .
    . . . .]αλ[. . . .]νε[.
10 . . .] παραλλὰ[ξ] γενό-
    μέν]ων δε[. . . .]ζε πα
    . . . .]νο[. . .] εἶναι λέγ[ε-
    ται ὅπ]ερ εἰ ἦν ἀγανακτ[η-
    τικόϲ], ὅθ[ε]ν οὐχ ὑπὸ τῆϲ ἀ-
15 νάγκηϲ . . . .]ϲαλλο̣
    . . . .]ται κα
    . . . .   γ]ὰρ ὑπὸ τῶν
    φί]λων, ὃ καὶ [δ]ούλοιϲ π[.
    . .]τ̣ειν οἷϲ ἐλευθέροιϲ

Fragment 20[35]

[*no significant words legible*]

Fragment 21[36]

... but they l[am]ent [if] a mourning song is performed (?), and by Zeus the ...

... [10] things happening alternately ...

... is said to be ... [which very thing,] if he were a quarrelsome person; therefore it is not by n[ecessity ...

... [17] for by their friends, which is for slaves also ... appears accessible to free men, but that which is for free

---

35. This column is the right *sezione* of the third *pezzo* in *cornice* 1; line beginnings are poorly preserved.

36. This is the first extant column on the first *pezzo* in *cornice* 2. This *cornice* unrolled cleanly, so the columns (though still called "fragments" by the earliest editors) are largely in the correct order.

20 γ' ἐ]πιβατὸc εἶναι δο-
κεῖ]· ὃ δ' ἐλευ[θ]έροιc καὶ
κρείτ]τοcιν, οὐχ ὁμοίω[c
. . .]τερον· ἔ[δ]ει τοίνυν
. . . .]των ἄλλων ἐχ[. . .
25 . . .]αλλον[.]εων ὀργί{{ζ}}-
26 ζε]ται κα[. . . . .(.)
margo adest

Frag. 21 = Indelli 10. ‖ 3 ἐφεν[ακ- vel φεν[ακ- Janko ‖ 4–5 ἤ]τ[το]ν ἢ | [μᾶ]λλον Janko ‖ 5 ἄ]λλον Henry : [ἔνο]χλον * ‖ 5 ὀ[δυρ]ονται Wilke ‖ 6 Wilke ‖]ταcι[.] ο[.]cαναγη O ‖ 7 Wilke ‖ 8]cυ[ν]ν[temptavit Wilke ‖ 10–11 γενο|[μέν]ων * : γενό|[μενοι] ὧν Wilke ‖ 11 δὲ leg. McO : δὶ Wilke, Indelli ‖ δ' ἐ[νόμι]ζε Janko ‖ 12–14 Wilke : λέγ[ε|θ' ὥcπ]ερ Janko ‖ 14–15 ἀ|[νάγκηc Gomperz, cf. frag. 24.5 : ἀ|[γανακ-τήcεωc Janko ‖ 17 Philippson :]αρυπογων O,]αρ ὑπογων Wilke ‖ 18 φί]λων McO, aeque possis ἄλ]λων * ‖ 18–19 π[ο|ρί]ζειν Janko ‖ 19 τ vel π vel γ sic Wilke legit ‖ 20–21 Wilke ‖ 22 κρεῖτ]τοcιν Philippson ‖ 23 ἐφ' ἕ]τερον Wilke : ἑκά]τερον Janko ‖ ἔ[δ]ει McO ‖ 25 μ]ᾶλλον [θ]εῶν Janko ‖ 25–26 ὀργί|[ζε]ται Janko : ὀργιc⟨θή⟩|[cε]ται Wilke ‖ 26 κα[ὶ *

Fragment 22

desunt ca. 30 lineae
1 ατρα[- - -
τατε[- - -
ἤδη [- - -
τητα [. . . . . ὑπο-
5 / ⟦δυc⟧`λήψ´εcι [
ματαίοι[c - - -
.]υροc[- - -
λογον [- - -
ελο[- - -
10 επι⟦ου⟧κ[- - -
margo adest

Frag. 22 = Indelli 11. ‖ 4–5 Wilke ‖ 6 vel μάταιοι [‖ 8 λόγον vel e.g. εὔ]|λογον * ‖ 10 Ἐπι⟦ου⟧κ[ουρ- Wilke legit et supp.; hodie non vidimus puncta expunctionis

and [more powerful?] men ... not similarly ...
... [23] it was necessary therefore ... of the others (?) ... he is angry ...

Fragment 22[37]

... already ... vain suppositions[38] ... reason (?) ...

---

37. This fragment stands on a small piece of papyrus adjacent to the previous fragment; it does not join with the following fragment.

38. For the conjunction of "suppositions" (ὑπολήψεcι) with "foolish" or "vain" (ματαίοιc, to be understood as synonymous with κεναῖc, "empty"), see 47.18–23 with Philippson 1916, 432. Epicurus already used the adjective as epicene in a similar phrase: τῆι ματαίωι δόξηι (*Kyr. dox.* 24). "Empty anger" makes its first appearance here. Philodemus and the maximalists agree that foolish suppositions (or perhaps the suppositions of fools) lead to empty anger (see 47.18–29).

Fragment 23

desunt ca. 16 lineae |[17] - - -] .ας| - - -]ον| - - -]ο .|[20] - - -]το| - - -]αι| - - - γ]ὰρ| - - -]ιας| - - -]ε̣δι| *margo non adest*

Frag. 23 = Indelli 11 app. ‖ **22** *

Fragment 24

      desunt ca. 13 lineae
1   εμ[. . . .   .
      κα[. . .]υcεα[. . . . .
      ε[. .]αθ[. . . . . ἀπο-
      φα[ί]νει τὸ λε[γόμενον,
5   ὡς οὐ τῆc ἀνάγκηc ἀλ-
      λὰ [τῶ]ν ὑπολήψεων τὰc
      ἀπ[α]τήcειc ἀπεργαζομέ-
      νῳ[ν], ὅπερ ἐπὶ τ[ῶ]ν κατη-
      ναγκαcμένων [πεπ]όν-
10   θαcι. κ[αθ' ὃν] λ[όγον] πένηc
      μὲν καὶ διωργιcμένο[c
      ὑφ' ἑνὸc οἰκέτου φέρει
      πολλάκιc ἐνεπηρεα-
      ζόμενοc ὑπ' α[ὐ]τοῦ. λο-
15   γιcμῶι τοί⟨νυν⟩ [κ]αταλειφθεὶc
      τῶν χρειῶ[ν ἀτ]ευκτή-
      cει. [καὶ πλούcιοc] δέ, ἅτε
      cεμνότεροc ὤν], καὶ πολ-
      λάκι[c ὀ]ρ[γί]ζεται καὶ κο-
20   λάζ[ε]ι, βα[c]ιλεὺc δὲ καὶ
      τὰc κεφαλὰc ἀφαιρεῖ, καὶ
      τὸν αὐτὸν δὲ πενόμε-
      νον μὲν ἄλλον ἔcτιν
      ἰδε[ῖν], πλου[τ]ήcαντα δ' ⟦ε⟧ `ὁ-´
25   πο[ίω]c ἂν μεταβεβλη-

Anger, Reasoning, and Timasagoras (Frags. 17–33, Cols. 1–7)

Fragment 23[39]

[*no words legible*]

Fragment 24[40]

... (this) proves what is [said], that they experience the same thing as in the case of things that are compulsory, because not necessity but their own suppositions create the deceptions.[41] [10] [For that reason,] a poor man, constantly angered by his one slave, must often endure being treated maliciously by him. [14] Therefore, because he failed to reason,[42] he will fail to get what he needs.[43] [17] [Even a rich man], since [he is more arrogant], often both is [an]gry and inflicts punishment, and a king even beheads people, and one can see the same man in poverty being one sort of person [24] and, after he has gotten rich, changed, in whatever way, (into another)....[44]

---

39. Remains of a column on the same piece and to the left of frag. 24.
40. This fragment is the last part of the second *pezzo*.
41. Fools make the excuse that they were compelled to act on their anger, but it was not compulsion but false suppositions that deceived them, and *logismos*, reasoning and reflection, would have set them straight. "Suppositions" (ὑπολήψεις, with its synonym δόξαι; cf. Diogenes Laertius, *Vit. phil.* 10.34) and "compulsion" (τὸ κατηναγκασμένον) are a recurrent theme in the later fragments (frags. 21, 28, 32, and 33). The word πεπόνθασι is a "gnomic perfect," or "empiric perfect" (Smyth §1948).
42. Literally "abandoned by reasoning."
43. For ἀτευκτεῖν τῶν χρείων, "fail to meet one's needs," see Indelli 1988, 140, and P.Herc. 222, col. 3.7 (from Philodemus's *On Flattery*). This phrase does not appear elsewhere in surviving Greek. Irascible masters and their slaves are discussed further in frag. 24.
44. Indelli's note on lines 10ff. suggests that there is a theatrical flavor to these various situations. Indeed, they all seem to feature what are called "blocking characters" in comedy or mime: the poor man always at odds with his one slave, the rich man always punishing his many slaves, the tyrant always saying "off with his head," the newly rich man suddenly turning from humility to aggression. They all fail to get their needs met, not by necessity, but because they cannot reflect and reason.

26   κότ[α . . . . .]δοταιc καὶ
     . .]ω[. . . . .]ε[. .
     margo adest

Frag. 24 = Indelli 12. ‖ 1-5 P legi non potest ‖ 1 εμ[N : ε[O ‖ 2 O : κα[. . .]με[N ‖ 3 ε[. .]αθ[N : ε[. .]αε[O ‖ 3-4 ἀπο]|φα[ί]γει Gomperz (φα[.]νει O, κ[. .]γει N ‖ 4 λε[γόμενον Gomperz : λε[λεγμένον * : λε[λογίcθαι Angeli (λε[O, λη[N) ‖ 6 Gomperz ‖ 7 ἀπ[α]τήcειc Wilke ‖ 7-8 Gomperz ‖ 9-10 [οὐ πεπ]όνθαcι Delattre (longius) ‖ 10 Gomperz : κ[αὶ ἄλ]λ[οc δὲ] Philippson : κ[ρατεῖ]γ [ἐcτί· Angeli ‖ 11 Wilke (ῳ : ο P) ‖ 14 Gomperz ‖ 14-15 λο|γιcμωι Gomperz (-μωc O,]c N) ‖ τοί⟨νυν⟩ Wilke (τo legit McO, το.[O, ται N) : γὰρ legit Delattre-Monet ‖ [κατ]αλειφθεὶc Bücheler ‖ 16 χρειῶ[ν Gomperz ‖ 16-17 ἀτ]ευκτή|cει Wilke ‖ 17 * post [πλούcιοc] Bücheler et [καὶ ἄλλοc] Indelli post Wilke ([καὶ ἕτεροc]) ‖ 18 * : πλούcιοc ὢν Wilke (brevius) : ὑβριcτὴc ὢν Angeli (brevius) ‖ 19-20 fere Gomperz (ὀργίζ]εται καὶ κο|λάc[ε]ι) : [πορίζ]εται {κα} κο|λαc[ι]γ Wilke : κο|λάc[ε]ι Indelli ‖ 20 βα[c]ιλεὺc Gomperz ‖ 24 ἰδε[ὶν Gomperz ‖ πλου[τ]ήcαντα Bücheler ‖ 24-25 ὁ´|πο[ίω]c ἂν DA (cf. Anon. Lond. 6.40-41: ὁποίωc ἂν ἡ μεταβολὴ γένηται) ‖ 25 in marg. sin. Giuliano vestigium noti legit ‖ 25-26 μετα . ε . η|κοτ[legit McO : μεταβεβλη|κα legit Wilke, qui μεταβεβλη|κ⟨ότ⟩α coni. : μεταβαλλη|κα[O ‖ 26 ἐν προ]δόταιc Janko

---

Fragment 25

|¹ - - -]πον[- - - | - - -]του[- - - | - - -]τεν[- - - | - - -]γωμ[- - - |⁵ - - -] κα[- - - | - - -]φε[- - - |⁷ - - -]cαι[- - - | (*desunt lineae ca. 13*) |²⁰ - - -]. αc| - - -]ογ| - - -]ο .| - - -]το[- - - | - - -]αι[- - - |²⁵ - - -]αρ[- - - | - - -]ιαc[- - - |²⁷ - - -]εδι[- - -| - - -

Frag. 25 = Indelli 12 app. ‖ 21 γ vel λ, δ, α

Fragment 26

vestigia plurium linearum |²⁴ - - -]κα[- - - |²⁵ - - -]νομεν[- - - | - - -]τ[- - - | - - -]νο[- - - |²⁸ - - -]πε[- - -

Frag. 26 = Indelli 12 app.

Fragment 25[45]

[*no words legible*]

Fragment 26[46]

[*no words legible*]

---

45. The right margin of this fragment appears to be extant, and line numbers are relative to frag. 23.
46. Mere traces; no margins are extant. Line numbers are relative to frag. 27.

Fragment 27

desunt ca. 9 lineae

1 ....]ταλ[..... .
....]ν[. .]ετ[. .
..... .] ἀνα[π]ηδᾶν οὐδὲ
.....]εγω[.] καρτερεῖν
5 ..... . οἰκ]ίας ἐξέλη
....]ις ἔνδον ε-
....]cθαι καὶ δει
....] ἀκμὴν οι
....]ακαδετειν
10 ....]οφιλαθοι
.... βε]βλημένος
....] γυμνῶ[ι
...]αισημ[..... .]αδε
...]μενων ἦι παρεῖται
15 κἂν] ἀπαντήσας τις εἴπηι
πρὸς] τοῦτον [δ]ή, ἐν ὧι λα-
.....]πτ[. .]εἰπεῖν και
. .]αις πολλ[ά]κις δεγα
.]ασις[. .]ν, ἐὰν δέ τις ἦ
20 τῶ[ν] τ[υχ]όντων ὁ εἰρηκὼς
αλ[..... .]χανε πολλά-
κι[ς] ου[.]ουλομαι αιροεν
π[. ἄξιο]ν οὐδενὸς παι-
δάριόν [τι] λαλῆσαν ἢ γι-
25 νόμενον ἐμποδὼν καὶ
τύπτειν καὶ λακτίζειν.
κἂν ἐμ βαλανείωι δὴ
...]τρα[. .]ετ[.] ὁμολογῆι
. .]ετα[. .]ον, ὁ [δὲ] νουθε-
30 τεῖν περὶ ἁπάντων ἤδη
31 δ[...] ἀεὶ τ[.] πολλά[κι]ς ὑ-
margo adest

Fragment 27[47]

... to leap up,[48] nor ... to endure ... take out of the ho[use] ... indoors ...

... peak (?) ...

... [11] struck ... naked ... whichever way he is going, [and if] someone were to meet him and say [to] this man, while ... to say ... often ... [19] if the person who has said it is an [ordin]ary person ... often... both to beat and to kick a [worth]less slave boy who has said something or gotten in his way. [27] Even if he should agree ... in the bathhouse ...

... but he ... to admonish about everything at that point ... always ... often ...

---

47. This fragment appears to join directly with the following one.
48. Cf. 10.21.

Frag. 27 = Indelli 13. ‖ 3 Wilke ‖ 4 λ]έγω[ν Janko ‖ 5 Bücheler, post quem [ἐκ τῆϲ Janko ‖ 6 το]ῖϲ Janko ‖ 9 sic legit McO :]ακαδεξειν N :]ικαδιζειν O : κ]ακὰ δ' ἕξειν Janko ‖ 10-11 θε]όφιλα θοι|[ν- Janko ‖ 11 Wilke post Bücheler (περιβε-) ‖ 12 Bücheler ‖ 14 παρεῖται legit Henry (ᾳ valde incertum) : πορευ⟨έ⟩ται * : ποθεῖται legit Wilke ‖ 15 Bücheler ‖ 16 Wilke ‖ 18-19 initia superposita esse suspicamur ‖ 18, 20 Bücheler ‖ 21 ἀλ[λ' ἐτύγ]χανε Gomperz ‖ 21-22 Gomperz ‖ 22 sic legimus (μαιδαι ?) :]ουλομαιταιρεν O : οὐ [β]ούλομαι δ' vel "οὐ [β]ούλομαι" Philippson, cf. col. 22.11-12 ‖ 23 π init. O tantum ‖ ἄξιο]ν McO ‖ 24 Wilke ‖ 28 ξύϲ]τρα Schoene : λου]τρά Philippson ‖ 29, 31 Wilke ‖ 31 τ[ὸ] Janko

Fragment 28

desunt ca. 15 lineae

1   δ[.]ζ[. . . . .
    τ[.]ιϲω[. . . . .
    . . .]ν[. .]νεϲ[. . . . .
    πι[.]ω[. .]νε[. . . . .
5   . . .]τοτηϲ[. . . . . ἐ]-
    πειδ[ὰν] ε[. . . . .
    α[.]γηνη πάϲηϲ [. . . . .
    ονοϲαμ[. . . . .
    τατηι[.]χ[. . . . .
10 αδυνατ[. . . . . .
    παθεῖν δόξ[αι, τὸ δὲ βε-
    βιαϲμένον [οὐκ ἔϲτιν.
    κἂν παθεῖν δό[ξαϲ δια-
    νοῆται τὸ κατη[ναγκαϲ-
15 μένον, καθὸ λέγε[ι, καὶ
    χ]ωρὶϲ ἁπάϲηϲ γ[νώϲεωϲ
    καὶ λογικῆ[ϲ ζητήϲεωϲ
    η[.]ναλαϲοι[. . . . .
    .]ν τελούμενον [. . . . .
20 τι τίνωμεν οὐ κατ[ηνάγ-
    καϲται. καὶ γὰρ εἰ μυρ[ιά-
    κιϲ βλάβηϲ μιᾶϲ γέ τ[ου
    ἢ φανταϲίαϲ βλά[βηϲ
    προπεϲούϲηϲ αὐ[τῶι δο-

Fragment 28

... whenever...all ...

... impossible ... [11] to app[ear] to suffer passively, [but the element] of compulsion [does not exist]. Even if he thinks, [15] as he says, that he app[ears] to have suffered what is com[pulso]ry, and (thinks this?) even apart from all [knowledge] and logical[49] [inquiry] ... (it) [has not been made compul]sory. [21] For even if, ten thousand times over,[50] because some one, single harm or appearance of harm has befallen hi[m, it se]ems ...

---

49. Another possibility is "verbal inquiry," that is, inquiry into the meanings of words (here, into what is called "compulsory"); cf. Diogenes Laertius, *Vit. phil.* 10.34: "of types of inquiry, there are those about reality and those about language alone" (τῶν τε ζητήcεων εἶναι τὰc μὲν περὶ τῶν πραγμάτων, τὰc δὲ περὶ ψιλὴν τὴν φωνήν). In Galen, *logikē zētēsis* is distinguished from practical inquiry, and he characterizes the first three books of Chrysippus's *On Emotions* as containing these only, whereas the fourth book, the *Therapeutikos,* is useful for *iasis*, practical therapy and healing (*SVF* 3.457).

50. For εἰ μυριάκιc, cf. κἂν μυριάκιc ... λανθάνηι (Epicurus, *Kyr. dox.* 35).

25   κεῖ cυνημε[. . . . .

Frag. 28 = Indelli 14. ‖ 4 π[̣]ω[O : πλω[N ‖ 5-6 Wilke ‖ 10-11 τὸ μόνον] | παθεῖν δόξ[αι Delattre : δόξ[ηι Gomperz ‖ 11 τὸ δὲ * : τό γε Philippson ‖ 11-12 βε]βιαςμένον Gomperz ‖ 12 οὐκ ἔcτιν Philippson ‖ 13 δό[ξας Janko : δο[κεῖν Wilke ‖ 13-14 δια]|-νοῆται Wilke ‖ 14-15 κατη[ναγκας]|μένον Gomperz ‖ 15 McO : λέγε[ται Gomperz : λέγε[ται καὶ Wilke ‖ 16, 17 Wilke ‖ 19 ἐ]ντελούμενον Wilke ‖ 19-20 ἐάν] | τι McO : ὅ]|τι Delattre-Monet ‖ 20-21 κατ[ηνάγ]|καcται Gomperz ‖ 22 τ[ου * (τ[ινος longius ut vid., cf. *MGH* 195-96) : τ[ις Philippson: γέ π[ως Wilke in editione : γε π[λὴν Wilke ‖ 24 προπεcούcης legit McO (cf. Demetri Laconis [*Sulla grandezza del sole*] P.Herc. 1013.12.4-5 Romeo; Philodemi, *Poem.* 2.99.6 Janko) ‖ αὐ[τῶι * (αυ[N : ατ[O : P hodie non exstat) ‖ 24-25 δο]|κεῖ Janko, fort. longius : κεῖ (=καὶ εἰ) cυνῆμε[ν *

Fragment 29

desunt ca. 22 vel pauciores lineae |¹ - - -] ̣ ̣ι ̣ ̣[- - - | - - -]ακις[- - - | - - -] τους[̣]αι[- - - | - - -]νποτε[- - - |⁵ - - -]μψατ̣ ̣ ̣ν[- - - | - - -]μ[̣ ̣ ̣]ν[̣] ντ̣[- - - | - - -]ν[- - - | - - -]κατ[̣ ̣ ̣]πιτα[- - - |⁹ - - -]ος οὐκ ἔcτ[ι - - - | (*una linea deest*) |¹¹ - - -]υcι[̣ ̣ ̣ ̣ ̣]ταλ[- - - | - - -]πϙντ[̣]ϲτορμη[- - - | - - -] ρ[- - - | - - -]cιcα[̣ ̣]ν[- - - |¹⁵ - - -]cαυτο[- - - | - - -]ητο[- - - | - - -]τ [̣ ̣ ̣ ̣]εδοκι[- - - | - - -]ενκ[̣]μα[- - - |¹⁹ - - -]μεν[̣]μο[- - - | (*incertum quot lineae desint*)

Frag. 29 = Indelli 15. ‖ 5 ἐμέ]μψατο̣ Janko : ἐπέμψατο * ‖ 12 τὸ Ὁμη[ρικὸν Philippson

---

Fragment 30

9   π[- - |¹⁰ - - -]και[- - - |παρη[
12   ̣]δ' ἔπεcτ̣ι καλο[ν - - -
      ̣]επας[̣ ̣]και τοὺς [- - -
      ̣]ομ[- - -
15   ενοις[- - -
      ἡ]μερ[ω]τάτοις [- - -
      ̣]θεν[̣ ̣]εcτας[- - -
18   . . . . .]νο[̣]ου[- - -

Frag. 30 = Indelli 15 app. ‖ 12 Wilke ‖ 16 Wilke

Fragment 29[51]

[*no significant words legible*]

Fragment 30[52]

... is on ... fine ...
... to very gentle-tempered[53] (persons?) ...

---

51. *Cornice* 3 unrolled mostly cleanly. The margins are absent, but it seems likely that this piece comes from near the bottom.
52. This column is partly visible as a *sottoposto* to the right of frag. 29. The left margin is visible at points, and the lineation is borrowed from frag. 28.
53. Probably "sages"; see 44.26 below.

Fragment 31

14 ..]μηταιτα[- - -
15 οὐ]κ αἰδουμ[εν- - - -
..]ειδες[- - -
λευσυ[- - -
.]υς ἐπιλέγω[ν - - -
"τέτλαθι δή, κραδίη [" - - -
20 ουμενος[- - -
ἐκθυμαν[εῖ - - -
.]αμεν[- - -
.]παρα[- - -
.]η[- - -
25 .]αθ[- - -

Frag. 31 = Indelli 17 app. ‖ 15 δουμ̣[legit Indelli : ἀθυμ̣[- legit Wilke : καιδουμ̣[εν- (= καὶ αἰδουμ[εν-) * : καὶ δοῦλ[ος Henry ‖ 16 ις̣.δες[‖ 16–17 βασι]|λεὺς Philippson ‖ 17 ὑ[πὲρ * ‖ 17–18 Ὀδυς|σε]ὺς fort. longius * ‖ 18 Wilke : ἐπιλέγω[μεν Rabbow ‖ 19 Gomperz primus citationem Homericam notavit, κραδίη add. Janko; cf. Aeliani, Nat. An. 5.54; Philostrati, Vit. Apoll. 1.14; Himerii, Or. 69.31 ‖ 19–20 νο]|ούμενος Janko ‖ 21 Wilke

Fragment 32

incertum quot lineae desint

1   ....]πα[..... .
....]αθαλ[.. κατη-
ναγκ]ασμέν[-..... ..
....] πάντ[ω]ς....
5   ..... .]α[.] ἀλλὰ καθ[...
...]μεν[.]ς[.]οις[.....]ν
....]οῦντας συν
....]ι πάντως
....] γὰρ δόξαις
10 .....]ουσιμαν [...]υ[.
....]κατα̣[..]σε

Fragment 31[54]

... not reverenc[ing (?) ...
... applying rational appraisal ... "endure, indeed, [O my heart"[55] ...
... he will be utterly enraged ...

Fragment 32[56]

... [compul]sory ... in every way ... but according (?) ...
... in every way ... [9] for by beliefs ...

---

54. This fragment is the rightmost in the *cornice*, and only the left margin survives. It stands a layer lower than frag. 32, which means that it comes from one or two columns before that fragment. Lineation is taken from frag. 32.

55. *Od.* 20.19, the opening of Odysseus's address to his own angry heart (κραδίη); see the introduction, pp. 50–52. *Epilogismos* ("rational appraisal") may be mentioned as a cure, like *logismos*, for the apparently "compulsory" influence of anger on the soul. Cols. 1–7 argue that the diatribe against anger provokes *epilogismos* in its audience, if done rightly.

56. Only the right margin is visible; it is likely that not much is missing from the bottom of the fragment.

```
12      . . ἀ]λλά τιcιν οὐ γ[ . . . ]ν
        . . μ]ηδ' ὀργα[ῖc] γο[ . . . ]α
        . . . . . ] ἀκολουθοῦ[cι]ν
15      . . . . . ]c πάντωc, [ἀ]λλ' οὐ
        . . . κατ]ηνα[γκα]cμένοιc
        . . . . . . . . . . . ]λ[ . ]γενη
        . . . ἠκ]ολού[θ]ηκεν δὲ
        . . . . . . . . . . ]ην cυναφθη-
20      . . . . . ]μεν δὴ τὰc τού-
        των ὑπ]ολήψειc ου νο
        κα[ . . . ἐ]νεῖναι τὴν ὀργὴν
        . . . ]κ[ . . ], ἧι δὲ νοεῖται φύ-
        cιc τ]οιοῦτο, ⌐ οὐ δεκτι-
25      κὴ π]άντωc, ἢ τοῦδέ τι-
        ν]ό[c] ἐcτιν φύcιc καὶ οὐ-
        κ ἄλλων] ἐcτίν, ἢ cὺν τού-
        τωι, κα]θάπερ καὶ cὺν τῶι
        ἄλλωι,] τὸν μὲν ὁρμᾶν
30      . . . . . . . ] ἀπὸ τοῦ ν[ . .
        . . . . . . . . . . . ]ω[ . . .
        incertum quot lineae desint
```

Frag. 32 = Indelli 16. ‖ 2 ἀγ]αθ' ἀλ[λὰ Janko (vel ἄλλα *) ‖ 2-3 * (]αc μεν[Willke) ‖ 11]γατ[N ‖ 12-15 Wilke ‖ 12-13 γ[ίνο]ν|[ται Janko, fort. longius ‖ 15 οὐ | [τοῖc * : οὔ|[τωc Janko ‖ 16 * ‖ 17-18 γένη vel γένη||[ται Janko ‖ 18 Philippson ‖ 19-20 cυναφθή|[cεcθαι] μὲν DA : cυναφθή|[cομαι] μὲν Janko : cυναφθῇ Philippson ‖ 20-21 * : τού|[του] Wilke ‖ 21 McO : ἐπιπλήξειc legit Wilke (επι[. .]ληψειc O, επι[. .]-ληξειc N, sed επι superpositas vidit McO) ‖ 21-22 οὔνε|κα [τοῦ] Janko ‖ 22 * : ν εἶναι Bücheler ‖ ad init. κα[.] N, fortasse superpositae ‖ ante νεινaι, litteras ταχ superpositas esse vidit McO ‖ 23 [φυcι]κ[ὴν Bücheler, fort. longius ‖ 23-24 φύ|[cιc Bücheler ‖ 24 τ]οιοῦτο leg. McO (τ)οιούτο[υ] Wilke) :]οιουτο . . ουδε O :]οιουcπ: . . ουδε N ‖ 24-25 Delattre-Monet (cf. 43.33, 44.1) : οὐδ' ἑκτι|κὴ Wilke (cf. 20.18) ‖ 25 π]άντωc Wilke ‖ 25-26 τοῦδέ τι|[ν]ό[c] Philippson : τοῦδ' ἔτι | [π]ο[ύ Wilke ‖ 26-27 * vel οὐ | [πάν-των] possis : οὐ|[χ ὁμοία] Wilke ‖ 27-28 τού|[τωι, κα]θάπερ Wilke ‖ 28 leg. McO : καὶ ουπτω legunt Wilke et Indelli ‖ 28-29 cὺν τῶι | [ἄλλωι] e.g. * (vel cύν τωι ἄλλωι, cf. MGH 195-96) ‖ 30-31 ν[ο]ουμένου Janko

... but to some not ... not even in fits of anger ... they follow ... in every way, but not ... [16] for those [com]pel[l]ed ...

... follow ... conjoined with ... the suppositions of these ... anger is in (him?) ... [23] but in the way such a thing is considered to be ["nature"], it is entirely incapable of this, or it is the nature of a given person and not [of others], or with this person [28] just as with [another] ... that the one desires ... from the ...[57]

---

57. These are the disappointing remains of an account of what sort of people's "nature" (lines 23–27) is irascible and thus might be thought (wrongly) to experience anger by compulsion. "Compulsion" (ll. 2–3 and 16) and "(mere) suppositions" (ll. 9 and 20–21) are visible or probable here and there in the text.

Fragment 33

(*incertum quot lineae desint*) |¹ τιν[- - - |μενως [- - - |φιλαυτ[- - - - |τ[.]c[-
- - |⁵ και φ[- - - |αcορο̣[- - - |τουc και[- - - |νυν τη[- - - |εcτιν̣ [- - - |¹⁰ οἵαc
α[. . .]υο[- - - |ημε[- - - |δεcε[- - - |μεναπ[- - - |του και [.]αc[- - - |
15   μαcαμεντ[. . . . .κατη-
      ναγκαcμένα̣ [- - -
      φύcει ταc[- - -
     —. . . .]ε̣γ̣μεν[- - -   εἰ-
      πόντεc ὅτ[ι ₍.₎. . . .ἀνέκ-
20   φευκτον [- - -
      τοῦτο δὲ κ̣[αὶ κατηναγ-
      καcμένου, ἧ̣ι̣[- - -
      οὕτω ηρα[- - -
      π[. . .]ον ὥcτε[- - -
25   . . . . .]α[- - -
      incertum quot lineae desint

Frag. 33 = Indelli 17. ‖ 3 Wilke ‖ 14-15 ἐθαύ]|μαcα μέν[τοι Janko : [ὠνο]|μάcαμεν Philippson ‖ 15-16 Wilke : -μένα̣[c Philippson ‖ 18-19 εἰ]|πόντεc ὅτ[ι Janko ‖ 19-20 ἀνέκ]|φευκτον Philippson : φευκτόν Wilke ‖ 21-22 * vel δ' ἐκ [τοῦ κατηναγ]|καcμέ-νου * ‖ 22 καcνενηυ[O , καιτωντη[N) ‖ 23 οὕτω, ηρα[- (ἢ ῥα-?) * potius quam οὕτω⟨c⟩ ηρα[- * (ουτωπ[. ₍.₎]ρα[O, ουτωc[.]ξ[N)

Column 1

desunt ca. 13 lineae

1   . . . .]γο̣ι̣
          . . . .]ηcα̣ι̣ την
          . . . .]πρ[.]υ̣cιν ων
          . . . .]ν̣ε̣ια̣ κατα
5   . . . . οὐ]δ̣' [ἀνα]ίνο`μαι´ `τοῦτο. πᾶcι γὰρ ὡc ἐκεῖνο´ φα-

1.5 μαι supra lineam et τοῦτο – ἐκεῖνο in margine dextro addidit librarius ‖ οὐ]δ' Philippson ‖ [ἀνα]ίνομαι Schoene

Fragment 33[58]

... self-lo[ve- (?) ...
... com]pulsory ... by nature ...
... saying that ... [in]escapable ...
... but this is characteristic [also of what is comp]ulsory, in the way that ...
... thus ...
... so as to ...

Column 1[59]

[*circa seventeen lines missing or untranslatable*]

"...[nor do] I [deny?] this. For it is obvious

---

58. Only the left margin is visible, but it is likely that the extant text is from near the bottom of the column.
59. From this point on, the papyrus unrolled very cleanly, and there are no major problems with stratigraphy or order, except for the fragments of tops pasted in above the columns (frags. A–H), some of which cannot be securely placed.

1.6 νερόν ἐςτιν] ὅτι κα-
κόν], ο[ὕ]τω κ[αὶ] τοῦτο. δι-
ὰ̣ [μ]ὲν̣ δὴ τοιούτων, ˇ ὅ-
τι ληρῶδές ἐcτι τὸ ψέ-
10 γειν ἐγκεχείρηκεν, ἀ-
δολέcχωc δὲ καὶ κα-
θάπερ εἴωθεν. ˇ εἰ μὲ-
ν οὖν ἐπ̣ετίμα{ι} τοῖc
ψέγουcι μ[ό]νον, ἄλλο
15 δὲ μηδὲ ἓν ποιοῦcιν
ἢ βαι̣[ό]ν, ὡc Βίων ἐν τῶι
Περὶ τῆc ὀργῆc καὶ Χρύ-
cιπποc ἐν τ[ῶ]ι Πε[ρ]ὶ παθῶν Θεραπευ[τι]κῶι, κἂν
20 μετρίωc ἵcτατο. νῦν
δὲ τ[ὸ] καθόλ[ο]υ̣ τὰ πα-
ρακολουθοῦν[τ]α̣ κακὰ
τιθέναι πρὸ ὀμμάτων
καταγέλαcτ̣[ο]ν εἶναι
25 καὶ ληρῶδεc ὑπολαμ-
βάνων, αὐ[τόc ἐcτι ληρώ-
27 δηc καὶ κα[ταγέλαcτοc ‖

1.6, 7 Wilke ‖ **8** Gomperz ‖ **13** del. Hayter ‖ **14** Gomperz, Spengel ‖ **16** Hayter : ἠβαι̣[ό]ν Hayter ‖ **18** Gomperz, Spengel ‖ **19, 21** Gomperz ‖ **22, 24** Gomperz, Spengel ‖ **26-27** αὐ[τὸc ληρώ]|δηc καὶ κα[ταγέλαcτοc Hayter; ἐcτι Gomperz

to all that, just as that is an evil, so is this." [7] By such arguments, indeed, he (sc. Timasagoras) undertook (to prove) that "blaming (anger) is ridiculous,"[60] but idly, as is his custom. [12] Now, if he were rebuking those who only blame (anger) and do little or nothing else about it, like Bion in his *On Anger* and Chrysippus in the *Therapeutikos Logos* of his *On Emotions*,[61] he would be taking a reasonable position. [20] As it is, in supposing that the general idea, (i.e.,) putting the consequent evils before one's eyes, is ridiculous and raving, he him[self is rav]ing and ri[diculous]....[62]

---

60. What Timasagoras meant is that the ψόγος ὀργῆς, the "diatribe" assailing anger, is not legitimate *therapeia,* but mere epidictic oratory (see the introduction, pp. 54–57). Cf. cols. 5.12 ψέγειν and 6.31 ψέγοντες (both in the section introducing Philodemus's own diatribe against anger).

61. Book 4 of his *On Emotions* was often cited separately under the title θεραπευτικὸς λόγος (see n. 49 above and n. 125 in the introduction). Philodemus may mean that Chrysippus and Bion did not suggest that anger could have any positive value (like his own "natural anger") or did not say enough about its therapy and that Timasagoras rebuked Basilides and Thespis, even though they did put forward such a theory.

62. Note the chiasmus, if the supplements are correct. On "before one's eyes," see n. 74. "Consequent evils" that follow the empty anger of fools, unforeseen by them, are a major theme of the diatribe. Near the end of the treatise, we find that the sage and others who feel natural anger can foresee and avoid them all (cf. 42.16–20).

Fragment A

1
---]μ[. . .]ν μ[---
---]τε καταλ[. . . .]ακ[---
---]γ[. . .]απν[---
---]ς ὥστε [---
5
---]αιτω[---
---]ω[---
---]γως[---

Column 2

desunt ca. 16 lineae

1   φυςικαι[. . . . .](.)
    πάθει γιγ[. . . . .](-)
    ςχετο[. . . . .]..-
    ςιν ως[. . . . .]..-
5   νομεθα[. . . . .]ον
    τῶν λογις[μῶν. ὁπό]ταν
    δὲ καταςτο[χάςη]ται
    τὸ λανθανόμ[ενον—τὰ
    δὲ ἔξω φανερ[ὰ κα]θέ-
10 ςτηκε καὶ μάλι[ςτ]α τῶι
    δυναμένωι πα[θο]λο-
    γεῖν—οὔτε π[αρῆχεν] ἡ-
    μᾶς, καὶ [πᾶςι]ν φανε-
    ρόν ἐςτι[ν ἔχειν] ὡς εἴ-
15 ρηκε· τό τε [τῆς δι]αθέ-
    ςεως, ἀφ' ἧς [περις]πῶ[ν-

2.1 φυςικαὶ Wilke vel φυςικαῖ[ς *, sc. ὀργαί, ὀργαῖς ‖ **1–3** ἐν] ǀ πάθει γιγ[όμενοι ἀνα]ǀςχετο[ί Wilke (fort. hiatus: γιγ[όμενον ἀνα]ǀςχετό[ν Philippson : γίγ[εςθαι vel sim. *) ‖ **4–5** (ἐ)γι]ǀνόμεθα Janko ‖ **6** Wilke ‖ **7** Philippson (ex καταςτο[ON) : fort. καταςτο[χάζη]ται * : καταςτή[ςει εἰς ὄψιν Wilke (hiatus) ‖ **8–9** [τὰ] ... φανερ[ὰ *: [τὸ] Wilke ... φανερ[ὸν Gomperz ‖ **9–11** Gomperz ‖ **12** π[αρῆχεν Philippson : π[αρῆγεν McO : π[αράγει Wilke ‖ **13–16** Wilke

Fragment A[63]

[no words legible]

Column 2

[circa sixteen lines missing]

... natural (angers?) ... by feeling com[es about (?)] ... of his reasonings. [6] [When]ever he (sc. the philosopher censuring anger) inf[ers] what is hidden from him[64]—what is external is obvious, especially to a person who can reason about emotions[65]—he has not m[isled] us, and it is "obvious to all"[66] that things [are] as he has said. [15] And that element of their disposition, from which they (angry people) become distraught,

---

63. On the placement of this fragment, see the introduction, pp. 108–9.
64. Medicine in antiquity was often called a cτοχαcτικὴ τέχνη, an art of plausible conjecture; see Ierodiakonou 1995. Philodemus in this respect compares it to ethical therapy by παρρηcία ("frankness"), which is also a stochastic art. See his *Lib.* frags. 1.5–10; 23.9–12; and especially 57.5–12: "reasonable conjectures [εὐλόγιcτα cτοχαcτά, sc. about one's pupils' feelings] do not always come out as was hoped, however strictly the elements of one's reasoning are based on likelihood."
65. Cf. Marcus Aurelius, 8.13 (to deal rightly with impressions, one must try three things: reasoning about natural causes, reasoning about passions, and logical argument: φυcιολογεῖν, παθολογεῖν, διαλεκτικεύεcθαι). At Epicurus, *Nat.* [34] [33].5–6 Arrighetti 1972, 358 = Laursen 1997, 48–49, the topic of the emotions (*pathologikos tropos*) is contrasted with that of their causes (*aitiologikos tropos*). Both verb and adjective are rare.
66. Philodemus sarcastically paraphrases Timasagoras's words πᾶcι ... φα|νερόν (see 1.5–6 above), as he will do yet again in 5.22 and in lines 9–10 of this column (and see n. 70).

2.17 ται, δι᾽ ἣν ἀγ[αριθμ]ήτοιc
συνεχόμ[ενοι] κακοῖc,
ἀναγεν[ν]ᾶ[ν πάλι]ν ἐπι-
20 cτάμεθα κα[κὰ ἐ]πὶ πο-
λύ, φιλολογια[..] ουχω
...]τρο[. ἐκ πί]cτε[[c]]ωc
....]τε[...]απε
24 ....]υδια[..]αλα‖

Column 3

desunt ca. 13 lineae

1 ....]ωcδ[..
....]θαι τὴν
....]εναπο
....]ρ ἤδη τ[.
5 ....]λλωι. ᵛ διόπερ
ἀναγράφ]ων τὰ μὲν ἀ-
γ]νοο[ύμεν]α τελέωc, τ[ὰ
δ᾽ εἰc λήθην ἀφιγμένα,
τὰ δ᾽ ἀνεπιλογιcτού-
10 μενα—τοῖc γε μεγέθε-
cιν, εἰ μηθὲν ἕτερον—τὰ
δ᾽ οὐκ ἀθρόωc γε θεωρού-
μενα, καὶ τιθεὶc ἐν ὄ-
ψει μεγάλ[ην] ἐνποιεῖ
15 φρίκην, ὥ[c]τε τοῦ πα-
ρ᾽ αὐτὸν εἶναι προcυ῾πο῾μνη-
῾c῾θέντοc ἀποφυγεῖν ῥᾳ-
δίωc· τοῦτ[ο] γὰ[ρ] δὴ προc-

2.17 ἀγ[αριθμ]ήτοιc Bücheler ‖ **18–20** Wilke ‖ **19** ἀναγεν[ν]ᾶ[cθαι ἡμῖ]ν Delattre (longius: -cθ᾽ possis) ‖ **21** φιλολογία Wilke ‖ [δὲ] * ‖ **22** ἰα]τρὸ[c McO (vel ἰα]τρο[ῖc) post Gomperz (ἰα]τρο[ὶ) ‖ ἐκ πίc]τεωc DA (cf. Sexti, *Pyr.* 2.141 = *Math.* 8.308) ‖ **3.4** ὥcπε]ρ Wilke ‖ **6** ἀναγράφ]ων Wilke : ὑπογράφ]ων * : παριcτάν]ων Gomperz ‖ **7, 14** Hayter ‖ **15** Bücheler ‖ **18** Gomperz

through which (they are) afflicted[67] by numberless evils, we know begets new evils all over again, in most cases.[68] [21] ... philosophical reasoning ... [from belief?] (can change this disposition?),

---

Column 3

[circa seventeen lines missing or untranslatable]

... [5] for which reason, [by describ]ing some things that are completely unknown (sc. to the patient), some that have been forgotten, others that are being left unappraised—at least with respect to their seriousness, if in no other regard—[11] and others that he never contemplated as a whole, and by putting all this in his sight, he (sc. the therapist) creates a great fright, so that (the patient), now that he has also been reminded that it is up to him,[69] can escape it with ease. [18] For this is what

---

67. For this use of the participle with εἰσί understood, see p. 119 in the introduction and λεγόμενοι in 43.40. Delattre suggested "through which, afflicted by numberless evils, we learn that new evils are begotten for us to a great extent; philosophical reasoning...."

68. The term ἀναγεννάω, first attested here, is used mostly in Christian texts influenced by 1 Pet 1:23. The philosophical therapist can interrupt this process; there is no reason to wait till the patient calms down (col. 7).

69. The construction παρά + accusative of a person is a standard formula in Epicurean language for indicating moral responsibility; see nn. 98 and 212 in the introduction.

3.19 τιθέασιν̣ [οἱ κ]α̣ὶ̣ μέτρι-
20 ο̣[ι] τῶν φιλ[οc]όφων, οἱ
δὲ] γενν[αῖοι] καὶ τοὺc τρό-
πο]υc, δ[ι' ὧν] ἂν ἥκιcτα
τοῖc ὀργί[λοιc] πάθεcιν
περιπίπτ̣[οι]μεν, ὑπο-
25 γράφουcιν. ⸏ ὅθεν δὴ καὶ
λέγων ὡc [ἄ]π̣[αcιν] φ[ανε-
27 ρώτερον καθ[έcτηκε ‖

Fragment B

1   - - -]θωcαντα ψ[- - -
    - - -]α̣ντουδε[- - -
    - - -]ο παθεῖν εγ[- - -
    - - -]α̣[.]πομενο̣ν[- - -
5   - - -]χολ[. .]θ[- - -

Column 4

desunt ca. 16 lineae

1   . .]πα[. . . . .
    γαιτα[. . . . .
    .]εγεcθ[. . . . .   -
    μ]ενοιc τ[ῶν ἰα]τρῶν τό τε
5   μέγεθοc [τῆc] νόcου καὶ
    τὰ γει[νόμεν]α δι' αὐτὴν
    πάθη καὶ [τὰc] ἄλλαc δυc-

3.19-20 οἱ κ]α̣ὶ̣ μέτρι|ο̣[ι Henry : κἀ]μ̣ μετρί|ω[c Wilke, fort. longius]αcμετ- N^ac :]μμετ- N^pc ‖ **20** φιλ[οc]όφων Gomperz ‖ **21** δὲ] Henry : δὴ] Crönert ‖ γενν[αῖοι Gomperz ‖ **21-22** τρό|[πο]υc Hayter ‖ **22** δ[ι' ὧν] Bücheler ‖ **23** Hayter (οργα[N) ‖ **24** Bücheler ‖ **26** λεγωνωc .τ[. . .]φ[O (P post νω non legitur) ‖ [ἄ]π̣[αcιν] Bücheler : []π̣ᾶcιν : τ[οῦτο] Gomperz (longius) ‖ **26-27** Bücheler : c]φ[αλε]|ρώτερον Gomperz ‖ **27** καθ[έcτηκε Gomperz ‖ **B.1** κατορ]θ- vel διορ]θ- * ‖ ψ[ευδ- vel ψυχ- Janko ‖ **3** τ]ὸ Wilke ‖ **4.2-3** ὀ|ρ]έγεcθ[αι Wilke : ψ]έγεcθ[αι * : λ]έγεcθ[αι Philippson **4** -μ]ένοιc Janko ‖ τ[ῶν ἰα]τρῶν Gomperz ‖ **5** Hayter ‖ **6** Bücheler ‖ **7** Gomperz

even ordinary philosophers present to him, but the really good ones also sketch out the behaviors by which we might fall prey to angry passions as little as possible. [25] That is, in fact, why, in saying that it is quite "obvious" to everyone⁷⁰ ... (sc. that Timasagoras is mistaken?) ...

Fragment B[71]

... to feel emotion ...

Column 4

[*circa nineteen lines missing or untranslatable*]

... [4] although some?] of the doctors (sc. point out?) the seriousness of the disease, the sufferings that happen because of it, and its other difficulties,[72]

---

70. If correctly restored, ἅπαϲιν φανερώτερον is Philodemus's mocking amplification of Timasagoras's πᾶϲι φανερόν.
71. On the placement of this fragment, see the introduction, p. 109.
72. For δυϲχρηϲτία in Philodemus, Polybius, and Cicero, see n. 141.

4.8   χ]ρηστίας, ἐ[νί]οτε [δ]ὲ καὶ
      τ]οὺς κινδύ[ν]ους, [[α]] λανθά-
10   ν]ει τὰ μὲν [κα]θόλου τοὺς
      κάμνοντ[ας], τὰ δ' ἐπιλο-
      γιστικῶς, ὅ[θ]εν ἀμελέσ-
      τεροι πρὸς τὴν ἀποφυ-
      γ]ὴν ὡς μετρίων ἐνεστη-
15   κότων καθίστανται, τε-
      θέντα δὲ πρὸ ὀμμάτων
      ἐ]πιστρ[εφ]εῖς πρὸς τὴν
      θ]εραπείαν παρασκευ-
      άζει. καὶ γὰρ ἐνταῦθα, τὰ
20   μὲν οὐδ' ὅλως ἐνθυμού-
      μ]ενοι, τὰ δ' [ο]ὐ καθαρῶς, οὐ-
      δὲ κεχρῆ[σθ]αι θέλουσιν εἰς
      θερ]απείαν ἑαυτούς,
24   μαθ]όντες δὲ κατὰ το‖

Column 5

      desunt ca. 10 lineae
1   ....]ατε[.......... .....
      καὶ τοῦτο κ[..... ...
      ουτο[.]προστ[..... .
      τεχ[....]οτ[..... ...
5   .]οντ[.]αλειπο[..... .
      ....]ν νῦν [..... .
      ....]ως, οἱ δὲ κα-
      λο]ῦσ[ι] προσέχειν ἐπι-

4.8 Hayter ‖ **9–10** λανθά|[ν]ει Gomperz ‖ **10–12** Hayter ‖ **11** ⟨ἀν⟩επιλογιστ{ικ}ῶς possis* ‖ **14** Gomperz ‖ **17** Hayter ‖ **18** Gomperz ‖ **21–23** Gomperz (22:]επεχρη[leg. Wilke, O; corr. iam N²: οὐ|[κ] ἐγχει[ρί]σαι Schoene) ‖ **24** Gomperz: διδ]όντες Bücheler ‖ ad fin. sic O : κατατων N : P legi nequit ‖ **5.2–3** χ[αὶ ἄλλο τοι]|οῦτο Wilke ‖ **7–8** Wilke (δεχα P, corr. iam N²)

and sometimes also its dangers, these things escape the sick men's notice—some generally, others by (failure of) rational appraisal,[73] [12] which is why they become too careless of their escape (sc. from these dangers), as if moderate (evils) were afflicting them, but these (evils), once put before their eyes,[74] render them attentive to their treatment. [19] In fact, in this case (i.e., philosophical therapy), because they do not consider some of these at all and others not clearly, they do not even want to commit themselves to therapy, but once they have learned ... according to (?) ...

Column 5

[circa sixteen lines missing or untranslatable]

... [7] and others call (on them)

---

73. Philodemus apparently means something like "others escape him for lack of appraisal," picking up τὰ δ' ἀνεπιλογιcτούμενα (3.9-10), but the use is strained and emendation is possible. Indelli compares Philodemus, *Rhet.* 1.254.33 (Sudhaus 1892-1896) (lib. inc., P.Herc. 1669), where the same adverb must mean "rationally" (see introduction, p. 56) and is used in opposition to παθητικῶc "emotionally": "what is [just] and good and [becoming] our philosophers affirm to be the same as what most people conceive them to be (τοῖc ὑπὸ τῶν πολλῶν νοουμένοιc), with the sole difference that we conceive them not just passively but by applying rational appraisal to them (τ[ῶι] μὴ παθητικῶc μόνον ἀλλ' [ἐ]πιλογ[ι]cτικῶc αὐτὰ κατανοεῖν)." Because they cannot vividly picture their disease, they cannot reason about it clearly and with due urgency, and they calculate incorrectly as a result. To use *epilogismos* on anger is to deal actively with one's plight (whether emotional or physical) rather than passively submit to it; *epilogismos* leads to seeing καθαρῶc (l. 21).

74. Putting the consequences of evildoing before one's eyes for rational appraisal (τιθέναι πρὸ ὀμμάτων; cf. 1.21-23 and 3.13-14), is key to Epicurean therapy; it also appears at *Lib.* frag. 26.4-5; cf. frag. 78N.1-3 (ἐπιδεικνύναι πρὸ ὀμμάτων) and col. 17a.4-14. Here it is defended as a paramedical virtue of the right kind of diatribe. See further Tsouna 2003.

5.9 μελέςτερον τῆι θερα-
10 πείαι καὶ μὴ παρολιγω-
ρεῖν οὐδ' ὧν ἕνεκεν ἰα-
τροῖς [ἐ]νχρῄζ[ει] τὸ ψέγειν
ἧττον ἀγνοουμένων,
εἰ δὲ μή γ', ἐπ' ἴςον, τῶν τε
15 μεγεθῶν καὶ τῶν ϲυνα-
πτομένων τα[ῖϲ] νόϲοιϲ
κακῶν καὶ ταῖϲ ὀργαῖϲ. αὐτῶι μ[ὲ]ν αἱ μέλ`λ´ουϲαι πα-
ρακολου[θήϲ]ειν ϲυμφοραὶ
20 διὰ τὴ[ν ὀργ]ὴν τὴν πρὸς
Βαϲιλεί[δ]ην καὶ Θέϲπιν
οὐκ ἦϲαν φανεραί, καίτοι
πέρατα, καθάπερ ᾤ[ι]ετο,
προϲ[τιθε]μένωι δριμύ-
25 τητο[ϲ]. οὕτω⟦ι⟧ δ' ἐϲτὶ τυ-
φλόϲ, ᾧ[ϲ]τε μακρῶι προύρ-
γιαίτε[ρ]ον ὑπάρχ⟦ει⟧`ο´ν τὰ
τ⟦α⟧`ο´ῖϲ λογίμοιϲ ϲοφ]οῖϲ νο-
μου[. . . . .
30 ῥαι[δίωϲ. . . .   . ǁ

5.12, 13, 16 Gomperz ǁ **18** Hayter : μ[ὴ]ν Philippson : μ[ὲ]ν ⟨δὴ⟩ Wilke (hiatus) ǁ **19–20** Hayter ǁ **21, 23** Crönert ǁ **24** Hayter ǁ **25, 26** Gomperz ǁ **27** Hayter : ὑπάρχοντα Wilke ǁ **5.28** Crönert ǁ **28–29** νο|μο⟨θετο⟩ύ[μενα ἐπιθεωρεῖν] Crönert : νο|ϲοὺ[ϲ ποιήϲαντα ἐφορᾶν] Delattre-Monet (29 ad init. ϲου[O) : νό|ϲου Janko : alia possis ǁ **30** ῥαι[δίωϲ λέγειν Indelli

to pay attention more carefully to this therapy and not to pass over lightly the seriousness and the evils attached to their diseases and to their fits of anger, since the reasons why it is indispensable for doctors to use blame are no less unknown (to Timasagoras?), or at any rate equally as unknown.[75] [17] So the misfortunes[76] that were going to follow from his anger toward Basilides and Thespis were not "obvious" (sc. to him),[77] even though, as he thought, he had s[e]t limits to his bitterness. [25] He is so blind that, though it is much more profitable ... (to pay attention to?) reputable [sages] ... easi[ly] ...

---

75. Indelli translates "e in àmbito diverso, ugualmente le dimensioni..." ("or in a different sphere, similarly the greatness..."). It is not clear who or what is the object of the comparison (no "less unknown to him" than to us?).

76. Although μέν looks forward and so strictly does not prevent asyndeton, Denniston (1950, 360) notes that "when [it] follows a pronoun at the beginning of a sentence which is not introduced by a connecting particle proper, it seems to acquire a quasi-connective, progressive force."

77. I.e., to Timasagoras, who attacked Basilides (scholarch at Athens ca. 200 BCE) and his contemporary at Athens, Thespis, his fellow Epicureans, for advocating vivid "diatribic" portrayals of anger, or so we suppose from the context; see Indelli's note on 5.17ff. and excursus 1 in the introduction.

Column 6

desunt ca. 9 lineae

1   . . . .]δ[. . . . .
    . . τ]ῶν ἀλόγως [βοηθούν-
    των] περιττο[. . . . .
    . . . .]α̣ι[.]π[. . . . .
5   . . . . . .]νεπ̣ι[. . . . . ..
    . . . .]ε[. . . . .
    ν̣[. . . . . ..]co[. . . . . ..
    δ[. . . . . ἀδύνα-
    το̣[ν γὰρ τὰς νόςους ἀπο-
10 φυ[γεῖ]ν οὐκ ἔστ[ι]ν, ἀλλὰ
    τῷ[ν εὐλ]όγως μ[ό]νον βο-
    ηθού[ν]των προ[ς]δεῖςθαι.
    τὰ [δ' ἐν τῆι ψ]υχῆι πάθη δι-
    ὰ τὴ[ν ἡμ]ετέραν ψευδο-
15 δοξ[ί]α̣ν παρακολουθοῦν-
    τα, τ[ι]νὰ μὲν καὶ τῶι γέ-
    νει, [τι]νὰ δὲ τ[ῶ]ι μεγέ-
    θε[ι, τὸ] ςυν[έ]χον [ἔ]χει τῆς
    ἀπ[ολύ]ςεως ἐν [τ]ῶι θεω-
20 ρῆς[αι τ]ὸ μέγεθος καὶ τὸ
    πλ[ῆθ]ος ὧν ἔχει καὶ ςυν-
    επι[ςπ]ᾶ̣τα̣ι κακῶν, ἀδια-
    νο[ήτ]ο̣υ καθεςτῶτος, ὅ-
    τι δ[. . (.)]επει κ[α]κὸν καὶ
25 . . .]ι̣ τοῦτο καὶ δύναται

6.1–7 P tantum ‖ 2–3 Wilke, cf. l. 11 ‖ 3 περιττο[ὶ λόγοι Wilke ‖ 7 ad init. ν O, μ N ‖ 8–9 ἀδύνα]|το̣[ν γὰρ Philippson : τοῦ]|το[ν γὰρ Janko ‖ 9 τὰς νόςους Indelli (e.g.) ‖ 9–10 ἀπο]|φυ[γεῖ]ν Gomperz ‖ 10–11 Gomperz ‖ 12–18 Hayter (15]ενπαρα N) ‖ 19 Asmis : ἀπ[οθέ]ςεως Gomperz ‖ 20, 21 Hayter ‖ 22, 23 Gomperz ‖ 23–24 ἔ|τι Gomperz ‖ 24 locus desperatus: δ[εῖ] Delattre-Monet : δ[έοι Janko : δ[ὲ] Gomperz ‖ ἐπεὶ vel βλ]έπει (e.g. *) possis ‖ 24 πρ]έπει Janko κ[α]κὸν Gomperz ‖ 25 ἐςτ]ι̣ Delattre-Monet : νοε]ῖ̣ Mewaldt : οὐχ ὅτ]ι̣ Bücheler

Column 6

[*circa ten lines missing or untranslatable*]

... [2] the] superfluous ... [of those trying to help] irrationally...

[*four lines missing or untranslatable*]

... [8] [for] it is not [impossible] to [escape the diseases], but one needs in addition only those who assist rationally. [13] But the emotions [in our] soul that torment us because of our own false suppositions,[78] which are consequent, some on the kind (sc. of emotions), others on their magnitude, [18] have the principal means[79] of release (from them) in our observing the greatness and the number of evils they have and bring along with them, since it is inconceivable that ... this ... an evil and (one)

---

78. Cf. frag. 23.5–10: anger is not compulsory but the result of false suppositions that *epilogismos* can correct. Here ψευδοδοξία stands for ψευδεῖc ὑπολήψεις/δόξαι. The emotions are "bad for us" because they are the wrong kind or of the wrong intensity, which is due to their being produced by false suppositions.

79. For τὸ cυνέχον, see *Lib.* frag. 45.7–9: καὶ τὸ cυνέχον καὶ κυριώτ[α]τον, Ἐπικούρωι καθ' ὃν ζῆν ἡρήμεθα, πειθαρχήcομεν ("and, what's most important and crucial, we shall obey Epicurus, according to whom we have chosen to live"); see also Cicero, *Att.* 9.7.1 (174 Shackleton Bailey 1968, 4:144): *plane τὸ cυνέχον effecisti* ("clearly, you did the most important thing"). Polybius uses the term about a dozen times.

6.26 ...ἀπ[ο]φεύγειν. ⌐ ἀλλὰ δὴ ⟦π⟧ `κ´αὶ
τὸ κύντατον, οὕτως ἐс-
τ[ὶ π]ᾶϲι φανερὸν τὸ τὴν
ὀργὴ]ν ὅλον εἶναι κακόν—
30 καὶ διὰ τοῦτο λογ[. . .]ι̣ν
οἱ ψ[έγ]ο̣ντεс—ὥ[с]τε καὶ με- ‖

Fragment C

1 οὔτε γὰρ[- - -
μαс ἐст[ι] τὸ παθε̣[ῖν - - -
.]α̣ ἕπεται, καθάπ[ερ καὶ ἡ-
μῖν, οἷόν ἐстι κα[κὸν - - -
5 . . . .]ινωс[- - -

Column 7

desunt ca. 14 lineae
1 δ̣[. . . . .
μ[. . . . .
τῶν ἄ[λλ]ων [ἡ διάθεсιс
τὰс ἄ[λλα]с ἔχει διαφορ[άс,
5 μὴ πρότ[ε]ρον αὐταῖс ἢ
θυμωθῆναι χρῆсθαι. κἂν
λέγῃ Τιμαсαγό⟦γ⟧`ρ´αс ἀνε-
πιλογίстουс αὐτοὺс γεγο-
νέναι τῶν παθῶν, καίπε[ρ
10 ἔχοντεс ἐπιδεικνύειν̣

6.26 Gomperz : ἀπ[ο]φ{ε}υγεῖν McO (cf. p. 124) ‖ **28** Gomperz ‖ **29** |[ὀργὴ]ν Hayter (spatio convenit, ut vid.) : ⟨ὀρ⟩|γὴ]ν Wilke ‖ **30** κἀιδία⟨ι⟩ (= καὶ ἰδίαι) Delattre-Monet ‖ ⟨ταὐτο⟩λογ[ουс]ιν Janko cf. Poem. 2.214.17 : ⟨ἀ⟩λογ[οῦс]ιν Bücheler, cf. 14.1 : λέγ[ουс]ιν Delattre-Monet : γο[οῦс]ιν Wilke (νο[legit Wilke; λο[O : λογ[N) ‖ **31** Gomperz ‖ **C.1-2** ἡ]|μᾶс DA ‖ **2** "an πάθο[с?" Wilke ‖ **3, 4** Wilke ‖ **5** ad init.]ενειс[(Wilke) vel]εγτε[(Indelli) subpositae sunt ‖ **7.2** [ὥст' ἐπεὶ] Philippson ‖ **3** ἄ[λλ]ων Croenert ‖ [ἡ διάθεсιс] Philippson : [ἡ θεραπεία] Delattre-Monet ‖ **4** Hayter ‖ **5, 9** Gomperz

can escape it (?). [26] But in fact this is the most shameless claim (sc. of Timasagoras): that it is so "obvious to all" that [anger] is entirely an evil, and because of this, those who blame it ... so that even ...

Fragment C[80]

... for neither ... (for us?) to suffer ... it follows, just as [for us also] what sort of evil it (sc. anger) is ...

Column 7

[circa sixteen lines missing or untranslatable]

... [3] [the disposition] of some people has some differences and other people's (has) other differences ... not to use these (methods?) before they have gotten angry.[81] [6] Even if Timasagoras should say that "they have become unable to use rational appraisal[82] about their emotions," although we can point out

---

80. This fragment probably belongs to the argument about the medical virtue of the diatribe (cols. 1–7) rather than the diatribe itself (cols. 8–31). On the placement of this fragment, see the introduction, p. 109.

81. The supplement in line 3 is not certain, nor is it clear to what αὐταῖc in line 5 refers. As restored, we take the sense to be that each person's disposition is different,

82. The term ἀνεπιλόγιcτοc is rare and used in philosophical contexts only by Epicureans: Epicurus, *Gnom. vat.* 63; Philodemus only here (cf. ἀνεπιλογιcτούμενα, a *hapax*, 3.19–20); Diogenianus frag. 3 apud Eusebius, *Praep. ev.* 6.8.30; [Plato], *Ax.* 365d2, 369e3 (drawn from Epicurean texts); otherwise, it is found only in Christian authors from Eusebius on. This is a strong indication that Timasagoras is a (heterodox) Epicurean.

Philodemus, *On Anger*

7.11 καὶ τῶν ἀποβαινόντων
ἃ γνωστὰ σαρκὸς θησόμε-
θ', ὅμως, ἐπειδὴ δέον τοῖ[c
προσφερομένοις τοὺς πα-
15 ραλογισμοὺς ὑποδεῖξ⟨αι π⟩άν-
τας, οὕτω δὲ τὴν εἰλικρί-
νειαν ἐπιλογίσασθαι τοῦ
κακοῦ, καθάπερ καὶ ἐπὶ
τῆς ἐρ[ωτ]ικ[ῆ]ς εἰώθα-
20 μεν ποιεῖν ἐπιθυμίας,
τότε̣ [δὴ] πᾶ[ν τὸ λυποῦν αὐτοὺς ἐξαριθμοῦμεν [καὶ
τὰ παρακολουθοῦντα [δυσ-
χερέ̣στα[τα . . .]ν̣η εστ[. . . . .
25]α[. . . . .] λυπη[. . .
. . . . .]υνει[. . . . . . .] ‖

Fragment D

1 . . . . .]πνη[. . . . .
ἄ]λλα γ' ἀρξαμ[έν]ης [. . . . .
γὰρ τῆς παρ' ἡμ[ᾶς . .
. . . .]παιδ[.]στηκα[. .
5 . . . . .]εστιν καὶ ου[. .
. . . .] οὐδὲν

7.15–16 ὑποδεῖξ⟨αι π⟩άν|τας Crönert ‖ 19 Hayter ‖ 21 τότε̣ [δὴ] Mewaldt (τοτο̣ π̣α̣ [O, τοτο̣ ν̣ [N) ‖ 21–22 Wilke ‖ 23–26 Gomperz : [δυσ]|χερέ̣στα[τ' αἴσ]χη, ἔστ[ι δ' ὅτε] | [κ]α[ὶ Mewaldt : [δυσ]|χερέ̣στα[τα κοι]ν̣ῇ, ἔστ[ι δ' ὅτε | κ]α[ὶ τὰ ἰδίαι] λυπή[σαν|τα κακά Philippson (24: χεριστα[O) ‖ **D.2** Wilke ‖ 3 ἡμ̣[ᾶς *

which of the consequences we can establish as recognizable physical symptoms,[83] [13] nevertheless, since one must demonstrate all their false reasonings to those who are carried away (sc. by anger), and thus rationally appraise the purity[84] of this evil, just as we are accustomed to do in the case of erotic desire,[85] [21] then, indeed, we number out everything [that is distressing them] and the very unpleasant consequences that follow ...[86]

[*two lines missing or untranslatable*]

THE DIATRIBE

Fragment D[87]

... other things ... (when anger?) has begun ...
... for that which is up to us ...

---

83. Physiognomonic symptoms (e.g., glaring eyes, redness of face, swelling veins) such as those discussed in frag. 18.

84. I.e., its unmitigated nature; εἰλικρίνεια implies pure evil from which an Epicurean cannot hope to get any good (unlike "natural" anger, which, though painful per se, is a good).

85. Philodemus indicates that he also wrote or lectured in diatribe style against erotic desire. His Περὶ ἔρωτος (*On Erotic Desire*) is not extant, though it is mentioned in *On Flattery* (book 2 of Philodemus's collection *On Vices*, P.Herc. 1457) at frag. 23.35.

86. The sentence is long and complicated and may need more textual correction than Crönert's reading at lines 15–16 provides. It begins at line 6 with κἄν and continues beyond the end of the surviving text. The main verb is ἐξαριθμοῦμεν in line 22, and the participle ἔχοντες in line 10 agrees with it. The participle and main verb are separated by a subordinate clause starting in line 13 with ἐπειδή. Its verb, δέον (sc. ἐστι), has two dependent infinitives: ὑποδεῖξ⟨αι⟩ in line 15 and ἐπιλογίςαςθαι in line 17.

87. See above on frag. C; Wilke 1914, 100; Indelli 1988, 69; and our introduction, p. 109. Drawn as part of col. 8 in N.

Column 8

desunt ca. 13 lineae

14   . . . .]πρ[.
15   . . . .]πα
         . . . .]οι τῶι θυ-
         μ. . . . .]ων ὀργ[.
         . . . .]ποτ[.]πανω
         . . . . .]υ[. .]α[. . .]γειν εἰ πα-
20   . .]ο[. . . .]μου[. .] ὅλον, ὡc-
         περεὶ cυνκείμενον ἐξ
         ἐκπυρώcεωc καὶ διοιδή-
         c]εωc καὶ διερεθιcμοῦ
         καὶ βριμώcεωc καὶ δεινῆc
25   ἐπιθυμίαc τοῦ μετελ-
         θεῖν καὶ ἀγωνίαc, εἰ δυ-
         νήcεται, καθάπερ ἀπο-
         δεί̣ξου[c]ι̣ν αἱ φωναί, τοτὲ
         μὲν εὐχομένων περιζώ-
30   cαcθαι τοῖc ἐντέροιc τοῦ λυ-
         πήcαντοc, τοτὲ δ̣' "ὠ̣μὰ δά-
         cαcθαι." εἶτ' ἐπὶ τὰc διαδι-
         δομέναc τῶι cώματι κει-
         νήcειc ἀcταθεῖc, οἷον λέ-
35   γω τὴν ὑπὸ τῆc κ[ρ]αυγῆc
         διάcταcιν [τ]οῦ πλεύμο-
         νοc cὺν αὐταῖc πλευραῖc,
         τὸ μετεωρότερον ἆcθμα
     /   τῶν χί{ν}⟦ηcεων⟧λ῾ί῾α δεδρα-
40   μηκότων cτάδια καὶ
41   τὴν πήδ[ηcι]ν τῆc [κ]αρδί-‖
9.1 [αc

8.14–15 legit Wilke (hodie non extant) ‖ **16–17** θυ|[μῶι Wilke ‖ **17–18** ὀργ[ι|ζομένων] Wilke ‖ **2** (τοῦ *) θυ]μοῦ [τὸ] Janko ‖ ὅλον legit McO, ut iam ci. Gomperz : λλον legit Wilke ‖ **23** Gomperz ‖ **28** Henry ‖ **32** εἶτ' Wilke : εἴτ' Gomperz ‖ **35, 36** Gomperz ‖ **39** κιν⟦ηcεων⟧λ῾ί῾α legit McO; χίλια iam ci. Gomperz ‖ **8.41–9.1** Hayter

Column 8

[circa nineteen lines missing or untranslatable]

... [16] the rage ... anger ... if ... whole ... [20] as if composed of raging fever and swelling and irritation and indignation and a dreadful desire to get revenge and anxiety [26] whether one will be able to, as the utterances of those people will demonstrate, who sometimes boast they will "gird themselves with the guts" of the one who hurt them and other times "tear him up raw."[88] [32] Then (their anger progresses) to unstable movements distributed throughout their bodies; I mean, for example, the dislocation of their lungs, ribs and all, from their shouting, their very rapid, shallow breathing like that of men who have just run a thousand stadia,[89] the throbbing of their heart ...

---

88. For the second quotation, two Homeric contexts, *Il.* 23.21, where Achilles threatens to feed Hector's body to the dogs, and *Od.* 18.87, Antinous's threat to Irus (cf. *Od.* 22.476), are both present to Philodemus's mind, as Indelli suggests. "Girding themselves with the guts" of the offender is not so easily paralleled.

89. Our reading is compatible with Gomperz's suggestion of χίλ'ι'α. We can read χι- and the second *iota* jammed in after the *lambda* on the papyrus. The distance, a thousand stadia, about 185 km or 115 miles, is deliberately exaggerated.

Column 9

post primam lineam suppletam, desunt ca. 16 lineae

18 τρόμους καὶ κ[εινήσεις
τῶν μερῶν κ[αὶ παραλύ-
20 σεις, οἷα συμβ[αίνει κ]αὶ
τοῖς ἐπιληπτ[ικ]οῖς, [ὥ]ς-
τε συνεχῶς π[α]ρακολου-
θούντων τὸν [ἅ]παντα βί-
ον ἐπιτρίβες[θα]ι καὶ τὸν
25 πλείω χρόνον̣ [εἰ]ς ἐκτρο-
φὴν κακο[δ]αιμ[ο]νίας λαμβάνειν. τὸ δ' ὅτ[ι] πολλοῖς
ἐγέννησεν α[ὐ]τό τε καὶ
τὰ γινόμενα δ̣[ι'] αὐτοῦ ῥή-
30 ξεις πλευμό[ν]ων καὶ
πλευρῶν πόν[ο]υς καὶ πολ-
λὰ τοιουτότρο[π]α πάθη
θανάτους ἐπ[ιφ]έροντα,
καὶ παρὰ τῶν ἰατρῶν ἀ-
35 κούειν ἔστι⟦σ⟧ν̣ καὶ παρα-
τηροῦσιν αὐτο[ὺς] ἐπιβλέ-
πειν. ᵛ καὶ πρὸς μελανχο-
λίας δὲ π⟦ε⟧`α´ρις[τ]άσιν ἅμ[α
συνεχεῖς, ὥ[στε] πολλά-
40 κις] κα[ὶ τὰς] μελαίνας γεν-‖
10.1 [νᾶν

9.18 Wilke (κ[ιν-, sed cf. 8.33) ‖ **19, 20** Gomperz (μερων O, με ων PN) ‖ **21–28** Hayter ‖ **29** Gomperz ‖ **30–33** Hayter ‖ **36** Wilke : αὐτο[ῖς Gomperz ‖ **38** π⟦ε⟧`α´ρις[τ]ᾶ-σιν Wilke ‖ ἅμ[α Gomperz ‖ **39** Hayter ‖ **39–40** πολλά‖[κις] Gomperz ‖ **9.40–10.1** γεν‖[νᾶν καρδίας Wilke : πικρίας McO

Column 9

[*circa seventeen lines missing*]

... [18] trembling fits and [movements] of their parts and [paraly]ses, such as hap[pen] to epileptics [as well], so that, since (these effects) continually follow them, they are afflicted for their whole lives and take the greater part of their time in nursing their misery.[90] [27] The fact is that it (sc. anger) and its consequences have produced breakings of lungs, pains in the sides, and many such afflictions that bring death in their wake—[34] as it is possible for those watching over them[91] to hear from their doctors and to notice. At the same time, (these circumstances) dispose them to continual bouts of melancholy as well, so as often [to produce] black[92] ...

---

90. A striking image: the angry man "nourishes" his own misery. Asmis compares Plato, *Resp.* 605a–b, where artistic mimesis is said to "nourish" (τρέφει) the evil passions of the soul and damage its faculty of reasoning.

91. The verb παρατηρέω means "to watch over (sc. a patient)" several times in Galen, a sense not recognized in LSJ.

92. The phrase μέλαινα καρδία, Wilke's conjecture, occurs elsewhere only in Pindar, frags. 123.5 and 225.2 (Snell and Maehler 1964).

Column 10

post primam lineam suppletam, ca. 10 lineae desunt

12 ..... .]ν[..... .....
..... .]μα[..... ....
..... .]δενι[..... ..
15 ..... .]ν ἐπὶ τὸ [.....
..... .]ακατας[.....
....] τοῖς μετρ[ίως
   ταρ[ακτοῖς]· ᵛ ἄρτι γὰρ ῥᾴι-
δ[ιον ἦν]. οὐκ ὀλιάκις δὲ
20 καὶ νοϲοῦντες ἀκμ[ὴ]ν
ἀναπηδῶϲιν, πολλάκ[ι
δὲ καὶ γυμνοί, καὶ κατα-
διώκουϲί τινας καὶ ϲυμ-
πλέκοντ̣[α]ι διὰ δὴ ⟨τὸ⟩ μεγά-
25 λοις ἐνκύκλιον ⟦τοις⟧ ϲυμ-
πτώμαϲιν. κἂν ἡϲυχά-
ζωϲιν ἐπὶ τῆς κλίνης,
διὰ τὴν [φλεγ]μονὴν καὶ
τὸν τῆς ψυχῆς διαϲπαϲ-
30 μὸν τρέπο[υ]ϲιν τὸ ϲωμά-
τιον φορῶς εἰς ἐπικιν-
δύνους ἀρρωϲτίας· ὅθεν
καὶ παραινοῦϲιν οἱ θερα-
πεύοντες αὐτοῖς τε τοῖς
35 ϲυνεχομέ[νο]ις φυλάττεϲ-
θαι τοὺς διερεθιϲμοὺς κ[αὶ
τοῖς παρεδρεύουϲ[ι] μη-
δὲν ὅλως ποιεῖν τῶν κι-
   νῆϲαι δυναμένων, τὸ δὲ
40 δυνατὸν [κ]αὶ τοῖς ἰατροῖς ‖

10.17–19 Wilke (cf. 3.17–20) ‖ **19** lege ὀλιγάκις ‖ **20** Hayter ‖ **21** Hayter (ανεπη P) ‖ **24** πλέκοντ̣[α]ι Gomperz ‖ δὴ ⟨τὸ⟩ DA : ⟨τὸ⟩ δὴ Diels : ⟨ἰ⟩δίᾳ δὴ Delattre-Monet ‖ **25** τοῖς def. McO (cf. p. 124) ‖ **28** Gomperz : ἐ]π[ι]μονήν Diels : διατην[. . . ₍.₎]τονην (]τ̣ vel]γ,]π̣) P ‖ **30** Gomperz ‖ **35–37, 40** Gomperz

Column 10

[*circa sixteen lines missing or untranslatable*]

... [unstable] ... in those moderate[ly distressed], for just now it [was ea]sy. [19] Not infrequently, even when still sick, they leap up, often quite naked, and chase people down and wrestle with them, obviously because of their liability to grave symptoms. [26] Even if they stay quiet in bed, because of their [inflammation[93]] and the agony of their souls, they accordingly[94] abandon their poor bodies to dangerous illnesses; [32] for this reason, their therapists advise the patients themselves to avoid irritations and their caregivers to do nothing whatever that could excite them. [39] What is possible even for the doctors ...

---

93. The word φλεγμονή, a fiery or inflamed condition, is appropriate for the context, but the traces do not support the *mu*.

94. The adjective φορός usually means "favorable, helpful," but in Philodemus the adverb means "in accordance with" and is used with the dative or with πρός + accusative; cf. *Sign.* 26.11 and 38.10. Here, "in accordance (with their mental condition)" is to be understood.

Column 11

desunt ca. 17 lineae

1   .]α[..... ....
     μεγ[...]αγ[..... ..]ας
     καὶ [κ]αθαρῶν ἀκο{υ}ῶν ἀ-
     νοιχείοις καὶ †προσταθει-
5   οις† κ[αὶ] τῶν προσώπων,
     ἀλλ[ὰ π]ανπόλλων ἐποι-
     στικὰς συμ[φ]ορῶν, ὅταν
     μηνί[σ]αντες [ἔ]χθρας ἀ-
     ναλάβωσιν [ἄν]θρωποι
10   καὶ πᾶν ἐπιμηχανῶν-
     ται, κἂν μὴ τὴν δίκην αὐ-
     τόθεν ἐπιθῶσι, πολλάκις
     δὲ καὶ θανάτων ἐπιπό-
     νων, ὅτ[α]ν βασιλεῦσιν ἢ
15   τυράννοις [ἐγ]κυρήσω-
     σιν ὁμοιο[τρόποι]ς ἀφυλά-
     κτως ὁμ[ι]λήσαντες, εἶ-
     τα κατὰ τὸν Πλάτ[ων]α
     κομί[ζ]ωνται "κούφων καὶ
20   πτηνῶν λόγων βαρυ- ⟦νε⟧
     τά⟦ι⟧τας ζημίας." οὐ γὰρ
     ἔστιν ἀναλαβεῖν τὴν
23   πρ[ο]ε[ι]μένην ἅπαξ φω- ‖
12.1 [νὴν

11.3 Delattre-Monet (]αθαρων ON) : μιαρῶν Wilke ‖ del. Wilke ‖ **4–5** προστα⟨χ⟩-θεῖ|ςιν ὑ[πὸ] Delattre-Monet : προςπαθεί|αις * ? ‖ **5** κ[αὶ] Wilke ‖ **6, 7** Gomperz ‖ **7** ὅταν ⟨γε⟩ Wilke ‖ **8** Henry : μὴν πάντ[ω]ς Wilke : μὴν πᾶν τ[ὰ]ς Delattre-Monet : μὴν παντ[ὸ]ς Wilke in apparatu ‖ **9** [ἄν]θρωποι Janko : [ἄν]- Gomperz ‖ **14–15** Hayter ‖ **16** Gomperz ‖ **17–18** Hayter ‖ **19** Gomperz ‖ **23** πρ[ο]ε[ι]μένην Bücheler ‖ **11.23–12.1** φω|[νὴν Hayter

Column 11

[circa nineteen lines missing or untranslatable]

... [3] and of unpolluted senses of hearing (?) ... unfitting and ... and of persons (?) ... but that bring about very many misfortunes, whenever people become enraged and take up enmities and plot everything against their enemies, even if they do not wreak their vengeance on the spot, [12] and (sc. that bring about their own) miserable deaths often as well, when they fall in and associate incautiously with kings or tyrants with characters like their own, and then, in Plato's words, they reap "for light and winged words very heavy penalties," [21] for one cannot take back the word once it has been sent forth[95] ...

---

95. *Leg.* 717d, on bearing patiently the anger (θυμός) of one's parents: "for light and winged speech brings a very heavy penalty; Justice has her appointed messenger Nemesis to keep watch over all such matters" (διότι κούφων καὶ πτηνῶν λόγων βαρυτάτη ζημία· πᾶcι γὰρ ἐπίcκοποc τοῖc περὶ τὰ τοιαῦτα ἐτάχθη Δίκηc Νέμεcιc ἄγγελοc). The context is that one should bear with one's parents when they feel angry and act out their anger in word or in deed. The passage is quoted or paraphrased also by Plutarch, *Cap.* 90c and *Cohib. ira* 456d as a commonplace of the diatribe against anger; see also *Garr.* 505d, *Quaest. conv.* 634f, Aelian *Var. hist.* 4.28, as catalogued by Indelli. For the many parallels to the next axiom, *nescit vox missa reverti*, "a word cannot come back after it is spoken," see Indelli 1988, 163–65.

Column 12

post primam lineam suppletam, desunt ca. 12 lineae

14   τιζ[..... ....
15   νες[..... ....
     μενο[.... ....
     ..] καὶ χείρ[ο]ν[ας δὲ δι-
     ατίθηςι δάκν̣[ων, ὥστ' ἐ-
     πῶν ἐπιλαμ[βάνεςθαι
20   ἀτόπων· ᵛ κατὰ [δὲ βαι-
     ὸν καὶ καταφέ[ρεςθ' εἰς
     λί[θ]ων̣ βολάς. οὐ μὴν [ἀλ-
     λ' ἐ[ν]ί[ο]τε καὶ παρὰ πολ[ὺ
     ςυμβάλλουςιν ἰςχυρ[ο-
25   τέρ[οι]ς—οὐ γὰρ ἐᾶι διακ[ρί-
     νειν ὁ θυμός, ὡς καὶ Τι-
     μοκράτην φηςὶν ὁ Μη-
     τρόδωρος τῶι πρεςβυ-
     τάτωι τῶν ἀδελφῶν Μ[εν-
30   τορίδηι—κἄπειτα τῆς
     προπετείας πικρὰ κο-
     μίζονται τἀπίχειρα.
     ςυμβαίνει δ' αὐ[τοῖς] ἐ[κ
     τῶν τοιούτων χειρο-
35   κραςιῶν καὶ μυριάκ̣ι
     ταῖς ἐκ τῶν νόμων πε-
     ριπίπτειν ζημίαις,
     ἐπειδὰν ὄφλωςιν δ[ί-
     κην ὕβρεως ἢ τραύμ[α-
40   τος ὁτὲ [μ]ὲν εἰς [..]ςυν̣[. ‖

12.17 Gomperz ‖ **18** δάκν̣[ων ὥστ' Gomperz : δακν[ηρῶν Wilke ‖ **18–19** ἐ]|πῶν Wilke ‖ **19** ἐπιλαμ[βάνεςθαι Gomperz : ἐπιλαμ[βάνειν ἢ Wilke : ἐπιλαμ[βάνειν καὶ Indelli ‖ **20–21** Henry : κατὰ [τελευταῖ]ον ⟨δὲ⟩ Wilke ‖ **21** McO : καταφε[ρεῖς εἰς Gomperz ‖ **22** λί[θ]ων Hayter ‖ **22–23** [ἀλ]|λ' Gomperz, Spengel ‖ **23** ἐ[ν]ί[ο]τε ... πολ[ὺ Gomperz ‖ **24–25** Gomperz ‖ **29–30** Wilke ‖ **33** αὐ[τοῖς Hayter ‖ ἐ[κ Spengel ‖ **35** -άκ̣[ις Hayter ‖ **38, 39** Gomperz, Spengel ‖ **40** Wilke

Column 12

[*circa sixteen lines missing or untranslatable*]

... [17] and it (sc. anger) makes them still worse as it bites at them, so that they take up vile language[96] and little by little sink so low as even to throw stones.[97] [22] Not only that, but sometimes they attack those much stronger than themselves—their rage does not allow them to distinguish, as Metrodorus tells us Timocrates did to his eldest brother, Mentorides[98]— [30] and then they get the bitter wages of their recklessness. It happens to them countless times, as a result of such acts of violence, that they fall foul of the penalties prescribed by the laws, whenever they are convicted of assault or battery, sometimes for ...

---

96. The meaning of ἄτοπος shifts from simply "out of place" to "strange" and from there to "monstrous, bad, wicked, vile" (see LSJ, s.v. 3); cf. ἀτοπία at 35.26 meaning "offense."

97. A traditional example, already used as an example in frag. 19.10 and in Chrysippus; see n. 31 above.

98. Epicurus's former disciple and relentless enemy Timocrates of Lampsacus, Metrodorus's brother; for full accounts, see Sedley 1976a; Roskam 2012; and the detailed entry "Timocrates" in *DPA* T156 (Angeli). Of course, this particular *exemplum* of extravagant anger will not have been used by Chrysippus or Bion; it is only suitable for an Epicurean "diatribe." Verde (2017) now connects this passage with the fragment of Metrodorus in 33.9–11.

Column 13

desunt ca. 12 lineae

1 . . . .]ιουτο
   . . . .] δὲ καὶ
   . . . .] τοῖc cω-
   . . . .]ε[.]c καὶ παν-
5 τα[χῶc τὸν] μὲν τυπτό-
   μενον ἥκιcτα βλάπτου-
   cιν, ⋎ αὐτοὶ δ' ἑαυτοὺc λυμαί-
   νονται παντοδαπῶc, καὶ
   διὰ τοῦτο πάλιν θυμοῦγ-
10 τα]ι καὶ cυμπλεκόμε[ν]οι
   προ]cπαροινοῦνται. τ[ί γ]ὰρ
   δ]εῖ λέγειν τὸ μηδ' ἀπ[ω]c-
   μένουc ἀλλ' ἐπιφερομέ-
   νουc ⋎ ἐν῾ί῾οτε διὰ τὴν ἀνε-
15 πιcταcίαν εἰc ξύλα καὶ
   τοίχουc καὶ τάφρουc ἤ τι
   τοιοῦτον ἐνπίπτειν; ἂν
   δὲ οὖν γενόμενοι κρείτ-
   τουc προβῶcιν, ὥcπερ εἰώ-
20 θ]α[cι]ν, ἕωc ὀφθαλμῶν
   ἐκκοπῆc ἢ μυκτήρων
   ἀποτρώξεωc ἢ καὶ φόνου,
   τὸ περιπίπτειν ἐκ τῶν
   νόμων τε καὶ τῶν cυνορ-
25 γιζομένων, τοτὲ μὲν τοῖc
   ὁμο[ί]οιc, το⟨τὲ⟩ δὲ φυγαῖc ἐκ τῶν

13.3–4 τοῖc cώ|[μαcι cυνεχ]ε[ῖ]c Wilke (brevius) ‖ 4–5 παν|τα[χῶc Wilke ‖ 5 [τὸν] Gomperz ‖ 9–10 Gomperz ‖ 10 ad fin. Hayter ‖ 11 ad init. McO :]ι ON : ἐπ]ιπαροινοῦνται vel ἔτ]ι παροινοῦνται Wilke (utrumque propter hiatum reiciendum), post ται, puncta super et sub lineam scripta sunt, spatio non relicto ‖ τ[ί Gomperz ‖ γ]ὰρ Hayter ‖ 12 Gomperz ‖ 20 Hayter ‖ 26 ὁμο[ί]οιc Hayter ‖ το⟨τὲ⟩ add. Gomperz

Column 13

[circa fifteen lines missing or untranslatable]

... [4] and in every [way] they barely harm the person they strike, while they themselves maltreat themselves in every sort of way and, because of that, get enraged again, and, while entangled (sc. with their enemies), they get involved in drunken brawls still further.[99] [11] Why should I mention[100] that that they do not retreat but rush forward and, because of their distraction, sometimes crash into wooden barriers and walls and ditches or something like that? [17] But if they *do* get the better (sc. of their enemies) and progress, as they are accustomed, to the point of tearing out eyes[101] or biting off noses or even murder, [23] (why should I mention) their falling foul, due either to the laws or to those whom they have angered,[102] sometimes of similar punishments (sc. to those they inflicted), but sometimes to exile from their

---

99. The word προσπαροινέω appears elsewhere only at Philostratus's *Imag.* 2.23.4 in the active, where it means "add a further indignity"; cf. παροινέω, to act drunk, to act with drunken violence, but in the passive "to be a victim of drunken violence." On wine and drunkenness in the ancient world, see Fitzgerald 2015.

100. For other examples of τί δεῖ λέγειν (*praeteritio*), Indelli notes 18.34–35, 20.28, and 28.35; cf. also τί δεῖ διατρίβειν at 33.24–25. Jensen and Wilke argued that this figure means that Philodemus is abridging his sources at these points; see n. 44 in the introduction.

101. I.e., those of their enemies.

102. The verb cυνοργίζομαι usually means "be angry together with someone," i.e., on their behalf, but that sense seems unsuitable here.

13.27 πατ[ρίδ]ων; εποϝ[. .]ι τοῖϲ
28   απε . [. . . .]αθ[. . . . .] ‖

Column 14

desunt ca. 7 lineae

1   . . . . ἀ]λογοῦϲιν [α]ὖ
         καὶ πικραίνο]νται[ι] καὶ
         θυμοῦνται τ]ὰϲ τῶν πα-
         ραδεδομέν]ων θεῶν ὀρ-
5   γὰϲ . . . . .] ἀπ[ο]μιμού-
         μενοι . . . . . κα]θάπερ ου
desunt duae lineae
         φινειϲϲυγ[. . . . . ταῖϲ
10   ἀληθείαιϲ, ὡϲ πολλ[οὶ] πα-
         ραπλήϲιοι τοῖϲ Οἰδίπ[ο]δοϲ
         υἱοῖϲ ᵛ καὶ τοῖϲ Πέλοποϲ
         ἢ Πλειϲθένουϲ τῶ[ν] τ' ἄλ-
         λων προϲηκ[ό]ντων, κα-
15   θάπερ μυρίοι καὶ πάλαι καὶ
         νῦν. ᵛ ἀμέλει γὰρ καὶ φιλο-
         τιμότερόν ἐϲτι καὶ τῆϲ
         ἐρωτικῆϲ [ἐ]πιθυμίαϲ
         τὸ κακόν, καὶ καταρχόμε-
20   νον ἀπ' ἐλαχίϲτου μέχρι
         καὶ τῶν ἐϲχάτων ἐξοκέλ-
         λειν ποιεῖ. ᵛ προάγεται δὲ
         καὶ ἀϲεβεῖν εἰϲ ἱερεῖϲ ὑ-
         βρίζονταϲ καὶ παροινοῦν-

13.27 πατ[ρίδ]ων Hayter ‖ **27–28** ἔπον[τα]ι τοῖϲ | ἀπέ[ραντ]α θ[υμουμένοιϲ Wilke : ἔπον[τα]ι ⟨δὲ⟩ * ‖ **14.1–6** e.g. tantum ‖ **1–2** Wilke (1 πολυ]λογοῦϲιν Delattre-Monet) ‖ **3** [θυμοῦνται Wilke : [ἀγανακτοῦϲι Indelli ‖ **3–6** Gomperz (5 ἀτόπωϲ] Wilke) ‖ **9** φινειϲϲυγ[P : Φινεῖ{ϲ} ϲύγ[γονοι Janko φϙνεῖϲ ϲυγ[γενῶν McO : Φινέωϲ υἱ[οί dub. Gomperz ‖ ϲυγ[γένειαν Philippson ‖ [ταῖϲ] ad fin. Gomperz ‖ **10, 11, 13, 14, 18** Gomperz, Spengel

fatherlands?

[*one and a half lines untranslatable*]

Column 14

[*circa seven lines missing*]

... [1] they are irrational [and embitter]ed and [they rage] ... imitating the an[gers] of the [traditional] gods,[103] just as ... not (?) ...

...[104] [9] [in] truth, as many resembling Oedipus's sons and those of Pelops or Pleisthenes and the rest of that family,[105] just like countless others, both in the past and now. [16] For certainly this evil is even more extravagant than erotic desire[106] and, beginning from the smallest trifle, makes one run oneself utterly aground. [22] It inspires people to commit sacrilege by insulting priests and outraging

---

103. For πα[ραδεδομένων], see Polystratus, *Cont.* 13.2–6: πότερον δυνατὸν ἢ οὐ δυνατὸν ὑπάρχειν ἐν τῆι φύσει (sc. τῶν θεῶν) τὰς τοιαύτας δυνάμεις οἷαι παραδέδονται ("whether is it possible or impossible that there should exist in the nature [of the gods] such powers as are given by tradition"); see also *Cont.* 15.7–11.

104. Janko suggests Φινεῖ {c} cύγ[γονοι ("relatives ... to Phineus"), a reference to the myth that Phineus allowed his second wife to blind his children by his first wife. McOsker's conjecture φονεῖc cυγ[γενῶν ("murderers of relatives") is along the same lines.

105. Oedipus's sons are Eteocles and Polynices; Pelops's family (the Atreidae) included at least one Pleisthenes, who is variously identified in the sources as his son or grandson.

106. Cf. 7.18–20 above, with note.

14.25 τας εἰς ἱκέτας καὶ τῶν
θείων αὐτῶν ἀφειδοῦν-
τας καὶ περὶ ἄλλα πολλὰ
τῶν τοιούτων ἐκβακχεύ-
οντας. ᵛ ὅθεν ἐπὶ πολλ[οῖς
30 τῶν συντελουμένων τε
καὶ ἀ̣π̣αντών⟨των⟩ {μενων} αἱ
ψυχ[αὶ τ]ῶν ὀργίλων cυν̣-
33 ταράττονται]. ἔχουcι [δὲ ‖

Column 15

desunt ca. 8 lineae
1 χθη[..... ....
γα.[.... ....
νευ[..... ....
του γε[.... ....
5 δόξας ε̣[..... .... .
το.[.]ογου[..... ...
ἔcτιν ἀεὶ κ[..... ...
ἐ]ὰ̣ν̣ θυμω[..... ...
τα[.]. καὶ γὰρ οὐδὲ μ[ε]τὰ
10 χρόνον ἐπὶ [πᾶcιν ἀμέ-
λει τοῖc πραχθεῖcιν, ἀλ-
λ' εὐθέωc κάθηνται τ[ι]λλό-
μενοι καὶ κλαίοντεc ἐφ' οἷc
ἐπαρῴνηcαν, ᵛ ἐν ί̔οτε δ' αὐ-
15 τοὺc ἐπικαταcφάττοντεc.
οὕτω δὲ κ[α]ὶ ἐ̣κ̣φ[έρε]ι τὸ
πάθοc, ὥcτε̣ καὶ προίεc-

14.29 Gomperz ‖ 31 καιαπαντωνμενωναιP,corr.Wilke:καὶἀπ̣α̣ντω{ν}μένωναἱGomperz ‖ 32 Hayter ‖ 33 Wilke ‖ 15.6 ἄ̣[λ]ογου Wilke : τοῦ̣ [λ]όγου Janko ‖ 8–9 ἐ]ὰ̣ν̣ θυμῶ̣[ι χαρίζων]|τα[ινεlcυνέχων]|τα[ιWilke:θυμῶ[νταικατ'αὑ]|τα[cJanko‖9 μ[ε]τὰGomperz‖ 10 ἐπὶ [πᾶcιν Henry : ἐπὶ [πᾶν (= καθόλου) McO ‖ 10–11 ἀμέ]|λει Gomperz : μετα-μέ]|λει Cobet, cf. 18.2 ‖ 12 Gomperz, Spengel ‖ 16 Hayter

suppliants and not sparing the holy things themselves[107] and going completely out of control about many other things of the sort. [29] For this reason, the souls of the irascible [are in turmoil] at many things that they have done and that happen to them. [33] [And] they have ...

Column 15

[*circa fifteen lines missing or untranslatable*]

... if in a rage.... [9] In fact, not even with the passage of time, and (sc. grieving) over all their doings in general, but immediately, they sit there pulling their hair out and sobbing over the insults they visited on people and sometimes butchering themselves.[108] [16] This emotion drives them so out of their mind that it makes

---

107. Apparently an allusion to Agamemnon's confrontation with the priest Chryses (Homer, *Il.* 1.22–33).
108. As Wilke noticed, this is probably a reference to Ajax's behavior after he lost the Judgment of the Arms. If so, Philodemus's attitude is not sympathetic.

15.18 θαι ποιεῖ ταῦθ' ὧν μάλισ-
τα δεινοὺς ἔχει τοὺς εἰ-
20 μέρους ὁ θυμούμενος.
Φοίνικα γοῦν τρώκτην,
ὃς ἕνα χαλκοῦν ἀποβαλὼν
αὐτὸν πνείγει ᵛ "χάσκων
βαδίζεις, οὐ προσέχεις
25 cαυτῶι" λέγων, ἀναγκάζει
διαριθμοῦντα πολλάκις
⟨τ⟩ἀργύριον ἐν πλοίωι καὶ
τετράχμον ἓν ἐπιζητοῦν-
τα [τὸ] πᾶν ε[ἰ]ς τὸ πέλαγος
30 ἐκχεῖν. κἄπειτα δῆλον
ὡς ἑαυτὸν καὶ φίλαρχον
32 ἢ φιλόδοξον, οὕτω [. . . ‖

Column 16

desunt ca. 8 lineae
9   . . . . .]καὶ τὸν ηγου[. .
10 . . . .]ηcειατ[. . .
παντι̣[. . .]δεε[.]ωμ̣[. .
Ὕπνος, ὦ̣[ι] γε Ζεὺς εχε̣[
.]η τῆς τυχούσης αἰτι-
ας] ῥεῖψαι, κἄπειτα πᾶσι
15 . . .]ον̣[. . ἕ]τερο[ν] "θαῦμα
ἰδέσθαι". . .₍.₎] . . [₍.₎ οὐ]χ οὕτως

15.27 add. Croenert ‖ 29 Hayter ‖ 15.32–16.2 οὕτω [καὶ | φιλοχρήματον ὄντα | βλάπτειν τὰ μέγιστα] supplevit Wilke, redegit Indelli in lineas ‖ 9–10 ἡγού[μενον] Gomperz ‖ 12 ὦ̣[ι] Wilke : ὦ̣[ς] Bücheler ‖ εχε̣[legit McO, ON: εχθ[legit Wilke, ex quo ἐχθ[ρός Bonn Seminar (saepius autem librarius scribebat ἐκθρός, sed cf. 26.21–22) ‖ 12–13 ὅ[ν] γε Ζευς ἔθε[|λε]ν ⟨ἐκ⟩ Janko (⟨ἐκ⟩ iam Wilke) ‖ 13 ν vel η ‖ ἢ]ν Delattre-Monet : ὤ]ν Bonn Seminar ‖ 13–14, 15, 16 Wilke ‖ 16]ηρ[vel]ηι̣[legit McO :]ι̣ο[leg. Wilke ‖ οὐ]χ οὕτως Philippson

the enraged man throw away the very things for which he cherished the most dreadful longings. [21] It compels the greedy Phoenician knave, at any rate,[109] who strangles himself because he lost a penny, "saying, 'you're walking about gaping; you're paying no attention to yourself,'"[110] to count, over and over, the coins in the ship and, because he cannot find one tetradrachm, to pour it all out into the sea. [30] And next, it is clear that ... himself ... the lover of power or the lover of glory, so ...

Column 16

[*circa eleven lines missing or untranslatable*]

... [12] Hypnos, to whom Zeus ... to throw him (down) for some random cause ... and then to all ... another "an amazement to see"[111] ... not thus ... as we do,

---

109. In some lost comedy, such as Menander's *Carchedonios*, with Carthaginian characters.

110. χάcκων βαδίζειc, οὐ προcέχειc cαυτῶι λέγων scans as a comic iambic trimeter (see Indelli ad loc.; Sauppe 1864, 5; Cobet 1878, 376). λέγων was probably not originally part of the line. The fragment is now *adespoton* 476 in Kassel and Austin 2001.

111. Cf. Homer, *Il.* 14.242-262: Zeus, angry that Hera and Hypnos drove Heracles off course in a storm while he was on his way to Troy, threatened to throw Hypnos down from heaven into the sea: καί κέ μ' ἄϊcτον ἀπ' αἰθέροc ἔμβαλε πόντωι ("he would have thrown me out of his sight from heaven into the sea"). The word ῥῖψε is used at 1.591 of Zeus's throwing Hephaestus out of heaven. Buecheler suggested the next phrase refers to Zeus's threat to make an example of any god who disobeys him (8.10-17) and enters the battle, though the formula θαῦμα ἰδέcθαι does not appear in the text there. Philodemus also invokes Apollo's punishment of the innocent Achaeans for Agamemnon's insult to Chryses (*Il.* 1.44-52) and two other examples of mythical gods in anger avenging themselves on the innocent.

16.17 . . . .]αν[. . . . ὡ]ς [ἡ-
μεῖς, [ἔνιο]ι δὲ καὶ τι[μω-
ροῦνται, καθάπερ Ἀπόλ-
20 λων τοὺς ἐπευφημοῦν-
τας "αἰδεῖσθαι θ' ἱερῆα" {ι}
καὶ τὰ τέκνα τῆς Νιόβης
ἡ ἀδελφὴ καὶ [τὸν] Κά- [[δ]]
δμον ὁ [Δι]όνυ[σος] ἕνε-
25 κα τῆς τῶν θυγ[ατέ]ρων
αὐτοῦ βλασφη[μίας]. οὐ-
δ', εἰ πρὸς τοῦ πάθο[υς] εὐα-
νάσειστοι γίνοντ[αι], καὶ τε-
λέως εὐπαραλόγ[ι]στοι
30 καὶ διαβολαῖ[ς τῶν] τυ-
χόντων, ᵛ ἐνίοτ[ε δὲ] καὶ
τῶν ἐχθρῶν, κ[ατὰ] τῶν
φιλτάτων π[ιστεύ]ον-
τες. μανίας τ[ο]ιγα[ρο]ῦν
35 οὐχ ὁμο[[ιτον]]γεν[ῆ γ'] εἶναι συμβέβηκε [τὴν] ὀρ-
γήν—⟨ὧ⟩δέ τις εἴρ[ηκεν—ἀ]λ-
λ' ἐνίοτ[ε] τὴν [κυρίως κα-
λουμένην μ[ανίαν ὀρ-
40 γὴν προσ[αγορεύομεν ‖

16.17 ὡ]ς Bücheler ‖ **17–18** ἡ]|μεῖς Wilke ‖ **18** Wilke : [θεο]ὶ Delattre-Monet ‖ **21** del. Gomperz ‖ **23, 24** Hayter ‖ **25** Gomperz ‖ **26–31** Hayter ‖ **32** Gomperz ‖ **32** lege ἐχθρῶν ‖ **33** Bücheler ‖ **34** Gomperz ‖ **35** * post Wilke (-γ]εν[ῆ], hiatus) : ὁμο[[ιτον]]γεν[ὲς] Crönert ‖ **36** Hayter ‖ **37** ⟨ὧ⟩δέ Delattre-Monet : ⟨ὀλιγοχρόνιον μανίαν⟩ δέ Wilke ‖ **37–38** εἴρ[ηκεν—ἀ]λ|λ' ἐνίοτ[ε] Gomperz ‖ **38** [κυρίως] Delattre-Monet : [ὄντως] Gomperz : [ἰδίως] Gand. ‖ **38 fin.–40** Gomperz (προσαγορεύουσιν Gand.)

[18] and [some] (sc. of the gods) also get revenge, just as Apollo did on those who cried "Respect the priest!"[112] and his sister on the children of Niobe and Dionysus on Cadmos for his daughters' blasphemy. [26] But if the gods are easily excited by this emotion, they are also not so utterly easy to cheat by the slanders of random people, sometimes even of their enemies, because they believe (them) against their closest friends.[113] [34] It is for that reason that it turns out that anger is not something similar in type to madness—someone[114] has put it ⟨that way⟩—but sometimes we [call madness, properly] so[-called, an]ger[115] ...

---

112. Homer, *Il.* 1.23. Although only Agamemnon was guilty of mistreating the priest, the whole army suffered for it.
113. That is, sometimes angry people are taken in by their enemies' slanders against their friends.
114. Horace (*Ep.* 1.2.62) and Seneca (*Ir.* 1.1.2) say that anger is a brief insanity.
115. I.e., the word ὀργή can be used to refer to insanity as well (originally, it was any temper of mind; see LSJ, s.v. A.I.).

Column 17

desunt ca. 8 lineae

1   . . . .]ζοντα
    . . . .]προσκο-
    . . . .]χοις εμ-
    . . . .]ν ἐπιστα-
5   . . . .] πάντων
    . . . .]ων[.
    . . . .] . . .παις
    .]γα[. . .]ης λ[ακτίζοντα τὰ
    τ]έκνα καὶ κατασχί[ζον-
10 τα{c} τοὺς χιτωνίσκου[ς ἢ
    καὶ μετὰ φωνῆς λοιδορού-
    μενον πρὸς τοὺς ἀπόντας
    ὡς πρὸς παρόντας, καὶ πάν-
    πολλα τούτοις παραπλή-
15 σια συντελοῦντα. περὶ
    μὲν γὰρ τοῦ μι[κ]ρὸ[ν] τό[δε
    εἶναι τὸ πάθο[ς] ἔργον λέ-
    γειν, ὅταν καὶ [μ]υίαις φό-
    νο[υ]ς μηχανῶνται δε[ι-
20 ν]οὺς ⟦αις⟧ ⟨καὶ⟩ κώνωψιν μετὰ
    βριμώσεως καὶ ἀπειλῶ-
    σι καὶ ῥαπίζωσιν ὡς κα-
    ταφρονούμενοι. ᵛ παρα-
    κολουθεῖ δ' αὐτοῖς [ἐξ ἐπι-
25 γενήματος καὶ [τοῖς φιλ-
    τάτοις συνοῦσιν [διαφω-
    νεῖν καὶ προσκ[. . . . . .(.)

17.7 ἢ ἄπαις Wilke ‖ **8–10** Wilke (9–10 κατασχί[ζον]|τας dub. Gomperz) ‖ **16** μι[κ]-ρὸ[ν] vel μι[α]ρὸ[ν] Wilke ‖ τό[δε Wilke : το[ῦτ' Philippson (elisione insolita) ‖ **17–19** Gomperz ‖ **20** Gomperz (αις P) : ⟨τ⟩αῖς Bücheler ‖ **24–25** Gomperz : [ἀντὶ] | γενήματος Delattre-Monet ‖ **25–26** [τοῖς φιλ]|τάτοις Gomperz ‖ **26–27** [διαφω]|νεῖν Bonn Seminar ‖ **27** προσκ[ρούειν dub. Gomperz

Column 17

[*circa twelve lines missing or untranslatable*]

... of all ... child (?) ... [8] [kicking their] children and ripping up their frocks, and abusing absent people out loud as if they were there, and doing a great many things very like those. [15] It is a task to describe the pettiness of this passion, when they devise the terrible murders of flies and mosquitoes with indignation and threaten (them) and take sticks to them as if they had been insulted (by them). [23] It follows as a consequence[116] for them that they [diff]er from their nearest and dearest to their faces,

---

116. The word ἐπιγέννημα often appears in manuscripts with one ν (e.g., Epictetus, *Diatr.* 3.7.7 *bis*; Philodemus, *Mort.* 22.29; 30.35; and 35.38).

17.28 ..]νειν καὶ μα̣[. . . . . ἔ-
       cτ̣' ⟨ἂν⟩ ἀπει̣λῶνται φιλοcο-
30   φία[. . .]ιcε[. . .]μενα
       . . . .]ετ[. . .].αυτ̣.
       . . . .]μ‖
       margo fortasse exstat

Column 18

1   . . . ν]⟦ο⟧υκτερεύουcα[ν
       τὴν μ]εταμέλειαν πα[.
       . . . .]γοντων ἀπάντων
       . . . .]οιποιουναπε
5   . . . .]πον ἐcτιν
       . . . .]αια
       desunt duae lineae
       μ[.]κρο[. . . . .] .
10   θ[. . .]μ̣[. . . . .] . .
       c[. .]ω[. . . . .] -
       νουντα̣[. . . . .] .
       κρεάδια̣ [. . . . .] -
       μενουλου[. . . . . . . πα-
15   ρὰ χαλκοῦν ἐc[τιν ἀνυ-
       πέρβατοc, ἐπ[ειδὰν τὴν
       γῆν οὐρ]ανῶι μιγνύωcι
       π]αραπεμφθέντεc ὑπό
       τ]ινοc ἐcτιῶντοc, ὥcπερ
20   ὁ] Σοφοκλέουc Ἀχιλλεύc,
       ἢ] κατά τι τοιοῦτο παρο-

17.28 μά̣[λιcτα Philippson ‖ 28–29 ἔ]|cτ̣' ⟨ἂν⟩ Wilke ‖ 29 Wilke (απελλ P) ‖ 18.1–2 Gomperz ‖ 2–3 πα[γ|κακω]γ̣ ὄντων Philippson (3 ad init. νο- O et legit Indelli, χο- N) ‖ 11–12 πο]|νοῦντα Janko ‖ 14–15 πα]|ρὰ Gomperz ‖ 15 ε[legit McO : εc vel εθ O, ex quo ἐc[τιν * : ιε[legit Wilke (ex quo ἱε[ρὸν) ‖ 15–16 [ἀνυ]|πέρβατοc * : ὑ]|περβατόc Wilke ‖ 16 ἐπειδὰν Gomperz ‖ 16–17 τὴν] | γῆν οὐρ]ανῶι Hayter : τὰ | κάτω] ἄνω{ι} Gomperz ‖ 18–19 Hayter ‖ 20–21 Gomperz

and ... [so long as] they threaten ... philosophy ...

Column 18

... [1] passing the night[117] ... their remorse

[*ten lines missing or untranslatable*]

... [13] morsels of meat ... because of a bronze coin it (sc. their anger) is [unsu]rpassable, whenever they mix [earth] with heaven[118] because they were passed over by someone giving a feast, [19] like Sophocles's Achilles,[119] or were slighted in similar circumstances—

---

117. In spite of the daring metaphor here, νυκτερεύω ("spend the night") is not a poetic word (seventy-four instances in the TLG, but only one is comic poetry; all the others are prose). It is found in a philosophical context at Xenophon, *Cyr.* 4.2.22, and P.Flor. 2.113, a *Sōkratikos logos*, perhaps Antisthenic; see Luz 2015.

118. Cf. Plutarch, *Rom.* 28.7: οὐρανῶι δὲ μειγνύειν γῆν ἀβέλτερον ("but it is stupid to mix earth with heaven").

119. These events may be from the *Syndeipnoi* (of which no relevant fragments survive) when Agamemnon forgot to invite Achilles to a symposium. The story was mentioned also in the *Cypria* (Proclus, *Chrestomathy*: Severyns 1938: 144–47 = West 2003, 76–77), and in Aristotle, *Rhet.* 2.24, 1401b16–20.

18.22 λιγωρηθέντ[[ο]]ες· οὔπω
γὰρ "ἀδικηθέντες" λέ-
γω. καὶ τῶν μὲν κυνῶν
25 οἱ πρὸς τὰς θήρας, ἂν οἰ-
κουρὸς αὐτοὺς ὑλακτῇ
παριόντας, οὐκ ἐπιστρέ-
φονται, ᵛ τὸν δ' Ἀλεξάν-
δρου φασὶ μηδ' [ὅ]ταν ἄλ-
30 λο κινηθῇ θηρίον ἀλλ' ὅ-
ταν λέων—οἱ δὲ τῶν ποι-
ητῶν θεοὶ μικροῦ καὶ
[[ταυ]] τα[ῖ]ς υἱσὶν ὀργίλως
διατίθενται. ᵛ τί γὰρ δεῖ
35 το[ὺς β]ασιλεῖς λέγειν; ἐμ-
πο[δίζ]ονται δὲ καὶ πρὸς
τὴν ἐν φιλοσοφίαι συν-
αύξησιν, οἷς μεταδιώ-
κεται τοῦτο, διὰ πολλὰς
40 αἰτία[ς . . . .] ‖

Column 19

desunt ca. 7 lineae
1 . . . (.)] ἐφιστάνειν διό[τι
ἐν] πολλοῖς ἐξί[στανται
κ]αὶ παρατηροῦντ[ες
εἰς] κόλας[ι]ν εὐφυε[ῖς
5 κα]ιροὺς περισπῶν[ται καὶ
μ]εταμελείαις συνεχό-
με]νο[ι] περὶ ταύτας γίνονται καὶ ὑπὸ τῶ]ν ὑβρισμέ-

not even treated unjustly at all,[120] I mean. [24] And as for dogs, if a guard dog barks at hunting dogs as they pass by, they do not pay any attention, and they say that Alexander's dog did not pay attention when any other beast than a lion was roused, but the poets' gods come near to behaving angrily to sows.[121] [34] Why should I mention kings? And those who have this goal are also hindered from growth in philosophy for many reasons ...[122]

Column 19

[circa seven lines missing]

... (one should?) [1] consider that in many things they are out of control and distracted (sc. from their studies) as they watch for opportune times for retaliation, and they come to be caught up in remorse and obsessed with it, and ... [8] [by those] who have been outraged ...

---

120. See the introduction, §§3 and 4, on ὀλιγωρία, ἀδικία, and βλάβη as incitements to anger in Aristotle, the Stoics, and Philodemus.

121. An allusion (so Wilke and Indelli) to the proverb ὕς ποτ' Ἀθαναίαν ἔριν ἤρισεν ("a sow once quarreled with Athena"; cf. Theocritus, *Id.* 5.23); in Latin, *sus Minervam*).

122. Here (18.35–21.40) Philodemus's diatribe becomes a more serious discussion of the problem that anger poses to students of philosophy. See Asmis 2001 on Philodemus' "school." It was no doubt these columns that most inspired Ringeltaube (1913, 39) to compare the diatribe to a voyage by time-travel into an ancient class

19.9   νων . . . .]λη[. .]ται
10   . .]αϲε[. . . . . . .]ϲ γεγονότων
       ἐχθρῶν οὐκ ἐ[ῶν]ται ϲχο-
       λάζειν. ἀπροβάτους δ' αὐ-
       τοὺς ἀνάγκη γίνεϲθαι καὶ
       τῶι μήτε καθηγητὰς
15   ἀνέχεϲθαι μήτε ϲυϲχο-
       λάζονταϲ, ἂν ἐπιτιμῶϲι
       καὶ διορθῶϲιν—ὡϲ τὰ [θ]η-
       ριώδη τῶν ἑλκῶν οὐδὲ
       τὰϲ τῶν ἠπιωτάτων
20   φαρμάκων ὑπομένει
       προϲαγωγάϲ—ἀλλὰ κἂν ἑ-
       τέροιϲ ἐπιπλήττωϲιν,
       ἀλογώτατα πρὸς ἑαυτοὺς
       ὑποπτεύειν ἀεὶ τὰ πάν-
25   τα λέγεϲθαι—μήτε [τ]οῦ
       διὰ ϲυζητήϲεωϲ με-
       τέχειν ἀγαθοῦ· τοῦτο
       μὲν οὐδενὸς ὑπομένον-
       τοϲ ϲυνκαταβαίνειν, τοῦ-
30   το δ', ἂν εὕρωϲι, τῶν διε-
       ρεθιϲμῶν οὐχ οἷον ἀνε-
       π[ι]ϲτάτουϲ παρεχομέ-
33   νων, ἀλλὰ καὶ μέχρ[ι τοῦ ‖

19.9 ληπται leg. Wilke ‖ **10** αϲειτ leg. Wilke ‖ **9–10** ἢ δι' οἵαϲ]δή[πο]τ' αἰ|[τί]αϲ ἑ[αυτοῖ]ϲ γεγονότων Gomperz ‖ **11** McO ‖ **17** Gomperz ‖ **25** Hayter ‖ **19.32, 33** Gomperz

those who have become enemies ... are not allowed to study. [12] They[123] necessarily become incapable of progress[124] because they can put up with neither their teachers nor their fellow students, whenever these rebuke and correct them, just as the malignant kinds of ulcers cannot endure the application of even the mildest medicines,[125] [21] but whenever they (sc. the teachers) reprove others (sc. students), they necessarily suspect, most unreasonably, that everything is always being said against themselves— nor can they share in the good of studying together: for one thing, because no one can endure associating with them, and for another, [30] even if they find (someone who can endure it), their irritations not only make them inattentive, but even to the point of

---

room (cf. note 51 in the introduction). On lexical parallels between this part of the diatribe and *On Frank Speech*, see n. 142 in the introduction.

123. In this long and complicated sentence, ἀνάγκη (l. 13) serves as the main verb and takes two infinitives (γίνεcθαι, l. 13; ὑποπτεύειν, l. 24, coordinated by ἀλλά, l. 21). The first of these infinitives is modified by a pair of articular infinitives dependent on only one τῶι: ἀνέχεcθαι in line 15 and μετέχειν in lines 26–27 (!). Interwoven into the infinitives are three μήτε's, the first two paired neatly with καθηγητάc (l. 14) and cυcχολάζονταc (ll. 15–16) but the third preceding the second infinitive: "by enduring neither their teachers nor fellow students ... nor by participating." Rounding out the sentence are several subordinate clauses: one conditional clause (ἄν in l. 16), from which a comparison hangs (ὡc in l. 17); and a second conditional clause in l. 21, onto which several other clauses are loosely attached. The end of the sentence is lost in the lacuna in col. 20.

124. "Incapable of progress" translates ἀπρόβατοc, from προβαίνω, the original Epicurean term for "to make progress (in philosophy)"; cf. Epicurus, *Hdt.* 35; Philodemus, *Mort.* 18.9–10 and 38.21–22. The Stoics originally used προκοπή and προκόπτω, but by Philodemus's day, these had become philosophical jargon; cf. *Lib.* frags. 10.10 and 33.3 (προκοπή), *Mort.* 17.33, 38 and 23.8 (προκόπτω). On moral progress in Hellenistic philosophy, see the papers collected in Fitzgerald 2008b, especially Fitzgerald 2008a and Armstrong 2008.

125. The medical metaphors in *On Frank Speech* about *therapeia* by means of "harsh" and "mild" frank speech are echoed here; see Konstan et al., 1998, 20–23; McOsker 2020a; and the explicit cross-reference to *On Frank Speech* at 36.23–28.

Column 20

1 ἐκτρέχ[ειν ἀπὸ τοῦ φιλ-
   τάτου τὴν ε[ὐθεῖαν (.)
   καὶ λοιδορεῖν [..... .
   ἐφισταμενο[..... .-
5 φοντα καὶ λακ[τιζ- ...
   .....]ουcον[..... .
   ....]οιc[..... ..
   deest una linea
   ....]πι[.
10 ....]ωνοι
   .... (-)κ]αλουμεν(-)
   ....]ε καὶ προc
   ....]ν cοφίαι
   ....]τι· κἂν γὰρ
15 ....]κιαc
   .... δ]εκ-
   τικόν, ὅταν [κατὰ πάν-
   των ἢ ἐπὶ μ[ικ]ροῖc [ἀναγ-
   κάζῃ cκυθρωπάζει[ν
20 / καὶ λοιδορεῖν ἀπ⟦α⟧`λ´ύτωc
   καὶ διαβάλλειν καὶ πλάτ-
   τειν τὰ μὴ γε[γ]ονότα καὶ
   τὰ μηδενὸ⟦θ⟧`c´ ἄξι⟦ο⟧`α´ λόγου
   μεγαλύνειν, ἵνα τὴν εὔ-
25 λογον ὀργὴν ἐπιδείξη-
   ται, καὶ μυcτικοὺc λόγουc
   καὶ πράξειc ἐ⟦ν⟧`κ´καλύπτειν.
   τί γὰρ δεῖ λέγειν τὸ πολ-
   λοὺc ε`ὐ´θέτουc ὄνταc εἰc

20.1-2 Gomperz : ἐκτρέ[χειν ἐκ Indelli ‖ **3** [μὴ] * ‖ τὸν]| Gand. ‖ **4** ἐφιcτάμενο[ν Gomperz ‖ [καὶ] Gand. : [μήτε] * ‖ **4-5** νή]|φοντα Gomperz ‖ **5** λακ[τίζοντα Janko : λακ[τίζειν Wilke ‖ **6** ὄν[ταc Janko ‖ **11** Janko ‖ **13** ἐ]ν Gomperz ‖ **16-17** δ]εκ-|τικὸν * (cf. ad frag. 16.24-25) :] ἐκ|τικόν Wilke ‖ **17** Henry, cf. *Lib.* frag. 79.4-6 ‖ **18-19** Hayter ‖ **22** Gomperz

Column 20

running away [from their dearest friend] [straight down the road?] ... and reviling ...

[*nine lines missing or untranslatable*]

... wisdom ... capable ... [17] whenever it compels him to glower at everyone or over trifles and to revile people in filthy language and slander them and make up things that have not happened and magnify things not worthy of any mention, to display (sc. to his teachers) his reasonable anger,[126] and reveal secret words and deeds.[127] [28] Why should I say that many who are well-suited to

---

126. "Reasonable" anger is natural anger. Philodemus means that the students try to justify their empty fits of anger to their teachers as "natural."

127. By Philodemus's day, μυστικός often meant simply "secret" or "private"; see Cicero, *Att.* 4.2.7 (74, Shackleton Bailey 1965, 2:74) *cetera quae me sollicitant* μυστικώτερα *sunt* ("the other things that worry me are more private") and 6.4.2 (118, Shackleton Bailey 1968, 3:122), where μυστικώτερον introduces a brief passage written allusively and in Greek for secrecy. The angry students blurt out the secrets that had been entrusted to them, which ruins existing friendships and makes forming future ones harder. See also Cicero *Amic.* 22 and *Fin.* 2.85; Seneca *Ep.* 3.2–3; and Pliny the Younger *Ep.* 5.1.12.

20.30 φιλίαν, μήπω δὲ παρει-
λημμένους, ἄ[c]τροις cη-
μαίνεcθαι τὴν καὶ μόνον
πρόcοδον καὶ θεωρίαν
τῶν τοιούτων; ὑπομέ-
35 νει δ' αὐτοῖc οὐδὲ cυμβου-
λεῦcαί γε τῶν ὁπωcδήπο-
τ' αὐτοῖc προcηκόντων
οὐδείc, οὔτε αὐτόκλητοc
οὔτε παραληφθείc, ἐφ' ἑ-
40 κάc]τọ[υc ἐρε]θ̣[[υ]]ι̣ζομένοιc ‖

Column 21

1 ἢ μι]c̣ουμένοιc ἐπαμύ-
νειν κ]αιροῦ τε παραπε-
cόντοc κ]αὶ cυνεπιτί-
θεcθαι]. ᵛ ἔχουcι δέ, καὶ
5 ὡc ἐγώ γ' οἶ]μαι, ἀνελευ-
θέρουc ψυχὰc . . .]φα
desunt duo lineae
λεμ[. . . . .
10 γενέcθ[αι . . . .
εcποδ[. . . . .
διαβ[. . . . .
εκ[.]ν[. . . . .
αν καὶ [. . . . .
15 ρικλεινιạ[. . . . .
μίαν τὴν ἑạ[υτῶν (.) μὴ δια-

---

20. 31 Gomperz ‖ **35** super αυτο, Indelli το legit (solum ο O) ‖ **39** ⟨φοβηθεὶc⟩ ἐφ' Gomperz ‖ **39–40** ἐ[[κάc]τọ[υc Wilke ‖ **40** ἐρε]θ̣[[υ]]ι̣ζομένοιc Gomperz, "]c̣ψιζο (ψ vel littera deleta)" Wilke, υ linea obliqua deletam esse coniecimus ‖ **21.1–3** Gomperz ‖ **3–4** cυνεπιτί|[θεcθαι] Cobet ‖ **5, 6** Wilke ‖ **6** καὶ] McO ‖ **6–7** φα|[νερ- Janko ‖ **21.10** Wilke ‖ **14–15** οἱ πε]|ρὶ Janko ‖ **15** Κλεινία[ν Wilke ‖ **15–16** ἐρη]|μίαν vel οὐδε]|μίαν *: μίαν Wilke ‖ **16** ἑα[υτῶν Gand. : ἑα[υτοῦ Henry : ἐλ[ευθερίαν dub. Wilke ‖ μὴ * ‖ **16–17** δια]|γ[αγ]ọ́ντεc * post ἀ]|γ[αγ]ọ́ντεc Delattre-Monet

friendship but have not yet become firm friends want to reckon even the approach and the sight of such people by the stars? [128] [34] Not one of those who have any relationship to them whatever wants even to give them advice, whether spontaneously or by request, irritated as they are with everyone,

---

Column 21

or to defend them when they are hated and, when occasion arises, to join with them in attack.[129] They have, [as I supp]ose, slav[ish souls] …

[*ten lines missing or untranslatable*]

… [16] [by not having led]

---

128. An amusing hyperbole: those who are well-suited for friendship want to be so far away from angry men that they must use astronomical methods of calculating long distances to determine where the angry men are or when they will next see them. See Indelli's note for a collection of parallels and discussion.

129. Or possibly "join with them in their defense," LSJ, s.v. "συνεπιτίθημι," II.1 and 2.

21.17 γ[αγ]ό̣γ̣τες ζωὴν ι̣[..
       νον τῶν οἰκείων ἐξ ἑ-
       κ]ά̣στου χρει[ῶ]ν ἀτευκτοῦc[ι,
20   μᾶλλ[ον] δὲ καὶ τῆς ἄνευ
       φιλίας καὶ συγγενείας ἐ-
       πιπλοκῆς ἐν ῾ί᾿οις καὶ συλ-
       λαλήσεως διαγωγὴν ἐ-
       χούσης καὶ μάλιστα τοῖς
25   ἰδιώταις ἐστέρηνται. το-
       σοῦτο γὰρ ἕκαστος ἀπο-
       λείπει τοῦ προσπελά-
       ζειν τοῖς τοιούτοις ὁμει-
       λήσων, ὡς καὶ φεύγει πε-
30   ριληφθεὶς ἀπὸ τύχης ἐν
       κο[υ]ρείοις ἢ μυροπωλί-
       οις [ἢ] συμποςίοις ἢ παρα-
       καθίσας ἐν θεάτροις ὡς
       κύων τετοκυῖα· παραπλη-
35   ςίω[ς δ]ὲ οὐδ' εἰς ταὐτὸ τολ-
       μᾶι π[λ]οῖον [ἐ]μβαίνειν
       οὐδὲ γειτονεύειν· ἔα γὰρ [[τ]]
       τὸ κοινωνεῖν τινος ἢ
       πρός τι τοιοῦτο συνκα-
40   ταβαίνειν [..... ...] ||

21.17 γ (vel ιο) [..]πατες leg. Wilke ‖ **17–18** χ[οι]|νὸν * ‖ **18–19** ἑ|[κ]ά̣στου χρει[ῶ]ν Gomperz, Spengel ‖ **19** ἀτευκτοῦς[ι] Wilke post Gomperz (ἀτευκτοῦς|ιν) ‖ **20** μᾶλ-λ[ον Spengel : κἄλλοι Wilke ‖ **31, 32, 35, 36** Gomperz, Spengel ‖ **37** ἔα Henry : ἐᾶ Spengel, Gand.

their life ... they fail to meet their own needs from anyone, or rather, they are deprived of even that involvement and conversation—without friendship or kinship[130]—with others that provides entertainment, particularly for normal people.[131] [25] Everyone avoids approaching such people to converse with them to such an extent that they even run away when by chance (such a person) is encountered in barber shops or perfume shops or at drinking parties or has sat down in the next seat in a theater "like a bitch that has just given birth."[132] [34] Similarly, no one dares to embark on the same ship or live next door, let alone engage in a business deal or go along with them in some such thing ...

---

130. I.e., they do not even have a superficial relationship (ἐπιπλοκή) or ability to converse (cυλλάληcιc) with other people, not to mention a close relationship like friendship or kinship, and cannot get the pleasure and utility that people usually do from their relationships.

131. An ἰδιώτηc is a "non-philosophical person, layperson" (LSJ, s.v. III). Such a one is contrasted with philosophy students at *Lib.* frags. 14.3, 31.11; col. 11b.1–2; and with ἰδιωτικόc, col. 8b.3.

132. The κύων τετοκυῖα may be a relic of a hexameter verse end, perhaps from a proverb in metrical form. Several proverbs and fables involving dogs are known, but not this one, though as Gigante (1987) points out, it must be akin to the description of a protective mother dog at *Od.* 20.14–15. Ennius may parody the proverb: *tantidem quasi feta canes sine dentibus latrat* ("worth as much as the barking of a toothless pregnant bitch [or "bitch protecting her litter"]). (frag. 528 Vahlen 1903, 96 = lxxxv Skutsch).

Column 22

desunt ca. 8 lineae

1 ευςπ[.]ρα[..... ....
   ....]ι τε καὶ προ[.....
   το]ύτοις ἐπιτη[..... .
   τ]οῦ διερεθίςα[ντος.. (.)
5 .] ποιῆςαι προ[.....
   ....]εν προςε[..... .
   ....]τειν παρ[..... .
   ....]ως αναξ[..... ..
   ....]ν[...
10 .]ηθε[..... ..]αδ[....
   εἰρηκὼ[ς ....] οὑτωςὶ
   ποίηςο[ν..... ... κ]ραυ-
   γ]άζειν [..... ...]ες
   ἢ] βριμ[ω]μέν[ους ἀδο]κή-
15 τως, τὰ [δ]ὲ πρ[ὸς αὐτο]ύς,
   ὅταν [εἰ]ρηκέν[αι τι δοκ]ῶ-
   ςιν ἢ πεπραχ[έ]να[ι κ]α-
   θ' αὑτῶν, ⟦οι⟧ εἶτ' ἐπακολου-
   θοῦςι μετὰ τῶν ςυνε-
20 πιςπωμένων ἐκκακχά-
   ζοντες καὶ πονπεύον-
   τες, ἄχρι ἂν καὶ παρακό-⟦ι⟧
   ψαι ταῖς ἀληθείαις τῶι
   χρόνωι ποιήςωςιν. πα-
25 ρακολουθεῖ δ' αὐτοῖς,
   κἂν μονότροπον ἔχω-

22.1 π[α]ρὰ Wilke ‖ 2–4 πρὸ[ς τοῖς τοι[ο]ύτοις ἐπιτη[ρεῖται ὑπὸ | τ]οῦ διερεθίςα[ντος Gomperz ‖ 3 το]ύτοις Indelli ‖ ἐπιτη[δει- * ‖ 6 μ]ὲν πρὸς ἑ[τέρους Gand. ‖ 8 ὡς ἀναξ[ίους Gand. ‖ 11 εἰρηκὼ[ς Gomperz ‖ 11–12 [αὐτῶι,] "οὑτωςὶ | ποίηςο[ν" Wilke ‖ 12–13 κ]ραυ|[γ]άζειν Gomperz ‖ 14 Wilke (ἢ) iam Gand.); vel βριμ[ού]μεν[ους possis ‖ 15 τὰ [δ]ὲ Wilke : τά [τ]ε Gomperz ‖ πρ[ὸς αὐτο]ύς Gomperz : πρ[ὸς πολλο]ύς Delattre-Monet ‖ 16 εἰ]ρηκέν[αι τι Hayter ‖ 16–17 δοκ]ῶ|ιν Gomperz ‖ 17–18 πεπραχ[έ]να[ι κ]α]θ' Hayter ‖ 21 lege πομπ-

Column 22

[*eleven lines missing or untranslatable*]

... [4] of the one who irritated ... to do ...

[*five lines untranslatable*]

... [11] having said ... "do thus" (?) ... to yell ...

... or [unex]pectedly indignant, but as for what concerns [themselves], whenever they [thi]nk that anyone has done or said [something] against them, [18] then they pursue (him), guffawing and yelling insults, with others dragged along, until in time they make (themselves) go mad in very truth. [24] And if they lead a solitary life,

22.27 ϲι βίον, ὑπὸ τῆϲ ἐρημί-
ας καὶ τῆϲ ἁρπαγῆϲ τῶν
ὑπαρχό[ν]τ[ω]ν [κ]αὶ τῆϲ
30 ὑφοράϲεωϲ τ[ῶ]ν κληρο-
νόμων ἐγβά[λλ]εϲθαι. 〚κ〛
κἂν γήμωϲι, τ[ῇ] ˋγυναιˊκὶ π[...] ‖

Fragment E

1 υμηϲ ἐκκαλο[υ- . . . .
προπίπτε[ιν . . . . . .
τὰ ϲυμβαίν[οντα . . . .
τι μεθοδευ[. . . . .
5 δευμα. περὶ δ[ὲ . . . .
. . . .] ἡμεῖϲ [. . . . . . .
. . . .]πον[. . . . .

Column 23

desunt ca. 9 lineae

10 . . . .] ἀφορη-
τ . . . . π]ρὸϲ ἅπανταϲ
. . . .]ϲι γερόντων
. . . .]ειν δυϲκολι-
. . . .]οι[. . . . .]ται
15 . . . .]ει
θε[. . . . .
μηδ[. . . . .

22.29, 30, 31 Gomperz ‖ **32** π[άλι(ν) *; cetera v. app. ad frag. E l. 1 ‖ **E.1** ἀ]|κμῆϲ Janko : πρὸϲ] | ⟨λ⟩ύμηϲ Schoene, περὶ] | ⟨λ⟩ύμηϲ Gand. ‖ εκκαλο legit Wilke, O (hodie P legi nequit) : ἐγκαλο[ῦνταϲ Bücheler : ἐκκαλο[υμένηι Gand. ‖ **2** Gomperz ‖ **3–5** ϲυμβαίν[οντα ἢ ἄλλο] | τι μεθοδεύ[ονταϲ μεθό]|δευμα Wilke ‖ **4–5** ἐπιτή]|δευμα * ‖ **5** δ[ὲ Philippsonx ‖ **23.10–11** ἀφορη|[τ- * ‖ **11** Gomperz ‖ **12** παι]ϲὶ Gomperz ‖ **13–14** ὑπογράφ]ειν δυϲκολί|[αϲ Gomperz

they come to be outcasts because of their isolation, the theft of their goods, and their suspicion of their heirs. [32] And if they marry, to their wife ...

Fragment E[133]

... accusing[134] ... to occur[135] ... things happening ... but about ... we ...

Column 23

[*circa ten lines missing or untranslatable*]

... [11] to(ward) all ... of old men ... bad temper[...

[*six lines untranslatable*]

---

133. On the placement of this fragment, see the introduction, p. 109.
134. This word (only ἐκκαλο[υ- in the Greek) and the end of the previous column have suggested the emendation ⟨λ⟩ύμης for the first word of the fragment. Emendation seems required: Homeric ὑμῆς (*Od.* 9.284), from ὑμός = ὑμέτερος, is hardly possible, and no other known word would divide this way across the line boundary. The scribe makes several errors of line division, but they are all corrected—perhaps the column-end interfered?
135. Cf. προπεcούcης αὐ[τῶι, frag. 28.24.

23.18 μοιρ[..... ....
   ⎯μονίας δ[..... ..... .
20 πολλὰ κα[ὶ τῶν προ]κειμέ-
    νων λόγο[ν αἰτ]οῦντές
    τε {ς} [κ]ατὰ [πυ]κνὸν προς-
    ενφυσάν[τω]ν παραγω-
    γάς, ἀπολλύοντές ᾽τε᾽ διὰ
25 τοὺς θυμοὺς ἑκουσίως
    οὐκ ὀλίγα, καὶ διὰ τὴν
    ἄρρητον ἐπιθυμίαν
    τοῦ μετελθεῖν τινας
    ὅλας τὰς οὐςίας ἐξανα-
30 λίςκοντες, ἐνίοτε δ' ὑ-
    πὸ τῶν γεγονότων ἐχθρῶν
    καταδικαζόμενοι καὶ
    παντελῶς ἀναγκαζό-
    μενοι τῶν ⟦ν⟧ ὑ⟦ν⟧᾽π᾽αρχόν-
35 των ἐκπίπτειν. ἀφίη-
    μι γὰρ τοὺς ἐκκοπτομέ-
    νους ὄμματα δούλους,
    πολλ[ά]κις δὲ φονευομέ-
    νου[ς, ἂ]ν δὲ βά᾽λω᾽ςι καλῶς,
40 δρα[πε]τεύοντας. παρέ-
    πεται δ'] αὐτοῖς καὶ τὸ ‖

23.18–19 (μετ') εὐδαι]|μονίας Gand. vel (μετὰ) κακοδαι]|μονίας * ‖ **19** post μονιας signum :- legitur ‖ **20–21** κα[ὶ τῶν προ]κειμέ|νων Gand., Indelli : κα[ὶ τῶν] κειμέ|νων Wilke : τῶν παρα]κειμέ|νων Delattre-Monet ‖ **21** λόγο[ν αἰτ]οῦντές Wilke : λογο[ποι]-οῦντές Delattre-Monet : λόγῳ[ν ὑφαιρ]οῦντές Gand. (longius) ‖ **22** τε {ς} Hayter : {τες} Wilke ‖ cetera supp. Wilke, Gand. ‖ **22–23** * post προς|ενφύςαν[τες] Wilke et προς|ενφυςάν[τω]ν Delattre-Monet ‖ **31** lege ἐχθρῶν ‖ **38–40** Gomperz ‖ **41** Wilke : παρέ|[χουςι δ'] Gand.

... [20] much of what is before them, both demanding an account from people who have often[136] implanted[137] falsehoods (?) and losing voluntarily not a few (of their possessions) because of their rages and spending their entire fortunes [26] because of their unspeakable desire for vengeance on others, and sometimes condemned by those who have become their enemies, and compelled to be deprived completely of their property. [35] For I pass over the slaves with their eyes knocked out or often murdered or, if they have good luck,[138] becoming runaways. [40] And another consequence for them is ...

---

136. The phrase κατὰ πυκνόν = πυκνόν, used adverbially (LSJ, s.v. "πυκνός," B.II).
137. It is not clear what force προc- has here.
138. Literally, "if they happen to throw well," a metaphor from dice or draughts.

Fragment F

1 ἀηδ]εῖϲ δὲ γίνονται καὶ
γονεῦ]ϲι καὶ ἀ[δ]ελφοῖϲ καὶ
τέκνο]ιϲ καὶ το[ῖ]ϲ ἄλλοιϲ ἅ-
παϲι φίλοι]ϲ, ἃ[ν] καὶ μήπο-
5 τ' αὐτοὺϲ ἀνα]γκάϲωϲιν
. . . . πο]λλάκιϲ
. . . .]τα[.]ται
8 . . . .] πολλὴν

Column 24

ca. 8 lineae desunt

9 τα[. . . . . -
τη[. . . . .
10 βον[. . . . .
και [. . . . .
ειτε[. . . . .
μενο[. . . . .
—εξων[. . . . . .]και[. . . .
15 πιτ[. . . . .]ρομ[. . .
φοδετο[. . . . .]παρο[. . .
—ϲυναϲπίζειν. ⸍ ὅϲα [δὲ πέφυκεν ἐξ οἰκετῶν, οὐκ [ἐ-
λαττώματα μόνον ἐν
20 ὑπηρεϲίαιϲ, ἀλλὰ καὶ δ[υϲ-
χρηϲτία⟨ι⟩ καὶ ϲυμφορῶν ε[ἴ-

F.1–3 Gomperz (1 βαρ]εῖϲ Gand.) ‖ 3–4 ἅ|[παϲι φίλοι]ϲ ἃ[ν Wilke post Gomperz (ἅ|[παϲιν) : ἀ|[ναγκαίοι]ϲ Gand. ‖ 5 Gomperz ‖ 6 Wilke ‖ 24.17 [δὲ Gand. : [τε Gomperz ‖ 17–18 πέ]|φυκεν Hayter ‖ 18–19 [ἐ]|λαττώματα Gomperz, Spengel ‖ 20–21 δ[υϲ]|χρηϲτία⟨ι⟩ (pl.) Hayter : δ[υϲ]|χρηϲτία Spengel : δ[υϲ]|χρηϲτία⟨ϲ⟩ Gand.

Fragment F[139]

... and they become [unpleas]ant to [parents] and brothers and [children] and [all] their other [friend]s, even if they never [co]mpel [them] ... often ... much ...

Column 24

[*circa sixteen lines missing or untranslatable*]

... (no one is willing?) [17] to share a shield (with him?) in battle. And as for what comes from slaves, not just failures in services performed,[140] but difficulties[141] and all sorts of

---

139. On the placement of this fragment, see the introduction, pp. 109–10.
140. As with the man who quarreled with his single slave; see frag. 24.10–17.
141. For δυςχρηςτία, cf. Polybius's usage of this noun and the verb δυςχρηςτέω (both first and frequent in him) and Cicero, *Att.* 16.7.6 (415 Shackleton Bailey 1967, 6:178): *mirifica enim* δυςχρηςτία *est propter metum armorum* ("for owing to the fear of war, there is marvelous difficulty [sc. in getting cash]"). On the possible Roman context for this, see n. 143 in the introduction.

24.22 δὴ πάντα παρ⟦η⟧`α´κολουθε[ῖ,
διά τε τὰς βριμώσεις καὶ
τὰς κακηγορίας καὶ τὰς ἀ-
25   πειλὰς καὶ τὰς ἀναιτίους
κολάσεις καὶ συνεχεῖς καὶ
ὑπερμέτρους εἰς πᾶν ἐκ-
καλουμένων τῶν δού-
λων, ἂν μὲν αὐτοὺς ἀπο-
30   κτεῖναι δύνωνται, σφόδρ' ἡ-
δέως ποιούντων, ἂν δ' ἀ-
δυνατήσωσι, τέκνα καὶ
γαμετάς, ἂν δὲ μηδὲ ταῦ-
τα, τὰς οἰκ[ί]ας ἐμπιμπράν-
35   των ἢ τἄλλα κτήματα
διαφθειρ[ό]ντων. ἀλλὰ μὴν
ἐὰν καὶ πολλὰς ἔχωσ[ιν
ἀφορμὰς εἰς φιλανθρ[ω-
πίαν ἢ δικαιοσύνην [ἢ προσ-
40   ήνειαν [. . . . .
. . . .]νην ἡνδήποτ[ε . . ‖

Fragment G

1   . . . .] ἐν τοῖς
       . . . .]αστε
       . . . .]ημε
4   . . . .]ηψι

24.22, 34, 36, 37, 38 Gomperz, Spengel ‖ **39–40** Bücheler ‖ **40–41** ἀ|φροσύ]νην Delattre-Monet (longius) ‖ **41** ἢ ἡδο]νὴν Janko ‖ ἡνδήποτ[ε Wilke post Gomperz (οἱανδήποτε) ‖ ad fin. ἀρετὴν Gand. ‖ **G.4** ψι|[λ- Janko

misfortunes result, because of their (sc. the masters') rages, abuse, threats, [25] and unmotivated, continual, and excessive punishments of their slaves, who are incited to anything and everything, who, if they can kill their masters, do it with great pleasure, and if they cannot, their children and spouses, or if not even those, they burn down their houses or destroy the rest of their property.[142] [36] But in fact, even if they should have many impulses to philanthropy, justice or mildness ... whichever ...

Fragment G[143]

[*nothing legible*]

---

142. Another of Philodemus's complicated sentences. The initial clause, ὅcα τε πέφυκεν, "as for what comes from slaves," provides the connection to the previous sentence. The main verb (παρακολουθεῖ, l. 22) is singular because εἴδη is the closest subject. Then we find a lengthy prepositional phrase (διὰ ... ὑπερμέτρους, ll. 23–27) somewhat loosely connected to an objective genitive: rages, abuse, threats, and punishments inflicted on the slaves, τῶν δούλων, who are provoked to every outrage (εἰς πᾶν). Then we have a series of further genitive participles, each with a subordinate conditional clause (ll. 29–36), each still depending on τῶν δούλων.

143. On the placement of this fragment, see the introduction, p. 110.

Column 25

desunt ca. 5 lineae

1 κἄνθρωπο[ι . . . . (.) τὰ
δίκαια κρι[. . . . . . (.) καὶ κα-
χόμιλοι γινόμε[νοι καὶ κα-
τὰ τῶν ἀπαντώ[ντων. πολ-
5 λὰ δὲ ἀνατρέπο[υσι . . . (.)
ἀνευ[δ]όκητα πᾶς[ιν οἱ ποι-
οῦντες ἀνθρώποι[c . . . .
ταῖc ἄλλαιc κατατ[. . . . (.)
. . . .]ιπ[. . . . .
10 . . . .]c[. κ]αὶ πα[ρὰ
τοῖc προcή]κουcιν καὶ παρὰ
τοῖc ὀθνείοιc, ἑκάcτου τοῖc
ὁμοίοιc εἰκότωc ἀμε⟦ρ⟧`ί´βεc-
θαι τὸν ἀcυμπερίφορον
15 ──δικαιοῦντοc. ⌶ ἀναφ⟦ρ⟧`α´[ί]νουcι
δὲ πολλάκιc ὑπ' ὀργῆc καὶ
γεγονυίαc ἑαυτῶν cυν-
ωμοcίαc καὶ πράξειc ἄλ-
λαc ἀπορρήτουc, ὥcτε καὶ
20 μεγάλα`ι´c δι' αὐτὸ τοῦτο
περιπίπτειν cυμφοραῖc.
ἡδεῖα δ' αὐτοῖc οὐδὲ θέα
γίνεται διὰ τὴν ὀργήν,
οὔτε λουτρὸν οὔτε cυμ-
25 πόcιον οὔτε ἀποδημία

25.1-8 valde difficiles ‖ **1** ἀφυεῖc Wilke : οὐδ' (καὶ οὐχ Gand.) οἷοί τε Gomperz : ἀδύνατοι * ‖ τὰ] Gomperz ‖ **2-3** κρί[νειν καὶ κα]χόμιλοι Gomperz ‖ **3-4** γινόμε[νοι κα]|τὰ Gomperz, καὶ ins. Janko ‖ **4** ἀπαντώ[ντων * (cf. 14.31) : ἀπάντω[ν Gomperz ‖ **4-5** πολ]|λὰ Gomperz : ἔπιπ]|λα * ‖ **6** ἀνατρέπο[υcιν Gomperz ‖ οἱ Janko ‖ **6-7** ποι]|οῦντεc Wilke ‖ **7** ἀνθρώποι[c Gomperz ‖ ad fin. κἀν Gomperz : ἐν Gand. ‖ **8** κατατ[ριβαῖc Wilke ‖ **10-11** κ]αὶ πα[ρὰ | τοῖc Gomperz ‖ **11** προcή]κουcιν Bücheler : cυνοι]κοῦcιν Gomperz ‖ **15** Gomperz

Column 25

[*circa five lines missing*]

.... and people ... the just ... and are bad company [even to those they casually meet.] And they cause much disturbance ... things discreditable in the eyes of all persons ... doing ...

[*two lines untranslatable*]

... (at odds?) [10] both among [his relatives] and among strangers, since each one deems it right to repay the uncompanionable man with similar actions, as he deserves. [15] In their anger, they often reveal conspiracies they have been part of and other secret practices,[144] so that for this very reason they fall victim to great misfortunes. [22] They cannot even enjoy a public spectacle because of their anger, or a bath or drinking party or a trip

---

144. On secrets, see 20.26–27 with n. 127. The students grow up and betray more dangerous confidences than mere school gossip.

25.26 μεθ' ὡνδήποτε ἀνθρώπων [ο]ὔτε ἄλλο τῶν ἐπι-
τερπῶν εἶναι δοκούντων
οὐδέν, ἀλλὰ πάντα πα-
30 ραμιϲγομένων τῶν ἐ-
ρεθιϲμῶν διὰ νεῦμα καὶ
ψιθυριϲμὸν καὶ γέλωτα
καὶ τῶν ἐφ' [ο]ἷϲ ἐθυμώθη-
ϲαν ὑπό τινοϲ ἀνάμνη-
35 ϲιν καὶ τῶν δια[.....] ‖

Fragment H

1   μα..ινα[....]μο[.....
κἂν περι[.....   ....
καταφρον[.....   .....   .
ἐπὶ πᾶϲιν [.....   .....
5   καὶ τὰ ϲυμ[.....   .....
...] εἶναι [.....   .....
...]νεοιϲ ου[.....   .....
...]ων ευ[.....   ....
....]πο[.....   ....
10 *deest una linea*
οϲω[.....   .....
τ[.....   ....
....]ϲονο[.....   .....
deest una linea
15 ..]ετ[.....   ....

25.27 Gomperz, Spengel ‖ **33** Hayter ‖ **35** δια[βολῶν Delattre-Monet : δι' ἃ [κακῶϲ ἐποίηϲαν, μετάγνωϲιν Wilke in apparatu ‖ **H.1–2** |κἂν Wilke : οὐ]|κ ἂν * ‖ **3** καταφρον[ῆι McO

with any sort of people whatever or any of the things considered pleasurable, [29] but in everything their irritations are mixed in because of a nod, a whisper, a laugh, or a reminder of the things over which they were enraged by someone, and of the ...

Fragment H[145]

... even if ... [have] contempt ... in all ... and the ... to be ... young (?) ...

---

145. On the placement of this fragment, see the introduction, p. 110.

Column 26–27.1

desunt ca. 6 lineae

1   κἂν κρ]αυγάϲωϲιν ἢ [γυ-
    ναῖ]χ᾽ ἢ παιδάριον ἤ τι
    ἄλλο] τῶν τοιούτων, κἂν
    μὴ ὅτι] ἀνθρώπους, ἀλλὰ
5   καὶ] ἄλογα [[ι]] ζῷα καὶ
    δὴ κἄ]ψυχα καὶ μικροῦ δεῖν
    . . . . . .(.)]η γὰρ ἐνίων ου
    . . . .]ρα
    . . . .]ϲ[.
10 γ᾽] ἔτ[ι] πικ[ρότερον] τῶν
    ὀργίλων παθῶν, ἥ τε φύ-
    ϲιϲ καὶ τὰ κιρνάμενα
    ταύτηι κακοδαιμονικῆϲ
    γέμει [π]ικρίαϲ. καὶ ϲυνοι-
15 κοῦϲι δὲ φόβοιϲ καὶ ἀγω-
    νίαιϲ καὶ ταραχαῖϲ, καὶ κα-
    θ᾽ ὃν ἐνεργοῦϲι χρόνον καὶ
    μετὰ ταῦτα, τοτὲ μὲν
    ἐπὶ τῶι μὴ δύναϲθαι με-
20 τελθ[ε]ῖν, τοτὲ δὲ ἐννο-
    οῦντεϲ ὅϲουϲ ἔχουϲιν ἐ-
    χθρούϲ, τοὺϲ δὲ μιϲοῦνταϲ
    ἄλλωϲ ἢ καταφρονοῦν-
    ταϲ, οἰκείουϲ τε καὶ τῶν ἔ-
25 ξωθεν ἀνθρώπουϲ. ⌐ πολ-
    λάκιϲ δὲ καὶ τὸν παρ᾽ ἑτέ-
    ρων οὐκ ἀναμένουϲιν θά-

26.1 κἂν Wilke ‖ ὑβρίϲωϲιν ἢ κρ]αυγάϲωϲιν Bücheler ‖ **1–2** [γυ|ναῖχ᾽] Wilke post Gomperz (γυ|ναῖκα in apparatu) ‖ **2–3** τι | [ἄλλο] Gomperz ‖ **4** Bücheler post Gomperz (οὐχ ὅτι) ‖ **5** Crönert ‖ **6** Wilke ‖ **7** ad init. [πάντα] Bücheler : [λίθουϲ] Janko : [ϲκιάϲ] Wilke : [αὐτοὺϲ] Gomperz ‖ ἤδ]η * ‖ **10** τί γὰρ ἔτι πικ[ρότερον Gomperz (γ᾽ ad init. Wilke) ‖ **14, 20** Gomperz, Spengel

Column 26–27.1

[circa six lines missing]

[... even if they] shout at their [wife] or slave or any[thing else] of that sort, and not just human beings but dumb brutes and indeed inanimate things, and well-nigh even ...

[two lines illegible]

... [10] a thing even more bitter than their angry emotions: both their nature and that which is mixed with it (sc. their nature) are filled with miserable bitterness. [14] They live with terrors and agonies and disturbances both while they are acting and afterwards, sometimes because they cannot get their revenge, sometimes because they consider how many enemies they have, and those who hate them especially or[146] despise them, both from among their kinsmen and people outside the family. [25] Often they do not even await death at the hands of others,

---

146. The phrase ἄλλως ἤ usually means "otherwise than, differently than," but it does not seem have that force here. Rather, the words are separate, with ἄλλως "especially" or "in particular" construed with the participle and ἤ meaning "or."

26.28 νατον, ἀλλὰ διὰ τὸ μὴ δύ-
να⟨σ⟩θαι μετελθεῖν ἢ διὰ
30 τὸ μετελθόντας ἀνήκεσ-
τα προσδοκᾶν ἢ διὰ τὴν
/ ἐφ' οἷς 〚τ〛 〚ἔ〛πραξαν μετάγνω-
c[ιν ἢ τι] τοιοῦτον ἑαυτοὺς
34 κατε]κρήμνιcαν ἢ κατέ- ‖
27.1 [cφαξαν

Column 27.12–28.5

desunt ca. 10 lineae
12 / δ[..... ....
δι[..... ....
νο[..... . λέγο]με[ν ἐγ-
15 γενέcθαι καὶ διαβολ〚η〛ʼὰcʼ καὶ
μωμητικὰ καὶ μυρίας ἄλ-
λας κακίας, δι' ὧγ καὶ αὐτῶν ὑπερμεγέθως κολά-
ζονται. τῆι γε μὴν ἀνεπι-
20 εικεῖ καὶ ἀνημέρωι καὶ
τραχείαι διαθέcει, παcῶν
ὀλεθριω〚ν〛τάταις νόcοις,
cυνέζευκται τὸ πάθος, ἀ-
φ' ὧν εἰς πᾶcαν αἰκείαν τοῦ
25 δοκοῦντος ἠδικηκέναι
προάγει, καὶ βιάζεται μη-
δὲ τῶν φιλτάτων ἀπέχεc-
θαι μετ' ἐπιθυμίας παν-
/ τὸς ὠνουμένης ἃ ποθεῖ
30 καὶ βριμώcεως θηριώδους
οʼὐʼδὲ παυομένης ὡς τῆς

26.32-34 Hayter ‖ 26.34-27.1 κατέ|[cφαξαν Bücheler : κατε|[πόντιcαν Gomperz ‖ 14-15 Indelli ‖ 15 sic legit Indelli, διαβολ〚η〛ʼαιcʼ legit Wilke)

but, because they cannot get their vengeance or because they got their vengeance and now expect fatal consequences [31] or because of their remorse for what they have done [or something] like that, they throw themselves off a cliff or [slit their own throats][147]...

Column 27.12–28.5

[after a restored first line, circa ten lines missing at the top of column 27; 28.1–5, which follow directly on 27.39 and form column 28 supra, were erroneously pasted above column 32]

... [14] [we say] that slanders and faultfinding and a myriad of other evils spring up, through which very things they are exceedingly severely punished. [19] And to this unyielding and ungentle and harsh disposition, the most destructive diseases of all,[148] the emotion is yoked, (characteristics) from which it (sc. the emotion) leads him on to every outrage against the one who appears to have wronged him, and it compels him not to spare even his dearest friends, with a craving that buys at any price [29] what it desires[149] and with a beastly rage that never rests, as that

---

147. Gomperz's supplement would mean "or throw themselves into the sea."
148. The plural ὀλεθριωτάταις νόcοις is surprising after the singular διαθέcει, but the plural refers to the characteristics of the bad *diathesis*: inflexibility, lack of gentleness, and harshness. The plural relative that follows has no antecedent if the phrase is emended to the singular.
149. Wilke rightly compares Heraclitus B85 D.-K.: "*thymos* is hard to fight with, for it buys whatever it wants at the price of spirit."

27.32 / τῶν λεόντων, ὅταν ἐκτὸς
ὁ βλάπτων γένηται τῆς
ὄψεως ἢ παύςωνται τῆς
35 ἐνδείας, ἀλλ' ἕως καὶ νε-
κρῶν προπηλακιςμοῦ βα-
διζούςης καὶ τὸ πέρας ὥς-
περ εἰς αὐτὴν τιμωρίαν
39 μετ]ατ[ρ]εποúςης. ͮ cυνήρ- ‖
28.1 τηται δὲ καὶ δυςκολίαι
καὶ] κατὰ βρῶςιν ʽκαὶ πόςινʼ καὶ κατὰ
cυμ]περιφορὰν φίλοις καὶ
κατὰ δ]ιακονίαν καὶ πᾶν τ[οι-
5 οῦτο. . . . . .]αι δὲ τὸ πα-

Column 28.7–40

post quinque lineas suppletas, una linea deest
7 απ[. . . . .
θοc[. . . . .
νανδ[. . . . .
10 χιcτα[. . . . .
περὶ το[. . . . .
cυμβαιν[. . . . .
δὲ καὶ καχ[. . . . .
τ[ῆ]c τε λοιδ[ορίας . . . . .
15 . . .]πε τὸν κ[. . . . .
καὶ φιλονικε[ῖν καὶ λυπ]εῖ[ν
καὶ] διαcύρειν καὶ πάν[π]ολ-
λα ποιεῖν ἕτερα δυςχερῆ,
cυναυξόμενον δὲ καὶ μι-

27.38 αὐτὴν ⟨τὴν⟩ Janko ‖ 39 Wilke ‖ 28.2 Hayter ‖ 3 Gomperz ‖ 4 init. supp. Hayter
‖ 4–5 τ[οι|οῦτο Wilke ‖ 5 βιάζετ]αι Wilke ‖ 5–6 δὲ τὸ πά|[θος Gomperz ‖
28.7–8 πά]|θος Janko ‖ 8–9 Μέ]|νανδ[ρος tempt. Wilke (cf. 38.27) ‖ 9–10 (τὰ) ἐλά]|-
χιστα * : τά]|χιστα Janko ‖ 12–13 cυμβαίν[ει, πολλάκις | δὲ καὶ καχ[ομίλοις εἶναι Wilke
(καχ[ύποπτος Gand.) ‖ 13 καχ[λάζ- Janko ‖ 14 Mewaldt ‖ 16–17 Gomperz

of lions does whenever the person harming them is out of sight, or whenever they cease from their hunger, but that progresses to defilement of corpses, and at last transforms (him) into something like vengeance herself.[150] [39] It is also conjoined with distemper in eating and drinking and relations with friends and performing one's duties and everything [like that] …

Column 28.7–40

[*after the five lines printed at the end of the last column, eight lines missing or untranslatable*]

… [14] of both reviling and … and to strive for victory, [give pain], disparage people, and do many other unpleasant things, and, as it grows stronger,

---

150. The absence of the article probably shows that Philodemus is using τιμωρία as a proper name, lightly personifying it.

252　　　　　　Philodemus, *On Anger*

28.20　　cανθρωπίας αἴτιον γίνε-
　　　 ται, ⟨ἐνίοτε⟩ δὲ καὶ ἀδικεῖν, ᵛ ἐπει-
　　　 δήπερ οὔτε δικαcτὴc οὔ-
　　　 τε βουλευτὴc οὔτ' ἐκκλη-
　　　 cιαcτὴc οὔτ' ἄρχων δύνα-
25　　 ται δίκαιοc εἶναι πάθεcιν
　　　 ὀργίλοιc cυνεχόμενοc, οὐ-
　　　 δ' ἄνθρωποc ἁπλῶc εἰπεῖν.
　　　 ἐπακολουθεῖ δὲ τοῖc ἔχου-
　　　 cιν αὐτὸ καὶ τὸ δεcποτικοῖc
30　　 γίνεcθαι καὶ καχυπ῾ό῾νοιc καὶ
　　　 ψεύcταιc καὶ ἀνελευθέροιc
　　　 καὶ δολίοιc καὶ ὑπούλοι῾c῾ καὶ
　　　 ἀχαρίcτοιc ᵛ καὶ φιλαύτοιc,
　　　 δι' ἃc αἰτίαc ῥᾴδιον cυνι-
35　　 δεῖν. ᵛ τί γὰρ δεῖ λέγειν ⟨τὸ⟩ βλε-
　　　 πόμενον, ὅτι τῶν ἀγαθῶν
　　　 εἰcιν ἄγευcτοι παρὰ τὸν βί-
　　　 ον ἅπαντα τῶν ἐκ ῥαθυμί-
　　　 αc τῆc ἀποδε⟦ι⟧κτῆc καὶ πρα-
40　　 ότητοc καὶ βαθύτητοc καὶ
　　　 νὴ τὸν Δ[ί]α̣ [...]ν[....]οc ‖

Column 29

　　　　 desunt ca. 5 lineae
1　　　]ωcαν[..... .....
　　　 ἐξαγριοῖ [..... ..
　　　 καὶ πρὸc τ̣[..... ..... .
　　　 ὀρθιάζε[ιν..... .....
5　　　 εἰ γένοιτο cω[τηρία διὰ

28.21 add. Wilke, post quem ⟨τοτὲ⟩ Janko : ⟨βιάζεται⟩ Henry : ⟨προάγεται⟩ Gomperz ‖ **35** * post Wilke (⟨τὸ πᾶcι⟩) ‖ **41** supp. Hayter ‖ sic legit Indelli : [....]ω[.]πος legit Wilke, cεμ]ν[ότητ]οc Janko : κοι]ν[ότητ]οc Mewaldt : ἀ]ν[άγωγ]ο̣ι tempt. Philippson ‖ **29.5** Gomperz

it becomes a cause even of misanthropy—[21] and ⟨sometimes⟩ even of doing injustice, since neither a juryman nor a council member nor a member of an assembly nor an archon can be just while in the grip of angry emotions, nor, to put it simply, can any human being. [28] Becoming despotic is the consequence for those who have it (a bad disposition? the emotion?), and suspicious, liars, slavish, tricky, false, ungrateful, and self-centered, for reasons it is easy to comprehend. [35] Why mention what is well known, that throughout their whole life they have no taste of the good things that come from the acceptable kind of good temper, mildness, self-control,[151] and by Zeus ...

Column 29

[*circa six lines missing*]

... [2] makes wild ... and to ... cry out ... if there could be sal[vation through]

---

151. The word βαθύτης is found three times as a description of character in letters of Cicero to Atticus (4.6.3 [= 83 Shackleton Bailey 1965, 4:98]; cf. 5.10.3 [= 103, 1968, 5:26]; and 6.1.2 [= 115, 1968, 5:78]): *et simul ne* βαθύτης *mea, quae in agendo apparuit, in scribendo sit occultior et aliquid satisfactio levitatis habere videatur* ("moreover the self-control I have shown in conduct might not be so apparent in writing, and such an apologia might seem rather lacking in dignity)." The word is said to be synonymous with εὐοργησία and πραότης at Σ Euripides, *Hipp*. 1038–1039. On the "acceptable kind of good temper" that is not lazy or overindulgent, see Indelli 1988, 199.

29.6 τῶν ἀναξα[ινόντων
      φαρμάκων· [ἂ]ν δ[ὲ μὴ ...
      καλῶς ἀποκρύπτ[ωσι
      πάντα τὰ] γεγονότα [...
10   ....]ιν[...
      π[..... ..]γαι δοκῇ[ι. αἰ-
      ϲχ[ύ]νεται [δ]ὲ καὶ φιλοσο-
      φία{ι} δι' αὐτὴν καὶ τὰς δι'
      αὐτὴν παρακολουθούσας
15   πράξεις, ὅταν οἱ προεστά-
      να[ι] δοκοῦντες αὐτῶν φω-
      ρῶνται τοιοῦτοι. κἀπαν-
      τῶ[σι] δὲ πολλάκι πολλαὶ
      συμφοραὶ καὶ φίλοις καὶ [[π]]
20   προσήκουσιν ἄλλοις, ἔς-
      τιν δ' ὅτε καὶ πατρίσι καὶ
      βασιλεία`ι´ς, οὐ πάλαι μόνον
      ὅθ' ἡ "μῆνις" ἐκείνη "μυρί'
      Ἀ[κ]χαιοῖς ἄλγη ἔθηκεν," ἀλ-
25   λ' ὁσημέραι· ͮ καὶ μικροῦ δεῖν
      "ὅσα τις ἂν νώσαιτο" κατὰ
      Δημόκρ[η]`ι´τον κα[τ]`κ´ὰ πάν-
      τα παρακολουθεῖ διὰ τὰς
      ὑπερμέτρους [ὀργάς. ἡ][μ]-
30   μεῖς δὲ τὰ δυνατ[ὰ π]ερι-
      γραφῆναι καὶ σύμμετρα
      καὶ πρόσχειρα μόνον ὑπε-
      μνήσαμεν. ͮ ἐπισημαινό-
      μεθα δὲ νῦν, [ἵ]να μᾶλλον
35   φοβώμεθα δ[..... ....] ‖

29.6 Gomperz ‖ **7** [ἂ]ν δ[ὲ Gomperz ‖ μὴ Janko ‖ **8–9** Wilke (ἀποκρύπτ[ηται Gomperz) ‖ **11–12** Gomperz (⟨κατ⟩αι|σχ[ύ]νεται Cobet) ‖ **13** del. Gomperz ‖ **16** Gomperz, Spengel ‖ αὐτῶν (i.e., 'qui semet ipsos gubernare videntur') Gomperz : αὐτων Spengel ‖ **18** Gomperz ‖ **29–30** Hayter ‖ **32** πρό{ς}χειρα Cobet et Gand. ‖ **34** Hayter

drugs that [tear open one's wounds],[152]... [7] but [i]f they should not conceal well [all that] happened ...

[one and a half lines untranslatable]

... [11] and philosophy is shamed because of it (anger) and the actions that follow because of it, whenever those who seem to be in command of themselves[153] are caught red-handed being such people. [17] Many times many misfortunes happen both to friends and others who are close (sc. to them), sometimes also to fatherlands and kingdoms, not only of old when that "wrath" "gave the Achaeans countless pains,"[154] but every day, and nearly, as Democritus says, "as many" evils "as one could conceive of"[155] all come about through excessive [fits of anger]. [29] But we have only mentioned those (sc. evils) that can be sketched out, the moderate and ordinary ones. [33] But now we point out, in order that we may fear more ...

---

152. The term ἀναξαίνω is frequently used in medical authors of tearing off scabs to get access to a wound, therefore a painful but occasionally necessary procedure.
153. Gomperz's reading (followed by Delattre-Monet); cf. LSJ, s.v. "προΐςτημι," A.II.1.
154. Homer, *Il.* 1.1–2.
155. Democritus B143 D.-K. Philodemus has a predilection for quotations from Democritus; cf. *Mort.* 29.27–30, 39.13–15; and *Mus.* 4.150.29–39 (Delattre 2007), as well as Gigante and Indelli 1980.

Column 30

desunt ca. 5 lineae

1   . . .]ιϲθ[. . . . .
    . . .]ινωϲ εἶπε λ[. . . . . .
    . . .] πάντας καὶ επ[. . . .
    . . .] καὶ διότι μάλιστ' [ἐρεθί-
5   ζον]ται πρὸς τοὺς φίλ[ους
    τε κα]ὶ ϲυνόντας, καὶ [τὴν
    ἔχθ]ραν ἢ τὴν ὀλιγωρίαν
    ἀφόρη]τον παρασκευά-
    ζουσιν ἑαυτοῖς . . . .]δε
10 . . . .]υωμεν
    . . . .]κοϲι μη-
    δ' ὡς οὐκ ἔχουσι τὸ πάθος, ὑ-
    πομιμνήϲκομεν, ὅτι οὐ
    μόνον συνεχῶς θυμοῦνταί
15 τινες, ᵛ ἀλλ' ἐνίοτε καὶ ταῖς
    κατ' ἀριθμὸν ὀργαῖς πολυ-
    χρονίοις ἐνέχονται καὶ
    δυϲαποκαταστάτοις, κἂν
    ἐπιϲχεθῶσι, πάλι καὶ πυ-
20 κνὸν ἀνοιδούσαις, τισὶ
    δὲ καὶ μέχρι τῆς τελευ-
    τῆς διαμενούσαις, πολλά-
    κις δὲ καὶ παρατιθεμέ- [ν]
    ναις παισὶ παίδων, καὶ δι-
25 ότι καὶ μεγάλους ἄνδρας
    ἐκβακχεύειν πεφύκασι,
    κἂν ἐπὶ ποσὸν ἐαθῶσι[ν],

30.1–2 [ἀ]|ληθ]ινῶϲ * ‖ **3** ad init. κατὰ] * : ἐπὶ] Philippson ‖ **3–4** ἐπ[ὶ πάν|των] Philippson ‖ **4–5** Wilke, qui etiam coni. [μά|χον]ται ‖ **5** φίλ[ους Gomperz ‖ **6, 7** Wilke (ἔχθ-) ‖ **8** ἀφόρη]τον Gomperz ‖ **8–9** παρασκευά|[ζουσιν Wilke ‖ **9** ἑαυτοῖς Philippson ‖ **9–10** ὅταν] δὲ Janko : ἵνα] δὲ | [μὴ Gand. ‖ **10** κωλ]ύωμεν Janko : -δεικν]ύ-ωμεν * ‖ **11** ad init. [ὡς τοῖς] * ‖ εἰρη]κόϲι Janko ‖ **13** ὅτε Gomperz

Column 30

[*circa seven lines missing or untranslatable*]

... [4] all and ... and because they are most [irritat]ed at both friends and companions and they rend[er] the enmity or the slight [unbearable to themselves] ... [11] nor as not having the emotion, we remind them that, not only are some continually enraged, but sometimes they are liable to separate[156] fits of anger that are of long duration and hard to recover from, and which, if they should be repressed, often swell up again, [20] and some stay with them even until death and are often handed down to children's children,[157] and that they naturally make even great men completely lose their minds, and if they relax for a while,

---

156. Here κατ' ἀριθμόν, "countable, individual" (Indelli: "singoli"), as opposed to cυνεχῶc, "continually."

157. For παῖδες παιδῶν, "descendants," cf. Plato, *Resp.* 2.363d4 and 366a7 with notes in Adam 1965. This part of the *Republic* is on Philodemus's mind in his peroration to the diatribe; see n. 160. The resentments and grudges held between two individuals are thus passed down to descendants and become feuds spanning generations (like that of the Hatfields and McCoys).

30.28 πάλ[ι]ν ἐπανατρέχουσι,
       / κἂν ἀμέτοχος ἦι τις ⟦ις⟧, ἐν-
30   γίνονται δι' αἰτίας πολλάς·
       καὶ διότι παντὸς ἅπτον-
       ται γένους ἀνθρώπων, ολο
       ..] .ν τῶν νωχελεστά-
       των], οὓς ια . . . α βαρυθυ-
35   μοτά]τους ἐνίοθ' ὁρῶ[μεν ‖

Column 31

desunt ca. 7 lineae

1   . . . .]καὶ διότι [. .
       . . . .] ὀρ[γ]αῖς μέτρον
       . . . .] .ατα δια ϲυγ-
       . . . .] .καὶ μέχρι
5   . . . .] . . .ονται[. .]ι
       . . . .] .ακειας με
       . . . .] .ις πτωμα
       . . . .] . . . . . διο

deest una linea

10   πλὴν τ[οῦ] καν[ονικοῦ
       λόγου. ᵛ τοὐναντίον δὲ
       πᾶς ἀντίδικος, ὁ μὲν ἔ-
       ξωθεν καὶ διερεθίζων
       παντοδαπῶς, γονεῖς δὲ
15   καὶ πᾶς προσήκων τὰ πολ-
       λὰ καὶ συνχαίροντες ὡς
       ἐπάνδροις, τῶν δὲ φιλοσό-
       φων οἱ μὲν φλυαροῦντες

30.28 Gomperz ‖ **32** ολο legit McO, ϲλο legit Wilke : ἀ̣δ̣ό|[λως Janko : ϲφό|[δρα ἂ]ν Philippson : ο̣ὐ̣χ̣ | [οἷο]ν Gomperz ‖ **33–34** νωχελεστά|[των, ο]ὓς Gomperz ‖ **34** υσιαι . . . α O : υσιαιδ̣ . .α N : υσιαλλια legit Wilke : τἆλλα Janko : κ[αὶ μάλ]α Bücheler : κ[αὶ ἅμ]α Gomperz ‖ **34–35** Gomperz ‖ **31.2** Wilke ‖ **6** κο]λακείας vel β]λακείας Gand. ‖ **7–8** το̣ῖς πτώμα|[σι(ν) Janko ‖ **10** Wilke ‖ **17** ἐπάνδρωι Spengel

they recur, and if ever a person is free from (sc. fits of anger?), [29] they can be engendered in him through many causes, and that they get hold of every kind of person ... of the most sluggish people, whom ... sometimes we see ... (are?) the most profoundly rage-filled ...

Column 31.1–24

[*circa seven lines missing*]

... and that[158] ... [2] a limit to fits of anger ... so far as ... (nothing can save a person from this?) [10] but can[onic] reasoning.[159] On the other hand, everyone is an opponent: the outsider who provokes anger in every imaginable way, parents and every relative who often rejoice as if over brave fellows,[160] [17] and the philosophers, the ones who babble

---

158. It may be that καὶ διότι in line 1 echoes ὅτι in 30.13 and καὶ διότι in 30.24–25 and 30.31, all following on ὑπομιμήσκομεν in 30.12. For Wilke's idea that a fragment from the top of col. 26 is to be placed between the end of col. 30 and the beginning of col. 31, see the introduction, p. 110.

159. The concluding sentences of the "diatribe" are in a tone of rhetorical seriousness: the final revelation is that not merely diatribe but the knowledge of canonic and the rest of Epicurean philosophy is necessary to conquer anger completely, as Philodemus already hinted in col. 2 (those who *only* censure anger). But notice the contemptuous drop back down to earth at the end.

160. Here Philodemus means to be taken as speaking to (or about) the younger students of his school (note "parents and other relatives"). He has a passage of Plato's *Resp.* 2 in mind, where Plato's brother Adeimantus complains to Socrates that fathers tell their sons that they must be just, but only for the material rewards that come from a good reputation: "for fathers say and recommend to sons, and all family members responsible for others tell them, that yes, one must be just, but not by praising justice for itself, but the good reputation to be got from it" (λέγουσι δέ που καὶ παρακελεύονται πατέρες τε ὑέσιν καὶ πάντες τινῶν κηδόμενοι, ὡς χρὴ δίκαιον εἶναι, οὐκ αὐτὸ δικαιοσύνην ἐπαινοῦντες ἀλλὰ τὰς ἀπ' αὐτῆς εὐδοκιμήσεις, 362e5–363a2). The relatives quote the poets, Homer, Hesiod, Pindar, and the rest, to support their argument (363a5–e3). The argument of material reward and punishment is all the praise and blame that these relatives and the poets offer when they recommend justice and discourage injustice (363e4–5). Indeed, if you press them, they do not really believe that

31.19 ἐν ταῖc παραμυθίαιc, οἱ δὲ
20 καὶ μετὰ cυνηγορίαc ἐ-
πιρρωννύντεc· ἀφ[ί]ημ[ι
μὲν ῥήτοραc καὶ ποιητὰc
καὶ πᾶcαν τὴν τοιαύτην
γρυμέαν. ⋎ ἔνιοι γοῦν τῶν
25 Περιπατητικῶν, ὥc που
καὶ πρότερον παρεμνήc-
θημεν διὰ προcώπων,
ἐκτέμνειν τὰ νεῦρα τῆc
ψυχῆc φαcι τοὺc τὴν ὀρ⟦ι⟧`γ´ὴν
30 καὶ τὸν θυμὸν αὐτῆc ἐξαι-
ροῦνταc, ὧν χ⟦α⟧`ω´ρὶc οὔτε κό-
λαcιν οὔτ' ἄμυναν εἶναι·
33 cυ[νε]πεζεῦχθαι γ[ὰ]ρ αὐ-

Column 32

1 τῶι τὸ μ]ετὰ τῆc πάcηc [ἀν-
ελευθε]ρίαc ὑποτρέχε[ιν
καὶ κο]λακ[ε]ύειν· ἔνιοι
δὲ καὶ α]ὐτο[μ]άταc ὑπ[οφέ-
5 ρειν ἀικεί]αc οὐδὲ [...
....]ρλοπ...

vacant 6 lineae

13 νε[..... ....
δρο[..... ....
15 απ[..... ..... ἐν τοῖc
πολέμοιc κα[ὶ τοῖc ἀνα-
λόγοιc καιροῖc ο[ὐκ εἴ-

31.21 Hayter ‖ **33** Wilke post Gomperz (ἐ]πεζ-, iam fere Gand.) ‖ **32.1** τῶι τὸ μ]ετὰ Wilke ‖ **1–2** [ἀν|ελευθε]ρίαc Schoene ‖ **2** ὑποτρέχε[ιν Wilke ‖ **3–5** Mewald ‖ **5** ἀικεί]αc Wilke ‖ **15–17** fere Gomperz (15 ἐν τε τοῖc Gomperz, 17 ο[ὐκ iam Hayter)

in their attempts to assuage it [anger] and the others who strengthen it by advocacy[161]—and I pass over orators and poets and all that kind of trash.

THE PERIPATETICS

Column 31.24–32.40

Now some of the Peripatetics, as we also mentioned at some point earlier with citations by name,[162] claim that people cut out the nerves of the soul when they deprive it of its anger and its wrath,[163] [31] without which there can be neither punishment nor self-defense, for conjoined with that[164] is [32.1] fawning and flattering with utter baseness; and some of them also (claim) [one submits to] unprovoked [assaults], and not even …

[*nine lines missing or untranslatable*]

… [15] [in] wars and at [comparable] crucial moments, it is n[ot

---

justice is always rewarded nor injustice punished, even materially (364a–366b2). This is an appropriate passage for Philodemus to evoke here at the end of his own diatribe against anger.

161. Philodemus briefly summarizes the opponents of the Epicurean view of anger: among nonphilosophers, there are close friends and family as well as outsiders; both groups provide harmful messages. Among philosophers, the inept "assuagers" are Stoics, advocating total suppression of all emotions, while the "advocates" are the Peripatetics (notice the chiasmus: babbling : attempts to assuage it :: strengthening it : advocacy).

162. The terms ἔνιοι and especially διὰ προςώπων suggest that in the earlier attack on the Peripatetics (see the notes on frags. 7–11) several Aristotelian philosophers were listed by name. Fleischer has shown that in the *Index Academicorum* Philodemus describes a hitherto unknown revival of the school in his day, converting several lifelong friends of his from the Academy to the Peripatos; for these, see the introduction, §6.4.

163. Here, as Philodemus will argue later and as often in Aristotle himself, *orgē* and *thumos* are clearly synonyms; see the introduction, pp. 77–78.

164. I.e., the soul deprived of anger.

32.18 ναι προσφέρεσθαι χω[ρὶς
ὀργῆς, ἢ θαρρεῖν ποιε[ῖ
20 καὶ πάντα ὄκνον ἀφα[ι-
ρεῖται καὶ δειλίαν κα[ὶ
ἀνικήτως ποιεῖ μέχρ[ι
καὶ θανάτου μένειν· [ὡς-
αύτως δὲ τὸ τιμωρητ[ι-
25 κὸν τῶν ἐκθρῶν κατα-
cκευάζειν, ὃ καλόν τε ὑ-
πάρχειν καὶ δίκαιον καὶ
cύμφορον ἰδίαι καὶ κοι-
νῆι καὶ πρὸς τούτοις ἡδύ.
30 διὸ τήν τε παράστασιν
/ τὴν εὔλογόν [[η]] τινων
καὶ τὸν ἄλογον οἶ[ον ἐν-
θουσιασμὸν οἴον[ται θυ-
μὸν εἶναι τὸν περὶ ο[ὗ δι-
35 αλεγόμεθα. καὶ παρο[ρᾶ
ὅτ[ι] χω[ρ]ὶς ὀργῆς ἔςτι [τὸ
πολεμε[ῖν κ]α[ὶ] ἀγω[νί-
ζε[c]θαι κ[αὶ πι]κρῶς χει[ροῦν,
/ μετ' ὀργ[ῆς δ]ὲ τον .[....
40 ....] ἐνέ[χ]εcθ[αι ‖

32.18–23 Gomperz ‖ **24** Wilke ‖ **25** lege ἐχθρῶν ‖ **32–34** Hayter ‖ **35** *post Wilke (παρ[ορῶ⟨cιν⟩, iam fere Gand.) : γὰρ ο[ὐχ Gomperz ‖ **36** ὅτ[ι] χω[ρ]ὶς Gomperz ‖ ἔcτι [τὸ Wilke : ἔcτι[ν Gomperz ‖ **37** πολεμε[ῖν Gand, Wilke ‖ **37–38** κ]α[ὶ] ἀγω[νί]-|ζε[c]θαι Gomperz ‖ **38–39** Wilke (ἄ)κρως enim brevius censuit) ‖ **32.39–40** τὸν [προcι|όντα βλάβαιc] ἐνέ[χ]εcθ[αι Indelli post Wilke (eadem, βλάβηι excepto)

pos]sible to go on the offensive without anger, which makes one courageous and takes away all shrinking and cowardice and makes one endure steadfastly even unto death. [23] In the same way, it creates a spirit of vengeance against one's enemies, a thing that is noble and just and profitable individually and communally and, in addition, pleasurable. [30] That is why they think that both the rational courage[165] of some people and their irrational "possession," so to speak, constitute the angry emotion[166] that we are talking about. [35] And (sc. this argument or he[167]) overlooks the fact that it is possible to fight and grapple and inflict bitter defeat without anger, but (that?) with anger…[168]

---

165. For εὔλογος … παράστασις, cf. εὔλογος ὀργή (20.24–5) and ῥαθυμία ἡ ἀποδεκτή (28.38–39); in Epicurean theory, emotions and behaviors can be vicious or acceptable, but the Peripatetic idea is different: the rational (εὔλογον) in the mature and wise is to the irrational (ἄλογον) as ruler is to subject and, like ruler and subject, they have different but complementary virtues (Aristotle, Pol. 1.12, 1260a3–7, Eth. nic. 1.13, 1102b13–28). For παράστασις, see LSJ, s.v. II.7.b, and Indelli's note on 32.23–29.

166. The word θυμός, here meaning just "anger," not "rage," is probably borrowed from his Peripatetic opponents.

167. Probably παρ[ορᾷ sc. ὁ λόγος "their argument overlooks" (or possibly παρ[ωρῶ⟨ςιν⟩ "they overlook").

168. The sentence continues in the next column, where ἐνέχεσθαι is translated. Wilke's suggested supplements are intended to mean "with anger that compels the person [who goes forth (into battle)] to be liable to [damages]…."

Column 33

1 βιαζομένης ⋎ καὶ πολλ[ά-
κις ἀνόπλους καὶ πρὸς τ[ὴν
φυλακὴν ἀποτυ[φλ]ούςης
καὶ τὸ c]ῶμα cυντριβούςης
5 καὶ μὴ]ν μᾶλλον α[ὐ]τοὺς
τῶν ἐναν]τίων κα[κ]ῶc δι-
ατιθείcης] καὶ κολα[. . . .
. . . . .].μηριcε.[. . . .
. . . .] διὰ τὰc α[. . . .
10 . . . .].ιμ[. . . .

desunt 6 lineae

17 . . . .] . . . [. . . . ..
. . . .] οὐχ ὅ[τι τὸ τι-
μω[ρεῖc]θαί τινα ἀλλὰ κ[αὶ
20 τὸ κολάζειν. ἔcται δ[ὲ] περὶ τούτου καὶ προβαίνου-
ςιν πλείων λόγοc. ⋎ πε[ρὶ δὲ
τῶν φληναφωμένω[ν
cτρατιωτῶν τί δεῖ [δια-
25 τρίβειν, ὡc ἀπειθ`ε΄ῖc [τῶι
cτρατηγῶι καὶ κρατ[οῦ]ν-
τεc αὐτοῦ καὶ πάντ' ἀ[περ-
γαζόμενοι κα{ι}κά, τ[ί δ]ὲ
περὶ τῶν νεύρων τῶν ἀ-
30 νεύρων καὶ ταχέως [ἐ-
γλυόντων [κ]αὶ κατ' ἄκριτον
ἐξόντων [β]ιαίως, ἀλλὰ

33.1–2 Hayter ‖ **3** Gomperz ‖ **4** Hayter ‖ **5** Wilke ‖ **6–7** Gomperz (qui etiam κολά[ζειν scripsit) ‖ **8** ἤριcε Janko ‖ **17–18** μ[ετὰ θυμοῦ] | καὶ ὀργῆc Indelli post Philippson (μ[ετ' ὀργῆc | θυμοῦ τε]) ‖ **18** ὅ[τι Janko : ο[ἷον Gomperz ‖ **18–19** τὸ τι]|μω[ρεῖc]θαί Gomperz ‖ **19** κ[αὶ Hayter ‖ **20, 22–26** Hayter (25 [εἰcι Gomperz) ‖ **27** Wilke post Gomperz (-τα [κάπερ-) ‖ **28** del. et supp. Wilke ‖ **30–33** Gomperz

Column 33

... that compels (the soldiers) to be liable to ... and often weaponless, and blinds them to keeping watch,[169] and wears down their bodies, and indeed [disposes] them worse than their enemies ... and ... punish ...

[*ten lines missing or untranslatable*]

... (prevents?) [18] [not only] getting vengeance on someone but even punishing him. [20] There will be more discussion of this as we go on. But why should we dwell on how the "soldiers" babbled about (sc. by them) are disobedient to their general, overpowering him and committing every evil,[170] [28] or why (dwell on) these nerveless "nerves" that are quick to collapse and will be in a state of violent confusion but

---

169. We take Philodemus to mean that soldiers who have lost their weapons must be even more cautious in battle but that anger can make them heedless of the precautions that they ought to take. Keeping watch requires calm and alertness, not distracting anger. Another possibility is to assume the loss of words such as cυμβάλλειν εἰc μάχην ἀναγκαζούcηc after ἀνόπλουc and translate "and often compels them to join battle unarmed and blinds them to their own protection," but supplementation is not really necessary.

170. More sarcasm about the supposed rule of the rational as commander over the irrational as its "soldiers," couched as yet another *praeteritio*.

33.33 οὐκ εὔτον[ί]αν ἐνποιούν-
των; ὁ δ' Ἀντίπατρος εἰ καὶ
35 πρὸς τὰ θηρία τοῖς ἀμυνο-
μένοις θυμοῦ χ⟦ε⟧ρεία πυν-
θάνεται ⟦α⟧ καὶ πρὸς τοὺς
ἀνταγωνιστάς, τῶν ἀλει-
πτῶν κραυγαζόντων "μὴ
40 —θυμοῦ." [κα]ὶ πρὸς τὸ κολάζειν ‖

Column 34

1 τοῖς ἱππικοῖς τοὺς ἵππ[ο]υς
καὶ τοῖς γραμματικοῖ[ς
καὶ] τοῖς ἄλλοις τεχνίταις
τοὺς μ]αθητάς, καί φησι
5 . . . . (.) χω]ρὶς ὀργῆς
. . . .]τέρων πολ-
desunt 9 fere lineae
16 [. . .ἐὰν τοὺς ἀοργήτους]
ὁμοίους ὁρῶ]μεν ὀρ-
—γίλοις, [ἰστ]έον ὅτι χω-
ρὶς αὐτ[οῦ τοῦ] πάθους καὶ
20 τῆς δια[θ]έσεως καὶ [τ]ῶν
ὅσα παρ' αὐτοὺς διὰ ταῦ-
τα γίνεται [τ]ἄλλα πάντα
ὅσων ἐποιησάμεθα τὴν

33.35 θηρία coni. Gomperz : θιτ[]ρι legit McO : ειτ[.] N : ειτρι O : ει .πι legit Indelli : ειτ[.]ρι legit Wilke, cui τ deleta videbatur) ‖ **40** [καὶ] Wilke : [φησὶ] Crönert ‖ πρὸς τὸ κολάζειν legit Crönert, P hodie haud legitur : τ]ὸ τε κ[ο]λά-[ζ]ειν Wilke (qui leg. ϙτςι) ‖ **34.1, 2** Gomperz ‖ **3-4** ad init. λει et εδω superpositas esse dispexit Crönert, ut vid., et Henry, v. 35.3-4 ‖ **3** Henry ‖ **4** Gomperz ‖ **5** κολάζειν χω]ρὶς Wilke ‖ **6-7** ἑ]τέρων πολ|[λῶν Gomperz, post quem 6 περὶ vel περὶ (δ')] Janko : ἐπὶ (δ')] McO ‖ **7** τεχνῶν] McO ‖ **16-17** Wilke in apparatu (e.g., cf. 24-31) ‖ **18** Hayter ‖ **19, 20** Gomperz ‖ **21-22** διὰ ταῦ|τά Delattre-Monet ‖ **22** Gomperz : γίνεται ⟨καὶ ταῦτα καὶ⟩ add. Mewaldt : γίνεται, ⟨ἔστι καὶ προσφέρεσθαι καὶ τιμωρεῖσθαι (vel sim.) καὶ⟩ dub. Gomperz

The "Anger" of Sages and Their Students (Cols. 34.16–37.9)   267

never create health in them? [34] Antipater[171] asks whether anger[172] is also of use for those defending themselves against wild beasts or against opponents in athletic contests, given that the trainers shout "Do not get angry!" and for horse trainers for punishing

Column 34.1–15

horses, and for grammarians [and] other craftsmen for punishing [their] students, and he claims ... [with]out anger ...

[*circa ten lines missing or untranslatable*]

THE "ANGER" OF SAGES AND THEIR STUDENTS

Column 34.16–40[173]

[... if we see those who are not irascible being like] the irascible, we must know that all the other things whose description we have set out occur without the emotion itself, the disposition, and all the things that are up to them personally because of those things (i.e., the emotion and disposition).[174]

---

171. Antipater of Tarsus (d. 130/129 BCE, *DPA* 1.220–23) was the student and successor of Diogenes of Babylon as head of the Stoic school in Athens. This is another sign, if it were needed, that Philodemus and his Epicurean sources use Stoic-Cynic diatribe sources freely in arguing against "empty" anger.

172. Again θυμός, not ὀργή; Philodemus is paraphrasing Antipater's argument against the Peripatetics and does not change his terms.

173. In the lacuna of eight to ten lines, the argument against the Peripatetics was concluded, and the topic of the Epicurean sage's "natural" anger, which lasts to the end of the treatise, was reintroduced with a view to combatting "minimalist" and "maximalist" views of it; see the introduction, pp. 66–71.

174. If the conditional clause is restored correctly, Philodemus is trying to explain why Epicurean sages, who are not irascible by disposition, sometimes appear to be. He

34.24　ἔκθεσιν. ˇ ἔστιν δ' ὅτε καὶ
25　περιΐστασθαι γίνεται δι-
　　ά τε τοὺς μαν[ι]οποιοῦντας
　　ἀνθρώπους καὶ διὰ τὸ τὰς
　　κοινότητας αὔξεσθαι,
　　δι' ἃς ὀργίλοι φαίνονται,
30　καὶ εἰς τὸ ταῖς ἀ[λ]ηθείαις
　　ὀργίλους εἶναι. ˇ καθόλου
　　δὲ ἰστέον, ὅτι καθαρῶς
　　τις ὢν ἀόργητος οὐ πο-
　　λὺν χρόνον ἀποδώσει
35　φαντασίαν ὀργίλου· πλεί-
　　ω δὲ ἀποδιδ[ο]ὺς οὐκ ἔσ-
　　τιν βαθύς, ἀλλὰ μόνον
　　οὐ τ[οι]οῦτος [ο]ἷος δοκεῖ.
　　φαί[νο]νται δ' [οὖ]ν πρὸς τό-
40　σον καὶ τὴν [ἐν]αντιωτά- ‖

Column 35

1　τη]ν ἔχοντες διάθεσιν,
　　ὥστε κἂν σοφός, καθάπερ
　　ἀμέ‵λει′ καὶ Ἐπίκουρος
　　ἀπέ‵δω′[κεν ἐ]νίοις τοιού-
5　του [φαντασ]ίαν. ἐ̣ίησαν
　　δ' ἂ[ν] αἱ πα[ρ]α[δεδειγ]μέναι
　　κοινότη[τες τόσαι] κ̣αὶ τοι-
　　αῦται γ[. . . . .]ω[.

34.26, 30, 36, 38, 39 Gomperz ‖ **39–40** τό|cον Wilke (τ ON, τ̣ potius quam π̣ P) : πο|cὸν Gomperz ‖ **40** Gomperz ‖ **35.1** Hayter ‖ **3–4** litteras λει et ε̣δω superpositas huc ex 34.3–4 transtulit Henry ‖ **3** Henry legit ut Hayter coni. ‖ **4** Gomperz ‖ **5** [φαντασ]ίαν Gomperz ‖ ἐ̣ίησαν Henry : [ἐ]πῆσαν Mewaldt ‖ **35.6** δ' ἂ[ν] Henry : δ' ἂ[ρ] Wilke : δ' [ἐν] Jensen (δ[.] O, δα̣[.] N) ‖ αἱ πα[ρ]α[δεδειγ]μέναι Henry : αἱ πα[ρ]α[δεδο]μέναι Wilke (ad init.,]αιτ[̣ leg. Indelli, sed αιπ[mavult McO : αιπα[ON) ‖ **7** κοινότη[τες Gomperz ‖ τόσαι] Wilke ‖ **8** γ[ενόμεναι Gomperz ‖ τ]ῶ[ν Janko

[24] Sometimes, however, it comes about that they even become irascible in truth, both because of people driving them crazy and because of the intensification of the characteristics because of which they appear irascible. [31] But generally we should know that someone who is, in the full sense of the words, "not irascible" will not give an impression of being irascible for a long time or, if he does give that impression for a longer time, will not be profoundly so, but just not the sort of person that he seems to be. [39] At any rate, people do appear (irascible) to that extent even when their disposition is quite opposite,[175]

Column 35

so that even a sage (sc. might give), as, for instance, even Epicurus gave the impression of (being) such a person to some.[176] [5] The characteristics [indicated] might be [so many] and such that …

---

says that they might give an appearance of being angry, but without the emotion, disposition, or their own moral responsibility for actions caused by "empty" anger being in play. Philodemus usually uses ὀργίλος in the meaning "irascible (by a bad disposition)." Thus, someone "who is, in the full sense of the word, not irascible (ἀόργητος)" is of a good disposition with regard to anger and experiences only natural anger, like the sage.

175. As Wilke notes (1914, xxviii), this is a deliberate reference to the Epicurean saying that "when once one has become a sage, it is impossible he should ever take on the opposite disposition" (τὴν ἐναντίαν...διάθεσιν, Diogenes Laertius, Vit. phil. 10.117).

176. One expects a potential optative after κἄν in the result clause: "so that even a sage might give the impression of being such," but Philodemus's use of Epicurus as an example led him to an aorist indicative ("for instance, even Epicurus gave this impression … to some," hence the odd construction. Philodemus knew very well that

35.9 . . . .]υ
10 . . . .].μ
desunt 6 lineae
17 . . . . x]ἄπ[ει-
τα διὰ τὸ φ[ιλεῖν] ἐπιτί-
μησις πυκν[ὴ καὶ] πᾶσι
20 τοῖς γγ[ωρ]ίμο[ις] ἢ τοῖς πλεί-
στοις καὶ ἐπιτεταμένη—
πολλάκις δὲ καὶ λοιδορη-
τικὴ ψυχῆς εὐκινησίαι—
καὶ πρὶν ἐνθυμηθῆναι
25 συντετελεσμένως τὴν
/ ἀτοπίαν ἐπὶ π⟨ο⟩ίων, ὀργαί
ποτε θεωρούμεναι κα-
τηξιωκότων ἐνίων ὅ-
λως ἀκίνητον εἶναι τὸν
30 σπουδαῖον, σύννοια κατὰ
τὰς ἐπιμειξίας ὡς ἐπὶ
τὸ πολὺ τὰς τοῖς πολλοῖς,
ἔλεγχος ἀκριβὴς ἔν τε
γραφαῖς καὶ διατριβαῖς
35 τῶν κατὰ τοὺς λ[ό]γους δι-
απεπτωκότων φιλο-
σόφων, ἀπόστασις ἐνίων
φίλων διὰ τὰς ὑπ' αὐτοῦ
παρρησίας ἢ καὶ τῶι πα-
40 ──ρητῆσθαι· ᵛ ποτὲ δὲ καὶ ‖

35.17 Gomperz ‖ **18** Mewaldt, ut iam Gand. coni, cf. *Lib.* 3b.10–14 : φ[ορὸν Bücheler ‖ **19** πυκν[ὴ Hayter ‖ καὶ Gand. : μὲν Hayter ‖ **20** Hayter ‖ **26** Henry post Jensen (ἐπὶ π⟨ο⟩ιῶν) : ἐπὶ π⟨ο⟩ςὸν Gand. ‖ **35** Gomperz

The "Anger" of Sages and Their Students (Cols. 34.16–37.9)   271

[*nine lines missing*]

... [17] [and] th[en] (there follows?), because of his (the sage's) af[fection] (for them),[177] frequent and quite intense rebuking of all or most of his disciples—often even reviling, out of quickness of spirit—and before fully realizing over what sort of things their misbehavior (occurred); [26] fits of anger occasionally seen in him, though some[178] have made it an axiom that the good person should be unmoved (sc. by emotion), [30] his reserved manner[179] in his relations—for the most part—with the public; a severe style of refutation, in both writing and lecturing, of those who have committed errors in their arguments; [37] desertion by some of his friends because of his frank speaking or their having been refused something; sometimes even

---

Epicurus had appeared irascible from time to time (e.g., when discussing his teachers) but denies that he was actually so.

177. For the supplement φ[ιλεῖν] here, see *Lib.* col. 3b.10–14. Here, 35.5–36.30 contain a list of possible instances of anger in a sage that may be forgivable or even praiseworthy. The definite article is omitted with ἐπιτίμησις, ὀργαί, cύννοια, ἔλεγχος, and ἀπόστασις; not any single sage but various sages show various instances of these behaviors. The list here parallels the defense of the Epicurean sages from accusations of being flatterers in *On Flattery*, P.Herc. 222 col. 2 and 1457 cols. 10–12, and in *Epic.* 1232 col. 2.8, and from accusations of arrogance in *Sup.* cols. 5–9; see Tsouna 2007a, 136–42.

178. The Stoics and heterodox Epicureans such as Nicasicrates.

179. For cύννοια ("a worried and downcast look"), see [Plato], *Alc.* 2 138a.

Column 36

1 .. (.) μῖcoc πρ]ὸc τοῦτον
πι[κραινο]μένων, ὥc
εἰcιν ἀκράχολοι—δούλοιc
περίπτωc[ιc] ἁμαρτωλοῖc
5 καὶ δι' ἄλ[λα π]ολ[λὰ] πράγματα [..... .....]γ-
.]αζουcι [..... ...]νοιc
ἄνευ δε[..... ....
9 ..]καν[..... ....
desunt ca. 7 lineae
17 .....]ε[...]ν, ᾧ[cπερ] τινὲc
co]φοί τινων μ[ᾶλ]λον ἀ-
ποδώcουcι φα[ντ]αcίαν
20 ὀ[ρ]γίλων, οἷc ἡ φυcικ[ή, καθ'
ἃ προείπαμεν, πρόcεc-
τ[ι] μᾶλλον, ἢ παρρηcι-
αcτικοὶ μᾶλλόν εἰcι, δι'
ἃ[c] αἰτίαc ἐν τῶι Περὶ [[π]]
25 π[αρ]ρηcίαc λόγωι κατε-
τάξαμεν, ἢ τὰ τοιαῦτα
cυνκεχύρηκεν αὐτοῖc
μᾶλλον. οἷc δ' οὐ πρόcεcτιν
οὐδὲ cυνέτυχεν ἃ λέ-
30 γομεν, οὐδ' ἀποδώcουcι.
τῶν δὲ μὴ cοφῶν μηδὲ
cυνεγγιζόντων ὑπολη-
φθήcονταί τινε[c] ὀργιλώ-
τεροι καὶ τῶι πικρῶc λα-
35 λεῖν καὶ ἐπιτετα{γ}μένωc,
ἐνίοτε δὲ καὶ λοιδόρουc

36.1–2 Wilke ‖ **4** Bücheler ‖ **5** Wilke post Gomperz ‖ **6** [παρέχει] Wilke ‖ **6–7** ἀνα]γ|[κ]άζουcι Wilke ‖ **17** Wilke ‖ **18–20** Hayter ‖ **22, 24, 25, 33, 35** Gomperz

Column 36

[hatred again]st him from those who are emb[ittered], because they (the sages) are sharp-tempered; falling afoul of servants who had done wrong; and because of many other actions ...

[*circa ten lines missing or untranslatable*]

... [17] just as some sages will present the impression of being irascible more than others, (namely,) those in whom there is more natural [anger] present,[180] as we said before, or who are more given to frank criticism for the reasons we listed at length in our *On Frank Speech*,[181] or because such things happen to them more often. [28] But those in whom it is not present, and to whom those things that we mention did not happen, will not present such an appearance.

[31] Now of those who are not sages and who do not approach their level,[182] some will be supposed to be more irascible because of the bitterness and intensity of their speech, [36] and sometimes also

---

180. On the interrelation of emotion with temperament and disposition, cf. Lucretius, *Rer. nat.* 3.288–323 (see excursus 3 in the introduction). Philodemus makes the same point about irascible and nonirascible dispositions, which do not affect one's ability to live happily or be a sage. Lucretius ascribes anger to heat, fear to cold, placidity to air (lion, deer, and cow, respectively), i.e., to different kinds of atoms predominating in the soul. No surviving text of *On Anger* corresponds to this claim, but the words καθὰ προείπαμεν ("as we said before") show that an earlier mention of the physical and ethical dimensions of *diathesis* may be lost.

181. A crucial passage of *On Frank Speech* argues at length that some philosophers use the angry style of frank criticism with their pupils more, others less, according to their "nature," but all mean well and are equally motivated by affection and good will (*Lib.* cols. 3a–7b). We give some of this passage of *On Frank Speech*, and some similar material from the fragments, in the introduction, pp. 67–71.

182. The description of the nonphilosophical *dyskolos*, or ill-tempered person, at 36.31–37.4 is a warning to those not yet perfect in Epicurean philosophical discipline, for example, the audience of students addressed in cols. 18–21, because of the potential for self-harm. Like the description of various kinds of harmless anger forgivable in sages, it sounds like a brief exercise in the genre of Theophrastus's *Characters*. Philodemus refers frequently to various "characters" of flatterers and parasites and the like in *On Flattery*. Philodemus does not accept Nicasicrates's view that the sage sometimes harms himself in his anger, if that means he does himself great or serious harm (cf. 39.31–33; see *DPA* N34 [Dorandi] for bibliography).

36.37 τιθέναι φωνὰς καὶ τῶι
κ[α]χυπόνουν ἔχειν τι καὶ
τῶι τὸν μεισοπόνηρον ἐ-
40 πιφαίνειν καὶ τῶι τὸν λογι- ‖

Column 37

1 ζόμ[ενον] ὑποκ[ρ]ίνεσθαι
χα[λεπότητα] ὅλην [πλεισ-
των ἢ κοινῶς ἀνθρώπων,
— ἢ τ[ῶ]ι βλά[π]τειν ἑαυτόν,
5 ὅ φ[η]ςι Νικας[ικ]ράτης [ἐ-
νίοτε ποιεῖν καὶ τὸ[ν] ϲο-
φ[ό]ν, καὶ παρ' ἄλλ[ας αἰτί]ας,
ὧν φυλακὴν ὕϲτ[ερον] πα-
ρα[ι]νέϲομε[ν . . . .]δε
10 . . . . .]οφ[. . . . .
desunt fere 5 lineae
16 οἱ μὲν τὸ πάθος ὑπάρχ]ειν
αὐ[τὸ μ]ακά[ρ]ιον [ὑπο]λαμ-
— βά[ν]οντες, ᵛ οἱ δὲ κακόν,
τῶ[ι] δακνηρῶι προς⟦ε⟧πί-
20 πτ'οντ'ες αὐτῆς. ἡμεῖς δὲ τῶι
καὶ κατὰ φωνήν τινα πα-
ραλογισμὸν ἐντρέχειν
οὐχ ἁπλῆν ποιούμεθα
τὴν ἀπόφασιν, ἀλλὰ τὸ
25 μὲν πάθος αὐτὸ κατὰ δι-
άληψιν ἀποφαινόμε-
θα κακόν, ἐπειδὴ λυπη-
ρόν ἐστιν ἢ ἀνάλογον

36.38 Gomperz ‖ **37.1** Gomperz ‖ **2** χα[λεπότητα Hayter (-τηθ' Wilke) ‖ **2–3** Delattre-Monet : τού]|των Gomperz ‖ **4–7** Gomperz ‖ **8** Bücheler ‖ **8–9** πα|ρα[ι]νέϲομε[ν Gomperz ‖ **9–10** μὴ]δὲ ‖[φιλος]οφ[- Janko ‖ παρὰ] δὲ | [τοὺς ϲ]οφ[οὺς Mewaldt ‖ **16** * e.g. post Delattre-Monet ([τὸ πάθος τι ὑπάρχ]ειν) ‖ **17–19** Gomperz

by their use of terms of revilement, by their having a certain tendency to think the worst, and by playing the (role of a) hater of base behavior,

---

Column 37

and by their acting the part of one who reckons on the complete [ill temper] of most people or of humanity in general, or by harming themselves, [5] which Nicasicrates says even the sage will sometimes do, and for other causes, against which we will later recommend precautions ...

[*circa six lines missing or untranslatable*]

ON THE PAINFULNESS OF NATURAL ANGER

... [16] [some] supposing [the emotion] itself to be a blessed thing, others an evil because they experience its sting. [20] But because a kind of false reasoning occurs because of the word,[183] we do not make a simple judgment but show that the emotion itself, taken in isolation, is an evil, since it is painful or is analogous

---

183. The τινα goes with παραλογιcμόν, not φωνήν, and the word in question is "anger," which is confusing because of its various significations; cf. 16.34–40.

37.29 λυπηρῶι, κατὰ δὲ τὴν
30 cυνπλοκὴν τῆι διαθέcει
κἂν ἀγαθὸν ῥηθήcεcθαι
νομίζομεν· cυνίcταται
γὰρ ἀπὸ το[ῦ] βλέπειν ὡc ἡ
φύcιc ἔχει τῶν πραγμά-
35 των καὶ μηδὲν ψευδο-
δοξεῖν ἐν ταῖc c[υ]μμε-
τρήcεcι τῶν ἐλα[ττ]ω-
μάτων καὶ ταῖc κολάcε-
cι τῶν βλαπτόντων. ὥcτε
40 καθ' [ὃ]ν τρόπον ἐλέγομ[εν ‖

Column 38

1 τὴν κ[ενὴν ὀρ]γὴν κακόν,
ὅτι ἀπὸ διαθέcεωc γί-
νεται παγπονήρου
καὶ μυρία δυcχερῆ cυν-
5 επιcπᾶται, δ[εῖ] λέγειν [οὐ
κακ[ὸν τὴ]ν φυcική[ν, ἀ]λ-
λά, καθὸ δηκτικόν ἐ[cτ]ί
τι, π[ερ]ὶ ἐλάχιcτ[α γ]ίν[ε-
ται, [κ]αὶ καθ' [ὃν τρόπον ἐ-
10 πιφ[ερ- . . . .
desunt 6 lineae
17 κ[. . . . .]ον
δὲ τ[ὸ] ἀπὸ cπουδαίαc, οὐ
κακόν, ἀλλὰ καὶ ἀγαθόν,
20 οὕτωc κακὸν ἐροῦμεν

37.33, 36, 37 Gomperz, Spengel ‖ 40 [ὃ]ν Gomperz ‖ ἐλέγομ[εν Bücheler : ἔλεγογ [Gomperz ‖ 38.1 Gomperz ‖ 3 legit McO, sic N : πα[ ]τιπονηρου O ‖ 5 δ[εῖ] λέγειν Hayter : τ[ῶι] λέγεc[θαι Wilke (λεγε[P hodie) ‖ οὐ Indelli ‖ 6 Wilke ‖ 6-7 ἀ]λ|λά Gomperz ‖ 7 ἐ[cτ]ί Gand., Wilke ‖ 8-9]ιν[legit McO, γινε]|ται iam Wilke (vel οὐ]ύ[κ ἐc]|ται McO) ‖ 9 Wilke ‖ 9-10 ἐ]|πιφ[έρομεν Mewaldt ‖ 18 Janko

to something painful, but if taken in conjunction with one's disposition, we think that it is something that may even be called[184] a good. [32] For it (anger) results from seeing what the nature of states of affairs is and from not having any false beliefs in our comparative calculations of our losses and in our punishments of those who harm us.[185] [39] And so, in the same way as we were calling

Column 38

em[pty] anger an evil because it results from an utterly base disposition and entails countless troubles, one must say that natural one is not an evil, but, insofar as it is something biting, [8] it happens in relation to very few things, and in the way in which we apply ...

[*seven lines missing or untranslatable*]

... [18] (as, when it comes?) from a good (disposition), it is not an evil but even a good, thus we will say it is an evil

---

184. Philodemus allows ἄν with the future infinitive or participle regularly (perhaps permissible even in Attic; cf. the introduction, §14.1 with n. 258).

185. Even natural anger, qua anger, is painful and an evil. To be accepted by the sage, it must survive the *symmetrēsis*, by which the Epicurean opts to endure pain to secure greater overall pleasure (Epicurus, *Men.* 130). Procopé (1998, 176–82) is very good on the *symmetrēsis* involved in the sage's accepting anger, though at 178 he wrongly considers Epicurean natural anger to be a natural desire. In Philodemus's view, if anger is experienced as a desire in any way, it is ipso facto empty and unnatural (see especially 43.41–44.35).

38.21 τὸ μὴ τὴν φυcικὴν ὀργὴν ἀναδέχεcθαι—"κα-
κῶc" γὰρ "ἀκούων" καὶ πάc-
χων "ὅcτιc οὐκ ὀργίζε-
25 ται, πονηρίαc πλεῖcτο[ν
τεκμήριον φέρει" κα[τὰ
τὸν Μένανδρον, ἐνίοτε
δὲ προκινηcίαc ἢ λύτ-
τηc περὶ ἕτερα· διὸ φα-
30 νερόc ἐcτ[ι]ν ἐπὶ τοῖc ἐ-
λαχίcτοιc παρὰ πόδαc
εὐθέωc ἐξcτηcόμε-
νοc ᵛ —ἀγαθὸν δὲ τὸ ἀνα-
δέχεcθαι. ᵛ παρὰ δὲ Νι-
35 καcικράτει λέγετα[ι] τὸ
τὴν φυcικὴν ὀργὴν μὴ
μόνον κατὰ τὴν ἰδίαν
φύcιν λυπεῖν, ἀλλὰ καὶ
ἐπιcκοτεῖν τοῖc λογι[c-
40 μοῖc, ὅcον ἐφ' ἑαυτῆι, κα[ὶ τὸ ‖

Column 39

1 πρὸc τὴν [μετὰ] φίλων
cυμβίωcι[ν] ἀν[ε]κτὸν κα-
τὰ πᾶν καὶ ἀπ[αρ]ενόχλη-
τον ἐμποδίζ[ειν, καὶ] πολ-

38.25 Hayter : πλείcτη[c Dobree ‖ **26, 30, 35** Gomperz, Spengel ‖ **32** lege ἐκcτ- ‖ **40** κα[ὶ Gomperz, Spengel ‖ τὸ Wilke ‖ **39.1** Wilke ‖ **2–3** Hayter ‖ **4** Hayter : ἐμποδιζ[ειν, τὰ δὲ] Gomperz

not to accept natural anger—[22] for he who "is not enraged when men speak ill of him" and maltreat him "is giving the greatest proof of baseness,"[186] as Menander says, and sometimes of a predisposition (to excitement) or of insanity regarding other matters; [29] that is why he obviously will fly out of his mind suddenly about utter trifles that appear in front of him,[187] but it is a good thing to submit to the natural kind of anger.

[34] Now in Nicasicrates it is said that "the natural kind of anger is painful not only in its own nature, but also it darkens one's reasonings, to the extent that is in its power,"

Column 39

and "impairs the perfect tolerability and untroubled character of one's communal life with friends" and brings with it many of the disadvantages

---

186. The quotation κακῶc ἀκούων ὅcτιc οὐκ ὀργίζεται / πονηρίαc πλεῖcτον τεκμήριον φέρει is a fragment of Menander (513 Kassel and Austin 1998, 288; they print Nauck's conjecture πιcτὸν for πλεῖcτον). Philodemus thinks not only the bite of "natural" anger but the impulse to "punish" those who have made one angry are painful (and therefore inherently bad); however, in the right circumstance and with the proper treatment, they can be good. According to the social contract not to harm or be harmed, people have the right to punish those who harm them. Philodemus is careful to specify that being actually harmed (κακῶc πάcχειν) is prerequisite to natural anger, not just being slandered (κακῶc ἀκούειν).

187. A digression clarifies the Menander quotation still further. For the meaning of the hapax προκινηcία, cf. Plutarch's use of προκινέω at Adol. poet. aud. 36d: "and moreover, poems preopen and premove the souls of the young to the arguments in philosophy" (ἔτι δὲ [sc. τὰ ποιήματα] προανοίγει καὶ προκινεῖ τὴν τοῦ νέου ψυχὴν τοῖc ἐν φιλοcοφίαι λόγοιc). Asmis (2011, 165) notices the air of uneasy self-correction here, which may be deliberate: Philodemus considers various alternatives for what to call natural anger—a good? a nonevil, even though painful?—and settles on "it is a good thing to submit to the natural kind of anger." Nothing painful is good in itself, though it may be choice-worthy after the alternatives are evaluated.

39. 5 λὰ τῶν κ[ατη]ριθμ[ημέ-
νω[ν] ἐλα[ττ]ωμάτω[ν
cυνε[πι]φέρε̣ι̣ν· μὴ cυ[ν-
κ[ρίνα]c δὲ τῆι κεν[ῆι
καὶ τ[. . . ₍.₎]ι . ἀγαθὰc [.
10   . . . .]υ[.]την[. . .
desunt 6 lineae
17 τὸ cοφ[ὸν] καλεῖcθαι, τῶν
δ' ἀερίων ἀπέχειν, μη-
δ' ἂν τεύξεcθαι ꞌτῆcꞌ προcη-
20 γορίαc ταύτηc, εἰ τηλικοῦ-
τόν ἐcτι κακόν. ἢ πῶc ἔ-
τι μετὰ παρρηcίαc ἐροῦ-
μέν τ[ι] πρὸc τοὺc λόγουc
τῶν ἀφαιρούντων τοῦ ⟦c⟧
25 cπουδαίου ⟦c⟧ πᾶcαν ὀργήν;
πῶc φυcικὸν τὸ πρὸc τὰ
τηλικαῦτα ἐμποδίζον
καὶ τοcούτων αἴτιον κα-
κῶν; εἰ δὲ ἀνέκφευκτον
30 καὶ διὰ τοῦτο φυcικὸν
λεγόμενον, πῶc οὐχὶ μέ-
γα κακὸν καὶ cοφοῖc ἐcτιν
ὑπομενητόν; ἢ πῶc οὐχὶ
καὶ περὶ τοὺc χαρίενταc
35 ὀργαί τινεc ὁρώμεναι; διότι παντὸc ἐcτέρηνται
τοῦ προc⟦ εν⟧ꞌανꞌαρτηθέντοc
ὑπὸ τούτων, ὀλίγον δέ
τι μόνον ἀνευδοκηcίαc
40 cυνε[πι]φέρονται τοῖc φυ- ‖

39.5–6 Gomperz ‖ **7** cυνε[πι]φέφε̣ι̣ν Hayter ‖ **7–8** cυ[ν]|κ[ρίνα]c Wilke ‖ **8** κεν[ῆι Gomperz ‖ **10** sub lineae initium, το O, iam deletae, quas Wilke superpositas censuit ‖ **17** Bücheler ‖ τῶν̣ Gomperz : τῶι Hayter ‖ **23** Gomperz ‖ **25** c expunctum in O (P non exstat hodie) ‖ **40** Gomperz, Spengel

that have been e[nu]merated.[188] [7] But since he did not compare it (natural anger) with empty (anger), even ... good ...

[*seven lines missing or untranslatable*]

... [17] being called a sage and keeping away from futile things, nor could it ever be given this appellation (sc. natural), if it is so great an evil. [21] Or how could we still say anything frankly against the arguments of those who take away anger entirely from the sage? [189] How can that which impedes such important things and causes so many evils be natural? [29] If it is inescapable, and therefore called natural,[190] then how is it not a great evil that must be endured even by sages?[191] Or how are there not outbursts of anger manifested even in the case of good men? [35] Because (sc. these outbursts) are free from everything that is attached to them by those (sc. other philosophers) and they bring only some little amount of embarrassment upon

---

188. In the diatribe, 8-31.24. For "enumerated," cf. ἐξαριθμοῦμεν (7.22): diatribes enumerate evils, and Philodemus has now enumerated them. Nicasicrates believes that sages experience natural anger, that the crucial objection to anger is that it is painful "in its very nature"; he believes in *ataraxia* and living in community with friends. Philodemus expects him to argue against the Stoics about emotion instead of siding with them. All these are strong indications that he is an Epicurean. Asmis (2011, 166) argues that he was an Academic satirizing the very idea of Epicurean natural anger. It seems to us that Philodemus reproaches him for agreeing too much with the Stoics and making the Epicurean view too nearly identical with theirs; he was "letting down the team." See further Ringeltaube 1913, 43–46; Procopé 1998, 188–89.

189. The Stoics. Nicasicrates's position is too close to theirs for Philodemus to distinguish them, he claims.

190. In conformity to the theory of what counts as natural given by Demetrius Laco, *On Textual and Exegetical Problems in Epicurus* (col. 67); see above, pp. 41–43.

191. As Philodemus refuses to believe. They do suffer pain in their anger but not serious anguish. The phrase πῶς οὐ introduces an incredulous question: "How is it not so?" meaning "It is surely so." A conversation with Nicasicrates is imagined, of which only his side is given: Nicasicrates: "How can something that impedes important activities and causes pain be natural?" Philodemus: "Because it is inescapable." Nicasicrates: "If it is natural because it is inescapable, then surely it is a great evil that even sages must endure, and surely good men have outbursts of anger, right?" Philodemus: "No, because anger is not as you (and the Stoics) describe it, and fits of anger are not really embarrassing for the angry man in the judgment of those who understand that the fit was of natural anger."

Column 40

1 cικὸν καὶ περὶ [τ]ὸν coφὸ[ν
ἀκαριαῖ[ον] ποιήcουcι; κα-
ταλείπ[ει δὴ] καὶ πολὺ μᾶλ-
λ]ον ὁ [διαπ]είθων λ[όγο]c, ἀ-
5 νέκφ]ευκτον [εἶναι τ]ὸ γέ-
νοc π]αντ[ί. ὡc γὰ[ρ ἐν ἀρ-
χῆι] μικρὸν φαίνε[ται, ὕ-
cτερον] δ' ὡc cυνηυξ[η-
μένον ἐ]κ τῶν προcθέ[cε-
10 ων . . . .]ενον τῳ[.
. . . .]ν ἀλλ[. .
tres lineae desunt
15 φευχ[. . . . . . .]ομεν, [φα-
νερόν, οἶc οὐκ ἂν εἴπαιμεν
ἐγκυρεῖν τὸν εὐλόγιcτον,
τῆι δὲ φυcικῆι πάντωc πε-
ριπίπτειν, δι' ἣν αἰτίαν
20 ἀνέκφευκτον αὐτὴν ἐ-
δείκνυμεν ἀνθρώπων
⟦η⟧ φύcει. ʽκαὶʼ γὰρ οὗτοc δήπου
μετέχων αὐτῆc οὐκ ἂν
οἷόc τ' εἴη {ι} πᾶcαν ἐκφεύ-
25 γειν, ἀλλά τινοc ἐπιδεκτ[ι-
κ[ὸ]c εἶναι πάντωc. ᵛ ἕξεc-

40.1 Gomperz ‖ **2** ἀκαριαῖ[ον Hayter ‖ **2–3** Gigante post Wilke (κα|ταλείπ[ε-ται] ⟨δὴ⟩) ‖ **4** Wilke post Gomperz (ὁ [ἡμᾶc π]είθων) : [cυμπ]είθων Delattre-Monet ‖ **5–6** εἶναι τ]ὸ γέ|[νοc Gomperz : [τοιοῦτ]ό γε | [ὂν Delattre-Monet ‖ **6** π]αντ[ί Wilke : ἅπ]αντ[ι Delattre-Monet ‖ **6–8** Wilke, qui etiam ci. ὡc γὰ[ρ ἀρχό⟨μενον⟩ | μὲν ‖ **7–8** μ]ικρὸν φαίνε[ται, ὕ|cτερον] Wilke ‖ **8–9** cυνηυξ[η|μένον δ' ἐ]κ Gomperz (δ' om. Wilke) ‖ **9–10** προcθέ[cε]ων Gomperz ‖ **10** ὀξὺ γενόμ]ενον Wilke : μέγα γενόμ]ενον Mewaldt ‖ **10–15** τῷ[ι | ματαίωι κακό]ν, ἀλλ' [οὐ | τῶι cοφῶι· ὅτι γὰρ τούτωι | τὰ τῶι πάθει παρακολου|θοῦντα κακὰ οὐχ ὡc ἀνέκ]|φευχτα cυνάψ]ομεν Philippson (15 "ἀνέκφευκτον?" iam Wilke, ἐκ]|φεῦχ[θ' Janko) ‖ **15** ἡμάρτο]μεν e.g. Janko ‖ **15–16** [φα]|νερόν Hayter ‖ **21** corr. Wilke (ανθρωπον P) ‖ **24** del. Gomperz ‖ **25–26** Gomperz, Spengel

Column 40

those who will make out that it (the emotion) is both natural and, in the case of the sage, brief.[192] The [convi]ncing ar[gume]nt, [then,] leaves much more in place, (namely) that this kind (sc. the "natural" one) is inescapable for every person. [6] For [at the beginning,] it appears small, but [later], after it has grown [from] the additions...

[*four lines missing or untranslatable*]

... [15] obvious ... (sc. evils?) with which we could not say the reasonable man meets, but assuredly he falls into natural (anger), and for that reason we showed that it is inescapable for human nature.[193] [22] In fact, even this man (sc. Nicasicrates), I suppose, since he shares in it (human nature), could not escape all anger but would as a matter of course be receptive to some of it.

---

192. The term ἀκαριαῖον is frequently glossed in ancient lexicons and scholia with βραχύ. Anger is βραχύc at 42.39, felt βραχέωc at 45.11 and 47.37, is ἀκαριαῖοc here, οὐ cύντονοc at 44.9, and felt οὐ cυντόνωc at 48.6 and 10. Asmis (2011, 167 n. 51) wishes her reading to mean "they" (i.e., the Stoics) "assign only something slight without (internal) approval (i.e. assent) to those who will make something natural and momentary [happen] also in the case of the sage." But how can "they" assign this to "those who," meaning themselves? Both ἀνευδοκηcία here and ἀνευδόκητοc in 25.6 are *hapax legomena*: it matters little or nothing to Philodemus (or any other ancient philosopher) if the sage does things that rouse murmurs in ordinary people.

193. As opposed to the Epicurean gods, as Wilke notes.

40.27 τι δ', εἴ τις βούλεται καὶ κα-
τ' ἰδίαν τούτου λόγον φέ-
ρειν, ἀντὶ τοῦ κοινοῦ τὸν
30 σοφὸν ἐντ[ά]ξαι, καὶ τοῦτον δὲ τὸν τρόπον κατα-
σκευάσαι ταὐτό· βλαβεὶς
ὑπό τινος ἑκουσίως ἢ
λαβὼν ἔνφασιν τοῦ βλα-
35 βήσεσθαι, πότερον ἀδι-
άφορον ἀναδέξεται πά-
θος, ᵛ ὥσπερ ἐμβλέψαν-
τος αὐτῶι τινος, ἢ ἀλλό-
τριον, ἐπειδὴ τό γε οἰκεῖ-
40 ον λέγειν ἀπόπληκτο[ν; ‖

Column 41

1 ἀδιάφ[ορον μὲν] οὖν φά-
ναι βίαιον, εἰ δ' ἀλλότριον
καὶ γινώσκει, διότι κολασθεὶς ἀνασταλήσεται καὶ
5 τοὺς ἄλλους ἐπιστήσει, μανικῶς οὐκ ἂν ἔλθοι πά[λι]ν
καθ' ἕνα γέ τινα τρόπο[ν
δακών. ᵛ τὸ δὲ τοιοῦτο[ν
ὀ]ργὴν [κ]αλοῦμεν. ᵛ ὁ δ' ἐν
10 ὀ]ργαῖ[ς πρ]ὸς τὰ μόνον βλ[ά-
π]τοντ[α, χ]ωρὶ[α]ς δὲ πρὸ[ς
τὴν ἀλ]λοτρίωσιν [.....
desunt 4 lineae

40.30 ἐντ[ά]ξαι Gomperz ‖ τοῦτον {δὲ} Janko : {τοῦ} τόνδε Spengel : τοῦ|τον δὲ Gomperz ‖ **40** Gomperz, Spengel ‖ **41.1** ἀδιάφ[ορον Hayter ‖ μὲν] Gomperz, Spengel ‖ **6** Wilke ‖ **7** Hayter ‖ **8** Gomperz ‖ **9** Gomperz, Spengel ‖ **10** ὀ]ργαῖ[ς Gomperz ‖ πρ]ὸς spatio convenit, ut vid., ⟨π⟩ρὸς sic Wilke : ε]ἰς Gomperz ‖ **10-11** βλ[ά|π]τοντ[α Gomperz ‖ **11** χ]ωρὶ[α]ς Wilke ‖ πρὸ[ς Gomperz ‖ **12** Gomperz

[26] It is possible, if someone wishes to offer an account[194] of this subject specifically, to insert "the sage" in place of "a human being in general" and in that way to arrive at the same result: [32] when he has been intentionally harmed by someone or has received the impression he will be harmed, will he experience an indifferent feeling, [37] as if someone looked at him, or a painful[195] one, since calling it attractive to him is senseless?

Column 41

Well, certainly calling it indifferent is forced, but if it is painful, and he (the sage) knows that, when punished, he (the adversary) will be checked and will rein in the others,[196] he (the sage) would be insane not to grit his teeth[197] and come back at him in one way or another. [8] We call that sort of thing anger. But the man who, in fits of anger against what merely harms him, but separately (?) ... against the alienation ...

[*four lines missing*]

---

194. For λόγον φέρειν, cf. [Plato], *Epin.* 973c2.
195. For ἀλλότριος "alienating," *ergo* painful, and οἰκεῖος "attractive," *ergo* pleasurable, see the introduction, pp 74–75.
196. Presumably his example will deter anyone else considering such a course of action, perhaps including the confederates of the enemy (if "the others" can bear that sense). Both the feeling of pain and the prospect of successfully punishing the adversary, thereby discouraging both him and others from further outrages, are essential to "natural" anger.
197. For this translation, see Procopé 1998, 180 with n. 41, who compares Menander's *Samia* 356: δακὼν ἀνάσχου, καρτέρηcον εὐγενῶc ("grit your teeth and endure it; bear up like a good fellow").

41.17 __θαι. ᵛ γί[νονται μ]ὲν οὖ[ν] περὶ τοὺc ἀγαθοὺc ὀργαί, κἂν
εἰc τοὺc φίλουc ἁμάρτῃ
20 τιc, κἂν εἰc ἑαυτὸν φίλοc
πλημμελήcῃ, τοῖc ὅλοιc
εἰc αὐτὸν οὔτε διειλημ-
μένωc οὔτ᾽ ἀδιαλήπτωc
καινοῦ κακοῦ προcδο-
25 κωμένου καταντήcειν.
ἀλλ᾽ ἡμεῖc ἐπὶ τῆc εἰc ἑ-
αυτὸν ἐρχομένηc ἔcτη-
__μεν βλάβηc. ᵛ ἀπόχρη γὰρ
ἐπιδεῖξαι τὸ κοινόν, ὅτι
30 cυcχεθήcεταί τιcιν ὀρ-
__γαῖc ὁ cοφόc. ᵛ καὶ φήcει τιc,
ἀλλ᾽ εἰ διὰ τὸ βλάπτεcθαι
καθ᾽ ἑκούcιον τρόπον ὀργίζεται, βλάπτεται δ᾽ ὑπό
35 τινων εἰc τὰ μέγιcτα, πῶc
οὐχὶ καὶ 〚ου〛 μεγάλην ὀργὴν
ἀναδέξεται καὶ cφοδρὰν
ἐπιθυμίαν ἕξει τοῦ μετελ-
θεῖν; ᵛ πρὸc ὃν ἐροῦμεν, ὅτι
40 τῶι βλάπτοντι τὰc τοιαύταc
β]λά[β]αc ἢ φανερῶι [γ᾽ ὄν]τι ‖

41.17 γί[νονται Hayter ‖ μ]ὲν οὖ[ν] Wilke ‖ **24** κοινοῦ Rabbow ‖ **30** Hayter : cυc-χεθηcεcθαι P ‖ **41** Hayter : φανερώc[αν]τι * post Spengel (-ον]τι) : φανερωι[O φανει[P, N

... [17] so, then, fits of anger do happen in the cases of good men, both whenever someone wrongs their friends and whenever a friend has behaved badly to his own loss, even when no fresh[198] ill is either distinctly or indistinctly expected to occur to him personally. [26] But we are focused on the case of harm coming to the man himself personally. For it is sufficient to demonstrate the general proposition that the sage will be liable to certain fits of anger. [31] Someone will say, "But if he is angered because he is harmed intentionally, and he is harmed by certain people to the greatest extent, how will he not experience a great anger and have a violent desire for revenge?" [39] We will reply to him that, toward the person who harms him in these ways or is obviously

---

198. I.e., "additional," beyond the harm that provoked the original fit of anger. Philodemus means that the sage does not expect to be injured by his friend, even though the friend has already injured himself or been injured. This is an interesting topic, but, unfortunately, Philodemus does not discuss it.

Column 42

1 διότι μ[ε]γά[λ]ως βλάψει,
προσαλλοτριοῦται μὲν ἄ-
κρως καὶ μισεῖ (τοῦτο γὰρ ἀ-
χ[όλο]υθον), οὐ μέντοι γε τα-
5 ρα[χ]ὴν ἀνα[δ]έχεται μεγά-
λη[ν], οὐ[δ'] ἔ[στ]ιν γέ [πώς] τ[ι] παρὰ [μέγα] τῶν ἔξωθεν, [ὅ]τ' οὐδὲ κ[α]τὰ τὰς παρουσία[ς] τῶν
μεγάλων ἀλγηδόνω[ν] με-
10 γάλαις συνέχεται τ[αρα-
χαῖς, [πο]λλῶι δὲ μᾶλλ[ο]ν
κατὰ [τὰ]ς ὀργάς· τὸ γὰ[ρ] δει-
νὰ [. . . . .]υεται[. . . .
deest una linea
15 ἔστι [. . . . .]ην[. .] τοῦτο δύναται, μυρίας τε συμ-
φορὰς ἔχει καὶ συμπεπλε-
γ]μένας καὶ συνακολουθού-
σας, ͮ ὁ μάλιστ' αὐτὰς θεω-
20 ρῶν σοφὸς οὐκ ἂν ἐμπίπτοι.
τό τε [] ἐπιθυμεῖν τῆς κολά-
σεως καθάπερ ἀπολαυ-
στοῦ τινος, ὃ συνέζευκται
ταῖς μεγάλαις ὀργαῖς, μάται-

42.1 μ[.]γα[.]ως legit McO (μ[εγ]ά[λ]ως iam Gomperz), sed hasta verticalis gammae longior et hasta horizontalis ad alpham ligata est: μ[. . .][α]ˋηˊ[.]ις O (η super α scripta) ‖ 4, 5 Gomperz, Spengel ‖ 6 μεγά|λη[ν] Gomperz, Spengel ‖ οὐ[δ'] ἔ[στ]ιν γέ [πώς] τ[ι] Wilke : οὐ[δὲ] [φης]ιν γ' ε[ἶν]αι Delattre-Monet ‖ 7 [μέγα] Gomperz, Spengel ‖ [ὅ]τ' Hayter : [ὅ]τ⟨ι⟩ Wilke in apparatu ‖ 8 κ[α]τὰ Hayter ‖ παρουσία[ς Gomperz, Spengel ‖ 10 Gomperz, Spengel ‖ 11 πο]λλῶι Spengel ‖ μᾶλλ[ο]ν ⟨ἢ⟩ Gomperz ‖ 12 Gomperz ‖ 13 [παθεῖν Philippson ‖ λ]ύεται[ι Gomperz : κωλ]ύεται[ι Janko : φ]ύεται[ι Philippson ‖ 13–14 ἐξ ἀ|νοίας] Philippson ‖ 14 [εἴ τις οὖν μάταιός] Indelli ‖ 15 [συναφθ]ῆν[αι] Philippson ‖ 18 Gomperz, Spengel ‖ 21 [δ'] Indelli

Column 42

going to harm him greatly, he is alienated in the highest degree and hates him[199]—that is consistent—but nonetheless he does not experience great disturbance in any way, [6] nor is any external thing all that important, seeing that he is not liable to great disturbances even through the presence of great pains, and much less through his fits of angers. For ... dreadful ...

[*about two lines missing or untranslatable*]

... [15] is ... this can ... and it has countless misfortunes both interwoven with and consequent on it. But the sage, who sees into these (misfortunes) most clearly, could not fall into them. [21] And desiring (to inflict) punishment as if it were something enjoyable, which is conjoined to great fits of anger,

---

199. In Epicurean terms, his being "alienated" means he expects only pain from further relations with the offender, which is explained as hatred: μιcέω and Latin *odi* imply aversion and avoidance as well as hatred. On the relation between hatred and anger in general, see Procopé 1985.

42.25 ὂν ἐ[c]τιν οἰομένων μέ-
γιcτον ἀγαθὸν εἶναι καὶ
καταcτρεφόντων ὡc εἰc
δι' αὐτὸ αἱρετὸν καὶ κο-
λάcε[ι]ν οὐκ ἄλλωc νομι-
30 ζόντων, καὶ ἀνημέρω[[c]]ι
cυμπέπλεκται διαθέ-
cει, κα[θ]άπερ ὑπεδεί`ξ΄αμεν
καὶ προϊόντεc ἔτι παρα-
cτήcομεν. ὥcτ' οὐκ ἂν εἴ-
35 η περὶ αὐτὸν ἅμα καὶ γι-
νώcκοντα διότι τὴν ἀ-
κροτάτην [[νο]] `κο΄[μ]ίζετα[ι] τι-
μωρίαν ὁ τοιοῦτοc ἐξ ἑ-
αυτοῦ. ᵛ διὸ καὶ βραχείαιc
40 ο[. .]τε[.]νεινα τελεωc[

Column 43

1 — .[. . . . . (.)] cυνέχεται, καὶ δι-
α[φ]ορᾳ[ῖc] μὲν ὀνόματοc,
ἀ[λ]λ' οὐ μὰ Δί[[cτ]]α [[δὲ]] cυνέγ-
γ[ι]ζον τ[ῶι] ὑπὸ τοῦτο τατ-
5 τομένω[ι δια]νοήματι ἢ [ἱ]
τοῖc ἄλλ[ο]ιc ⟨ἃ⟩ τούτωι π[ρ]οcα-
γορεύ]ομεν. [οὐδὲ χρ]ὴ τὴν
δ[ι]αφοράν, ἣν τὸ π[άθο]c ἔ-

42.25, 29, 32 Gomperz, Spengel ‖ **37** Gomperz ‖ **39** ad fin. ⟨καὶ⟩ Wilke ‖ **40** sic legit Wilke, fere O, ͺ ͺ ͺτε ͺνειν ͺ ͺτεμθωc N; ἐ[πι]τέμνειν ἀτέλε[cιν Wilke : ὡ[c ἔ]ποc εἰπεῖν ἀτέλεcιν Delattre-Monet : ὀ[ργ]αῖc coni. Janko ‖ **43.1** ὁ [cοφὸc Janko : ὀ[ργαῖc] Wilke (vel c[), fort. τ[leg. McO dub. ‖ **2** Wilke, qui etiam de δι|α[φ]ορρ[ιc cog. ‖ **3** ἀ[λ]λ' Wilke ‖ i.e., μαλιcταδε correxit librarius in μὰ Δία ‖ ⟨τὸ⟩ cυν- Philippson ‖ **3–4** cυ-νεγ|γ[ί]ζον Gomperz (cυνεγ| P) : cυνεπ[ό]|μ[ε]νον perperam Wilke ‖ **4–5** τ[ῶι] … τατ|τομένω[ι Gomperz ‖ **5** δια]νοήματι Henry : ἢ ἐν]νοήματι Gomperz : ἐν]νόημά τι Delattre-Monet ‖ **6** ⟨ἃ⟩ * ‖ **6–7** π[ρ]οcα|[γορεύ]ομεν Gomperz ‖ **7** [οὐδὲ Indelli et χρ]ὴ Philippson : κατὰ δ]ὴ Wilke post Gomperz ‖ **8** Hayter

is the folly of those who think[200] it the greatest good and who turn to it as to a thing in itself worthy of pursuing and who believe they cannot punish others in any other way, and it is interwoven with an untamed disposition, as we have demonstrated and will further establish as we go on. [34] And so, it could not happen to him (the sage), who, at the same time, knows that the bitterest vengeance such a person takes is on his own self. Thus ... brief ...

Column 43

... is liable, and with differences of name, but by Zeus it is not something that resembles either the concept that underlies this name or the other things ⟨that⟩ we call by this (name).[201] [7] [Nor shou]ld one, [on account of the name, ignore] the difference that the emotion

---

200. The Peripatetics.
201. Only the feeling, not its further developments, which are inevitable in fools, is "natural" and "inevitable" to the wise man. The text of 42.39–43.7 is difficult, and we are not convinced that any of the attempts to make sense of it are satisfactory. The scribe perhaps found the passage too technical for him. Our supplement makes τοῦτο in line 4 and τούτωι in line 6 refer to an ὄνομα (cf. l. 2), that of "rage" or "great anger." The phrase τὸ ὑπὸ τοῦτο ταττόμενον would then be equivalent to τὸ ὑποτεταγμένον τούτωι τῶι φθόγγωι ("what underlies this word," Epicurus, Hdt. 37). For other texts and exegesis, see Arrighetti 1993 and Verde 2010b ad loc., as well as Long and Sedley (1987, 1:87–90, 2:91–93).

43.9 χει πρὸς τὸ γινόμε[ν]ον πε-
10 ρὶ [τ]οὺς πολλούς, ἐπ[ις]τῆςαι
ἢ [μετ]ελθεῖν τιν[α, μ]ηδ' ἂν
θυμὸν] αὐτὸ προς[αγο]ρεύ-
ωμεν, τ]ο[ῦ] ὀν[όματος ἕνε-
[κεν ἀγνοεῖν. τὸ δ' ἀσθενές]
15 τι [λέγειν ὀργὴν] γ[ί]ν[ες-
θαι καὶ τῶι σοφῶι περιά- 〚π〛
πτειν, ὥστε καὶ τοῦτον
ἀσθενῆ ποιεῖν, οὐ παρενο-
χλήςει, καθάπερ ἐν[ί]οις, οἳ
20 πάνδεινον ἡγήσαντο, ταῖς
Κυρίαις Δόξαις ἀντιγρά-
φοντες, εἰ τετόλμηκέ τις
ἐν ἀσθενείαι λέγειν ὀργὴν
καὶ χάριτα καὶ πᾶν τὸ τοι-
25 οῦτον, ᵛ Ἀλεξάνδρο[υ] τοῦ
πάντων πλεῖστον ἰσχύσαν-
τος ὀργαῖς τε πολλαῖς συν-
εσχημένου καὶ κεχαρις-
μένου μυρίοις. οὐ γὰρ ἡ 〚ι〛 τῆι
30 τῶν ἀθλητῶν καὶ βασι-
λέων ἀντίθετος ἀ[ς]θέ-
νεια λαμβάνεται κατὰ
τ〚ι〛`ὸν´ λόγον, ἀλλ' ἡ δεκτικὴ
κατασκευὴ καὶ φύσις θανά-
35 του καὶ ἀλγηδόνων, ἧς καὶ
Ἀλέξανδρος δήπου καὶ
πᾶς ὅλως ἄνθρωπος με-
τέσχηκεν, εἰ μὴ καὶ μάλις-
θ' οἱ κατ' ἐκεῖνο δυνατώ-

43.9 Gomperz ‖ **10–11** Hayter (ἐπ[ις]τῆσαι cf. 41.5) ‖ **11** i.e., ἐάν ‖ **12** θυμὸν] Delattre-Monet : ὀργὴν] Wilke ‖ **12–13** προς[αγο]ρεύ|[ωμεν Wilke ‖ **13–14** Philippson post Wilke (τ]ὸ [δ'] ὄν[ομα) ‖ **15** [λέγειν ὀργὴν] Indelli ‖ **15–16** γ[ί]ν[ες]|θαι Wilke ‖ **19** Gomperz ‖ **25** Gomperz, Spengel

has in comparison with the case of what happens in the cases of many people, (sc. namely, their) putting a halt to someone's actions and getting vengeance on him—not even if we should call it [rage].[202]

[14] But [saying that anger is] a [weakness] and applying it to the wise man, so as to make him weak too, will not trouble us, as it does some,[203] who, writing against the *Kyriai Doxai*, thought it was outrageous that someone[204] had dared to say that "anger, gratitude, and all that sort of thing are in weakness," [25] since Alexander, by far the strongest of all, was liable to frequent fits of anger and conferred favors on countless men. For it is not the weakness opposite to the (strength) of athletes and kings that is meant[205] in his (sc. Epicurus's) argument, but the constitution and nature that is capable of death and pains, [35] which Alexander, one would suppose, and every human being in general share,[206] although they most of all (sc. athletes and kings)

---

202. A difficult sentence: without the verb, it is not clear to which type of anger "the emotion" (τὸ πάθος) refers, and the infinitives in lines 10–11 do not have a clear grammatical relationship to the rest of the sentence. "We must recognize in the name the difference the emotion has with respect to that which in most men springs up to restrain someone or avenge oneself on him, nor can we call that [anger]," so Indelli. We would rather take the alpha in ἄν as long (= ἐάν); [ὀργὴν] ("anger") is equally possible as a supplement.

203. Peripatetics are the obvious choice. Heterodox Epicureans such as Nicasicrates or Timasagoras are also possible, but why would they write against a summary work by the school founder? The contention, however, that Alexander's violent angers and extravagant favors were a sign of strength, not weakness, sounds more like a rhetorical point against the Epicureans than a philosophical argument. For the "philosophical" tradition about Alexander, see p. 76 of the introduction.

204. Epicurus did say that in *Kyr. dox.* 1, part of which Philodemus closely paraphrases here.

205. For λαμβάνω meaning "understand (sc. in a certain sense)," see LSJ, s.v. A.I.9.c.

206. A gnomic perfect.

43.40 τατοι λεγόμενοι, καθάπερ οὗτος. ᵛ καὶ θυμ[οῦ τοί- ‖

Column 44

1   νυν δεκτικὸς εἶναι ῥηθή-
    cετα[ι] ὁ coφόc, ἤ ̓ί ̓ που κἀπὶ τὸ
    κοινότατον εἰώθαμεν φέ-
    ρειν ταύτην τὴν προςηγο-
5   ρίαν· ἧι δ' ἐπὶ τὸ cύντονον
    κατὰ [τ]ὸ μέγεθος ἢ καὶ ἐπὶ
    τὴν ὡc πρὸ[c] ἀπ[ολ]αυcτὸν ὁρ-
    μήν, οὐ δήπουθε[ν ε]ἴπαιμ⟨εν⟩ ἄν.
    ο]ὔτε γὰρ cυντόν[οι]c περιπί-
10 π]τει πάθεcι το[ιού]τοιc· μα-
    νί]α γάρ, ἐπεὶ κ[αὶ] μυρίων
    ὅcων κ]ακῶν [.] παρ' αυτο[.
    . . . . .]ια[. . . . ₍.₎] φευξόμ[ε-
    [θα . . . .
15 deest una linea
    [. . . . . οὔτε ὡc πρὸc]
    ἀ]π̣ο̣[λαυcτ]όν (οὐδὲ γὰρ ἡδ[ύ
    τι προcφέρεται) ἀλλ' ὡc πρὸ[c
    ἀναγκαιότατον, ἀηδέcτα-
20 τον δὲ παραγίνεται, καθά-
    περ ἐπὶ πόcιν ἀψινθίου καὶ
    τομήν. ἀνήμεροc γάρ, κα-

43.41 Hayter ‖ **44.2, 6, 7** Gomperz, Spengel ‖ **8** ε]ἴπαιμ⟨εν⟩ ἄν Wilke : ε]ἴπαιμ' ἄν Gomperz (elisione insolita) ‖ **9–10** Gomperz, Spengel ‖ **11** Gomperz ‖ **12** ad init. ὅcων] Janko : γέμει] Gomperz ‖ κ]ακῶν Gomperz, Spengel ‖ [ἢ] Philippson ‖ παρ' αὐτὸ[ν Indelli : παρ' αὐτὸ[ὺc Gomperz, Spengel : παραυτό[θεν Delattre-Monet (fort. longius) ‖ **13** τιμωρ]ία Delattre-Monet (spatio quadrat) : ἐπιθυμ]ία Philippson (fort. longius) ‖ [ἣν καὶ] φευ- Philippson ‖ **13–14** φευξόμ[ε|θα Wilke ‖ **14–15** [πᾶcαν ὡc μέγιcτον οὖ|cαν κακόν] Philippson ‖ **15–16** [οὔτε πρὸc (τὴν) | κόλαcιν ὁρμᾶι, ὡc πρὸc] Bücheler (τὴν ins. Indelli) ‖ **16** * e.g. post Bücheler et Indelli ‖ **17** ἀ]π̣ο̣[λαυcτ]όν Bücheler ‖ ἡδ[ύ Gomperz ‖ **18** Gomperz, Spengel

are called[207] the most "powerful" in that regard. So, then,

Column 44

the wise man will also be said to be capable even of rage; in one way, I suppose, we are accustomed to use this appellation for the most general case, but in another we could certainly not use it for something intense in its greatness or for an impulse (to revenge) as if to something enjoyable.[208] [9] For he neither falls prey to intense emotions of such a sort, because that is madness, because ... of myriads of evils in his power (?) ... we will avoid ...

[*one line missing*]

... [16] [nor as to something enjoyable]—because it offers nothing sweet—but he approaches it as something most necessary but most unpleasurable, like drinking wormwood or the doctor's knife.[209] [22] For the untamed man is,

---

207. For a participle used like this without εἰσί, see the introduction, p. 119.

208. The question is, "In what sense can an Epicurean say 'the sage is capable of *thymos*'?" In its most common sense, *thymos* is synonymous with *orgē* and just means anger without further specification; this usage is acceptable. But if *thymos* is used to mean rage (i.e., empty anger or a type of it), then Epicureans could not say that the sage is capable of *thymos*.

209. For this imagery, see *Lib.*, col. 2b.2–7: "if one asks which [sc. the sage; cf. 2a.10–11] does with more pleasure [i.e., praise or blame his students], he is asking the obvious, for it is obvious the sage does the one with great pleasure and endures the other with no pleasure at all, like a drink of wormwood." See also *Lib.* 17a.1–8: "but when they (the students) see that their disposition is faulty, they are stung (δάκνονται), and (become) like those who call in wise physicians for an operation, who apply the scalpel to the sick."

44.23 τὰ τὸν Ὅμηρον "ἀφρήτωρ"
καὶ "ἀθέμιστος," ὄντως "ἔρα-
25 ται πολέμου" καὶ τιμωρίας
ἀνθρώπων, ὁ δὲ σοφὸς ἡμε-
ρώτατος καὶ ἐπιεικέστα-
τος. ὅ τε ἐπιθυμῶν τῆς κο-
λάσεως οὕτω⟦ι⟧ παρίσταθ' ὡς
30 πρὸς αἱρετὸν δι' αὐτὸ τὴν
τιμωρίαν, εἴ γε καὶ συνκα-
ταδύνειν προαιρεῖται, co-
φὸν δὲ μανία καὶ διανοεῖς-
θαι παριστάμενον ὡς πρὸς
35 τοιοῦτο τὴν κόλασιν. ἔξες-
τιν δὲ καὶ τῶν προενεχθη-
σομένων εἰς τὴν παραμυ-
θίαν ἐνίοις χρήσασθαι λό-
γοις ἐπιλογιστικοῖς τοῦ προ-
40 κειμένου χειρισμῶι διαλ-
λάξαντας. ᵛ ἀρέσκει δὲ καὶ ‖

Column 45

1 τοῖς καθηγεμόσιν οὐ τὸ
κατ[ὰ] τὴν πρόληψιν [τ]αύ-
την θυμωθήσεσθαι τὸν co-
φ]όν, ἀλλὰ τὸ κατὰ τὴν κοι-
5 ν]οτέραν. καὶ γὰρ ὁ Ἐπίκου-
ρ]ος ἐν ταῖς Ἀναφωνήσεσιν
δ]ιασαφεῖ [τό] τε θυμωθή-
σεσθαι καὶ [τὸ] μετρίως· καὶ

45.2 Gomperz, Spengel ‖ **4** Hayter ‖ **5, 6** Gomperz, Spengel ‖ **7** τό] τε Gomperz, Spengle [πο]τε Delattre-Monet ‖ **8** Spengel : καί[τοι] Delattre-Monet

as Homer says, "tribeless and lawless" and genuinely "loves war" and getting vengeance on people, but the sage is the most gentle and most reasonable. [28] And the person who desires punishment is thus inclined toward vengeance, as if toward a thing choice-worthy in itself,[210] even if he is choosing to drown himself together with (his victim), but it is insanity even to imagine a sage being inclined to punishment as if it were such a thing.

THE MAXIMALISTS

[35] It is possible also to make use of arguments for the explanation[211] (of this problem) that take account of the present subject, among which are those we will presently bring forward in its support,[212] changing the treatment. But also

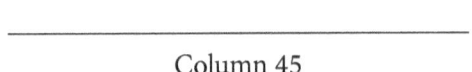

Column 45

the Founders accept the idea that "the wise man will be enraged," not according to that preconception, but according to the more general one.[213] [5] In fact, Epicurus makes clear in his *First Appellations*[214] both that the sage "will experience rage" and (will experience it) "in moderation," and

---

210. "Something choice-worthy in itself" to Epicureans can only be something pleasurable. Philodemus sets punishment as the goal of natural anger, as vengeance is the goal of empty anger, and it becomes as contemptible as vengeance, if pursued for its own sake as a pleasure.

211. The term for argument is ἐπιλογιcμόc, though Philodemus does not appear to be using its technical meaning; if he is, it is in a way that escapes us. He calls one of their arguments a λόγoc (49.27). For "explanation," see LSJ, s.v. "παραμυθία," A.4.

212. See below, 46.16–47.41.

213. Philodemus means that the Founders understood *thymos* not in the sense in which Philodemus's opponents use it, "rage," but in a more general one, as a synonym for "anger" generally. See n. 208. On the quotation from Metrodorus, see n. 98.

214. The *Anaphōnēseis* is mentioned only here, and this is its only fragment. Sedley

298 Philodemus, *On Anger*

45.9 ὁ Μητρόδω[ρ]ος, εἰ κυρ[ί]ως
10 λέγει τὸ [τοῦ] σοφοῦ θυμός,
συνεμφα[ίνε]ι τὸ λίαν βραχέως. ᵛ τ[ὸ] δ' [ὅτ]ι θυμωθή[ς]ε-
ται ᵛ καὶ τῷ[ι Ἑρ]μάρχωι π[. .]αι
. .]τον[. . . . .]ην
15 deest una linea
ὥστε θαυμάζειν ἐπ[ὶ τοῖς
βυβλ'ι'ακοῖς εἶναι θέλουσιν,
ὅτι ταῦτα καὶ τὰ πρότερον
ἐπισημανθέντα παρα-
20 λιπόντες ἐξ ἀκολουθίας
τὸ θυμωθήσεσθαι κατὰ
τοὺς Ἄνδρας τὸν σοφὸν ἀ-
πεδείκνυον. ᵛ αἵ τε πίστεις
αὐτῶν αἱ περὶ τοῦ θυμωθή-
25 σεσθαι ᵛ τοσοῦτον ἀποδέουσι
τοῦ κατὰ πᾶσαν ἔννοιαν θυμοῦ
θυμωθ[ήσεσθα]ι προσάγειν,
ὅπερ ὤφειλον, εἰ διὰ παν-
τὸς οὐ καὶ τὴν ὀργὴν καὶ τὸν
30 θυμὸν κατηγορουμένως οὐδὲ τὸ κοινῶς ὀργισθήσες-
θαι, καθάπερ ὑποδείξομεν,
παριστάνουσι. δῆλον δ' ὅτι
καὶ καθὸ μεγέθει καὶ καθὸ
35 ποιότητι διαφέρει τῆς
ὀργῆς, οὐδὲ φυσικός ἐστιν
ὁ θυμός· οἱ δὲ μὴ καλῶς πό-
τ' ἐπὶ ταὐτὸ καὶ πότ' οὐκ ἐπὶ
ταὐτὸ φέρετ' ὀργὴ καὶ θυ- ⟦μ⟧

45.9 ὁ Μητρόδω[ρ]ος Gomperz, Spengel ‖ κυρ[ί]ως Gomperz **10** τὸ [τοῦ] Henry : τὸ [μὲν] * post Spengel (τὸ [μὲν ὡς]) : τρ[ῦ δὲ] Gigante : τή[χει] Delattre-Monet ‖ **11-12** Hayter ‖ **13** τῷ[ι Ἑρ]μάρχω[ι Gomperz ‖ ad fin. π legit Wilke : x O ‖ **13-14** π[αραι]|[τη]τὸν [μὲν οὐ δοκεῖ, ἀλλὰ Wilke ‖ **14-15** τ]ὴν | [σύντονον μόνον ὀργήν·] Philippson ‖ **16** Spengel ‖ **27** Hayter

Metrodorus, if he says "the rage of the wise man" in its proper sense, shows also that he feels it "very briefly." [12] That "he will feel rage"... also to Hermarchus ...

[*two lines missing or untranslatable*]

... [16] so that I am amazed at those who want to be textbook Epicureans,[215] that they ignored these and the things I mentioned before, and as a result[216] tried to demonstrate that, according to our Founders, "the sage will become wrathful." [23] And their proofs that he will become enraged are very far from establishing that he will become enraged according to every notion of rage, as they ought to have, since nowhere do they establish both anger and rage as separate categories,[217] nor that "he (the wise man) will become angry" in the sense common (to both words), as we will show. [33] It is clear that both in magnitude and quality rage differs from anger and is not natural. [37] But they have reasoned wrongly about when anger and rage are referred to the same thing and when they are not,

---

(1973, 5) argued that these ἀναφωνήϲειϲ should be identified with the "natural" and primal meanings of words; cf. Demetrius Laco, *On Textual Criticism*, 67.7–9: φύϲει τὰϲ πρώταϲ τῶν ὀνομάτων ἀναφωνήϲειϲ γεγονέναι λέγομεν ("we say that the first appellations of words came into being by nature"); see further in the introduction, pp. 41–43.

215. The βιβλιακοί are "Epicureans by the book," or at least so they claimed. The school encouraged verbal disputations over the texts of the founders like those in Demetrius Laco's *Textual Problems*. See Sedley 1998, 62–93; and Del Mastro's (2014, 184–87) reconstruction of the title Πρὸϲ τοὺϲ φαϲκοβιβλιακούϲ A, in P.Herc. 1005/862 (partially published in Angeli 1988a).

216. LSJ (s.v. "ἀκολουθία") singles out this passage for ἐξ ἀκολουθίαϲ "as a consequence." According to the TLG, it occurs in Galen fifteen times also, frequently of erroneous as well as correct inference (as opposed to observation).

217. For the translation of εἰ as "since," see Smyth §§2246 and 2698b and d. κατηγορουμένωϲ should mean something like "categorically" or perhaps "by categories," which is what it appears to mean in its only other appearance in the TLG, in the anonymous commentary on Aristotle's *On Interpretation* edited by Tarán (1978).

45.40 μὸc ἐπιλελογιcμένοι, κα-
θ]ὸ διαπίπτουcι κἀν τῶι πε- ‖

Column 46

1 ριπίπτειν ἢ μὴ περιπί-
πτειν θυμῶι δοξάζειν
τὸν cοφόν [[δ]] ⱽ —εὔcημ[ον] οἶμαι
τοῖc παρηκολουθηκό[c]ιν οἷc
5 ἐν τῶι λόγωι τῶι περὶ τούτων ἐπεcημηνάμεθα. ⱽ ταῦ-
τα μὲν ο[ὖ]ν τὰ παρ' ἡμῶ[ν
ἢ κα[ὶ] τὰ περὶ [ἡ]μῶν [ὑπὲρ
τοῦ φυ[cι]κήν τι[ν]α ὀρ[γὴν εἶ-
10 ναι καταcκευάζουc[ι] λόγοιc [π]ροθέντε[c] ἀντείπα-
μεν [δὴ] τὸ τὸν cο[φ]ὸν ὀργιc-
θήcε[cθαι]. τινὲc [δὲ καὶ] θυμωθή[cεcθαι τὸν cοφό]ν φα-
15 cι . . . .(.)]ν καὶ
. (.)]ον. ἐπὶ τούτ[οιc οὖν κέ-
χρηνται καὶ τοι[ούτοιc ἐ-
πιλογιcμοῖc. εἰ τ[οῖ]c καλῶc
παρ' ἑαυτοὺc κ[εχ]ρημένο[ιc
20 εὐχαριcτήcει cοφὸc ἀνήρ,
καὶ τοῖc ἑκουcί[[οι]]`ω´c βλάψα-
cιν αὐτὸν ὀργιcθήcεται· [εἰ
δ' οὐκ ὀργιcθήcεται τού-

45.41 Gomperz ‖ **46.3, 4** Gomperz, Spengel ‖ **7** Gomperz, Spengel ‖ **8** κα[ὶ] ... [ἡ]μῶν Wilke ‖ ad fin. [ὑπὲρ Delattre-Monet : [τε καὶ Gomperz ‖ **9–10** Gomperz, Spengel ‖ **11** Wilke post Gomperz ([οἷc π]ρο-) ‖ **12** [δὴ] Wilke ‖ cο[φ]ὸν Gomperz, Spengel ‖ **12–13** ὀργιc|θήcε[cθαι Gomperz ‖ **13** [δὲ καὶ] Gomperz, Spengel : [δ' ἡμῶν] Delattre-Monet ‖ **14** θυμω|θή[cεcθαι Gomperz, Spengel ‖ **14–15** τὸν cοφό]ν φα[cίν Wilke ‖ **15** οὐχ ἧττον ἢ τὸ]ν Philippson : οὐχ οὕτωc ὡc τὸ]ν Delattre-Monet ‖ **15–16** κρι[ν]όν Indelli ‖ **16** Wilke ‖ **17–19, 22,** Gomperz, Spengel ‖ **22** αὐτῷν McO (cf. p. 124)

just as they fail in their opinion about whether

Column 46

the sage does or does not fall into a "rage"—I think this clear to those who have followed what we have indicated in our discussion of the subject.[218] [6] So, then, having laid down these things on our own behalf and concerning us, with arguments that prove it, in support of there being a natural kind of anger, we have [indeed] replied that the sage will become angry.

[13] But certain (philosophers) (claim that that the sage?) will become "enraged" ...

[*most of two lines missing*]

... [So,] in addition to these arguments, they use arguments by analogy su[ch as the following]:[219]

[18] (A) If a sage will feel gratitude to those who have treated him well of their own free will, he will also become angry with those who have intentionally harmed him. If he will not get angry with

---

218. Wilke supposes that Philodemus refers especially to 39.41–44.35.
219. For analysis of the arguments, see the introduction, §6.7. We mark the paired parts of each of the three *epilogismoi* with A, B, and C to make the structure clearer.

46.24 τοις, οὐδ' ἐκείνοις εὐχαρι[c-
25 τήcει. τὸ γὰρ ἀντίcτρο- 〚φ〛
φον γίνεται πάθοc ἐπὶ θα-
τέρου πρὸc θάτερον, καὶ
κινεῖ, καθάπερ τὴν εὐχα-
ριcτίαν, οὕτω καὶ τὴν ὀρ-
30 γὴν τὸ ἑκούcιον. ὡc γὰρ εὐ-
χαριcτοῦμεν ο[ὔ]τε τοῖc ἀψύ-
χοιc τῶν ποιητικῶν οὔτε
τοῖc ἀπροαιρέτ〚οι〛`ω´c τι πα-
ραcκευάζουcι τῶν [ἐμ]ψύχων,
35 οὕτωc οὐδ' ἀγανακτοῦμεν.
οἱ δὲ φυcικῶc φαcιν ἡμᾶc
ἐπὶ τὴν ὀργὴν ὥcπερ ἐπὶ
τὴν εὐχαριcτίαν ὁ[ρ]μᾶν
διὰ τὴν ἀντίcτροφο̣ν αἰ-
40 τίαν. ᵛ ὥcπερ τε πολ[λο]ῖc πε-
ριπεcόντεc, ὅτ[α]ν οἶνο[ν] 〚π〛 ‖

Column 47

1 προcενέγκωνται, μεθυc-
κομένο̣ιc—[οὐ] μόνον ἄφρο-
cιν, ἀλλὰ κα̣ὶ cυνετοῖc, καὶ
οὐ μᾶλλ[ον ἐ]κείνοιc ἢ τού-
5 τοιc—καταλαμβάνομεν ὅ-
τ[ι] τὸ μεθύειν ο̣[ὐ] cυμβαί-
ν[ει] πα[ρ'] ἀλογιcτίαν, ἀλλά, κἂν
οἱ] cοφ[οὶ μεθύωcι, π]α̣ρα̣ [cοφί-

46.24 Gomperz, Spengel ‖ 31, 34 Gomperz ‖ 38 Gomperz, Spengel ‖ 40 Hayter ‖ 41 Gomperz, Spengel ‖ 47.2 Hayter ‖ 4 Gomperz, Spengel ‖ 6 Hayter ‖ 7 Gomperz ‖ 8–9 Wilke : π]αρά[λογον, | οὕτω καὶ cαφ]ὲc Delattre

the latter, he will not feel gratitude to the former.[220] [25] For the one emotion appears in the one case to correspond to the other in the other case, and just as the intentional element provokes gratitude, so also it provokes anger. For as we are grateful neither to inanimate active causes nor to those animate ones that achieved something by no choice of their own, so also we are not annoyed at them. [36] Others say that we are naturally impelled to anger, as to gratitude, through the corresponding cause.[221] (B) And, because we have encountered many men,

Column 47

who, whenever they take wine, get drunk—not just fools, but also intelligent men, and the latter no less than the former—we understand that their drunkenness happens not because of irrationality, [7] but, whenever even the sag[es are drunk,] because [of wisdom] …

---

220. This argument relies on the implication of *Kyr. dox.* 1 that, though the gods, being incorruptible, are free of anger and gratitude, humans are not; indeed, their weakness compels them to feel both emotions. If the wise man is liable to anger (δεκτικὸc ὀργῆc), as *Kyr. dox.* 1 implies, he must also be liable to gratitude (δεκτικὸc χάριτοc) on the same grounds, set forth already in 43.14–44.14. So far Philodemus agrees. Note that παρ' ἑαυτούc (46.19), ἑκουcίωc (46.21, 48.7–8), τὸ ἑκούcιον (46.30), and κατὰ προαίρεcιν (48.11–12; cf. 39.29) are used throughout the first *epilogismos* as synonyms for "intentional(ly), voluntary/voluntarily." Philodemus takes for granted, along with the maximalists, that gratitude is felt because of good intentionally done to us.

221. Harm done us intentionally, as opposed to good done us intentionally. *Kharis* is the emotional response to good done to us intentionally. So both for the maximalists and for Philodemus, *kharis* and *orgē* are to that extent mirrors of each other.

47.9 αν, ...]ες οὐ μόνο[ν
10   . . . .]ιους, ὅταν ἑκο[υ-
      cίως ὑπό τι]νος βλαβῶς[ιν,
      . . . .]ης τῆς τοὺς [. .
      . . . .]το μὲν οὖ[ν] ερου-
14   . . . .]αται ο[. . . . .
      desunt 2 lineae
17   αἰτίαν ο[. . . . .] προc-
      άπτεcθα[ι]. ᵛ cυνέχεταί τε
      οὐδὲ τ[αῖc] ματαίοιc ὀργαῖc
20   ὁ μάταιος [γε]νόμενος κε-
      ρ]αυνόπλ[ηκ]τος, ἀλλὰ κα-
      τὰ τὰς ὑπολήψεις τὰς προ-
      η]γουμένας· ᵛ ὁ μὲν βεβλά-
      φ]θαι δοκ[ῶ]ν, ὁ δὲ καὶ μεγά-
25   λ[[οι]]`ω´ς, [. . ₍.₎]εν[. .τ]ὰς ὑπολήψεις
      οὐκ ἔχων [ταύ]τας, ὑπὲρ ἄλ-
      λων δ' ἔχω[ν], ἐπ' ἐκείνοις
      μὲν ἀόργητός ἐστιν, ἐπὶ
      δὲ τούτοι[ς ἐ]ξίσταθ'· ὥστ' εἰ
30   τὸ διερεθί[ζε]cθαι κοινῶς [[υ]]
      ὑπολήψε[cι]ν ἐπακολουθεῖ,
      βλαπτόμ⌜ενος⌝ δ' ὁ σοφὸς ὑ-
      πό τινος [ἑ]⌜κου⌝cίως ὑπο-
      λαμβάνει βλάπτεσθαι, τη-
35   λικοῦτο δὲ μόνον ὅσον βέ-

47.9–18 οὕτως cαφ]ὲς οὐ μόνο[ν |¹⁰ τοὺς ματα]ίους, ὅταν ἑκο[υ|cίως ὑπό τι]νος βλαβῶς[ιν, | ἐπιδεκτικο]ὺς τῆς ⟨ὀργῆς εἶναι, ἀλλὰ καὶ⟩ τοὺς [co|φούς. διὰ τοῦ]το μὲν οὖ[ν] ἐροῦ|μεν, ὥσπερ δύν]αται ὁ [cοφὸς |¹⁵ μεθύcκεcθαι κατὰ φύcιν, | οὕτως χρὴ διὰ τὴν αὐτὴν] | αἰτίαν ὀ[ργὴν αὐτῶι] προc|άπτεcθα[ι] Philippson post 10–11 ἑκο[υ]cίως Wilke et 13–14 διὰ τοῦ]το μὲν οὖ[ν] ἐροῦ[[μεν Gomperz ‖ **13–14** οὐ[κ] ἐροῦ[[cι Janko ‖ **14** τοῖc μ]αταίο[ιc Gomperz ‖ **17–18** περι|άπτεcθα[ι Delattre-Monet, cf. 43.16–17 ‖ **20** Hayter : γι]νόμενος Spengel ‖ **21** Spengel ‖ **23** Gomperz ‖ **24** Hayter ‖ **25** [. . ₍.₎]εν[. . .]αc P : [ἐν] ἐν[ίοιc Delattre-Monet (longius?) : παρ'] ἔν[ια DA : ἐφ'] ἐν[ίων McO : κ]εν[ὰc Janko : τῶν μ]ὲν [τ]ὰc Gomperz (non quadrat) : [ὑπὲρ μὲν ἐνίων τ]ὰc Wilke (e.g., valde longius) ‖ **26** Spengel : [πιc]τὰc Delattre-Monet ‖ **27, 29, 30, 31** Gomperz, Spengel ‖ **32–33** collocavit hic litteras subpositas ex col. 48 Wilke, ut coni. Hayter

not only ... whenever they are intentionally harmed by someone ... then ... say ... cause.²²² [18] (C) And it is not because lightning hit the foolish person²²³ that he is liable to foolish fits of anger but according to the suppositions²²⁴ that lead him on: [23] one man thinking that he has been harmed, or another thinking even (that he has been harmed) greatly ... not having these suppositions, but having them concerning other things, he is not angered by the former but is driven mad by the latter; and so, if being irritated follows generally on suppositions, [32] and the wise man, being harmed by someone intentionally, supposes that he is harmed,²²⁵ but only to that extent that he has actually been

---

222. Here, too, Philodemus agrees with his opponents: that the wise man can in some sense get drunk is analogous to his being in some sense capable of anger.

223. I.e., not for an arbitrary or random reason.

224. "Suppositions" last appeared as the cause of "compelled" behavior by fools in frags. 24, 28, and 32, but see n. 78 above on ψευδοδοξίαν at col. 6.14–15. They now reappear as necessary parts of the definition both of natural and empty anger.

225. The phrase ὑπό τινος ἑκουσίως is placed ambiguously between βλαπτόμενος and ὑπολαμβάνει βλάπτεσθαι, and word order suggests that it should go with the main verb rather than the participle. But the rebuttal at 48.27–33 divides the prerequisites for anger into (1) "a supposition of being harmed" and (2) "the sage's being harmed intentionally," which shows that the translation printed above is most likely how Philodemus understood it.

47.36 βλαπται, πάντως μὲν ὀργις-
θήσεται, βραχέως δὲ διὰ
τὸ μηδέποτε μεγάλης ἔμ-
φασιν βλάβης λαμβάνειν, οὐ-
40 δὲν εἶναι παρὰ μέγα τῶν ἔ-
ξωθεν ἡγού[με]νος. ἔνιοι δὲ ‖

Column 48

1 καὶ περὶ τοῦ θυμωθήσε[c-
/ θαι τὸν σοφὸν ˋτούˊτοις προσεχρή-
— σαντο. τῶι πρώτωι τοιγαρ-
οῦν παραβληθήσεται τ[οι-
5 οῦτος λόγος· εἰ φυσικῶς ὁρμῶμεν ἐπὶ τὸ συντόνως
εὐχ[αρισ]τεῖν τ[ο]ῖς ἑκουσίως εὐ[εργετήσα]σιν, ἐκκα-
λού]μεθα φ[υσικ]ῶς κὰ[πὶ
10 τὸ] συ[ν]τόνω[ς ὀρ]γίζεσθαι
τ[ο]ῖς β[λ]άψ[ασ]ι κατὰ [π]ρο-
αίρε]σι[ν]· ὡς [δὲ κ]αὶ σοφὸ[ς
13 εὐχα]ρ[ι]στεῖ [. . . . .
desunt 4 lineae
18 . . . ἐ]πειδὴ καὶ τ[ὰς ὠφε-
λίας ἡγεῖται τὰς ἔξωθ[εν
20 βαιάς· οὐκ ἐπὶ τῶν κακῶν
γοῦν, ἀλλὰ καὶ ἐπὶ τῶν ἀγαθῶν τίθεται τὸ μηθὲν εἶ-
ναι παρὰ μέγα τῶν ἔξω-
θεν. ἀλλ' οὐ μόνον τοῖς σο-
25 φὸν ποιήσασιν εὐχαρισ-

47.41 Hayter ‖ 48.1, 4 Gomperz, Spengel ‖ 7 Hayter ‖ 8 Gomperz ‖ 8–9 ἐκ-κα|[λού]μεθα φ[υσικ]ῶς Hayter ‖ κ[ἀπὶ Wilke ‖ 10–11 Gomperz ‖ 11–12 [π]ρο-|[αίρε]σι[ν] Wilke ‖ 12–13 [δὲ κ]αὶ σοφὸ[ς | εὐχα]ρ[ι]στεῖ Gomperz : σοφὸ[ν] | εὐχα-]ρ[ι]στεῖ[σθαι Janko vel εὐχα]ρ[ι]στεῖ[ν * ‖ 18–19 Gomperz

harmed, as a matter of course he will be angered, but briefly, because he never receives an impression of being greatly harmed, as he never takes any external thing to be all that important.[226] But some

Column 48

have used these arguments about (the possibility of) the sage becoming enraged as well. [3] (A) Very well, then, as for the first (argument), an argument such as the following can be set alongside it: if we are naturally impelled to intense gratitude to those who have voluntarily done us good, we are also naturally provoked to intense anger against those who have harmed us intentionally. [12] But as even a wise man is thankful …

[*four lines missing*]

… [18] since he considers even external benefits unimportant. The rule "nothing external is important" is laid down not only with reference to evils alone but also to goods. "But he is greatly thankful not just to those who made him a sage,

---

226. Here also Philodemus agrees with the argument—but only as he qualifies it.

48.26 τεῖ μεγάλως, ἀλλὰ καὶ τοῖς
ἔνια τῶν ἄλλων παρα-
σκευάσασιν. εἰ δ' ἐρεῖ τις
εἰς [τ]ὴν προαίρεσιν [ἀ]τε-
30 νίζοντα τοῦτο πράττε[ι]ν,
ταὐτὸ δηλονότι καὶ ἐ-
/ πὶ τῆς ὀργῆς προσδέξεται.
φανερὸν δ' ὃ χρὴ λέγειν καὶ
πρὸς [τὸ]ν̣ ἑξῆς, χειρισμῶι
35 δὲ μ[ό]νον διαλλάττον-
τα λόγον. ⌐ ἄθλιόν γε μὴν
οἰητέον εἶναι τὸν ἑξῆς·
περί τε γὰρ τοῦ μεθυσθή-
σεσθαι καὶ τὸν σοφόν, εἰ μὲν
40 ἀποφαίνονται τοὺς πε-
ρὶ τὸν Ἐπίκουρον κ[ε]χρῆσθαι ‖

Column 49

1   τῶι καὶ τοὺς χα[ρ]ίεν[τας, φλ]υ-
αροῦσιν· ⌐ εἰ δ' ἑα[υ]τούς, ἀτόπως
περὶ ἐκείνου φ[ανερὸ]ν ἐκ τούτων συλλογίζ[ε]σ[θ]αι· ⌐ τῶι τε
5   παραπλησίωι τρόπωι πορευ-
όμενός τις ἀποδ[εί]ξει τὸ
καὶ φ[ιλ]οδοξ[ή]σει[ν ἢ ἐρασ-
θήσε[σθ]αι τὸ[ν σο]φὸν [καὶ μυρίοι[ς ἄ]λλοις σ[υσ]χεθήσ[εσθαι

48.29, 30 Hayter ‖ **34** Spengel ‖ **35, 41** Gomperz, Spengel ‖ **49.1** Hayter ‖ ⟨αὐ⟩τῶι add. et καὶ τοὺς χαρίεντας del. Gomperz ‖ **3** Wilke : φ[αῖεν ἂ]ν Henry ‖ **4** Gomperz ‖ **6** Hayter ‖ **7** φ[ιλ]οδοξ[ή]σει[ν Gomperz ‖ ἢ Wilke : καὶ Gomperz ‖ **7–8** ἐρας]|θήσε[σθ]αι Gomperz, Spengel, sed μα . ‖ legit Wilke (μ habet O) quae fortasse ad lineam sequentem pertinent ‖ **8–10** Gomperz (9 ἄ]λλοις iam Hayter)

but also to those who provided certain other things for him." [28] But if someone will claim that he does this looking to their intentions, then obviously he will accept the same claim concerning anger.[227]

[33] (B) And it is obvious what one must say against the next (argument), changing the argument only in the manner of handling it.[228] Indeed, one should consider the next argument simply wretched. For concerning the claim that the wise man, too, will get drunk, [39] if they mean Epicurus's circle

---

Column 49

used (the argument) that intelli[gent] people,[229] too, (will get drunk), they are talking [no]nsense; but if they mean themselves, it is obvious from the following (considerations) that they are reasoning about that man (sc. the sage) illegitimately: [4] by proceeding in a similar way, someone will demonstrate that he (sc. the sage) will be anxious for glory, will fall in love, and will be afflicted by innumerable other

---

227. In fact, the wise man is chiefly thinking about results—damage done or benefits conferred—not other people's intentions, however essential it is to anger and gratitude that the damage or benefit be intentional. Wisdom is the greatest gift, but no harm that can be done to the sage compares with it in importance.

228. Philodemus "changes the manner" because, if the opponents claimed that drunkenness was appropriate to the sage, they could justify any other vice by the analogy, which, he implies, is not worth arguing against.

229. The term χαρίεις, literally "endowed with graces, accomplished" (Asmis suggested "people of finer feelings" to us), is used here and in lines 11–12 as a synonym of cυνετός ("intelligent"), which appeared in the parallel passage at 47.3, where *epilogismos* B was first stated.

49.10 ⟦το[ν co]φον⟧ π[άθ]εcιν, εἴ[περ ἄλλο[ι κ]αὶ τῶν [πά]νυ χα[ριέν-
τῳ[ν cυ]νεχ[ῶc πό]νουc ἔ[χου-
13 cιν . . . .]ε ολοc[. . .
desunt 4 lineae
18 τὸ μεθύει[ν . . . . . .]ι[. .]ι[. .]δ[.
θαι πρόχειρό[ν ἐcτ]ι, καὶ ⟨τὸ⟩ τὸν co-
20 φὸν προcδε[κ]τέον εὐεμπτωτότερον ἐνίων ἀλογίcτων
εἰc τὰc ὀργὰc ὑπάρχειν. ᵛ καὶ
τὸ μὴ τῶν ἀφρόνων ἧττον
τοῦτο πάcχειν, ἐπειδήπερ
25 οὐχ ἧττον αὐτῶν μεθύc-
κεται, καθὸ λέ[γ]εται μεθύειν.
ὁ δ[ὲ] τελευταῖοc λόγοc ἀπέ-
ραντόc ἐcτιν ἐκ τοῦ τὴν
ὀρ[γ]ὴν χωρὶc ὑπολήψεωc τοῦ
30 βε[β]λάφθαι μὴ γίνεcθαι καὶ
τοῦ τὸν coφὸν ἑκουcίω[c] βλάπτεcθαι cυνά[γ]ων τὸ καὶ [ὀ]ργί-
⟦c⟧`ζ´εc[θ]αι. καθάπ[ε]ρ γὰρ χωρὶc
τοῦ γράμματα μαθεῖν οὐχ οἷ-
35 όν τ[ε] {μαθεῖν οὐχ οἷόν τε} γενέcθαι coφόν, ἀλλ' οὐκ, εἰ γράμ-
ματά τιc ἔμαθεν, ἐποιcθή-
cεται τὸ καὶ {τὸν} coφὸν αὐτὸν ὑπάρχειν, οὕτωc οὐδὲ

49.10 εἴ[περ Philippson : εἴ [γε Delattre-Monet : εἰ [γὰρ Janko ‖ **10–11** ἄλ]|λο[ι Philippson : πολ]|λο[ὶ Delattre-Monet ‖ **11–12** κ]αὶ τῶν [πά]νυ χα[ριέν]|τῳ[ν Hayter (12 ad init. το[P, τοι[legit Wilke) ‖ **12–13** cυ]νεχ[ῶc πό]νουc ἔ[χου]|cιν Philippson ‖ cυ]νεχ[εῖc McO ‖ **18** Gomperz ‖ **18–19** ἤ]δ[εc]|θαι Janko ‖ **19** πρόχειρό[ν ἐcτ]ι Gomperz, Spengel ‖ ⟨τὸ⟩ add. McO ‖ **20, 26** Gomperz, Spengel ‖ **27** Hayter ‖ **29–33** Gomperz, Spengel ‖ **35** τ[ε] Gomperz, Spengel ‖ del. Gomperz, Spengel ‖ **35–36** γί|νεcθαι Bücheler ‖ **38** del. Gomperz

passions, [10] if indeed others among highly intelligent men constantly have troubles (like those?) ...

[*five lines missing*]

... [18] getting drunk ...

... is easy, and it is necessary to accept that "the sage is more liable than some unthinking people to fall into fits of anger" [22] and that "he suffers this no less than fools, since he gets drunk no less than they do," in the sense they are using "be drunk."[230]

[27] (C) The last argument is invalid,[231] since from the statements that "anger cannot occur without a supposition of having been harmed" and that "the sage is intentionally harmed"[232] it leads to the statement "he is angered." [33] For just as without learning one's letters it is not possible to become a sage, but, if someone has learned his letters, it will not be concluded that he is also a sage, [39] so also (it does) not

---

230. The opponents are accused of arguing that the sage will get extremely drunk, not merely tipsy, in order to support their thesis that he will also get extremely angry, or "enraged." Philodemus replies by *reductio ad absurdum*.

231. So in Peripatetic logic; cf. Mates 1953, 134.

232. Gomperz noted that we might have expected this to read in its full form "the sage <supposes he> is being intentionally harmed."

49.40 τῶι προςτηςαμέν[ωι τὸ ὑ]πο-
λήψεcιν τοῦ βεβλάφθαι ‖

Column 50

1 τὴν ὀργὴν ἐπακολουθεῖν,
ἄλλωc δ' ἀδυνατεῖν, τὸ
πά]ντωc ὀ[ργ]ιcθήcεc[θ]αι
τὸν ἔμφαcιν εἰληφότα
5 βλάβηc, ἂμ μή τιc ἐπιδεί-
ξηι κ[α]ὶ δραcτικὸν αἴ[τι-
ον ὀργῆc εἶναι τ[ὴ]ν ὑπό-
ληψιν τ[ῆ]c [βλ]άβηc. ‖

Subscriptio

1 Φιλοδ]ή[μου
πε]ρὶ ὀργῆc
ἀ[ρι]θ᾽]XXXⲢHḤΔΔΔΠ

49.40 Hayter (τὸ add. Henry) ‖ **50.3** πά]ντωc Gomperz ‖ ὀ[ργ]ιcθήcεc[θ]αι Hayter ‖ **6** κ[α]ὶ Gomperz ‖ **6-8** Hayter ‖ **s.1** Genovesi ‖ **2** περὶ παθῶν ὅ ἐcτι] Indelli : ὑπόμνημα] Genovesi : περὶ ἠθῶν ὅ ἐcτι] Wilke, v. intro., §12

(follow) for him who has established

Column 50

that "anger follows upon suppositions of having been harmed, but is impossible otherwise" that "he who has received an impression of being harmed will as a matter of course[233] be angered," [5] unless someone should demonstrate that the supposition of harm is indeed an efficient cause of anger.[234]

Philodemus's
On] Anger
3,735 stichoi[235]

---

233. For πάντως, cf. 40.18–19, 25–26, and 47.36–37. Here it means "in every case," "as a (strict) rule."

234. The phrase δραστικὸν αἴτιον occurs only here in an Epicurean context; it means that the supposition of being harmed intentionally is a sufficient cause of anger. By contrast, Philodemus holds that it is only a necessary antecedent condition to feeling anger, which we can refuse to feel for many reasons. More usually, the expression is ποιητικὸν αἴτιον, as opposed to παθητικὸν αἴτιον "passive cause." The phrases δραστικὸν αἴτιον and ποιητικὸν αἴτιον are used as synonyms, e.g., in Galen, Caus. puls. 9 (Kühn 1821–1833, 9:5,9–10): ἡ ... δραστική τε καὶ ποιητικὴ καὶ δημιουργικὴ [note explanatory τε καί ... καί "that is ... and"] τῆς ἐνεργείας αἰτία ("a 'drastic,' that is, active and creative cause"); and Plen. 34.5–6 Otte = Kühn 1821–1833, 7:524,13–15: φάσκοντες αὐτὴν αἰτίαν εἶναι δραστικήν, ὡς οὐδὲν διάφερον εἰπεῖν ἤτοι δραστικὴν ἢ ποιητικήν ("we claim it is an active cause, as it makes no difference whether we say drastikēn or poiētikēn"). See the introduction, pp. 79–80.

235. On the subscription, see the introduction, §12.

Bibliography

Adam, James. 1965. *The Republic of Plato*. 2nd ed. Cambridge: Cambridge University Press.
Alberti, Antonina. 1995. "The Epicurean Theory of Law and Justice." Pages 161–90 in *Justice and Generosity: Studies in Hellenistic Social and Political Philosophy*. Edited by André Laks and Malcolm Schofield. Cambridge: Cambridge University Press.
Angeli, Anna, ed. 1988a. *Filodemo: Agli amici di scuola (PHerc. 1005)*. La scuola di Epicuro 7. Naples: Bibliopolis.
———. 1988b. "Il concetto di esattezza scientifica in Filodemo." Pages 551–59 in *Atti del XVII Congresso internazionale di papirologia (Napoli, 19-26 maggio 1983)*. Naples: Centro internazionale per lo studio dei papiri ercolanesi.
———. 2000. "Necessità e autodeterminazione nel *De Ira* di Filodemo." *PapLup* 9:15–63.
Angeli, Anna, and Maria Colaizzo. 1979. "I frammenti di Zenone sidonio." *CErc* 9:47–133.
Annas, Julia. 1989. "Epicurean Emotions." *GRBS* 30:145–64.
———. 1992. *Hellenistic Philosophy of Mind*. Hellenistic Culture and Society 8. Berkeley: University of California Press.
———. 1993. *The Morality of Happiness*. Oxford: Oxford University Press.
Armstrong, David. 1993. "The Addressees of the *Ars Poetica*: Herculaneum, the Pisones, and Epicurean Protreptic." *Materiali e discussioni per l'analisi dei testi classici* 31:185–230.
———. 2004. "All Things to All Men: Philodemus' Model of Therapy and the Audience of *De Morte*." Pages 13–54 in Fitzgerald, Obbink, and Holland 2004.
———. 2008. "'Be Angry and Sin Not': Philodemus versus the Stoics on Natural Bites and Natural Emotions." Pages 79–121 in *Passions and Moral Progress in Greek and Roman Thought*. Edited by John T. Fitzgerald. Oxford: Routledge.

———. 2011. "Epicurean Virtues, Epicurean Friendship: Cicero vs the Herculaneum papyri." Pages 105–28 in *Epicurus and the Epicurean Tradition*. Edited by Jeffrey Fish and Kirk R. Sanders. Cambridge: Cambridge University Press.

———. 2014. "Horace's Epicurean Voice in the *Satires*." Pages 91–127 in *The Philosophizing Muse*. Edited by Myrto Garani and David Konstan. Cambridge: Cambridge University Press.

———. 2016. "Utility and Affection in Epicurean Friendship: Philodemus *On the Gods* 3, *On Property Management,* and Horace, *Satires* 2.6." Pages 182–208 in *Hope, Joy and Affection in the Classical World*. Edited by Ruth R. Caston and Robert A. Kaster. New York: Oxford University Press.

Armstrong, David, Jeffrey Fish, Patricia A. Johnston, and Marilyn B. Skinner, eds. 2004. *Vergil, Philodemus, and the Augustans*. Austin: University of Texas Press.

Arrighetti, Graziano. 1973. *Epicuro opere*. 2nd ed. Classici della filosofia 4. Turin: Einaudi.

Asmis, Elizabeth. 1984. *Epicurus' Scientific Method*. Cornell Studies in Classical Philology 42. Ithaca, NY: Cornell University Press.

———. 1990. "Philodemus' Epicureanism." *ANRW* 2.36.4:2369–406.

———. 1991. "Philodemus' Poetic Theory and *On the Good King according to Homer*." *CA* 10:1–45.

———. 2001. "Basic Education in Epicureanism." Pages 209–39 in *Education in Greek and Roman Antiquity*. Edited by Yun Lee Too. Leiden: Brill.

———. 2004. "Epicurean Economics." Pages 133–76 in Fitzgerald, Obbink, and Holland 2004.

———. 2011. "The Necessity of Anger in Philodemus' *On Anger*." Pages 152–82 in *Epicurus and the Epicurean Tradition*. Edited by Jeffrey Fish and Kirk R. Sanders. Cambridge: Cambridge University Press.

Bailey, Cyril. 1926. *Epicurus: The Extant Remains*. Oxford: Clarendon.

Bassi, Domenico. 1909. "La sticometria nei papiri Ercolanesi." *RFIC* 37:321–62, 481–515.

Bénatouïl, Thomas. 2016. "Aristotle and the Stoa." Pages 56–80 in *Brill's Companion to the Reception of Aristotle in Antiquity*. Edited by Andrea Falcon. Leiden: Brill.

Benferhat, Yasmina. 2005. *Cives Epicurei: Les épicuriens et l'idée de monarchie à Rome et en Italie de Sylla à Octave*. Collection Latomus 292. Brussels: Latomus.

Besnier, Bernard. 1994. "Épicure et la définition." Pages 117–30 in *Ainsi parlaient les Anciens: In honorem Jean-Paul Dumont*. Edited by Lucien Jerphagnon, Jacqueline Lagrée, and Daniel Delattre. Lille: Presses universitaires de Lille.
Blank, David. 2007a. "Aristotle's 'Academic Course on Rhetoric' and the End of Philodemus, *On Rhetoric* VIII." *CErc* 37:5–47.
———. 2007b. "The Life of Antiochus of Ascalon in Philodemus' History of the Academy and a Tale of Two Letters." *ZPE* 162:87–93.
———. 2019. "Philodemus." *Stanford Encyclopedia of Philosophy*. https://plato.stanford.edu/entries/philodemus/
Bloch, Olivier-René. 1986. "Un imbroglio philologique: Les fragments d'Aristote sur la colère." Pages 135–44 in *Energeia: Études aristotéliciennes offertes à A. Jannone*. Paris: Vrin.
Blomqvist, Jerker. 1969. *Greek Particles in Hellenistic Prose*. Lund: Gleerup.
Braund, David. 1996. *Ruling Roman Britain: Kings, Queens, Governors and Emperors*. London: Routledge.
Brittain, Charles. 2001. *Philo of Larissa: The Last of the Academic Skeptics*. Oxford: Oxford University Press.
———. 2006. "Philo of Larissa." *Stanford Encyclopedia of Philosophy*. https://plato.stanford.edu/archives/fall2008/entries/philo-larissa/.
Brouwer, René. 2104. *The Stoic Sage: The Early Stoics on Wisdom, Sagehood and Socrates*. Cambridge: Cambridge University Press.
Broughton, T. Robert S. 1951–1986. *The Magistrates of the Roman Republic*. 3 vols. American Philological Association Philological Monographs 15.1–3. Atlanta: Scholar's Press.
Bücheler, Franz. 1864. Review of Gomperz 1864. *Zeitschrift f. d. öster. Gymnasium* 15:578–95. Repr. with updated references to Wilke's text as pages 510–30 in vol. 1 of *Kleine Schriften*. Leipzig: Teubner.
———. 1888. "Der Philosoph Nikasikrates." *RhM* 43:151–53.
Burnyeat, M. F. 2002. "Excuses for Madness." *London Review of Books*. 17 October. Online: https://www.lrb.co.uk/v24/n20/mf-burnyeat/excuses-for-madness.
Bury, Robert Gregg. 1915. Review of Wilke 1914. *CR* 29:156.
Cairns, Douglas. 2003. "Ethics, Ethology, Terminology: Iliadic Anger and the Cross-Cultural Study of Emotion." *YCS* 32:11–59.
Cameron, Alan. 1993. *The Greek Anthology: From Meleager to Planudes*. Oxford: Oxford University Press.
Cantarella, Eva. 2013. *"Sopporta, cuore…:" La scelta di Ulisse*. Bari: Laterza.

Capasso, Mario. 1988. *Carneisco: Il secondo libro del "Filista" (PHerc. 1027).* La scuola di Epicuro 10. Naples: Bibliopolis.

———. 1989. "Primo supplemento al Catalogo dei Papiri Ercolanesi." *CErc* 19:193–264.

———. forthcoming. "Philodemus and the Herculaneum Papyri." In *The Oxford Handbook of Epicureanism.* Edited by Phillip Mitsis. Oxford: Oxford University Press.

Carruesco, Jesús. 2010. "Le nain d'Alexandrie (Philodème, *De signis* col. 2, 4 ss.)." Pages 133–36 in *Miscellanea Papyrologica Herculanensia: Volumen I.* Edited by Agathe Antoni, Graziano Arrighetti, and M. Isabella Bertagna. Pisa: Serra.

Castiglioni, L. 1925. "Verisimilia ad Philodemi de ira librum." *BFC* 32:136–37.

Cavallo, Guglielmo. 1983. *Libri scritture scribi a Ercolano: Introduzione allo studio dei materiali greci.* Cronache ercolanesi Supplement 1. Naples: Macchiaroli.

Cirillo, Ida. 2008. *Lo iato nelle opere filodemee di storiografia e biografia filosofica.* Università degli Studi di Napoli - Federico II BA thesis.

Clark, Albert C, ed. 1907. *Q. Asconii Pediani Orationvm Ciceronis qvinqve enarratio.* Oxford: Clarendon.

Clay, Diskin. 2009. "The Athenian Garden." Pages 9–28 in *The Cambridge Companion to Epicureanism.* Edited by James Warren. Cambridge: Cambridge University Press.

Cobet, Carel Gabriel. 1878. "Φιλοδήμου Περὶ Ὀργῆς ex voluminibus Herculanensibus." *Mnemosyne* 6:373–86.

Cooper, John M. 1999. *Reason and Emotion: Essays on Ancient Moral Philosophy and Ethical Theory.* Princeton: Princeton University Press.

Corti, Aurora. 2016. "PHerc. 454 (Epicuro, *Sulla Natura* XXV): Edizione, traduzione, commento." *RhM* 159:28–59.

Courtney, Edward, 1993 *The Fragmentary Latin Poets.* Oxford: Oxford University Press.

Crönert, Wilhelm. 1906. *Kolotes und Menedemos.* Leipzig: Teubner.

———. 1903. *Memoria Graeca Herculanensis.* Leipzig: Teubner.

Del Mastro, Gianluca. 2014. *Titoli e annotazioni bibliologiche nei papiri greci di Ercolano.* Cronache ercolanesi Supplement 5. Naples: Centro internazionale per lo studio dei papiri ercolanesi.

Delattre, Daniel. 2007. *Philodème de Gadara Sur la Musique Livre IV.* Paris: Belles Lettres.

———. 2009a. "Philodème, témoin des discussions doctrinales entre épicuriens grecs aux IIe-Ier siècles avant notre ère." Pages 31–46 in *Transmettre les savoirs dans les mondes hellénistique et romain*. Edited by F. Le Blay. Rennes: Presses universitaires de Rennes.

———. 2009b. "Le Sage épicurien face à la colère et à l'ivresse: Une lecture renouvelée du *De ira* de Philodème." *CErc* 39:71–88.

———. 2010. "Le *Franc-parler* de Philodème (*PHerc*. 1471): Reconstruction bibliologique d'ensemble du rouleau." Pages 271–91 in *Miscellanea Papyrologica Herculanensia*. Edited by Agathe Antoni et al. Pisa: Giardini.

———. 2015. "La pratique maîtrisée du franc-parler: Philodème de Gadara, Le Franc-parler (col 151–62 D.)." Pages 435–53 in *Poïkiloï Karpoï: Exégèses païennes, juives et chrétiennes*. Edited by Mireille Loubet and Didier Pralon. Aix-en-Provence: Presses universitaires de Provence.

Delattre, Daniel, and Jackie Pigeaud. 2010. *Les Épicuriens*. Bibliothèque de la Pleiade 564. Paris: Gallimard.

Denniston, John Dewar. 1950. *The Greek Particles*. 2nd ed. Revised by K. J. Dover. London: Duckworth.

De Simone, Antonio. 2010. "Rediscovering the Villa of the Papyri." Pages 1–20 in *The Villa of the Papyri at Herculaneum: Archaeology, Reception, and Digital Reconstruction*. Edited by Mantha Zarmakoupi. Berlin: de Gruyter.

Diano, Carlo. 1974. "La Psicologia D'Epicuro e la teoria della passioni." Pages 129–280 in *Scritti epicurei*. Edited by Carlo Diano. Florence: Olschki. Reprint of *Giornale cirico della filosofia italiana* 39 (1939): 105–45; 40 (1940): 151–65; 22 (1941): 5–34; and 23 (1942) 5–49 and 121–50.

Diels, Hermann. 1879. *Doxographi Graeci*. Berlin: Reimer.

Dillon, John. 2016. "The Reception of Aristotle in Antiochus and Cicero." Pages 181–201 in *Brill's Companion to the Reception of Aristotle in Antiquity*. Edited by Andrea Falcon. Leiden: Brill.

Dobree, Peter Paul. 1831–1833. *Adversaria Critica*. Cambridge: Cambridge University Press.

Dorandi, Tiziano. 1982. *Filodemo: Il buon re secondo Omero*. La scuola di Epicuro 3. Naples: Bibliopolis.

———. 1987. "La Patria di Filodemo." *Philologus* 131:254–56.

———. 1991. *Filodemo: Storia dei Filosofi [.] Platone e l'Academia (PHerc. 1021 e 164)*. La scuola di Epicuro 12. Naples: Bibliopolis.

———. 1996. "Gaio Bambino." *ZPE* 111:41–42.

———. 1997. "Lucrèce et les Épicuriens de Campanie." Pages 35–48 in *Lucretius and His Intellectual Background*. Edited by Keimpe Algra, Piet Schrijvers, and Mieke Koenen. Amsterdam: Koninkligke Nederlandse Akademie van Wetenschappen.

———. 2015. Review of Del Mastro 2014. *BMCR*: http://bmcr.brynmawr.edu/2015/2015-04-55.html.

———. 2016. "Due titoli ercolanesi." *ZPE* 199:29–32.

———. 2017. "La nuova cronologia della 'Villa dei Papiri' a Ercolano e le sorti della biblioteca di Filodemo." *WJA* 41:181–203.

Dow, Jamie. 2015. *Passions and Persuasion in Aristotle's* Rhetoric. Oxford: Oxford University Press.

Dürr, Edeltraud. 1988. "Sulla catalogazione di alcuni papiri ercolanesi." *CErc* 18:215–17.

Eliasson, Erik. 2008. *The Notion of* That Which Depends on Us *in Plotinus and Its Background*. Philosophica Antiqua 113. Leiden: Brill.

———. 2013. "Plotinus on Fate (EIMAPMENH)." Pages 199–220 in Masi and Maso 2013.

Erler, Michael. 1992a. "Orthodoxie und Anpassung. Philodem, ein Panaitios des Kepos?" *MH* 49:171–200.

———. 1992b. "Der Zorn des Helden: Philodems 'De Ira' und Vergils Konzept des Zorns in der 'Aeneis.'" *GB* 18:103–26.

———. 1993. "Philologia medicans: La lettura delle opere di Epicuro nella sua scuola." Pages 513–26 in vol. 2 of *Epicureismo greco e romano: Atti del congresso internazionale Napoli 19–26 Maggio 1993*. Edited by Gabriele Giannantoni and Marcello Gigante. 3 vols. Naples: Bibliopolis.

———. 2003. "*Exempla Amoris*: Der epikureische Epilogismos als philosophischer Hintergrund der Diatribe gegen die Liebe in Lukrez *De Rerum Natura*." Pages 147–63 in *Le jardin romain: Épicurisme et poésie à Rome; Mélanges offerts à Mayotte Bollack*. Edited by Annick Monet. Lille: Presses universitaires.

———. 2009. "Epicureanism in the Roman Empire." Pages 46–64 in *The Cambridge Companion to Epicureanism*. Edited by James Warren. Cambridge: Cambridge University Press.

———. 2011. "Autodidact and Student: On the Relationship of Authority and Autonomy in Epicurus and the Epicurean Traditon." Pages 9–28 in *Epicurus and the Epicurean Tradition*. Edited by Jeffrey Fish and Kirk R. Sanders. Cambridge: Cambridge University Press.

Essler, Holger. 2006. "Bilder von Papyri und Papyri als Bilder." *CErc* 36:103–43.

Falcon, Andrea. 2013. "Aristotelianism in the First Century BC: Xenarchus of Seleucia." Pages 78–94 in *Aristotle, Plato and Pythagoreanism in the First Century B.C.: New Directions for Philosophy*. Edited by Malcolm Schofield. Cambridge: Cambridge University Press.

———. 2016a. "Aristotelianism in the First Century BC." Pages 101–19 in *Brill's Companion to the Reception of Aristotle in Antiquity*. Edited by Andrea Falcon. Leiden: Brill.

———. ed. 2016b. *Brill's Companion to the Reception of Aristotle in Antiquity*. Leiden: Brill.

Fillion-Lahille, Janine. 1970. "La colère chez Aristotle." *REA* 72:46–79.

———. 1984. *Le De Ira de Sénèque et la philosophie stoïcienne des passions*. Paris: Klinksieck.

Fine, Gail. 2014. *The Possibility of Inquiry: Meno's Paradox from Socrates to Sextus*. Oxford: Oxford University Press.

Fish, Jeffrey. 2004. "Anger, Philodemus' Good King, and the Helen Episode of *Aeneid* 2.567–589: A New Proof of Authenticity from Herculaneum." Pages 111–38 in *Vergil, Philodemus, and the Augustans*. Edited by David Armstrong, Jeffrey Fish, Patricia A. Johnston, and Marilyn B. Skinner. Austin: University of Texas Press.

———. 2011. "On Orderly Symposia in Homer: A New Reconstruction of *De bono rege* (*PHerc.* 1507), col. 19." *CErc* 41:65–68.

Fitzgerald, John T. 2004. "Gadara: Philodemus' Native City." Pages 343–97 in Fitzgerald, Obbink, and Holland 2004.

———. 2008a. "The Passions and Moral Progress: An Introduction." Pages 1–27 in *Passions and Moral Progress in Greek and Roman Thought*. Edited by John T. Fitzgerald. New York: Routledge.

———, ed. 2008b. *Passions and Moral Progress in Greek and Roman Thought*. New York: Routledge.

———. 2015. "Paul, Wine in the Ancient Mediterranean World, and the Problem of Intoxication." Pages 331–56 in *Paul's Graeco-Roman Context*. Edited by Cilliers Breytenbach. BETL 277. Leuven: Peeters.

Fitzgerald, John T., Dirk Obbink, and Glenn S. Holland, eds. 2004. *Philodemus and the New Testament World*. NovTSup 111. Leiden: Brill.

Fleischer, Kilian. 2015. "Der Stoiker Mnesarch als Lehrer des Antiochus im Index Academicorum." *Mnemosyne* 68:413–23.

———. 2016. "New Readings in Philodemus' *Index Academicorum*: Dio of Alexandria (P. Herc. 1021, col. XXXV, 17–19)." Pages 459–70 in *Proceedings of the 27th International Congress of Papyrology. Edited by Tomasz Derda, Adam Łajtar, and Jakub Urbanik. Journal of Juristic Papyrology Supplement 28. Warsaw: University of Warsaw.

———. 2017a. "Die Lokalisierung der Verso-Kolumnen von PHerc. 1021 (Philodem, *Index Academicorum*)." *ZPE* 204:27–39.

———. 2017b. "New Evidence on the Death of Philo of Larissa (PHerc. 1021, col. 33,42–34,7)." *Cambridge Classical Journal* 63:73–85.

———. 2017c. "The Pupils of Philo of Larissa and Philodemus' Stay in Sicily (PHerc. 1021, col. XXXIV 6-19)." *CErc* 47:73–85.

———. 2017d. "Starb Philo von Larissa im Alter von 63 Jahren? (PHerc. 1021 col. 33)." *AfP* 63:335–66.

———. 2018. "Dating Philodemus' Birth and Early Studies." *BASP* 55:119–27.

———. 2019. "Zenone di Sidone nacque intorno al 160 a.C." *RIFC* 147:43–50.

Fordyce, C. J. 1961. *Catullus: A Commentary*. Oxford: Oxford University Press.

Fortenbaugh, William W. 1984. *Quellen zur Ethik Theophrasts*. Amsterdam: Grüner.

———. 1985. "Theophrastus on Emotions." Pages 209–30 in *Theophrastus of Eresus: On His Life and Work*. Edited by William W. Fortenbaugh, Pamela M. Huby, and Anthony A. Long. Rutgers Studies in Classical Humanities 2. New Brunswick: Transaction.

———. 2002. *Aristotle on Emotion*. 2nd ed. London: Duckworth.

———. 2008. "Aristotle and Theophrastus on the Emotions." Pages 29–47 in *Passions and Moral Progress in Greek and Roman Thought*. Edited by John T. Fitzgerald. New York: Routledge.

Fortenbaugh, William W., P. M. Huby, R. W. Sharples, and D. Gutas. 1992. *Theophrastus: His Psychological, Doxographical and Scientific Writings*. 2 vols. Philosophia Antiqua 54. Leiden: Brill 1992.

Fowler, Donald P. 1997. "Epicurean Anger." Pages 16–35 in *The Passions in Roman Thought and Literature*. Edited by Susanna Morton Braund and Christopher Gill. Cambridge: Cambridge University Press.

Frede, Dorothea. 1996. "Mixed Feelings in Aristotle's *Rhetoric*." Pages 258–85 in Rorty 1996.

Friedrich, Gustav. 1908. *Catulli Veronensis Liber*. Leipzig: Teubner.

Furley, David J. 1967. *Two Studies in the Greek Atomists*. Princeton: Princeton University Press.

Galinksy, Karl. 1988. "The Anger of Aeneas." *AJP* 109:321–348. Reprinted as pages 434–57 in vol. 4 of *Vergil: Critical Assessments of Classical Authors*. Edited by Philip R. Hardie. 4 vols. London: Routledge.

———. 1994. "How to Be Philosophical about the End of the *Aeneid*." *BICS* 19:191–201.

Gardner, Robert. 1958. *Cicero, "Pro Caelio," "De provinciis consularibus," "Pro Balbo."* LCL. Cambridge: Harvard University Press.

Gargiulo, Tristano. 1981. "*PHerc*. 222: Filodemo sull'adulazione." *CErc* 10:103–27.

Gastaldi, Silvia. 2014. *Aristotele* Retorica*: Introduzione, traduzione e commento*. Classici 36. Rome: Carocci.

Ghisu, Sebastiano. 2015. *Filodemo di Gadara: Sulla franchezza*. Saonara: Il prato.

Gigante, Marcello. 1983. *Ricerche filodemee*. 2nd ed. Naples: Gaetano Macciaroli.

———. 1987. "Atakta: La grecità di John Hayter." *CErc* 17:108–9. Reprinted as pages 16–17 in Gigante, *Atakta: Contribuiti alla papirologia ercolanese*. Naples: Gaetano Macciaroli, 1993.

Gigante, Marcello, and Mario Capasso. 1989. "Il ritorno di Virgilio a Ercolano." *SIFC* 7:3–6

Gigante, Marcello, and Giovanni Indelli. 1978. "Bione e l'epicureismo." *CErc* 8:124–31.

———. 1980. "Democrito nei Papiri Ercolanesi di Filodemo." Pages 451–66 in *Democrito e l'atomismo antico: Atti del convegno internazionale, Catania, 18–21 Aprile 1979*. Edited by Francesco Romano. Catania: Università di Catania. Special issue of *Siculorum Gymnasium* NS 33.1.

Gill, Christopher. 2003. "Reactive and Objective Attitudes: Anger in Virgil's *Aeneid* and Hellenistic Philosophy." *YCS* 32:208–29.

———. 2009. "Stoicism and Epicureanism." Pages 143–66 in *The Oxford Handbook of Philosophy of Emotion*. Edited by Peter Goldie. Oxford: Oxford University Press.

Giovacchini, Julie. 2003. "Le refus épicurien de la définition." *Les Cahiers philosophiques de Strasbourg* 15:71–89.

Giuliano, Laura. 2005. "Segni e particolarità grafiche nel *PHerc*. 182 (Filodemo, *De ira*)." *CErc* 35:135–59.

Gomperz, Theodor. 1864. *Philodemi Epicurei De ira liber*. Leipzig: Teubner.

———. 1876. *Beiträge zur Kritik und Erklärung griechischer Schriftsteller III*. Vienna: Karl Gerold's Sohn. Online: https://archive.org/details/beitragezurkriti1234gomp/page/n79/mode/2up.

Gordon, Pamela. 2012. *The Invention and Gendering of Epicurus.* Ann Arbor: University of Michigan Press.

Graver, Margaret. 1999. "Philo of Alexandria and the Stoic *Propatheiai.*" *Phronesis* 44:300–325.

———. 2002. *Cicero on the Emotions: Tusculan Disputations 3 and 4.* Chicago: University of Chicago Press.

———. 2007. *Stoicism and Emotion.* Chicago: University of Chicago Press.

Grilli, Alberto. 1983. "ΔΙΑΘΕΣΙΣ in Epicuro." Pages 93–109 in ΣΥΖΗΤΗΣΙΣ: *Studi sull'epicureismo greco e romano offerti a Marcello Gigante.* Naples: Gaetano Macchiarioli. Reprinted as pages 47–63 in Grilli, *Stoicismo, epicureismo e letteratura.* Brescia: Claudiana, 1992.

Grillo, Luca. 2015. *Cicero's "De provinciis consularibus oratio."* American Philological Association Texts and Commentaries. Oxford: Oxford University Press.

Guidobaldi, Maria Paola, and Domenico Esposito. 2010. "New Archaeological Research at the Villa of the Papyri in Herculaneum." Pages 21–62 in *The Villa of the Papyri at Herculaneum: Archaeology, Reception, and Digital Reconstruction.* Edited by Mantha Zarmakoupi. Berlin: de Gruyter.

Hammerstaedt, Jürgen. 1992. "Der Schlussteil von Philodems drittem Buch über Rhetorik." *CErc* 22:9–117.

———. 2003. "Atomismo e libertà nel XXV Libro περὶ φύσεως di Epicuro." *CErc* 33:151–58.

Hammerstaedt, Jürgen, and Martin Ferguson Smith. 2014. *The Epicurean Inscription of Diogenes of Oinoanda: Ten Years of New Discoveries and Research.* Bonn: Habelt.

Harris, William V. 1997. "Saving the φαινόμενα: A Note on Aristotle's Definition of Anger." *CQ* 47: 252–54

———. 2001. *Restraining Rage: The Ideology of Anger Control in Classical Antiquity.* Cambridge: Harvard University Press.

Hatzimichali, Myrto. 2011. *Potamo of Alexandria and the Emergence of Eclecticism.* Cambridge: Cambridge University Press.

———. 2016. "Aristotelianism and the Construction of the Aristotelian Corpus." Pages 81–100 in *Brill's Companion to the Reception of Aristotle in Antiquity.* Edited by Andrea Falcon. Leiden: Brill.

Heinze, Richard. 1890. "Ariston von Chios bei Plutarch und Horaz." *RhM* 45:497–523.

Henry, W. Benjamin. 2009. *Philodemus,* On Death. WGRW 29. Atlanta: Society of Biblical Literature.

———. 2017. "Notes on Philodemus, *On Anger*." *ZPE* 201:59–63.
Heßler, Jan Erik. 2014. *Epikur, Brief an Menoikeus: Edition, Übersetzung und Kommentar*. Schwabe Epicurea 4. Basel: Schwabe.
———. 2015. "Das Gedanken an Verstorbene in der Schule Epikurs in der Tradition der ἐπιτάφιοι λόγοι." Pages 95–112 in *Questioni epicuree*. Edited by Dino De Sanctis, Emidio Spinelli, Mauro Tulli, and Francesco Verde. Sankt Augustin: Academia.
Hoffman, Adolf, and Susanne Kerner, eds. 2002. *Gadara – Gerasa und die Dekapolis*. Mainz: von Zabern.
Hollis, Adrian S. 2007. *Fragments of Roman Poetry c. 60 BC–AD 20*. Oxford: Oxford University Press.
Hulton, Angus O. 1957. "AN with the Future: A Note." *CQ* 7:139–42.
Hutchinson, Gregory O. 2018. *Plutarch's Rhythmic Prose*. Oxford: Oxford University Press.
Ierodiakonou, Katerina. 1995. "Alexander of Aphrodisias on Medicine as a Stochastic Art." *Clio Medicus* 28:473–85.
Indelli, Giovanni. 1982a. "Il lessico filodemeo nell'opera *Sull'ira*." *CErc* 12:85–89.
———. 1982b. "Citazioni poetiche nel libro filodemeo *Sull'ira*." Pages 493–508 in *La regione sotterrata dal Vesuvio: Studi e prospettive; Atti del convegno internazionale 11–15 novembre 1979*. Naples: Università degli studi.
———. 1984. Considerazioni su linguaggio e stile del libro filodemeo *Sull'ira (PHerc. 182)*." Pages 561–67 in *Atti del XVII Congresso Internazionale di Papirologia*. Naples: Centro internazionale per lo studio dei papiri ercolanesi.
———. 1988. *Filodemo: L'ira*. La scuola di Epicuro 5. Naples: Bibliopolis.
———. 2001. "Filodemo e Virgilio sull'ira." *CErc* 31:31–35.
———. 2004. "The Vocabulary of Anger in Philodemus' *De ira* and Vergil's *Aeneid*." Pages 103–10 in *Vergil, Philodemus, and the Augustans*. Edited by David Armstrong, Jeffrey Fish, Patricia A. Johnston, and Marilyn B. Skinner. Austin: University of Texas Press.
———. 2010. "Il lessico di Filodemo in alcune opere morali: gli ἅπαξ λεγόμενα." *CErc* 40:87–93.
———. 2014. "Lingua e stile nell'opera *Sull'ira* di Filodemo (*PHerc. 182*)." *CErc* 44:109–16.
Isaac, Benjamin H. 2017. *Empire and Ideology in the Graeco-Roman World: Selected Papers*. Cambridge: Cambridge University Press.

Janko, Richard. 2011. *Philodemus, On Poems Books 3–4, with the Fragments of Aristotle,* On Poets. Oxford: Oxford University Press.
Jensen, Christian Cornelius. 1911. "Ariston von Keos bei Philodem." *Hermes* 49:393–406.
Kassel, Rudolf, and Colin Austin. 1998. *Menander: Testimonia et Fragmenta apud scriptores servata.* Vol. 6.2 of *Poetae comici Graeci.* Berlin: de Gruyter.
———. 2001. *Adespota.* Vol. 8 of *Poetae comici Graeci.* Berlin: de Gruyter.
Kaufman, David H. 2014. "Seneca on the Analysis and Therapy of Occurrent Emotions." Pages 111–33 in *Seneca Philosophus.* Edited by Jula Wildberger and Marcia L. Colish. Trends in Classics—Supplementary Volume 27. Berlin: de Gruyter.
———. Forthcoming. "Philodemus and the Peripatetics on the Value of Anger."
Kindstrand, Jan Fredrik. 1976. *Bion of Borysthenes: A Collection of the Fragments with Introduction and Commentary.* Studia Graeca Upsaliensia. Uppsala: Acta Universitatis Upsaliensis.
Kondo, Eiko. 1971. "I *Caratteri* di Teofrasto nei papiri ercolanesi." *CErc* 1:73–87.
Konstan, David. 2003. "Aristotle on Anger and the Emotions: The Strategies of Status." *YCS* 32:99–120.
———. 2008. *A Life Worthy of the Gods: The Materialist Psychology of Epicurus.* 2nd ed. Las Vegas: Parmenides.
Konstan, David, et al. 1998. *Philodemus: On Frank Criticism.* SBLTT 43, Greco-Roman 13. Atlanta: Society of Biblical Literature.
Kroll, Wilhelm, ed. 1923. *C. Valerius Catullus.* Leipzig: Teubner.
Kühn, Carl Gottlob, ed. 1821–1833. *Claudii Galeni Opera Omnia.* 20 vols. Leipzig: Cnobloch. Repr., Hildesheim: Olms, 1964–1965.
Landolfi, Luciano. 1982. "Tracce filodemee di estetica e di epigrammatica simpotica in Catullo." *CErc* 12:137–43.
Lapatin, Kenneth, ed. 2019. *Buried by Vesuvius: The Villa dei Papiri at Herculaneum.* Los Angeles: J. Paul Getty Museum.
Larson, Matthew D. C. 2018. *Gospels before the Book.* Oxford: Oxford University Press.
Laursen, Simon. 1995. "The Earlier Parts of Epicurus, *On Nature,* 25th Book." *CErc* 25:5–109.
———. 1997. "The Later Parts of Epicurus, *On Nature,* 25th Book." *CErc* 27:5–82.

Lévy, Carlos. 2012. "Other Followers of Antiochus." Pages 290–306 in *The Philosophy of Antiochus*. Edited by David Sedley. Cambridge: Cambridge University Press.

Long, Anthony A. 1986. *Hellenistic Philosophy*. 2nd ed. Berkeley: University of California Press.

Long, Anthony A., and David Sedley. 1987. *The Hellenistic Philosophers*. 2 vols. Cambridge: Cambridge University Press.

Longo Auricchio, Francesca. 1977. Φιλοδήμου Περὶ ῥητορικῆς *libros primum et secundum*. Naples: Giannini.

———. 2013. "Filodemo e i nani di Antonio: valore di una testimonianza." *CErc* 43:209–14.

Longo Auricchio, Francesca, and Tepedino Guerra, Adele. 1981. "Aspetti e problemi della dissidenza epicurea." *CErc* 11:25–40.

———. 1982. "Chi è Timasagora?." Pages 405–13 in *La regione sotterrata dal Vesuvio: Studi e prospettive; Atti del convegno internazionale 11–15 novembre 1979*. Naples: Università degli studi.

Luz, Menahem. 2015. "Socrates, Alcibiades, and Antisthenes in PFlor 113." Pages 192–210 in *From the Socratics to the Socratic Schools: Classical Ethics, Metaphysics, and Epistemology*. Edited by Ugo Zilioli. New York: Routledge.

Macleod, Matthew D. 1956. "AN with the Future in Lucian and the *Solecist*." *CQ* 6:102–11.

Masi, Francesca Guadalupe. 2005. "La nozione epicurea di ἀπογεγεννημένα." *CErc* 35:27–51.

———. 2006a. *Epicuro e la filosofia della mente: Il XXV libro dell'opera "Sulla Natura."* Studies in Ancient Philosophy 7. Sankt Augustin: Academia.

———. 2006b. "Libertà senza *clinamen*: Il XXV libro del Περὶ Φύσεως di Epicuro." *CErc* 1996:9–46.

Masi, Francesca Guadalupe, and Stefano Maso. 2013. *Fate, Chance and Fortune in Ancient Thought*. Lexis Ancient Philosophy 9. Amsterdam: Hakkert.

Mates, Benson. 1953. *Stoic Logic*. University of California Publications in Philosophy 26. Berkeley: University of California Press.

McConnell, Sean. 2015. "Epicurean Education and the Rhetoric of Concern." *ACl* 58:111–45.

———. 2017. "Demetrius of Laconia and the Debate between the Stoics and the Epicureans on the Nature of Parental Love." *CQ* 67:149–62.

McNamee, Kathleen. 1992. *Sigla and Select Marginalia in Greek Literary Papyri*. Brussels: Fondation égyptologique Reine Élisabeth.

McOsker, Michael. 2017. "Hiatus in Epicurean Authors." *CErc* 47:145–61.
———. 2020a. "τὰ τῆς cωτηρίας φάρμακα: Epicurean Education as Therapy." Pages 307–18 in *Routledge Handbook of Hellenistic Philosophy*. Edited by Kelly Arenson. New York: Routledge.
———. 2020b. "Demetrius Laco and the Authority of Epicurus." In *Authority and Use of Authoritative Texts in the Epicurean Tradition*. Edited by Michael Erler, Jan Erik Heßler, and Federico Maria Petrucci, with Michael McOsker.
———. forthcoming a. "Poetics." Pages 347–76 in *Oxford Handbook of Epicurus and Epicureanism*. Edited by Phillip Mitsis. Oxford: Oxford University Press.
———. forthcoming b. "Philodemus of Gadara's Rhythmic Prose." *Rheinisches Museum*.
Monet, Annick. 1996. "[Philodème, *Sur les sensations*], PHerc. 19/698." *CErc* 26:27–126.
Moorhouse, Alfred C. 1946. "AN with the Future." *CQ* 1:1–10.
———. 1959. "A Reply on AN with the Future" *CQ* 9:78–9.
Moss, Jessica. 2012. *Aristotle on the Apparent Good: Perception, Phantasia, Thought and Desire*. Oxford: Oxford University Press.
Muehll, Peter von der. 1922. *Epicuri Epistulae Tres et Ratae Sententiae: Accedit Gnomologium Epicureum Vaticanum*. Leipzig: Teubner.
Nachstädt, Wilhelm. 1895. *De Plutarchi declamationibus quae sunt "De Alexandri Fortuna."* Berlin: Vogt.
Németh, Attila. 2017. *Epicurus on the Self*. Issues in Ancient Philosophy. London: Routledge.
Nicolardi, Federica. 2018. *Filodemo: Il primo libro della* Retrorica. La scuola di Epicuro 19. Naples: Bibliopolis.
Obbink, Dirk. 1996. *Philodemus* On Piety *Part 1: Critical Text with Commentary*. Oxford: Oxford University Press.
———. 2001. "Le livre I du *De natura deorum* de Cicéron et la *De pietate* de Philodème." Pages 203–25 in *Cicéron et Philodème: La polemique en philosophie*. Edited by Clara Auvray-Assayas and Daniel Delattre. Paris: Rue d'Ulm.
———. 2002. "'All Gods Are True' in Epicurus." Pages 183–221 in *Traditions of Theology: Studies in Hellenistic Theology, Its Background and Aftermath*. Edited by Dorothea Frede and André Laks. Leiden: Brill.
Ohly, Kurt. 1924. "Die Stichometrie der Herkulanischen Rollen." *AfP* 7:190–220.

O'Keefe, Tim. 2005. *Epicurus on Freedom*. Cambridge: Cambridge University Press.

———. 2009. "Action and Responsibility." Pages 142–57 in *The Cambridge Companion to Epicureanism*. Edited by James Warren. Cambridge: Cambridge University Press.

———. 2010. *Epicureanism*. Slough: Acumen.

Olivieri, Alexander. 1914. *Philodemi Περι Παρρησιας Libellus*. Leipzig: Teubner.

Otte, Christoph, ed. 2001. *"De plenitudine": Kritische Edition, Übersetzung und Erläuterungen*. Weisbaden: Reichert.

Parsons, Peter J. 1989. "The Palaeography of the Herculaneum Papyri." Review of Cavallo 1983. *CR* 39:358–60.

Pease, Arthur Stanley. 1955. *M. Tulli Ciceronis "De natura deorum": Liber primus*. Cambridge: Harvard University Press.

Peek, Werner. 1988. *Greek Verse Inscriptions: Epigrams on Funerary Stelae and Monuments*. Chicago: Ares. Orig. Berlin: Akademie, 1953.

Philippson, Robert. 1912. Review of, inter alia, Wilke 1911. *BPW* 32:390–94.

———. 1915. Review of Wilke 1914. *BPW* 35:645–62.

———. 1916. "Philodems Buch über den Zorn." *RhM* 71:425–60.

———. 1918. "Der Epikureer Timasagoras." *BPW* 38:1072–73.

Polleichtner, Wolfgang. 2009. *Emotional Questions: Vergil, the Emotions, and the Transformation of Epic Poetry*. Bochumer Altertumswissenschaftliches Colloquium Band 82. Trier: Wissenschaftlicher Verlag.

Price, Anthony W. 2009. "Emotions in Plato and Aristotle." Pages 121–42 in *The Oxford Handbook of Philosophy of Emotion*. Edited by Peter Goldie. Oxford: Oxford University Press.

Prioux, Évelyne. 2019. "Meleager of Gadara." Pages 389–405 in *A Companion to Ancient Epigram*. Edited by Christer Henriksén. Medford MA: Wiley Blackwell.

Procopé, John. 1985. "Haß." *RAC* 12:678–714.

———. 1993. "Epicureans on Anger." Pages 363–86 in *Philanthropia kai Eusebeia: Festschrift für Albrecht Dihle zum 70. Geburtstag*. Edited by Glenn W Most, Hubert Petersmann, and Adolf Martin Ritter. Göttingen: Vandenhoeck & Ruprecht.

———. 1998. "Epicureans on Anger." Pages 171–96 in *The Emotions in Hellenistic Philosophy*. Edited by Juha Sihvola and Troels Engberg-Pedersen. Dordrecht: Kluwer, 1998. Reprint of Procopé 1993.

Puglia, Enzo. 1988. *Aporie testuali ed esegetiche in Epicuro (PHerc. 1012)*. Scuola di Epicuro 8. Naples: Bibliopolis.

———. 2000. "Le biografie di Filone e di Antioco nella storia dell'Academia di Filodemo." *ZPE* 130:17–28.

———. 2013 Review of Del Mastro 2014. *Aegyptus* 93:235–42.

———. 2015. "Il misterioso titolo del ΠΡΟΣ ΤΟΥΣ di Filodemo (*PHerc. 1005/862, 1585*)." *Papyrologica Lupiensia* 24:121–24.

Purinton, Jeffrey S. 1999. "Epicurus on Free Volition and the Atomic Swerve." *Phronesis* 44:253–99.

Rabel, Robert J. 1977. "The Stoic Doctrine of Generic and Specific *Pathē*." *Apeiron* 11:40–42.

———. 1981. "Diseases of Soul in Stoic Psychology." *GRBS* 22:385–93.

Rabbow, Paul. 1914. *Antike Schriften über Seelenheilung und Seelenleitung: Auf ihre Quellen untersucht: I. Die Therapie des Zornes*. Leipzig: Teubner.

Radt, Stefan. 1980. "Noch einmal Aischylos, Niobe Fr. 162 N.^{2} (278 M.)." *ZPE* 38:47–58. Reprinted as pages 236–48 in *Kleine Schriften von Stefan Radt zu seinem 75. Geburtstag*. Edited by Annette Harder et al. Leiden: Brill 2002.

Ranocchia, Graziano. 2007a. *Aristone "Sul modo di liberare dalla superbia" nel decimo libro "De vitiis" di Filodemo*. Accademia toscana di scienze e lettere "La colombaria" 237. Florence: Olschki.

Rawson, Elizabeth. 1985. *Intellectual Life in the Late Roman Republic*. Baltimore: Johns Hopkins University Press.

Reeve, Michael D. 1971. "Hiatus in the Greek Novelists." *CQ* 21:514–39.

Ringeltaube, Hermann. 1913. *Quaestiones ad veterum philosophorum de affectibus doctrinam pertinentes*. Göttingen: Huth.

Rorty, Amélie Oksenberg, ed. 1996. *Essays on Aristotle's Rhetoric*. Philosophical Traditions 6. Berkeley: University of California Press.

Rose, Valentin. 1886. *Aristotelis quae ferebantur librorum fragmenta*. Leipzig: Teubner 1886.

Roskam, Geert. 2007. *Live Unnoticed (Λάθε βιώσας): On the Vicissitudes of an Epicurean Doctrine*. Philosophia Antiqua 111. Leiden: Brill.

———. 2012. "Will the Epicurean Sage Break the Law If He Is Perfectly Sure That He Will Escape Detection? A Difficult Problem Revisited." *TAPA* 142:123–40.

Russell, Donald A., and David Konstan. 2005. *Heraclitus:* Homeric Problems. WGRW 14. Atlanta: Society of Biblical Literature.

Rusten, Jeffrey, and I. C. Cunningham 2003. *Theophrastus: Characters. Herodas: Mimes. Sophron and Other Mime Fragments*. 2nd ed. LCL. Cambridge: Harvard University Press.

Sauppe, Hermann. 1864. *Commentatio de Philodemi libro, qui fuit de pietate*. Göttingen: Officina Academica Dieterichiana. Repr. as pages 387–403 in *Ausgewählte Schriften*. Berlin: Wiedmann. 1896.

Schofield, Malcolm. 1996. "*Epilogismos*: An Appraisal." Pages 221–37 in *Rationality in Greek Thought*. Michael Frede and Gisela Striker. Oxford: Oxford University Press.

———. 1999. "Social and Political Thought." Pages 739–70 in *The Cambridge History of Hellenistic Philosophy*. Edited by Keimpe Algra et al. Cambridge: Cambridge University Press.

Scott, Walter. 1885. *Fragmenta Herculanensia: A Descriptive Catalogue of the Oxford Copies of the Herculanean Rolls*. Oxford: Clarendon.

Sedley, David. 1973. "Epicurus, *On Nature*, Book XXVIII." *CErc* 3:5–83.

———. 1976a. "Epicurus and His Professional Rivals." Pages 119–59 in *Études sur l'épicurisme antique*. Edited by Jean Bollack and André Laks. Lille: Presses universitaires de Lille.

———. 1976b. "Epicurus and the Mathematicians of Cyzicus." *CErc* 6:23–54.

———. 1983. "Epicurus' Refutation of Determinism." Pages 11–51 in ΣΥΖΗΤΗΣΙΣ: *Studi sull'epicureismo greco e romano offerti a Marcello Gigante*. Naples: Gaetano Macchiarioli.

———. 1997. "Philosophical Allegiance in the Greco-Roman World." Pages 97–119 in *Philosophia Togata I*. 2nd ed. Edited by Miriam Griffin and Jonathan Barnes. Oxford: Clarendon.

———. 1998. *Lucretius and the Transformation of Greek Wisdom*. Cambridge: Cambridge University Press.

———. 2003. "Philodemus and the Decentralization of Philosophy." *CErc* 33:31–41.

———. 2009. "Epicureanism in the Roman Republic." Pages 29–45 in *The Cambridge Companion to Epicureanism*. Edited by James Warren. Cambridge: Cambridge University Press.

———. ed. 2012. *The Philosophy of Antiochus*. Cambridge: Cambridge University Press.

Severyns, Albert. 1938. *Texte, traduction, commentaire*. Vol. 2 of *Recherches sur la Chrestomathie de Proclos*. Paris: Droz.

Shackleton Bailey, D. R., ed. and trans. 1965–1970. *Cicero's* Letters to Atticus. Cambridge Classical Texts and Commentaries 3–9. 7 vols. Cambridge: Cambridge University Press.

Shapiro, Susan O. 2014. "Socration or Philodemus? Catullus 47 and Prosopographical Excess." *CJ* 109:385–405.

Sider, David. 1997. *The Epigrams of Philodemos: Introduction, Text, and Commentary*. Oxford: Oxford University Press.

Skutsch, Otto. 1985. *The Annals of Quintus Ennius*. Oxford: Clarendon.

Smith, Martin Ferguson. 1993. *Diogenes of Oinoanda: The Epicurean Inscription*. La scuola di Epicuro supplement 1. Naples: Bibliopolis.

———. 2003. *Supplement to Diogenes of Oinoanda: The Epicurean Inscription*. La scuola di Epicuro supplement 3. Naples: Bibliopolis.

Snell, Bruno, and Herwig Maehler, eds. 1964. *Pindari Carmina cum fragmentis*. BSGRT. Leipzig: Teubner.

Sorabji, Richard. 2000. *Emotion and Peace of Mind: From Stoic Agitation to Christian Temptation*. Oxford: Oxford University Press.

Spengel, Leonhard. 1863. "Die herculanischen Rollen." *Philologus* Supplement-Band 2:493–525.

Spinelli, Emidio, and Francesco Verde. Forthcoming. "'La rage du Sage': Philodème et la conception épicurienne de la colère." In *Lectures plurielles du* De ira *de Sénèque: Interprétations, contextes, enjeux*. Edited by Valéry Laurand, Ermanno Malaspina, and François Prost. Berlin: de Gruyter.

Stoneman, Richard. 2003. "The Legacy of Alexander in Ancient Philosophy." Pages 325–47 in *Brill's Companion to Alexander the Great*. Edited by Joseph Roisman. Leiden: Brill.

Strathmann, Gustav. 1892. *De hiatus fuga quam invenimus apud Philodemum Epicureum*. Jahres-Bericht 16 über das Real-Progymnasium der Stadt Viersen, 1891/92. Viersen: Stoffels.

Striker, Gisela. 1996. *Essays on Hellenistic Epistemology and Ethics*. Cambridge: Cambridge University Press.

Sudhaus, Siegfried, ed. 1892–1896. *Philodemi Volumina rhetorica*. 2 vols. BSGRT. Leipzig: Teubner.

———. 1895. *Philodemi Volumina rhetorica: Supplementum*. BSGRT. Leipzig: Teubner.

Swan, P. Michael. 1976. "A Consular Epicurean under the Early Principate." *Phoenix* 30:54–60.

Syme, Ronald. 1956. "Piso and Veranius in Catullus." *C&M* 17:129–34. Reprinted as pages 300–304 in vol. 1 of Syme, *Roman Papers*. 7 vols. Oxford: Oxford University Press, 1979–1991.

Tait, Jane Isabella Marion. 1941. "Philodemus' Influence on the Latin Poets." PhD diss. Bryn Mawr College.

Tarán, Leonardo. 1978. *Anonymous Commentary on Aristotle's "De interpretatione."* Meisenheim am Glan: Hain.

Tepedino Guerra, Adele. 1977. "Filodemo *Sulla gratitudine*." *CErc* 7:96–113.

———. 1994. "L'opera filodemea *Su Epicuro* (*PHerc*. 1232, 1289 β)." *CErc* 24:5–53.

Threatte, Leslie. 1980–1996. *The Grammar of Attic Inscriptions*. 2 vols. Berlin: de Gruyter.

Tieleman, Teun. 2003. *Chrysippus' "On Affections": Reconstruction and Interpretations*. Philosophia Antiqua 94. Leiden: Brill.

Travaglione, Agnese. 2003. "Incisori e curatori della *Collectio Altera*: Il contributo delle prove di stampa alla storia dei Papiri Ercolanesi." Pages 87–156 in *Contributi alla Storia della Officina dei Papiri Ercolanesi 3*. Edited by Mario Capasso. Naples: Graus.

———. 2008. *Catalogo descrittivo dei papiri ercolanesi*. Napoli: Centro internazionale per lo studio dei papiri ercolanesi.

Tsouna, V. 2001. "Philodemus on the Therapy of Vice." *OSAP* 21:233–58.

———. 2003. "'Portare davanti agli occhi': Una tecnica retorica nelle opere 'morali' di Filodemo." *CErc* 33:243–47.

———. 2007a. *The Ethics of Philodemus*. Oxford: Oxford University Press.

———. 2007b. "Philodemus and the Epicurean Tradition." Pages 339–97 in *Pyrrhonists, Patricians, Platonizers: Hellenistic Philosophy in the Period 155–86 BC*. Edited by Anna Maria Ioppolo and David N. Sedley. Naples: Bibliopolis.

———. 2009. "Epicurean Therapeutic Strategies." Pages 249–65 in *The Cambridge Companion to Epicureanism*. Edited by James Warren. Cambridge: Cambridge University Press.

———. 2012. *Philodemus: On Property Management*. WGRW 33. Atlanta: Society of Biblical Literature.

———. 2016. "Epicurean Preconceptions." *Phronesis* 61:160–221.

Turner, Eric G. 1987. *Greek Manuscripts of the Ancient World*. 2nd ed. Revised by P. J. Parsons. BICS Supplement 46. London: Institute for Classical Studies.

Usener, Hermann. 1887. *Epicurea*. Leipzig: Teubner.

———. 1977. *Glossarium Epicureum*. Edited by Marcello Gigante and Walter Schmid. Rome: Edizione dell'Ateneo e Bizzarri.
Vahlen, Johannes, ed. 1903. *Ennianae poesis reliquiae*. Leipzig: Teubner.
Van den Hoek, Annewies. 1996. "Techniques of Quotation in Clement of Alexandria: A View of Ancient Literary Working Methods." *VC* 50:223–43.
Verde, Francesco. 2010a. "Ancora su Timasagora epicureo." *Elenchos* 31:285–317.
———. 2010b. *Epicuro: Epistola a Erodoto*. Classici 5. Rome: Carocci.
———. 2013a. *Epicuro*. Pensatori 36. Rome: Carocci.
———. 2013b. "ΤΥΧΗ e ΛΟΓΙΣΜΟΣ nell'Epicureismo." Pages 177–97 in Masi and Maso 2013.
———. 2016. "Aristotle and the Garden." Pages 35–55 in *Brill's Companion to the Reception of Aristotle in Antiquity*. Edited by Andrea Falcon. Leiden: Brill.
———. 2017. "An Unrecognized Fragment of Metrodorus of Lampsacus' *Against Timocrates*? Some Reflections on Philodemus' *De Ira* (Coll. 12.22–32, and 45.8–12)." *ASNP* 9:248–56.
———. 2018. "I *pathē* di Epicuro tra epistemologia ed etica." *Elenchus* 39:205–230.
———. Forthcoming. "Il saggio epicureo e il controllo delle passioni." In *Les philosophes face au vice, de Socrate à Augustin*. Edited by Christelle Veillard, Olivier Renaut, and Dimitri El Murr. Philosophia Antiqua. Brill: Leiden.
Viano, Cristina. 2016. "Materia e causa materiale delle passioni: Aristotele e la definizione fisica della collera." Pages 61–76 in *Materia e causa materiale in Aristotele e oltre*. Edited by Cristina Viano. Studi di storia della Filosofia antica 3. Rome: Edizioni di Storia e Letteratura.
Vlastos, Gregory. 1945. "Ethics and Physics in Democritus (Part One)." *PhR* 54:578–92.
———. 1946. "Ethics and Physics in Democritus (Part Two)." *PhR* 55:53–64.
Webb, Ruth. 1997. "Imagination and the Arousal of Emotions in Greco-Roman Rhetoric." Pages 112–27 in *The Passions in Roman Thought and Literature*. Edited by Susanna Morton Braund and Christopher Gill. Cambridge: Cambridge University Press.
Weber, Thomas M. 2002. *Gadara Decapolitana: Untersuchungen zur Topographie, Geschichte, Architektur und der Bildenden Kunst einer*

"Polis Hellenis" im Ostjordanland. Vol. 1 of *Gadara – Umm Qēs*. Wiesbaden: Harassowitz.

Wendland, Paul. 1895. "Philo und die kynische-stoiche Diatribe." Pages 1–75 in *Beiträge zur Geschichte der griechischen Philosophie und Religion*. Edited by Paul Wendland and Otto Kern. Berlin: Reimer.

West, Martin L. 1982. *Greek Metre*. Oxford: Oxford University Press.

———. 2003. *Greek Epic Fragments*. LCL. Cambridge: Harvard University Press.

White, L. Michael. 2009. "Ordering the Fragments of *PHerc*. 1471: A New Hypothesis." *CErc* 39:29–70.

Wilke, Karl. 1905. *Polystrati Epicurei* ΠΕΡΙ ΑΛΟΓΟΥ ΚΑΤΑΦΡΟΝΗCEΩC *Libellus*. Leipzig: Teubner.

———. 1911. "Zu Philodems Schrift über den Zorn." Pages 94–117 in *Wissenschaftliche Aufsätze zur Feier des 350-jährigen Jubiläums des Gymnasiums und der Realanstalt zu Greifswald*. Greifswald: Bärwolff.

———. 1914. *Philodemi De ira liber*. BSGRT. Leipzig: Teubner.

———. 1915. "Zu Philodems de ira." *BPW* 23:732–33.

Yona, Sergio. 2015. "Some Epicurean Aspects of Horace's Upbringing in *Satires* 1.4." *CP* 110:227–51.

———. 2017. "Ofellus, Horace and Philodemus of Gadara in *Satires* 2.2." *Mnemosyne* 70:613–30.

———. 2018a. *Epicurean Ethics in Horace: The Psychology of Satire*. Oxford: Oxford University Press.

———. 2018b. "An Epicurean 'Mesure of Wealth' in Horace, *Satires* 1.1." *ClAnt* 37:351–78.

———. 2018c. "A Manual for Flatterers, a Proof of Candor: Philodemus' *On Flattery* and Horace, *Satires* 2.5." *AJP* 139:605–40.

Zarmakoupi, Mantha, ed. 2010. *The Villa of the Papyri at Herculaneum: Archaeology, Reception, and Digital Reconstruction*. Berlin: de Gruyter.

Zilch, G. 1866. *Observationum de Philodemi* περὶ ὀργῆς *libri specimen*. Marburg: Elwert.

Index Verborum

All fragments are explicitly marked as such; "col." is used to mark the point in the list where references to column numbers begin. We have not indexed καί, δέ, τε, οὐ, μή, or the article, nor γε, μέν, or δή except in combination with other particles. Citations are to the line on which the word begins. Words that are badly damaged, wholly restored, or the result of emendation are enclosed in square brackets; words that may not actually belong to the lemma under which they are listed or are otherwise questionable for some reason are marked with a question mark. Words that are (or are suspected of being) quotations are marked with the name of the author or, failing that, the note (poet.); (tit.) stands for title. The apparatus has not been systematically indexed, but some important or interesting readings have been included with the note (ap.). Regular comparatives and superlatives and regular adverbs are included under the positive form of the adjective; irregular forms are indexed separately. All verb forms are found under the dictionary entry (e.g., εἶπον is indexed under λέγω).

ἀγαθός	19.27; 28.36; 37.31; 38.19, 33; 41.18; 39.9 (?); 42.26; 48.21	ἀδικέω	frag. 5.7; col. 18.23; 27.25; 28.21
		ἀδοκήτως	22.14
ἀγανακτέω	14.3 (ap.); 46.35	ἀδολέσχως	1.10
ἀγανάκτησις	frag. 21.14 (ap.)	ἀδυνατέω	frag. 28.10 (?); col. 24.31; 50.2
ἀγανακτητικός	frag. 21.[13]	ἀδύνατος	6.[8]
ἄγευστος	28.37	ἀεί	frag. 27.31; col. 15.7; 19.24
ἀγνοέω	3.6; 5.13; 43.[14]	ἀέριος	39.18
ἄγριος	frag. 18.11 (ap.)	ἀηδής	frag. F.[1]; col. 44.19
ἀγωνία	8.26; 26.15	ἀθέμιστος	44.24 (Homer)
ἀγωνίζομαι	32.37	ἀθλητής	43.30
ἀδελφή	16.23	ἄθλιος	48.36
ἀδελφός	12.29; frag. F.2	ἀθρόως	3.12
ἀδιαλήπτως	41.23	αἰδέομαι	frag. 31.15 (?); col. 16.21 (Homer)
ἀδιανόητος	6.22		
ἀδιαφόρητος	23.10	αἰκία	27.24; 32.[5]
ἀδιάφορος	40.35; 41.1	αἱμηρός	frag. 18.15

αἱρετός 42.28; 44.30
αἶςχος 7.24 (ap.)
αἰςχύνω 24.11
αἰτέω 23.21
αἰτία 16.13; 18.40; 19.9 (ap.); 28.34; 30.30; 36.24; 37.[7]; 40.19; 46.39; 47.17
αἴτιος 28.20; 39.28; 50.6
ἀκαριαῖος 40.2
ἀκίνητος 32.23; 35.29
ἀκμή frag. 27.8; col. 10.20
ἀκοή 11.3
ἀκολουθέω frag. 32.14, 18
ἀκολουθία 45.20
ἀκόλουθος 42.3
ἀκούω 9.34; 38.23 (Menander)
ἀκράχολος 36.3
ἀκριβής 35.33
ἄκριτος 33.31
ἄκρος 42.2, 36
ἀλγηδών 42.9; 43.35
ἄλγος 29.24 (Homer)
ἀλείπτης 33.38
ἀλήθεια 14.10; 22.23; 34.30
ἀληθινός 30.1 (ap.)
ἁλίςκομαι frag. 12.15 (ap.)
ἀλλά frag. 3.34; frag. 20.16; frag. 24.5; frag. 32.5, 12, 15; 6.10, 26; frag. D.2; col. 11.6; 13.13; 15.11; 16.37; 18.30; 19.21, 33; 24.20; 25.29; 26.4, 28; 27.35; 29.24; 30.14; 33.19, 32; 34.37; 37.24; 38.6, 19, 38; 40.11 (?), 25; 41.26, 32; 43.3, 33; 44.18; 45.4; 47.3, 7, 21; 48.21, 24, 26; 49.36; ἀλλὰ μήν 24.36; οὐ μὴν ἀλλά 22.22
ἀλλαγή frag. 23.27
ἄλλος frag. 5.5; frag. 12.[13]; frag. 21.24, 25 (?); frag. 24.23; frag. 32.[27], [29]; col. 1.14; 4.7; 7.[3], 4; 14.13, 27; 18.29; frag. F.3; 24.35; 25.8, 18, 27; 26.[3], 23; 27.16; 29.20; 34.3, 22; 36.[5]; 37.7, 41.5; 42.29; 43.6; 47.26; 48.27; 49.9, 10; 50.2
ἀλλότριος 40.38; 41.2
ἀλλοτρίωςις 41.12
ἁλμυρός frag. 18.[19]

ἀλογέω 6.30 (ap.); 14.1
ἀλογιςτία 47.7
ἀλόγιςτος 49.21
ἄλογος 6.2; 15.6 (ap.); 19.23; 26.5; 32.32
ἅμα 9.38; 42.35
ἁμαρτάνω 41.19
ἁμαρτωλός 36.4
ἀμείβω 25.13
ἀμέλει 14.16; 15.[10]; 35.3
ἀμελής 4.12
ἀμέτοχος 30.29
ἄμυνα 31.32
ἀμύνω 33.35
ἄν (cf. ἐάν) frag. 24.25; col. 1.19; 3.22; 17.29; 22.22; 29.26 (Democritus); 30.33 (ap.); 35.2, 6; 37.31; 39.19; 40.16, 23; 41.6; 42.20, 34; 43.11; 44.8
ἀναγεννάω 2.19
ἀναγκάζω 15.25; 20.[18]; 23.33; frag. F.5; 36.6 (ap.)
ἀναγκαῖος 44.19
ἀνάγκη frag. 21.[14]; frag. 24.5; col. 19.13
ἀναγράφω 3.[6]
ἀνάγω frag. 21.6
ἀνάγωγος 28.41 (ap.)
ἀναδέχομαι 38.22, 33; 40.36; 41.37; 42.5
ἀναίνομαι 1.[5]
ἀναίτιος 24.25
ἀναλαμβάνω 11.8, 22
ἀνάλογος 32.16; 37.28
ἀναμένω 26.27
ἀνάμνηςις 25.34
ἀναξαίνω 29.[6]
ἀνάξιος 22.8 (ap.)
ἀναπηδάω frag. 27.3; col. 10.21
ἀναρίθμητος 2.17
ἀναςτέλλω 41.4
ἀναςχετός 2.2 (ap.)
ἀνατρέπω 25.5
ἀναφαίνω 25.15
ἀναφώνηςις 45.6 (tit.)
ἀνεκτός 39.2
ἀνέκφευκτος frag. 33.[19]; col. 39.29; 40.4, 14 (ap.), 20

Index Verborum

ἀνελευθερία	32.[1]	ἀπειλή	24.24
ἀνελεύθερος	21.5; 28.31	ἄπειμι	17.12
ἀνεπιεικής	27.19	ἀπέραντος	13.28 (ap.); 49.27
ἀνεπιλογιστέω	3.9	ἀπεργάζομαι	frag. 24.7; col. 33.27
ἀνεπιλόγιστος	7.7	ἀπέχω	frag. 7.5 (ap.); col. 27.27; 39.18
ἀνεπιстасία	13.14	ἁπλοῦς	28.27; 37.23
ἀνεπίсτατος	19.31	ἁπλύτως	20.20
ἄνευ	21.20; 36.8	ἀπό	frag. 32.30; col. 2.16; 14.20; 21.30; 27.23; 37.33; 38.2, 18; 20.[1];
ἀνευδοκηсία	39.39		
ἀνευδόκητος	25.6	ἀποβαίνω	7.11
ἀνέλευθερος	21.[5]; 28.31	ἀποβάλλω	15.22
ἄνευρος	33.29	ἀποδείκνυμι	8.27; 45.22; 49.6
ἀνέχω	19.15	ἀποδεκτός	28.39
ἀνήκεстος	26.30	ἀποδέω	45.25
ἀνήμερος	27.20; 42.30; 44.22	ἀποδηλόω	frag. 19.[7]
ἀνήρ	30.25; 45.22; 46.20	ἀποδημία	25.25
ἄνθρωπος	11.9; 25.1, 7, 26; 26.4, 25; 28.27; 30.32; 34.27; 37.3; 40.21; 43.37; 44.26	ἀποδίδωμι	34.34, 36; 35.[4]; 36.18, 30
		ἀπόθεсις	6.19 (ap.)
		ἀποκρύπτω	29.8
ἀνικήτως	32.22	ἀποκτείνω	24.29
ἄνοια	42.13 (ap.)	ἀπολαυстός	42.22; 44.7, [17]
ἀνοιδέω	frag. 18.17; col. 30.20	ἀπολείπω	21.26
ἀνοίκειος	11.3	ἀπόλλυμι	23.24
ἄνοπλος	33.2	ἀπόλυсις	6.[19]
ἀνταγωνιστής	33.38	ἀπομιμέομαι	14.5
ἀντί	17.24 (ap.); 40.29	ἀπόπληκτος	40.40
ἀντιγράφω	43.21	ἀπόρρητος	25.19
ἀντίδικος	31.12	ἀπόстасις	35.37
ἀντίθετος	43.31	ἀπότρωξις	13.22
ἀντιλέγω	46.11	ἀποτυφλόω	33.3
ἀντίстροφος	46.25, 39	ἀποφαίνω	frag. 24.[3]; col. 37.26; 48.40
ἀνυπέρβατος	18.[15]	ἀπόφασις	37.24
ἄξιος	frag. 27.23; col. 20.23	ἀποφεύγω	3.17; 6.9 (ap.), 26
ἀόργητος	34.[16], 33; 47.28	ἀποφυγή	4.13
ἄπαις	17.7 (ap.)	ἀποχράω	41.28
ἀπαντάω	frag. 27.15; col. 14.31; 25.4; 29.17	ἀπροαιρέτως	46.33
		ἀπρόβατος	19.12
ἅπαξ	11.23	ἅπτω	frag. 7.[5]; col. 30.31
ἀπαρενόχλητος	39.3	ἀπωθέω	13.12
ἅπας	frag. 13.29; frag. 27.30; frag. 28.16; col. 3.[26]; 9.23; 18.3; 23.11; frag. F.[3]; 25.4 (ap.); 28.38	ἀργύριον	15.27
		ἀρέскω	44.41
		ἀριθμός	30.16
ἀπάτησις	frag. 24.7	ἁρπαγή	22.28
ἀπειθής	33.25	ἄρρητος	23.27
ἀπειλέω	17.21, 29	ἀρρωстία	10.32

ἄρτι	10.18	ἀφυλάκτως	11.16
ἀρχή	40.[6]	Ἀχαιός	29.24 (Homer)
ἄρχω	frag. D.2	ἀχάριστος	28.33
ἄρχων	28.24	ἄχρι	22.22
ἀσάφεια	frag. 11.1 (ap.)	ἀψίνθιον	44.21
ἀσεβέω	14.23	ἄψυχος	26.6; 46.31
ἀσθένεια	43.23, 31		
ἀσθενής	43.[14]; 18	βαδίζω	15.24 (poet.); 27.36
ἆσθμα	8.38	βαθύς	frag. 19.9; col. 34.37
ἀσταθής	8.34	βαθύτης	28.40
ἄστρον	20.31	βαιός	1.16; 12.[20]; 48.20
ἀσυμπερίφορος	25.14	βαλανεῖον	frag. 27.27
ἅτε	frag. 24.17	βάλλω	frag. 27.11 (?); col. 23.39
ἀτελής	42.40 (ap.)	βαρύθυμος	30.34
ἀτενίζω	48.29	βαρύνω	frag. 15.[6]
ἀτευκτέω	frag. 24.16; col. 21.19	βαρύς	frag. 15.5 (?); col. 11.20 (Plato)
ἀτοπία	35.26	βασιλεία	29.22
ἄτοπος	12.20; 14.5 (ap.); 49.2	βασιλεύς	frag. 24.20; frag. 31.16 (ap.); col. 11.14; 18.35; 43.30
αὖ	14.[1]		
αὐξάνω	34.28	βιάζω	frag. 28.11; col. 27.26; 28.5 (ap.), 21 (ap.); 33.1
αὐστηρός	frag. 6.8 (ap.)		
αὐτόθεν	11.11	βίαιος	33.32; 41.2
αὐτόκλητος	20.38	βιβλιακός	45.17
αὐτόματος	32.4	βίος	9.23; 22.27; 28.37
αὐτός (et ὁ αὐτός)	frag. 6.7 (?); frag. 13.26; frag. 15.16; frag. 19.12; frag. 24.14, 22; frag. 28.2[4]; col. 1.[26]; 3.16; 4.6; 5.17; 7.5, 8, 21; 8.37; 9.28, 29, 36; 10.34; 12.[33]; 13.7; 14.26; 16.26; 17.24; 18.26; 19.12; 20.35, 37; 21.35; 22.25; 23.41; frag. F.[5]; 24.29; 25.20, 22; 27.17, 38; 28.29; 29.13, 14; 31.30, [33]; 33.5, 27; 34.19, 21; 35.38; 36.27; 37.[17], 20, 25; 40.20, 23, 32, 38; 41.22; 42.19, 35; 43.12; 45.24, 38, 39; 46.22; 48.31; 49.25, 38	βλάβη	frag. 1.4; frag. 28.22, 23; col. 32.40 (ap.); 41.28, [41]; 47.39; 50.5, 8
		βλακεία	31.6 (ap.)
		βλάπτω	13.6; 15.32 (ap.); 27.33; 37.4, 39; 40.32, 34; 41.10, 32, 34, 40; 42.1; 46.21; 47.11, 23, 32, 34, 35; 48.11; 49.30, 31, 41
		βλασφημία	16.26
		βλέπω	frag. 18.10; col. 28.35; 37.33
		βοηθέω	6.[2], 11
		βολή	12.22
		βουλευτής	28.23
ἀφαιρέω	frag. 24.21; col. 32.20; 39.24	βούλομαι	frag. 27.22 (ap.); col. 40.27
ἀφειδέω	14.26	βραχύς	42.39; 45.11; 47.37
ἀφίημι	23.35; 31.21	βριμάομαι (vel -όομαι)	22.14
ἀφικνέομαι	3.8	βρίμωσις	frag. 19.9; col. 8.24; 17.21; 24.23; 27.30
ἀφόρητος	23.[10]; 30.[8]		
ἀφορμή	24.38	βρῶσις	28.2
ἀφρήτωρ	44.23 (Homer)	βυβλιακός	45.17
ἀφροσύνη	24.40 (ap.)		
ἄφρων	47.2; 49.23	γαμετή	24.33

Index Verborum

γαμέω 22.32
γάρ frag. 13.27; frag. 21.17; frag. 23.[22]; frag. 32.9; col. 1.5; 6.[9], frag. C.1; frag. D.3; col. 10.18; 11.21; 12.25; 13.11; 14.16; 18.23, 34; 20.14, 28; 21.26, 37; 23.36; 26.7; 28.35; 31.[33]; 37.33; 38.23; 40.6; 41.28; 42.3, 12; 43.29; 44.9, 11, 17, 22; 46.25, 30; 48.38; 49.33
γὰρ δή 3.18
καὶ γάρ frag. 28.21; col. 4.19; 15.9; 40.22; 45.5
μὲν γάρ 17.16
γε μήν 27.19; 48.36
γέ πως frag. 28.22 (ap.); col. 42.[6]
γειτονεύω 21.37
γέλως 25.32
γέμω 26.14; 44.12 (ap.)
γενναῖος 3.21
γεννάω 9.28, 40
γέν(ν)ημα 17.25 (ap.)
γένος frag. 32.17 (ap.); col. 6.16; 30.32; [40.5]
γέρων 23.12
γῆ frag. 17.[16]; col. 18.[17]
γίγνομαι frag. 17.20; frag. 21.10; frag. 27.24; frag. 32.17 (ap.); col. 2.2 (ap.); 4.6; 7.8; 9.29; 13.18; 16.28; 19.7, 10, 13; 20.22; 21.10; 23.31; frag. F.1; 25.3, 17, 23; 27.33; 28.20, 30; 29.5, 9; 34.22, 25; 38.2, [8]; 41.[17]; 43.9, [15]; 46.26; 47.20; 49.30, 35
γιγνώσκω 41.3; 42.35
γνώριμος 35.[20]
γνῶσις frag. 28.[16]
γνωστός 7.12
γονεύς frag. F.[2]; col. 31.14
γοῦν 15.21; 31.24; 48.21
γράμμα 49.34, 36
γραμματικός 34.2
γραφή 35.34
γρυμέα 31.24
γυμνός frag. 27.12; col. 10.22
γυνή 22.32; 26.[1]

δαίομαι 8.31 (poet.)
δακνηρός 37.19
δάκνω frag. 19.[4]; col. 12.18; 41.8
δεῖ frag. 21.23; col. 7.13; 13.12; 18.34; 19.1 (ap.); 20.28; 26.6; 28.35 (bis); 29.25; 33.24; 34.6 (ap.); 38.[5]
δείκνυμι 30.10 (ap.); 40.20
δειλία 32.21
δεινός 8.24; 15.19; 17.19; 42.12
δεκτικός frag. 32.24; col. 20.[16]; 43.33, 44.1
δέρκομαι frag. 18.9 (poet.)
δεσποτικός 28.29
δή frag. 27.[16], 27; frag. 31.19 (Homer); frag. 32.20; col. 3.[21]; 6.26; 7.[21]; 26.[6];
μὲν δή 1.8
δηκτικός 38.7
δηλονότι 48.31
δῆλος 15.30; 45.33
δήπου 40.22; 43.36
δήπουθεν 44.8
διά 31.3 (?) (gen.) 1.7; 3.22; 9.29; 19.26; 27.17; 29.[5]; 31.27; 45.28; (acc.) 2.17; 4.6; 5.20; 6.13, 30; 10.24, 28; 13.9, 14; 18.39; 23.24, 26; 24.23; 25.20, 23, 31; 26.28, 29, 31; 28.34; 29.13 (bis), 28; 30.30; 33.9; 34.21, 25, 27, 29; 35.18, 38; 36.4, 23; 39.30; 40.19; 41.32; 42.28; 44.30; 46.39; 47.37
διαβάλλω 20.21
διαβολή 16.30; 25.35 (ap.); 27.15
διάγω 21.[16]
διαγωγή 21.23
διαδίδωμι 8.32
διάθεσις 2.15; 7.[3]; 27.21; 34.20; 35.1; 37.30; 38.2; 42.31
διακνίζω frag. 17.3 (?)
διακονία 28.4
διακρίνω 12.25
διαλαμβάνω frag. 7.7
διαλέγομαι 32.34
διάληψις 37.25
διαλλάττω 44.40; 48.35
διαμένω 30.22
διανοέω frag. 28.[13]; col. 44.33

διανόμημα	43.5
διαπείθω	40.[4]
διαπίπτω	35.35; 45.41
διαριθμέω	15.26
διαρρίπτω	frag. 19.10
διασαφέω	frag. 11.1; col. 45.7
διασπασμός	10.29
διάστασις	8.36
διασύρω	28.17
διατίθημι	12.17; 18.34; 33.[6]
διατριβή	35.34
διατρίβω	33.24
διαφέρω	45.35
διαφθείρω	24.36
διαφορά	7.4; 43.1, 8
διαφωνέω	17.[26]
δίδωμι	34.4
διειλημμένως	41.22
διερεθίζω	22.4; 31.13; 47.30
διερεθισμός	8.23; 10.36; 19.30
δίκαιος	25.2; 28.25; 32.27
δικαιοσύνη	24.38
δικαιόω	25.15
δικαστής	28.22
δίκη	11.11; 12.38
διό	32.30; 38.29; 42.39;
διόπερ	3.5
διοίδησις	8.22
διοργίζομαι	frag. 24.11
διορθόω	frag. B.1 (ap.); col. 19.17
διότι	19.[1]; 30.4, 24, 31; 31.1; 39.35; 41.3; 42.1, 36
δοκέω	frag. 21.[20]; frag. 28.11, 13, [24]; col. 22.16; 25.28; 27.25; 29.11, 16; 34.38; 47.24
δόλιος	28.32
δόξα	frag. 19.20, 23 (?); frag. 32.9; col. 15.5 (?); 43.21 (tit.)
δοξάζω	46.2
δοῦλος	frag. 21.18; frag. 31.15 (ap.); col. 23.37; 24.28; 36.3
δραπετεύω	23.40
δραστικός	50.6
δριμύτης	5.24
δύναμαι	2.11; 6.25; 8.26; 10.39; 24.30; 26.19, 28; 28.24; 42.16
δυνατός	10.40; 29.30; 43.39
δυσαποκατάστατος	30.18
δυσκολία	23.13; 28.1
δυσχερής	7.23; 28.18; 38.4
δυσχρηστία	4.7; 24.20
ἐάν	(ἄν) frag. 21.[6]; frag. 27.[15], 19, 27; frag. 28.13, 19 (ap.); col. 3.19 (ap.); 7.6; 10.26; 11.11; 13.17; 15.[8]; 18.25; 19.16, 21, 30; 20.14; 22.26, 32; 23.[39]; frag. F.4; 24. 29, 31, 33, 37; 26.[1], 3; 29.[7]; 30.18, 27, 29; 24.[16]; 41.18, 20; 47.7; 50.5
ἑαυτοῦ	frag. 6.7 (?); col. 4.23; 13.7; 15.14, 23, 31; 19.23; 21.[16]; 22.[16], 18; 25.17; 26.33; 30.[9]; 37.4; 38.40; 41.20, 26; 42.28, 38; 44.12 (ap.), 30; 46.19; 49.2
ἐάω	12.25; 19.[11]; 21.37; 30.27
ἐγγίγνομαι	27.14; 30.29
ἐγκαλέω	frag. E.1 (ap.)
ἐγκύκλιος	10.25
ἐγκυρέω	11.15; 40.17
ἐγχειρέω	1.10
ἐγχρῄζω	5.12
ἐγώ	21.[5]
ἐθέλω v. θέλω	
ἔθω v. εἴωθα	
εἰ	frag. 16.26; frag. 19.3, 9; frag. 21.13; frag. 24.25 (ap.); frag. 28.21; col. 1.12; 3.11; 5.14; 8.19, 26; 16.27; 29.5; 33.34; 39.20, 29; 40.27; 41.2, 32; 43.22, 38; 44.31; 45.9, 28; 46.18, [22]; 47.29; 48.5, 28, 39; 49.2, 36
εἶδον (v. ὁράω)	
εἶδος	24.21
εἰκότως	25.13
εἰλικρίνεια	7.16
εἰμί	frag. 6.4; [frag. 7.1]; frag. 18.5; frag. 21.12, 13, 20; frag. 24.[18], 23; frag. 27.19; frag. 28.[12]; frag. 29.9; frag. 32.26, 27; col. 1.6, 9, 24, [26]; 2.14; 3.16; 5.22, 25; 6.10, 25, 27, 29; frag.

Index Verborum

C.2, 4; 7.24 (?); 9.35; 11.22; 14.17; 15.7; 16.13 (ap.), 35; 17.17; 18.3 (ap.), 5, [15]; 20.29; 25.28; frag. H.6; 28.25, 37; 29.20; 30.29; 31.32; 32.[17], 34, 36; 33.20; 34.24, 31, 33, 36; 35.5, 29; 36.3, 23; 37.28; 38.[7], 30; 39.21, 32; 40.5, 24, 26; 41.[41]; 42.[6], 15 (?), 25, 26, 34; 44.1; 45.17, 36; 46.9; 47.28, 40; 48.22, 37; 49.[19], 28; 50.7

εἴπερ 49.[10]
εἶπον v. λέγω
εἰс frag. 7.[3]; frag. 18.11; col. 3.8; 4.22; 9.[25]; 10.31; 12.21, 40; 13.15; 14.23, 25; 15.29; 19.[4]; 20.29; 21.35; 24.27, 38; 27.24, 38; 34.30; 41.19, 20, 22, 26, 35; 42.27; 44.37; 48.29; 49.22
εἷс frag. 24.12; frag. 28.22; col. 15.22, 21.16 (ap.); 28; 41.7; μηδὲ εἷс 1.15
εἶτα 8.32; 11.17; 22.18
εἴωθα 1.12; 7.19; 13.19; 44.3
ἐκ, ἐξ 2.22; 8.21; 12.33, 36; 13.[23], 26; 16.13 (ap.), [24]; 21.18; 24.18; 28.38; 40.9; 42.38; 45.20; 49.3, 28
ἕκαστος frag. 5.5 (ap.); frag. 19.16 (?); col. 20.[39]; 21.18, 26; 25.12
ἐκβακχεύω 14.28; 30.26
ἐκβάλλω 22.31
ἐκεῖνος 1.5; 29.23; 43.39; 46.24; 47.4, 27; 49.3
ἔκθεсις 34.24
ἐκθυμαίνω frag. 31.21
ἐκκαγχάζω 22.20
ἐκκαλέω frag. E.1; col. 24.27; 48.8
ἐκκαλύπτω 20.27
ἐκκληсιαстής 28.23
ἐκκοπή 13.21
ἐκκόπτω 23.36
ἐκλύω 33.30
ἑκούсιος 23.25; 40.33; 41.33; 46.21, 30; 47.[10], 33; 48.7; 49.31
ἐκπίπτω 23.35
ἐκπύρωсις 8.22
ἐκτέμνω 31.28
ἐκτικός frag. 32.24 (ap.); col. 20.16 (ap.)
ἐκτός 27.32

ἐκτρέχω 20.1
ἐκτροφή 9.25
ἐκφέρω 15.[16]
ἐκφεύγω 40.24
ἐκχέω 15.30
ἐλάττωμα frag. 15.7; col. 24.18; 37.37; 39.6
ἐλάχιстος 14.20; 28.9 (ap.); 38.8, 30
ἔλεγχος 35.33
ἐλεύθερος frag. 21.19, 21
ἕλκος 19.18
ἐμβαίνω 21.36
ἐμβλέπω 40.37
ἐμπίμπρημι 24.34
ἐμπίπτω 13.17; 42.20
ἐμποδίζω 18.35; 39.4, 27
ἐμποδών frag. 27.25
ἐμποιέω 3.14; 33.33
ἔμφασις 40.34; 47.38; 50.4
ἔμψυχος 46.34
ἐν frag. 18.3; frag. 27.16, 27; col. 1.16, 18; 3.13; 6.[13], 19; 15.27; 18.37; 19.[2]; 21.30, 33; 24.19; 31.19; 32.[15]; 35.33; 36.24; 37.36; 40.[6]; 41.9; 43.23; 45.6, 41; 46.5
ἐναντίος 31.11; 33.6; 34.40
ἔνδεια 27.35
ἔνδον frag. 27.6
ἔνειμι frag. 32.22
ἕνεκα 16.24
ἕνεκεν 5.11; 43.[13]
ἐνεπηρεάζω frag. 24.13
ἐνεργέω 26.17
ἐνευρεθής frag. 18.14
ἐνέχω 30.17; 32.40
ἐνθουсιασμός 32.32
ἐνθυμέομαι 4.20; 35.24
ἔνιοι frag. 18.14, [15]; col. 16.[18]; 21.22; 26.7; 31.24; 32.3; 35.4, 28, 37; 43.19; 44.38; 47.41; 48.27; 49.21
ἐνίοτε 4.8; 12.23; 13.14; 15.14; 16.31, 38; 23.30; 28.[21]; 30.15, 35; 36.36; 37.5; 38.27
ἐνίстημι 4.14
ἐννοέω 26.20

ἐννόημα	43.5 (ap.)	ἐπιβατός	frag. 21.20
ἔννοια	45.26	ἐπιβλέπω	9.36
ἐντάττω	40.30	ἐπιγέν(ν)ημα	17.24
ἐνταῦθα	4.19	ἐπιδεικνύω	7.10; 20.25; 41.29; 50.5
ἐντείνω	frag. 18.16	ἐπιδεκτικός	40.25
ἐντελέω	frag. 28.19 (ap.)	ἐπιεικής	44.27
ἔντερον	8.30	ἐπιζητέω	15.28
ἐντρέχω	37.22	ἐπιθεωρέω	5.29 (ap.)
ἐξαργιόω	29.2	ἐπιθυμέω	42.21; 44.28
ἐξαιρέω	frag. 27.5; col. 31.30	ἐπιθυμία	7.20; 8.25; 14.18; 23.27; 27.28; 41.38; 44.13 (ap.)
ἐξαναλίςκω	23.29		
ἐξαριθμέω	7.22	ἐπικατασφάττω	15.15
ἔξειμι	40.26; 44.35	ἐπικίνδυνος	10.31
ἑξῆς	48.34, 37	ἐπιλαμβάνω	12.19
ἕξις	frag. 12.17	ἐπίλεγω	frag. 31.18
ἐξίςτημι	19.[2]; 38.32; 47.29	ἐπιληπτικός	9.21
ἐξοκέλλω	14.21	ἐπιλογίζομαι	7.17; 45.40
ἔξω	2.9	ἐπιλογιςμός	46.17
ἔξωθεν	frag. 18.2; col. 26.24; 31.12; 42.7; 47.40; 48.19, 23	ἐπιλογιστικός	4.11; 44.39
		ἐπιμελής	5.8
ἔοικα	frag. 18.7	ἐπιμηχανάομαι	11.10
ἐπαΐω	frag. 1.2 (?)	ἐπιμιξία	35.31
ἐπακολουθέω	22.18; 28.28; 47.31; 50.1	ἐπιπλήττω	19.22
ἐπαμύνω	21.1	ἐπιπλοκή	21.21
ἐπανατρέχω	30.28	ἐπίπονος	11.13
ἔπανδρος	31.17	ἐπιρρώννυμι	31.20
ἐπεί	6.24; 44.11	ἐπισημαίνω	frag. 18.9; col. 29.33; 45.19; 46.6
ἐπειδάν	frag. 28.[5]; col. 12.38; 18.[16]		
ἐπειδή	7.13; 37.27; 40.39; 48.18	ἐπισκοτέω	38.39
ἐπειδήπερ	28.21; 49.24	ἐπίςταμαι	2.19
ἔπειμι (εἰμί)	frag. 30.12; col. 35.5 (ap.)	ἐπιστρεφής	4.17
ἔπειμι	(εἶμι) frag. 1.2 (?);	ἐπιστρέφω	18.27
ἔπειτα	12.30; 15.30; 16.14; 35.[17]	ἐπιτείνω	35.21
ἐπευφημέω	16.20	ἐπιτέμνω	42.40 (ap.)
ἐπέχω	30.19	ἐπιτερπής	25.27
ἐπί	frag. 5.6; frag. 13.33; (gen.) frag. 24.8; col. 7.18; 10.27; 26.35; 30.3 (ap.); 41.26; 46.26; 48.20, 21, 31; (dat.) col. 14.29; 15.10, 13; 20.18; 25.33; frag. H.4; 26.19, 32; 38.30, 40; 45.16; 46.16; 47.27, 28; (acc.) frag. 18.13; frag. 19.19; col. 2.20; 5.14; 8.32; 10.15; 20.39; 30.3 (ap.), 27; 35.31; 44.2, 5, 6, 21; 45.38 (bis); 46.37 (bis); 48.6, [9]	ἐπιτεταμένως	36.35
		ἐπιτήδειος	22.3 (ap.)
		ἐπιτήδευμα	frag. E.4 (ap.)
		ἐπιτηρέω	22.3 (ap.)
		ἐπιτίθημι	11.12
		ἐπιτιμάω	1.13; 19.16
		ἐπιτίμηςις	35.18
		ἐπιτρίβω	9.24
		ἐπιφαίνω	36.39
ἐπιβάλλω	frag. 12.14 (ap.)	ἐπιφέρω	9.33; 13.13; 38.[9]; 49.37

Index Verborum

ἐπίχειρος	12.32
ἐποιστικός	11.6
ἕπομαι	frag. C.3; col. 13.27 (ap.)
ἔπος	12.18
ἔραμαι	44.24 (Homer); 49.[7]
ἔργον	17.17
ἐρεθίζω	20.40; 30.[4]
ἐρεθισμός	25.30
ἐρέω v. λέγω	
ἐρημία	21.15; 22.27
ἔριον	frag. 19.17 (ap.)
ἔρχομαι	41.6, 27
ἐρωτικός	7.19; 14.18
ἔστε	17.[28]
ἑστιάω	18.19
ἔσχατος	14.21
ἕτερος	3.11; 16.15; 19.21; 26.26; 28.18; 34.6 (ap.); 38.29; 46.26, 27
ἔτι	frag. 32.25 (ap.); col. 26.10; 39.21; 42.33
εὐανάσειστος	16.27
εὐδαιμονία	23.18 (ap.)
εὐέμπτωτος	49.20
εὐεργετέω	48.[8]
εὔθετος	20.29
εὐθύς	15.12; 20.[2]; 38.32
εὐκινησία	35.23
εὐλόγιστος	40.17
εὔλογος	6.11; 20.24; 32.31
εὐπαραλόγιστος	16.29
εὑρίσκω	19.30
εὔσημος	46.3
εὐτονία	33.33
εὐφυής	19.4
εὐχαριστέω	46.20, 24, 30; 48.7, [13], 25
εὐχαριστία	46.28, 38
εὔχομαι	8.29
ἐφιστάνω (ἐφίστημι)	19.1; 20.4 (?); 41.5; 43.10
ἐφοράω	5.29 (ap.)
ἔχθρα	11.8; 30.[7]
ἐχθρός	16.12 (ap.), 32; 19.11; 23.31; 26.21; 32.25
ἔχω	frag. 18.4; col. 2.[14]; 6.18, 21; 7.4, 10; 14.33; 15.19; 21.4, 23; 22.26; 24.37; 26.21; 28.28; 30.12; 33.32; 35.1; 36.38; 37.34; 41.38; 42.17; 43.8; 47.26, 27; 49.[12]
ἕως	13.20; 27.35
ζημία	11.21 (Plato); 12.37
ζήτησις	frag. 28.[17]
ζωή	21.17
ζῷον	26.5
ἤ	frag. 20.8, 11; frag. 27.24; frag. 28.23; frag. 32.25, 27; col. 1.16; 7.5; 11.14; 12.39; 13.16, 21, 22; 14.13; 15.32; 17.7 (ap.), 10; 18.[21]; 20.18; 21.[1], 31, 32 [bis], 38; 22.[14], 17; 24.35, 39 [bis]; 26.1.,2 (bis), 23, 29, 31, [33], 34; 27.34; 30.7; 35.20, 39; 36.22, 26; 37.3, 4, 28; 38.28; 39.21, 33; 40.33, 38; 41.41; 43.5, 11; 44.6; 46.1, 8; 47.4; [49.7]
ᾗ v. ὅς	
ἠβαιός	1.16 (ap.)
ἡγέομαι	16.1 (ap.); 43.20; 47.41; 48.19
ἤδη	frag. 18.12; frag. 22.3; frag. 27.30; col. 3.4
ἡδύς	24.30; 25.22; 32.29; 44.17
ἠθικός	frag. 2.1
ἥκιστα	3.22; 13.6
ἡμεῖς	2.12; frag. D.[3]; 16.17; frag. E.6; 29.29; 37.20; 41.26; 46.7, 8, 36
ἥμερος	frag. 30.16; col. 44.26
ἡμέτερος	6.14
ἤπιος	19.19
ἡσυχάζω	10.26
ἥττων	5.13; 49.23, 25
θάνατος	9.33; 11.13; 26.27; 32.23; 43.34
θαρρέω	32.19
θαῦμα	16.15 (Homer)
θαυμάζω	frag. 33.14 (ap.); col. 45.16
θέα	25.22
θέατρον	21.33
θεῖος	14.26
θέλω	4.22; 45.17
θεός	14.4; 16.18 (ap.); 18.32
θεόφιλος	frag. 27.10 (ap.)

θεραπεία	4.18, 23; 5.9; 7.3 (ap.)	καθόλου	1.21; 4.10; 34.31
θεραπεύω	10.33	καθοράω	frag. 19.15
θεωρέω	3.12; 6.19; 35.27; 42.19	καινός	frag. 13.[28]; col. 41.24
θεωρία	20.33	καίπερ	7.9
θήρα	18.25	καιρός	19.5; 21.2; 32.17
θηρίον	18.30; 33.[35]	καίτοι	5.22
θηριώδης	19.17; 27.30	κακηγορία	24.24
θοίνη	frag. 27.10 (ap.)	κακία	27.17
θυγατήρ	16.25	κακοδαιμονία	9.26; 23.18 (ap.)

θυμός   8.16 (?); 12.26; 15.8; 23.25; 31.30; 32.33; 33.36; 43.[12], 41; 45.10, 26, 30, 37, 39; 46.2

κακοδαιμονικός   26.13
κακοπαθέω   frag. 18.21 (ap.)

θυμόομαι   frag. 19.4; col. 7.6; 13.9, 28 (ap.); 14.[3]; 15.20; 25.33; 30.14; 33.40; 45.3, 7, 12, 21, 24, [27]; 46.13; 48.1

κακός   1.[6], 22; 2.18, [20]; 5.17; 6.22, 24, 29; frag. C.[4]; 7.18; 14.19; 29.27; 33.6, 28; 37.18, 27; 38.1, [6], 19, 20, 22 (Menander); 39.21, 28, 32; 41.24; 44.12; 48.20

θύρα	frag. 19.[5], 13	καλέω	col. 5.7; 16.38; 39.17; 41.9

καλός frag. 30.12 (?); col. 23.39; 29.8; 32.26; 45.37; 46.18

ἰατρός	2.22 (ap.); 4.4; 5.11; 9.34; 10.40	κάμνω	4.11
ἴδιος	frag. 18.12; col. 6.30 (ap.); 32.28; 38.37; 40.28	κανονικός	31.[10]
ἰδιότης	21.25	καρδία (v. κραδίη)	8.41; 10.[1] (ap.)
ἱερεύς	14.23; 16.21 (Homer)	καρτερέω	frag. 27.4
ἱερός	18.15 (ap.)		

κατά   4.24; 1.4 (?); (gen.) 16.[32]; 22.17; 25.3; (acc.) frag. 12.10; frag. 13.31; frag. 19.21; frag. 24.10; col. 11.18; 12.20; 18.21; 20.[17]; 23.22; 26.16; 28.2 (bis), 4; 29.26; 30.16; 33.31; 35.30, 35; 37.21, 25, 29, 40; 38.9, 26, 37; 39.2; 40.27; 41.7, 33; 42.8, 12; 43.32, 39; 44.6, 22; 45.2, 4, 21, 26; 47.21; 48.11

ἱκέτης	14.25		
ἵμερος	15.19		
ἵνα	20.24; 29.34		
ἱππικός	34.1		
ἵππος	34.1		
ἴσος	5.14		
ἵστημι	1.20; frag. D.4 (?); 41.27		
ἰσχυρός	12.24		
ἰσχύω	43.26	καταγέλαστος	1.24, [27]
		καταδικάζω	23.32
καθά (καθ' ἅ)	36.20	καταδιώκω	10.22
καθάπερ	frag. 32.28; col. 1.11; 5.23; frag. C.3; 7.18; 8.27; 14.6; 14; 16.19; 35.2; 42.22, 32; 43.19, 40; 44.20; 45.32; 46.28; 49.33	κατακρημνίζω	26.34
		καταλαμβάνω	47.5
		καταλείπω	frag. 24.15; col. 40.2
		καταναγκάζω	frag. 24.8; frag. 28.14, 20; frag. 32.[2], [16]; frag. 33.15, 21
καθαρός	4.21; 11.3; 34.32		
καθηγεμών	45.1	κατανταω	41.25
καθηγητής	19.14	καταξιόω	35.27
κάθημαι	15.12	καταποντίζω	26.34 (ap.)
καθίστημι	2.7 (ap.), 9; 3.[27]; 4.15; 6.23	καταριθμόω	39.5
καθό	frag. 28.15; col. 38.7; 45.34 (bis), 40; 49.26	κατάρχω	14.19
		κατασκευάζω	32.25; 40.31; 46.10

κατασκευή	43.34	κρατέω	33.26
καταστοχάζομαι	2.7	κραυγάζω	22.12; 26.1; 33.39
καταστρέφω	42.27	κραυγή	8.35
κατασφάττω	26.[34]	κρεάδιον	18.13
κατασχίζω	17.9	κρείττων	frag. 21.[23]; col. 13.18
κατατάσσω	36.25	κρίνω	25.2 (ap.)
κατατέμνω	frag. 19.13	κτῆμα	24.35
κατατριβή	25.8 (ap.)	κύντατος	6.27 (poet.)
καταφερής	12.21 (ap.)	κύριος	16.[38]; 43.21 (tit.); 45.9
καταφέρω	12.21	κύων	18.24; 21.34 (paroem.?)
καταφρονέω	17.22; frag. H.3; 26.23	κωλύω	30.10 (ap.)
κατηγορουμένως	45.30	κώνωψ	17.20
κατισχύω	frag. 7.[4]		
κατορθόω	frag. B.1 (ap.)	λακτίζω	frag. 27.26; col. 17.[8], 20.5 (ap.)
καχλάζω	frag. 6.1; col. 28.13 (ap)	λαλέω	frag. 20.15; frag. 27.24; col. 36.34
καχόμιλος	25.2; 28.13 (ap.)	λαμβάνω	9.26; 40.34; 43.32; 47.39; 50.4
καχυπόνους	28.30; 36.38	λανθάνω	2.8; 4.9
καχύποπτος	28.13 (ap.)	λέγω	frag. 7.[1]; frag. 13.30; frag. 17.18; frag. 21.[12] frag. 24.[4]; frag. 27.15, 17 (?), 20; frag. 28.15; frag. 33.19; col. 2.14; 3.26; 7.7; 8.34; 13.12; 15.25; 16.[37]; 17.17; 18.23, 35; 19.25; 20.28; 22.11, 16; 27.[14]; 28.27, 35; 30.2; 36.29; 37.31, 40; 38.5, 20, 35; 39.22, 31; 40.16, 40; 41.39; 43.[15], 23, 40; 44.1, 8; 47.13 (ap.); 48.28, 33; 49.26
κενός	38.[1]; 39.8		
κεραυνόπληκτος	47.20		
κεφαλή	frag. 24.21		
κίνδυνος	4.9		
κινέω	10.38; 18.30; 46.28		
κίνησις	8.33; 9.[18]		
κιρνάω	26.12		
κλαίω	frag. 4.15 (ap.); col. 15.13		
κλείς	frag. 19.3	λέων	18.31; 27.32
κλείω	frag. 19.[5]	λήθη	3.8
κληρονόμος	22.30	ληρώδης	1.9, 25, [26]
κλίνη	10.27	λίαν	45.11
κοινός	7.24 (ap.); 21.17 (ap.); 32.28; 37.3; 40.29; 41.24 (ap.), 29; 44.3; 45.4, 31; 46.15 (ap.); 47.30	λίθος	frag. 19.[10]; col. 12.22; 26.7 (ap.)
		λογίζομαι	36.40
		λογικός	frag. 28.17
κοινότης	28.41 (ap.); 34.28; 35.7	λόγιμος	5.28
κοινωνέω	21.38	λογισμός	frag. 24.14; col. 2.6; 38.39
κολάζω	frag. 24.19; col. 27.18; 33.7 (ap.), 20, 34.5 (ap.); 40; 41.3; 42.28	λογοποιέω	23.21 (ap.)
		λόγος	frag. 22.8 (?); frag. 24.1; col. 11.20 (Plato); 20.23, 26; 23.21; 36.25; 31.11; 33.22; 35.35; 39.23; 40.[4], 28; 43.33; 44.38; 46.5, 10; 48.5, 36; 49.27
κολακεία	31.6 (ap.)		
κολακεύω	32.[3]		
κόλασις	19.4; 24.26; 31.31; 37.38; 42.21; 44.16 (ap.), 28, 35		
		λοιδορέω	17.11; 20.3, 20
κομίζω	11.19; 12.31; 42.37	λοιδορητικός	35.22
κουρεῖον	21.31	λοιδορία	28.14
κοῦφος	11.19 (Plato)	λοίδορος	36.36
κραδίη (v. καρδία)	frag. 31.[19] (Homer)	λοξός	frag. 18.[11]

λουτρόν frag. 27.28 (ap.); col. 25.24
λυμαίνω 13.7
λύμη 23.1 (ap.)
λυπέω frag. 7.8; col. 7.21, 25 (ap.); 8.30; 28.[16]; 38.38
λύπη frag. 7.2
λυπηρόc 37.27, 29
λύττα 38.28

μά frag. 21.7; 43.3
μαθητήc 34.4
μαίνομαι frag. 18.[3]
μακάριοc frag. 7.6; 37.17
μακρόc 5.26
μάλιcτα 2.10; 15.18; 21.24; 30.4; 42.19; 43.38
μᾶλλον 21.20; 29.[34]; 33.5; 36.18, 22, 23, 28; 40.3; 42.11; 47.4
μανθάνω 4.[24]; 49.34, 37
μανία 16.34, 37 (ap.), [39]; 44.10, 33
μανικῶc 41.5
μανιοποιέω 34.26
μάταιοc frag. 22.6; col. 42.24; 47.10 (ap.), 19, 20
μάχομαι 30.4 (ap.)
μεγαλύνω 20.24
μέγαc frag. 7.[2]; col. 3.14; 10.24; 25.20; 30.25; 39.31; 41.35, 36; 42.5, [7], 9 (bis), 24, 25; 47.38, 40; 48.23; μεγάλωc 42.[1]; 47.24; 48.26
μέγεθοc 3.10; 4.5; 5.15; 6.17, 20; 44.6; 45.34
μεθόδευμα frag. E.4 (ap.)
μεθοδεύω frag. E.4
μεθύcκω 47.1; 48.38; 49.25
μεθύω 47.6, [8]; 49.18, 26
μειγ-, μειξ- v. μιγ-, μιξ-
μελαγχολία 9.37
μέλαc 9.40
μέλλω frag. 5.8 (?); col. 5.18
μέμφομαι frag. 29.5 (ap.)
μὲν οὖν 1.12; 41.[1], 17; 46.7; 47.13
μέντοι γε 42.4
μένω 32.23
μέροc frag. 13.27 (ap.); col. 9.19

μετά (gen.) 17.11, 20; 22.19; 25.26; 27.28; 31.20; 32.1, 39; 39.[1], 22; (acc.) 15.9; 26.18
μεταβάλλω frag. 24.25
μεταγιγνώcκω 25.35 (ap.)
μετάγνωcιc 26.32
μεταδιώκω 18.38
μεταμέλεια 15.10 (ap.); 18.2; 19.6
μετατρέπω 27.[39]
μετέρχομαι 8.25; 23.28; 26.19, 29, 30; 41.38; 43.11
μετέχω 19.26; 40.23; 43.37
μετέωροc 8.38
μέτριοc 1.20; 3.19; 4.14; 10.[17]; 45.8
μέτρον 31.2
μέχρι 14.20; 19.33; 30.21; 31.4; 32.22
μηδέ frag. 32.13; col. 13.12; 18.29; 24.33; 27.26; 30.11; 36.31; 39.18; 43.11; μηδὲ ἕν 1.15
μηδείc (μηθείc) 3.11; 10.37; 20.23; 37.35; 48.22; μηδὲ εἷc 1.15
μηδέποτε 47.38
μήν 11.8 (ap.); 33.[5]
μῆνιc 29.23 (Homer)
μηνίω 11.8
μήποτε frag. F.4
μήπω 20.30
μήτε frag. 17.15 (?); col. 19.14, 15, 25
μηχανάομαι 17.19
μιαρόc 11.3 (ap.)
μίγνυμι 18.17
μικρόc 17.16; 18.32; 20.18; 26.6; 29.25; 40.7
μιcανθρωπία 28.19
μιcέω 21.1; 26.22; 42.3
μιcοπόνηροc 36.39
μῖcοc 36.[1]
μόνον frag. 13.27 (ap.); frag. 20.18; col. 1.14; 6.11; 20.32; 24.19; 29.22, 32; 30.14; 34.37; 38.37; 39.39; 41.10; 47.2, 9, 35; 48.24, 35
μονότροποc 22.26
μυῖα 17.18
μυκτήρ 13.21
μυριάκιc frag. 28.21; col. 12.35

Index Verborum

μυρίος 14.15; 27.16; 29.23 (Homer); 38.4; 42.16; 43.29; 44.11; 49.8
μυροπώλιον 21.31
μυστικός 20.26
μωμητικός 27.16
νεκρός 27.35
νέος frag. H.7 (?)
νεῦμα 25.31
νεῦρον 31.28; 33.29
νή 28.41
νήφω 20.4 (ap.)
νοέω frag. 32.23; col. 29.26 (Democritus)
νομίζω 37.32; 42.29
νομοθετέω 5.28 (ap.)
νόμος 5.28 (?); 12.36; 13.24
νοσέω 10.20
νόσος 4.5; 5.16, 28 (ap.); 6.[9]; 27.22
νουθετέω frag. 27.29
νυκτερεύω 18.1
νῦν 1.20; 5.6 (?); 14.16; 29.34
νωχελής 30.33

ξύλον 13.15
ξύστρα frag. 27.28 (ap.)

ὅδε frag. 32.25; col. 17.[16]
ὀδύρομαι frag. 21.[5]
ὅθεν frag. 21.14; col. 3.25; 4.12; 10.32; 14.29
ὀθνεῖος 25.12
οἶδα 24.[18], 32
οἰκεῖος 21.18; 26.24; 40.39
οἰκέτης frag. 24.12; col. 24.18
οἰκία frag. 27.[5]; col. 24.34
οἰκουρός 18.25
οἶνος 46.41
οἴομαι 5.23; [21.5]; 32.33; 42.25; 46.3; 48.37
οἷος frag. 33.10; frag. C.4; col. 8.34; 9.20; 19.31; 32.32; 33.18 (ap.); 34.38
οἷοσδήποτε 19.10 (ap.); 24.41 (ap.)
οἷός τε 40.24; 49.34
ὄκνος 32.20
ὀλέθριος 27.22

ὀλιγάκις 10.19
ὀλίγος 23.26; 39.38
ὀλιγοχρόνιος 16.37 (ap.)
ὀλιγωρία 30.7
ὅλος frag. 13.30, 31; col. 4.20; 6.29; 8.20; 10.38; 23.29; 37.2; 35.28; 41.21; 43.37
Ὁμηρικός frag. 29.12 (ap.)
ὁμιλέω 11.17; 21.28
ὄμμα 1.23; 4.16; 23.37
ὁμογενής 16.35
ὅμοιος frag. 21.22; col. 13.26; 25.13; 34.[17]
ὁμοιότροπος 11.16
ὁμολογέω frag. 27.28
ὅμως 7.13
ὄνομα 43.2, [13]
ὀνομάζω frag. 33.14 (ap.)
ὄνος frag. 13.24 (ap.)
ὄντως frag. 16.28 (ap.); col. 44.24
ὀξύς 40.10 (ap.)
ὁποίως frag. 24.[24]
ὁπόταν 2.[6]
ὁπωσδήποτε 20.36
ὁράω frag. 17.14; frag. 24.24; col. 16.16 (Homer); 30.[35]; 34.[17], [18], 32; 39.35
ὀργή frag. 7.1, frag. 18.3; frag. 32.13, 22; col. 5.17, [20]; 6.[29]; 14.[4]; 16.36, [39]; 20.25; 25.16, 23; 29.[19]; 30.16; 31.2, 29; 32.19, 36, 39; 34.5; 35.26; 38.1, 21, 36; 39.25, 35; 41.9, 10, 18, 30, 36; 42.12, 24; 43.[15], 23, 27; 45.29, 36, 39; 46.[9], 29, 37; 47.19; 48.32; 49.22, 29; 50.1, 7
ὀργίζομαι frag. 6.2, 4; frag. 7.3; frag. 18.11; frag. 21.25; frag. 24.[19]; col. 38.24 (Menander); 41.33; 45.31; 46.12, 22, 23; 47.36; 48.10; 49.32; 50.3
ὀργίλος frag. 16.28; col. 3.[23]; 14.32; 18.33; 26.11; 28.26; 34.17, 29, 31, 35; 36.20, 33
ὀρθιάζω 29.4
ὁρμάω frag. 32.29; col. 44.16 (ap.); 46.38; 48.5
ὁρμή 44.7

ὅς frag. 18.11; frag. 21.18, 19, 21; frag. 24.10; frag. 27.14, 16; frag. 32.23; col. 2.16, 17; 3.[22]; 5.11; 6.21; 7.12; 15.13, 18, 22; 16.12; 18.38; 25.[33]; 26.17,
ὅς (cont.)
  32; 27.17, 24, 29; 28.34; 30.34; 31.31; 32.19, 26, [34]; 34.29; 36.20, [24], 28, 29; 37.5, 8, [40]; 38.[9]; 40.16, 19; 41.39; 42.23; 43.6, 8, 19, 35; 44.2, 5; 46.4; 48.33
ὁσδήποτε 24.41; 25.26
ὁσημέραι 29.25
ὅσος 24.17; 26.21; 29.26 (Democritus); 34.21, 23; 38.40; 44.[12]; 47.35
ὅσπερ frag. 13.34; frag. 18.6; frag. 12.[13]; frag. 24.8; col. 45.28
ὅστις frag. 5.3; frag. 7.[6]; col. 38.24
ὅταν frag. 7.4; col. 11.7, 14; 17.18; 18.29, 30; 20.[17]; 22.16; 27.32; 29.15; 46.41; 47.10
ὅτε frag. 18.5; col. 29.21, 23; 34.24; 42.7
ὁτέ 12.40; 28.21 (ap.)
ὅτι frag. 7.[7]; frag. 33.19; col. 1.6, 8; 6.23; 9.27; 26.[4]; 28.36; 30.13; 32.36; 33.[18]; 34.18, 32; 38.2; 41.29, 39; 42.[7]; 45.[12], 18, 33; 47.5
οὐδέ frag. 27.3; col. 1.5; 4.20, 21; 5.11; 15.9; 16.26; 19.18; 20.35; 21.35, 37; 25.22; 27.31; 28.26; 32.5; 36.29, 30; 42.6, 7; 43.[7]; 44.17; 45.30, 36; 46.24, 35; 47.19; 49.39
οὐδείς frag. 12.14 (ap.); frag. 13.30; frag. 27.23; frag. D.6; col. 19.28; 20.38; 21.15 (ap.); 25.29; 47.39
οὖν frag. 7.[6]; col. 13.18; 34.[39]
οὔπω 18.22
οὐρανός 18.[17]
οὐσία 23.29
οὔτε 2.12; Fr. C.1; 20.38, 39; 25.24 (bis), 25, 27; frag. H.7 (?); 28.22 (bis), 23, 24; 31.31, 32; 41.22, 23; 44.9, [16]; 46.31, 32
οὗτος frag. 20.10, 11 (?), 12; frag. 27.16; frag. 32.[20], [27]; frag. 33.21; col. 1.5, 7; 3.18; 5.2; 6.25, 30; 13.9; 15.18; 17.14; 18.39; 19.7, 27, 29; 22.3; 24.33; 25.20; 26.13, 18; 32.29; 33.21; 34.21; 36.1; 37.2 (ap.); 39.20, 30, 38; 40.22, 28, 30; 42.3, 15; 43.4, 6, 17, 41; 44.4; 45.2, 18; 46.5, 6, 16, 23; 47.4, [26], 29; 48.2, 30; 49.3, 24
οὕτω(ς) frag. 33.23; col. 1.7; 5.25; 6.27; 7.16; 15.16, 32; 16.16; 38.20; 44.29; 46.29, 35; 49.39; οὑτωcί 22.11
ὀφείλω 45.28
ὀφθαλμός frag. 18.4; col. 13.20
ὀφλιςκάνω 12.38
ὄψις 2.7 (ap.); 3.13; 27.34
πάγκακος 18.2 (ap.)
παθολογέω 2.11
πάθος 2.2; 3.23; 4.7; 6.13; 7.9; 9.32; 15.17; 16.27; 17.17; 26.11; 27.23; 28.5 (ap.), 7 (ap.), 25; 30.12; 34.19; 37.[16], 25; 40.36; 43.8; 44.10; 46.26; 49.10
παιδάριον frag. 27.23; col. 26.2
παῖς frag. D.4 (?); col. 23.12 (ap.); 30.24 (bis)
πάλαι 14.15; 29.22
πάλιν 2.[19]; 13.9; 30.19, 28; 41.6
πάμπολυς 11.6; 17.13; 28.17
παμπόνηρος 38.3
πάνδεινος 43.20
πανταχῶς 13.4
παντελῶς 23.33
παντοδαπῶς 13.8; 31.14
πάνυ 49.[11]
παρά (gen.) 9.34; 26.26; 46.7; (dat.) 25.10, 11; 38.34; (acc.) 3.15; frag. D.3; 12.23; 18.[14]; 28.37; 34.21; 37.7; 38.32; 42.6; 44.12 (ap.); 46.19; 47.7, 8, 40; 48.23
παραβάλλω 48.4
παραγίγνομαι 44.20
παραγωγή 23.23
παραδείκνυμι 34.[6]
παραδίδωμι 14.[3]; 35.6 (ap.)
παραινέω 10.33; 37.8
παραιτέομαι 35.39
παραιτητός 45.13 (ap.)
παρακαθίζω 21.32

Index Verborum 351

παρακολουθέω 1.21; 5.18; 6.15; 7.23; 9.22; 17.23; 22.24; 24.22; 29.14, 28; 46.4
παρακόπτω 22.22
παραλαμβάνω 20.30, 39
παραλείπω 45.19
παραλλάξ frag. 21.10
παραλογισμός 7.14; 37.21
παράλυσις 9.[19]
παραμιμνήσκομαι 31.26
παραμίσγομαι 25.29
παραμυθία 31.19; 44.37
παραπέμπω 18.18
παραπίπτω 21.2
παραπλήσιος 14.10; 17.14; 21.34; 49.5
παρασκευάζω 4.18; 30.8; 46.33; 48.27
παράστασις 32.30
παρατηρέω 9.35; 19.3
παρατίθημι 30.23
παραυτόθεν 44.12 (ap.)
παρεδρεύω 10.37
πάρειμι [εἰμί] 17.13
πάρειμι [εἶμι] 18.27
παρενοχλέω 43.18
παρεντίθημι frag. 19.19
παρέπομαι 23.[40]
παρέχω 2.[12]; 19.32; 36.6 (ap.)
παρίημι frag. 27.14 (?)
παρίστημι 9.38; 42.33; 44.29, 34; 45.33
παροινέω 13.11 (ap.); 14.24; 15.14
παρολιγωρέω 5.10; 18.21
παροράω 32.35
παρουσία 42.8
παρρησία 35.39; 36.25 (tit.); 39.22
παρρησιαστικός 36.22
πᾶς (cf. ἅπας) frag. 1.4; frag. 12.17; frag. 28.7; frag. 32.4, 8, 15, 25; col. 1.5; 2.[13]; 6.28; 7.15, 21; 11.10; 15.[10], 29; 16.14; 17.5; 19.24; 20.[17]; 24.22, 27; 25.6, 29; frag. H.4; 27.21, 24, 28; 28.4; 29.[9], 27; 30.3 (bis ap.), 31; 31.12, 15, 23; 32.1, 20; 33.27; 34.22; 35.19; 39.3, 25, 36; 40.[6], 18, 24; 26; 43.24, 26, 37; 45.26, 28; 47.36; 50.3
πάσχω frag. 24.9; frag. 14.11 (?), 13; frag. B.3; frag. C.2; col. 38.23; 49.24

πατρίς 13.27; 29.21
παύω 27.31, 34
πέλαγος 15.29
πέμπω frag. 29.5 (?)
πένης frag. 24.10
πένομαι frag. 24.22
πέρας 5.23; 27.37
περί col. 28.11; frag. E.5 (gen.) frag. 13.28; frag. 27.30; col. 17.15; 32.34; 33.20, 22, 29; 36.24 (tit.); 45.24; 46.5, 8; 48.1, 38; 49.3; (acc.) 14.27; 19.7; 38.[8], 29; 39.34; 40.1; 41.17; 42.35; 43.9; 48.40
περιάπτω 43.16
περιβάλλω frag. 13.11 (ap.)
περιγράφω 29.30
περιζώννυμι 8.29
περιίστημι 34.25
περιλαμβάνω 21.29
Περιπατητικός 31.25
περίπικρος frag. 18.19
περιπίπτω 3.24; 12.36; 13.23; 25.21; 40.18; 44.9; 45.41; 46.1, 40
περίπτωσις 36.4
περισπάω 2.[16]; 19.5
περιττός 6.3
πήδησις 8.41
πικραίνω 14.[2]; 36.[2]
πικρία 26.14
πικρός 12.31; 26.[10]; 32.38; 36.34
πιστεύω 16.[33]
πίστις 2.[22]; 45.23
πλάττω 20.21
πλεῖστος frag. 18.14; col. 35.20; 37.[2]; 38.25 (Menander); 43.26
πλείων 9.25; 33.22; 34.35
πλεύμων 8.36; 9.30
πλευρά 8.37; 9.31
πλῆθος 6.[21]
πλημμελέω 41.21
πλήν 31.10
πλοῖον 15.27; 21.36
πλούσιος frag. 24.[17]
πλουτέω frag. 24.24
πνίγω 15.23

ποθέω 27.29
ποιέω frag. 13.[26]; col. 1.15; 7.20; 10.38; 14.22; 15.18; 22.5, 13, 24;
ποιέω (cont.)
  24.31; 25.[6]; 28.18; 32.19, 22; 34.23; 37.6, 23; 40.2; 43.18; 48.25
ποιητής frag. 18.8; col. 18.31; 31.22
ποιητικός 46.32
ποῖος 35.[26]
ποιότης 45.35
πολεμέω 32.37
πόλεμος 32.16; 44.25 (Homer)
πολλάκις frag. 19.8; frag. 24.13, 18; frag. 27.18, 21, 31; col. 9.39; 10.21; 11.12; 15.26; 23.38; frag. F.6; 25.16; 26.25; 29.18; 30.22; 33.1; 35.22
πολυλογέω 14.1 (ap.)
πολύς frag. 19.[8]; col. 2.20; 9.27, 31; 12.23; 14.10, 27, 29; 18.39; 19.2; 20.28; 23.20; frag. F.8; 24.37; 25.[4]; 29.18; 30.30; 31.15; 34.6 (?), 33; 35.32 (bis); 36.[5]; 39.4; 40.3; 42.11; 43.10, 27; 46.40
πολυχρόνιος 30.16
πομπεύω 22.21
πονηρία 38.25 (Menander)
πόνος 9.31; 49.12
πορεύω 49.5
πόσις 28.2; 44.21
ποσός 30.27; 34.39 (ap.); 35.26 (ap.)
πότε 45.37, 38
ποτε 35.27, 40
πότερον 40.35
που frag. 32.26 (ap.); col. 31.25; 44.2
πούς 38.31
πρᾶγμα 36.5; 37.34
πρᾶξις 20.27; 25.18; 29.15
πραότης 28.39
πράττω 15.11; 22.17; 26.32; 48.30
πρέσβυς 12.28
πρίν 35.24
πρό 1.23; 4.16
προάγω 14.22; 27.26; 28.21 (ap.)
προαιρέομαι 44.32
προαίρεσις 48.[11], 29

προβαίνω 13.19; 33.21
πρόειμι frag. 20.9; col. 42.33
προηγέομαι 47.22
προΐημι frag. 18.6; col. 11.23; 15.17
προΐστημι 29.15; 49.40
πρόκειμαι 23.20; 44.39
προκινησία 38.28
προλέγω 36.21
πρόληψις 45.2
προπέτεια 12.31
προπηλακισμός 27.36
προπίπτω frag. 28.24; frag. F.2
πρός frag. 19.6 (?); col. 29.3; (gen.) 16.27; 22.32 (ap.); (dat.) 32.29; (acc.) frag. 27.[16]; col. 4.13, 17; 5.20; 9.37; 17.12, 13; 18.25, 36; 19.23; 21.39; 22.[15]; 23.11; 30.5; 33.2, 35, 37, 40; 34.39; 36.[1]; 39.1, 23, 26; 41.[10], 11, 39; 43.9; 44.7, [16], 18, 30, 34; 46.27; 48.34
προσαγορεύω 16.[40]; 43.6, 12
προσάγω 45.27
προσαγωγή 19.21
προσαλλοτριοῦμαι 42.2
προσαναρτάω 39.37
προσάπτω 47.[17]
προσδέομαι 6.12
προσδέχομαι 48.32; 49.20
προσδοκάω 26.31; 41.24
πρόσειμι 36.21, 28
προσεμφύω 23.22
προσεπιπολεμέω frag. 19.2 (ap.)
προσεπιπονέω frag. 19.[2]
προσέχω 5.8; 15.24 (com.)
προσηγορία 39.19; 44.4
προσήκω 14.14; 20.37; 25.11; 29.20; 31.15
προσήνεια 24.[39]
πρόσθεσις 40.9
προσκρούω 17.26 (ap.)
πρόσοδος 20.33
προσπάθεια 11.4 (ap.)
προσπαροινέω 13.11
προσπελάζω 21.27
προσπίπτω 37.19

προστάττω	11.4 (ap.)	στάδιον	8.40
προστίθημι	frag. 15.16 (ap.); col. 3.18; 5.24	στάσιμος	frag. 21.6
προσυπομιμνήσκω	3.16	στερέω	21.25; 39.36
προσφέρω	7.14; 32.18; 44.18; 47.1	στιλβηδών	frag. 18.5
πρόσχειρος	29.32	στρατηγός	33.26
προσχράομαι	48.2	στρατιώτης	33.24
πρόσωπον	frag. 18.13; col. 11.5; 31.27	συγγένεια	14.9 (ap.); 21.21
πρότερον	7.5; 31.26; 45.18;	συγγενής	14.9 (ap.)
προτίθημι	46.11	σύγγονος	14.9 (ap.)
προὔργου	5.26	συγκαταβαίνω	19.29; 21.39
προφέρω	44.36	συγκαταδύνω	44.31
πρόχειρος	49.19	σύγκειμαι	8.21
πρῶτος	frag. 18.8; col. 48.3	συγκρίνω	39.[7]
πτηνός	11.20 (Plato)	συγκυρέω	36.27
πτῶμα	31.7 (ap.)	συγχαίρω	31.16
πτῶσις	frag. 17.6 (ap.)	συζεύγνυμι	27.23; 42.23
πυκνός	23.22; 30.19; 35.19	συζήτησις	19.26
πυνθάνομαι	33.36	συλλάλησις	21.22
πῶς	39.21, 26, 31, 33; 41.35	συλλογίζομαι	49.4
		συμβαίνω	frag. 4.16; col. 9.[20]; 12.33; 16.36; frag. E.3; 28.12 (?); 47.6
ῥᾴδιος	3.17; 5.[30]; 10.18; 28.34	συμβάλλω	12.24
ῥᾳθυμία	28.38	συμβίωσις	39.2
ῥαπίζω	17.22	συμβουλεύω	20.35
ῥῆξις	9.29	συμμέτρησις	37.36
ῥήτωρ	31.22	σύμμετρος	29.31
ῥίπτω	16.14	συμπείθω	40.4 (ap.)
		συμπεριφορά	28.3
σάλιον v. σίαλον		συμπλέκω	10.23; 13.10; 42.17, 31
σάρξ	7.12	συμπλοκή	37.30
σεαυτοῦ	15.25 (com.)	συμπόσιον	21.32; 25.24
σεμνός	frag. 24.[18]	σύμπτωμα	10.25
σεμνότης	18.21 (ap.)	συμφορά	5.19; 11.7; 24.21; 25.21; 29.19; 42.16
σημαίνω	20.31		
σίαλον	frag. 18.[18]	σύμφορος	32.28
σκιά	26.7 (ap.)	σύν	frag. 32.27, 29; col. 8.37
σκυθρωπάζω	20.19	συνάγω	49.32
σοφία	20.13, 47.[8]	συνακολουθέω	42.18
σοφός	frag. 19.21 (ap.); col. 5.[28]; 35.2; 36.18, 31; 37.6, 10 (ap.); 39.17, 32; 40.1, 30; 41.31; 42.20 43.16; 44.2, 26, 32; 45.3, 10, 22; 46.3, 12, [14], 20; 47.[8], 32; 48.2, 12, 24, 39; 49.8, 19, 31, 36, 38	συνάπτω	frag. 32.19; col. 5.15; 40.15 (ap.); 42.15 (ap.)
		συναρτάω	27.39
		συνασπίζω	24.17
		συναυξάνω	28.19; 40.8
		συναύξησις	18.37
σπουδαῖος	35.30; 38.18; 39.25	συνεγγίζω	36.32; 43.3

σύνειμι	frag. 28.25 (ap.); col. 17.26; 30.6
συνεμφαίνω	45.11
συνεπιζεύγνυμι	31.33
συνεπισπάω	6.21; 22.19; 38.4
συνεπιτίθημι	21.3
συνεπιφέρω	39.7, 40
συνέπομαι	43.3
συνετός	47.3
συνεχής	9.22, 39; 13.3 (ap.); 24.26; 30.14; 49.[12]
συνέχω	2.18; 6.18; 10.35; 15.8 (ap.); 19.6; 28.26; 41.30; 42.10; 43.1, 27; 47.18; 49.9
συνηγορία	31.20
συνίστημι	37.32
σύννοια	35.30
συνοικέω	26.14
συνοράω	28.34
συνοργίζομαι	13.24
συνταράττω	14.[32]
συντελέω	14.30; 17.15
συντετελεσμένως	35.25
σύντονος	44.5, 9; 48.6, 10
συντρίβω	33.4
συντυγχάνω	36.29
συνωμοσία	25.17
συσχολάζω	19.15
σφαλερός	3.26 (ap.)
σφόδρα	24.30
σφοδρός	frag. 1.3; col. 41.37
σχολάζω	19.11
σῶμα	frag. 7.9 (ap.); col. 8.33; 13.3 (ap.); 33.4
σωμάτιον	10.30
σωτηρία	29.[5]
ταρακτός	10.[18]
ταραχή	26.16; 42.4, 10
τάττω	43.4
ταυτολογέω	col. 6.30 (ap.)
τάφρος	13.16
ταχέως	33.30
τεκμήριον	38.26 (Menander)
τέκνον	16.22; 17.9; frag. F.[3]; 24.32
τελευταῖος	49.27
τελευτή	30.21
τελέω	frag. 28.19 (?)
τελέως	3.7; 16.28; 42.40 (?)
τετράχμον	15.27
τέχνη	35.7 (ap.)
τεχνίτης	34.3
τηλικοῦτος	39.20, 27; 47.34
τίθημι	1.23; 3.13; 4.14; 7.12; 29.24 (Homer); 36.37; 48.22
τίκτω	21.34 (paroem.?)
τίλλω	15.12
τιμωρέω	16.18; 33.[18]
τιμωρητικός	32.24
τιμωρία	frag. 7.5; col. 27.38; 42.37; 44.13 (ap.), 25, 31
τίνω	frag. 28.20
τις	frag. 18.20; frag. 19.4; frag. 27.15, 19, [24]; frag. 28.20 (?), 22 (?); frag. 32.12, [25], 28 (ap.); col. 6.16, 17; 10.23; 13.16; 16.37; 18.19, 21; 21.38, 39; 22.16; frag. E.4 (?); 23. 28; 25.34; 26.2, [34]; 29.26; 30.15, 20, 29; 32.31; 33.19; 34.33; 36.17, 18, 33, 38; 37.21; 38.8; 39.23, 35, 39; 40.25, 27, 33, 38; 41.7, 20, 30, 31, 35; 42.[6], 23; 43.11, 15 (?), 22; 44.18; 46.9, 13, 33; 47.[11], 33; 48.28; 49.6, 37; 50.5
τίς	13.11; 18.34; 20.28; 28.35; 33.24, 28
τίσις	frag. 13.29
τλάω	frag. 31.19 (Homer)
τοιγαροῦν	16.34; 48.3
τοίνυν	frag. 21.23; frag. 24.[15]; col. 43.[41]
τοιοῦτος	frag. 18.[20]; frag. 32.24; col. 1.8; 12.34; 13.17; 14.28; 18.21; 20.34; 21.28, 39; 26.3, 33; 28.[4]; 29.17; 31.23; 34.38; 35.4, 7; 36.26; 41.8, 40; 42.38; 43.24; 44.10, 35; [46.17]; 48.4
τοιουτότροπος	9.32
τοῖχος	13.16
τολμάω	frag. 17.23 (ap.); col. 21.35; 43.22
τομή	44.22
τόσος	34.39; 35.[7]
τοσοῦτος	21.25; 39.28; 45.25

Index Verborum

τότε	frag. 7.[7]; col. 7.21
τοτέ	8.28, 31; 13.25, 26; 26.18, 20
τραῦμα	12.39
τράχηλος	frag. 18.16
τραχύς	27.21
τρέπω	10.30
τρέχω	8.39
τρόμος	9.18
τρόπος	frag. 18.21; col. 3.21; 37.40; 38.[9]; 40.31; 41.7, 33; 49.5
τρώκτης	15.21
τυγχάνω	frag. 27.20; col. 16.13, 30; 39.19
τύπτω	frag. 17.17; frag. 27.26; col. 13.5
τύραννος	11.15
τυφλός	5.25
τύχη	21.30
ὑβρίζω	14.23; 19.8; 26.1 (ap)
ὕβρις	12.39
υἱός	14.12
ὑλακτέω	18.26
ὑπάρχω	5.27; 22.29; 23.34; 32.26; 37.[16]; 49.22, 39
ὑπέρ	46.[8]; 47.26
ὑπερβατός	18.15 (ap.)
ὑπερμεγέθως	27.18
ὑπέρμετρος	24.27; 29.29
ὑπηρεσία	24.20
ὑπό	(gen.) frag. 21.14, 17; frag. 24.12, 14; col. 8.35; 18.18; 19.[8]; 22.27; 23.30; 25.16, 34; 35.38; 39.38; 40.33; 41.34; 47.[11], 32 (acc.) 43.4
ὑπογράφω	3.6 (ap.), 24; 23.13 (ap.)
ὑποδείκνυμι	7.15; 42.32; 45.32
ὑποκρίνω	37.1
ὑπολαμβάνω	1.25; 36.32; 37.17; 47.33
ὑπόληψις	frag. 22.4; frag. 24.6; frag. 32.21; col. 47.22, 25, 31; 49.29, 40; 50.7
ὑπομενητός	col. 39.33
ὑπομένω	19.20, 28; 20.34; 39.33
ὑπομιμνήσκω	29.32; 30.12
ὑποπτεύω	19.24
ὑποτρέχω	32.2
ὕπουλος	28.32
ὑποφέρω	32.[4]
ὗς	18.33
ὕστερον	37.[8]; 40.[8]
ὑφαιρέω	23.21 (ap.)
ὑφόρασις	22.30
φαίνω	34.29, 39; 40.7
φανερός	1.[5]; 2.9, 13; 3.26; 5.22; 6.28; 38.29; 40.15; 41.41; 48.33; 49.[3]
φανερόω	41.41 (ap.)
φαντασία	frag. 28.23; col. 34.35; 35.[5]; 36.19
φάρμακον	19.20; 29.7
φέρω	frag. 24.12; col. 38.26 (Menander); 40.28; 44.3; 45.39
φεύγω	21.29; 44.13
φευκτός	frag. 33.19 (ap.); col. 40.15 (ap.)
φημί	frag. 12.16; col. 12.27; 18.29; 31.29; 34.4; 37.5; 41.1, 31; 46.14, 36
φιλανθρωπία	24.38
φίλαρχος	15.31
φιλαυτ-	frag. 33.2
φίλαυτος	28.33
φιλέω	35.[18]
φιλία	20.30; 21.21
φιλοδοξέω	49.7
φιλόδοξος	15.32
φιλολογία	2.21 (?)
φιλονικέω	28.16
φίλος	frag. 21.[18]; col. 16.33; 17.25; 20.[1]; frag. F.[4]; 27.27; 28.3; 29.19; 30.5; 35.38; 39.1; 41.19, 20
φιλοσοφία	17.29; 18.37; 29.12; 37.10 (ap.)
φιλόσοφος	3.20; 31.17; 35.36; 37.10 (ap.)
φιλότιμος	14.16
φιλοχρήματος	15.32 (ap.)
φλεγμονή	10.[28]
φλέψ	frag. 18.17
φληναφάω	33.23
φλυαρέω	31.18; 49.1
φοβέω	20.39 (ap.); 29.35
φόβος	26.15
Φοῖνιξ	15.21
φονεύς	14.9 (ap.)

φονεύω	23.38
φόνος	13.22; 17.18
φορός	10.31; 35.18 (ap.)
φρίκη	3.15
φυγή	13.26
φυλακή	33.3; 37.8
φυλάττω	10.35
φυσικός	2.1; 36.20; 38.6, 21, 36; 39.26, 30, 40; 40.18; 45.36; 46.9; φυσικῶς 46.36; 48.5, [9]
φύσις	frag. 32.[23], 26; frag. 33.17; col. 26.11; 37.34; 38.38; 40.22; 43.34
φύω	24.17; 30.26; 42.13 (ap.)
φωνή	8.28; 11.23; 17.11; 36.37; 37.21
φωράω	29.16
χαλεπότης	37.[2]
χαλκοῦς	15.22; 18.15
χαρά	frag. 3.2 (ap.)
χαρίεις	39.34; 49.1, 11
χαρίζομαι	15.8 (ap.); 43.28
χάρις	frag. 3.[2]; col. 43.24
χάσκω	15.23 (com.)
χειρισμός	44.40; 48.34
χειροκρασία	12.34
χειρόω	32.[38]
χείρων	12.17
χίλιοι	8.[39]
χιτωνίσκος	17.10
χράομαι	4.22; 7.6; 44.38; 46.16, 19; 48.41
χρεία	frag. 24.16; col. 21.19; 33.36
χρή	43.[7]; 48.33
χρόνος	9.25; 15.10; 22.24; 26.17; 34.34
χωρίς	frag. 28.16; col. 31.31; 32.[18], 36; 34.[5], 18; 41.11; 49.29, 33
ψέγω	1.9, 14; 5.12; 6.31
ψευδοδοξέω	37.35
ψευδοδοξία	6.14
ψεῦδος	frag. B.1 (ap.)
ψεύστης	28.31
ψιθυρισμός	25.32
ψι[λ-	frag. G.4
ψυχή	6.13; 10.28; 14.32; 21.[6]; 31.29; 35.23
ὧδε	16.37
ὠμός	8.31 (poet.)
ὠνέομαι	27.29
ὡς	frag. 16.28; frag. 18.13; frag. 24.5; col. 1.5, 16; 2.14; 3.26; 4.14; 12.26; 14.10; 15.31; 16.[17]; 17.13, 22; 19.17; 21.[5], 29, 33; 27.31; 30.12; 31.16, 25; 33.25; 35.31; 36.2; 37.33; 40.6, 8; 42.27; 44.7, [16], 18, 29, 34; 46.30; 48.12
ὡσαύτως	32.23
ὥσπερ	13.19; 18.19; 27.37; 35.[17]; 40.37; 46.37, 40
ὡσπερεί	8.20
ὥστε	frag. 33.24; frag. A.4; 3.15; 5.26; 6.31; 9.21, [39]; 12.[18]; 15.17; 25.19; 35.2; 37.39; 42.34; 43.17; 45.16; 47.29
ὠφέλεια	48.[18]

Personal Names

Ἀλέξανδρος	18.28; 43.25, 36
Ἀντίπατρος	33.34
Ἀπόλλων	16.19
Ἀχιλλεύς	18.20
Βασιλείδης	5.21
Βίων	1.16
Δημόκριτος	29.27
Διόνυσος	16.24
Ἐπίκουρος	frag. 22.10 (ap.); col. 35.3; 45.5; 48.41
Ἕρμαρχος	45.13
Ζεύς	frag. 21.7; col. 16.12; 28.[41]; 43.3
Θέσπις	5.21
Κάδμος	16.23
Κλεινίας	21.15 (ap.)
Μένανδρος	28.8 (ap.); 38.27
Μεντορίδης	12.29
Μητρόδωρος	12.27; 45.9
Νικασικράτης	frag. 15.15; col. 37.5; 38.34
Νιόβη	16.22
Οἰδίπους	14.11
Ὅμηρος	frag. 29.12 (ap.); 44.23
Πέλοψ	14.12
Πλάτων	11.18

Πλειcθένηc	14.13
Cοφοκλῆc	18.20
Τιμαcαγόραc	7.7
Τιμοκράτηc	12.26
Ὕπνοc	16.12
Φινεύc	14.9 (ap.)
Χρύcιπποc	1.17

Ancient Authors and Works

Antipater	33.34-40
Bion, Περὶ τῆc ὀργῆc	1.17
Chrysippus, Περὶ παθῶν θεραπευ-τικὸc (λόγοc)	1.18
Democritus	29.26
Epicurus, Ἀναφωνήcειc	45.6
Epicurus, Κύριαι Δόξαι	43.21
Epicurus, *Rata Sententia I*	43.22-24
Fragmentum comicum adesp.	15.23–25
Heraclitus	27.28 sq.
Hermarchus, *Opus incertum*	45.12–15
Homer, *Ilias*	
1.2	29.23 sq.
1.23 sq.	16.21
8.63 sq.	44.23–25
23.21 (= *Odyssea* 18.87)	8.31
Menander	28.8 (ap); 38.22–26
Metrodorus	12.26–29
Philodemus, Περὶ παρρηcίαc	36.24
Plato, *Leges*	
4.717d	11.19–21
Sophocles, Cύνδειπνοι (?)	18.20

www.ingramcontent.com/pod-product-compliance
Lightning Source LLC
Chambersburg PA
CBHW032012300426
44117CB00008B/1000